[redacted]

THE ARAB-ISRAEL DISPUTE

LIBRARY IN A BOOK

THE ARAB-ISRAEL DISPUTE

Don Peretz

Facts On File, Inc.

LIBRARY IN A BOOK: THE ARAB-ISRAEL DISPUTE

Facts On File, Inc.
11 Penn Plaza
New York NY 10001

Library of Congress Cataloging-in-Publication Data

Peretz, Don, 1922–
The Arab-Israel dispute / Don Peretz.
p. cm. — (Library in a book)
Includes bibliographical references (p.) and index.
ISBN 0-8160-3186-X
1. Jewish-Arab relations. 2. Jewish-Arab relations—Bibliography.
3. Jewish-Arab relations—1917- —Sources. I. Title. II. Series.
DS119.7P4497 1996
956.04—dc20 96-4362

Facts On File books are available at special discounts when purchased in bulk quantities for businesses, associations, institutions, or sales promotions. Please call our Special Sales Department in New York at 212/967-8800 or 800/322-8755.

You can find Facts On File on the World Wide Web at **http://www.factsonfile.com**

Text design by Ron Monteleone

Printed in the United States of America

MP FOF 10 9 8 7 6 5 4 3 2

This book is printed on acid-free paper.

CONTENTS

PART III
DOCUMENTS **235**

MAPS

PALESTINE, 1878: TOWNS, VILLAGES, AND SETTLEMENTS

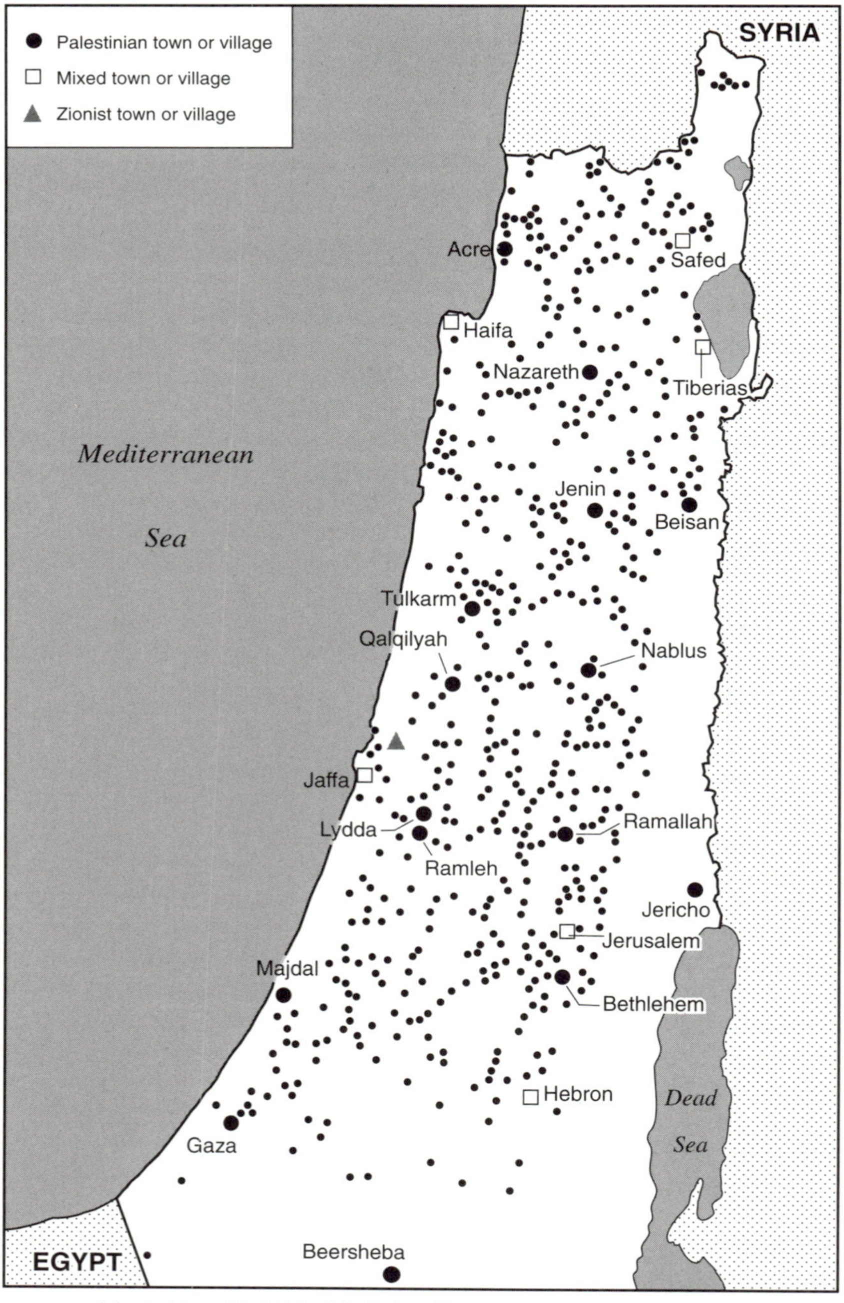

Adapted from Walid Khalidi, *Before Their Diaspora*. © 1984, 1991 by The Institute for Palestine Studies. Used with permission.

Maps

PALESTINE, 1920: TOWNS, VILLAGES, AND SETTLEMENTS

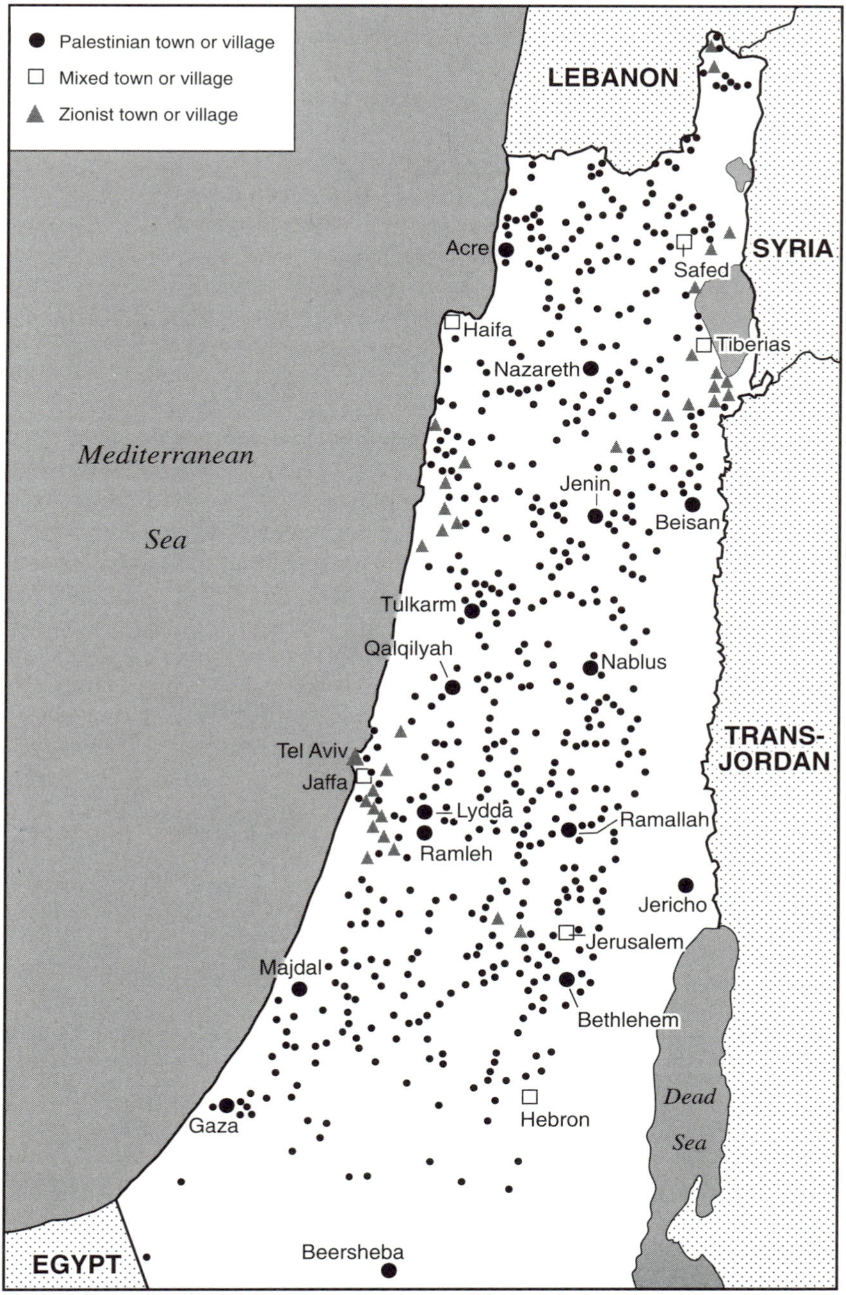

Adapted from Walid Khalidi, *Before Their Diaspora*. © 1984, 1991 by The Institute for Palestine Studies. Used with permission.

PALESTINE, 1946: POPULATION BY DISTRICT

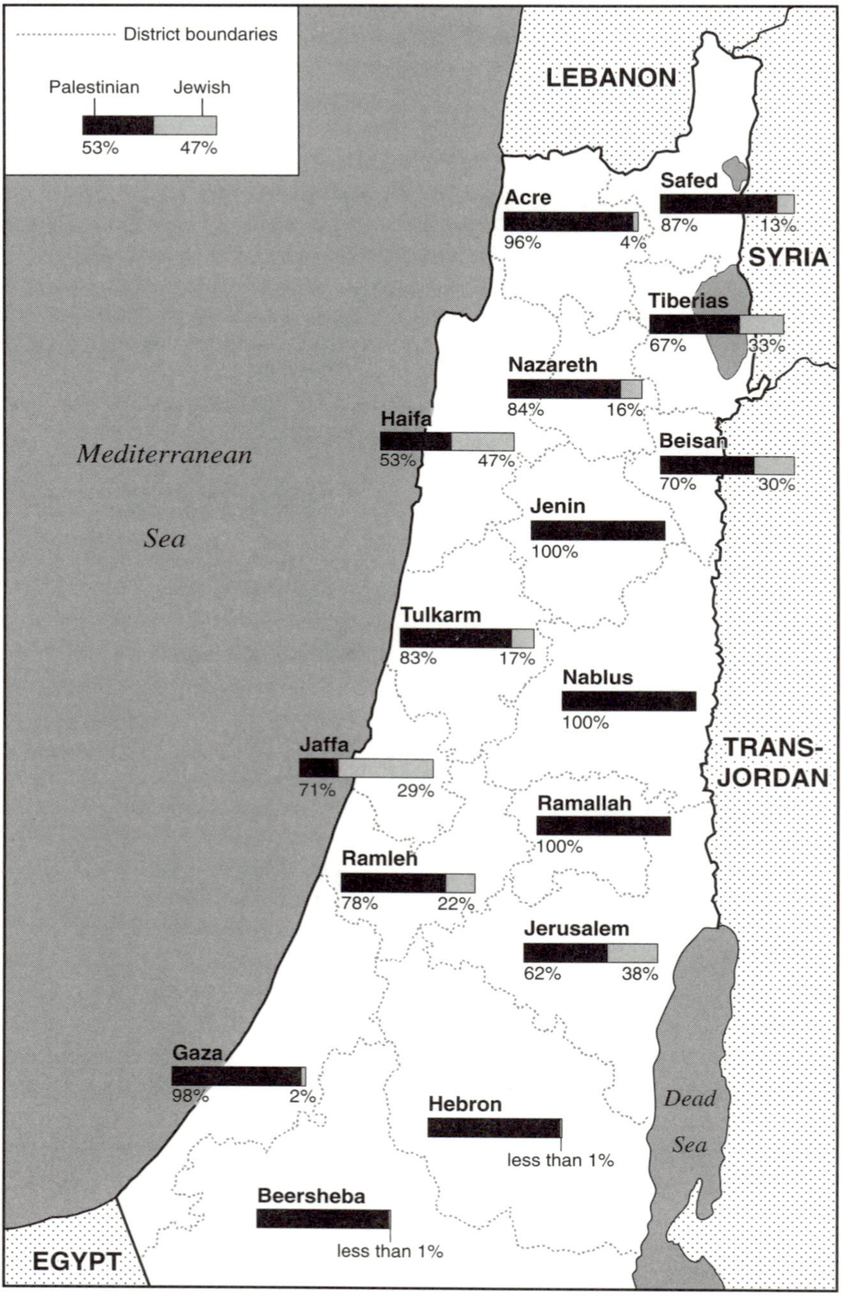

Adapted from Walid Khalidi, *Before Their Diaspora*. © 1984, 1991 by The Institute for Palestine Studies. Used with permission.

Maps

ISRAEL, 1949: THE ARMISTICE BOUNDARIES

ISRAEL, 1996: ISRAEL AND THE OCCUPIED TERRITORIES

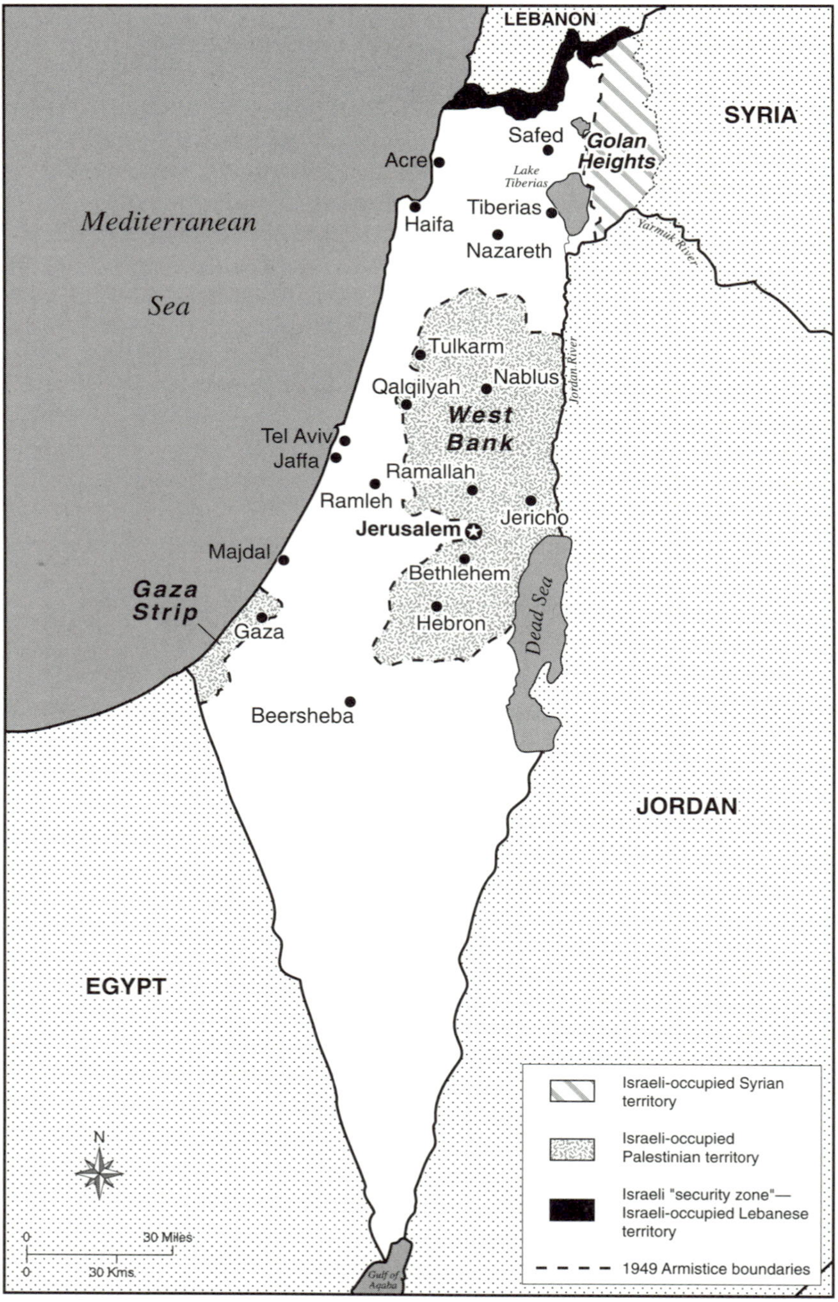
LEBANON
SYRIA
Safed
Golan Heights
Acre
Lake Tiberias
Tiberias
Haifa
Mediterranean
Sea
Nazareth
Yarmuk River
Jordan River
Tulkarm
Nablus
Qalqilyah
West Bank
Tel Aviv
Jaffa
Ramallah
Ramleh
Jericho
Jerusalem
Majdal
Bethlehem
Gaza Strip
Gaza
Hebron
Dead Sea
Beersheba
JORDAN
EGYPT
N
0
30 Miles
0
30 Kms.
Gulf of Aqaba
Israeli-occupied Syrian territory
Israeli-occupied Palestinian territory
Israeli "security zone"—Israeli-occupied Lebanese territory
1949 Armistice boundaries

THE ARAB-ISRAEL DISPUTE

PART I

HISTORICAL OVERVIEW

INTRODUCTION

The conflict between Zionism and the Arab states has been the focus of international attention since the end of World War I. It was a subject of major concern to the old League of Nations; after World War II, it was one of the first disputes in which the United Nations (U.N.) was involved. The conflict has been on the agenda of every session of the U.N. General Assembly since 1946 and is perhaps the item that has been most discussed in the U.N. Security Council. There have been several special sessions of the United Nations convened to cope with crises arising from conflict between Israel and its Arab neighbors. For many years, it was a factor in the Cold War between the Soviet Union and the West. More than half a dozen special U.N. organizations have been created to deal with the situation, including the U.N. Special Commission on Palestine, U.N. Truce Supervision Organization, U.N. Conciliation Commission on Palestine, U.N. Relief and Works Agency for Palestine Refugees in the Near East, U.N. Emergency Force, U.N. Observers Group in Lebanon and several more. The conflict has centered on the struggle between Zionism, or Jewish nationalism, and Arab nationalism for control of Palestine. It has involved not only the Jewish and Arab inhabitants of Palestine but also their respective supporters around the world, that is, both Jewish and non-Jewish advocates of a Jewish state and the 21 members of the Arab League and their supporters throughout the Islamic and many Third World nations.

Palestine did not exist as a separate political entity until Great Britain took over the country at the end of World War I. From 1517 until 1918, Palestine was part of the Ottoman Empire. Prior to the Ottoman era, the country had several rulers—Canaanites, Egyptians, Persians, Romans and various Arab dynasties. Jewish, and later Zionist, claims to Palestine derive from biblical accounts of ancient Hebrew tribes and Israelite kingdoms that existed in the country.

Most of the historical events recorded in the Old Testament took place in Palestine; thus it became the focus of many Jewish religious practices, customs and traditions. Many aspects of Jewish religious and cultural life were intimately linked with Palestine. Jewish rabbinical law favored settlers in the ancient homeland; religious literature echoed with sayings such as "it is better to dwell in the deserts of Palestine than in palaces abroad" and "whoever lives in Palestine lives sinless." Holidays, feasts and fasts commemorated events in the Bible and in Jewish religious history, such as the destruction of the first and second Jewish temples in Jerusalem.

Palestine is also important to Christianity and Islam. Jesus Christ was born and died in Palestine and lived most of his life there. Thus it is the scene of most events in the New Testament and the site of scores of shrines and churches built to commemorate events in the life of Christ. Christians from around the world have made pilgrimages to the Holy Land for nearly 2,000 years. In the Middle Ages, Christian rulers in Europe sent their armies to wrest Palestine from Islamic rule.

Palestine became an Arab and Islamic country some 1,300 years ago when tribes from the Arabian peninsula conquered it during their sweep through the Middle East after the death of the Prophet Muhammad. The country became holy to all Muslims because the Prophet initially designated Jerusalem as the first *qibla* (direction Muslims face during prayer) and because he was believed to have ascended to heaven from the site of King Solomon's temple. To commemorate the event, Muslims built a mosque called the Dome of the Rock on the place from which he ascended. Jerusalem became the third holiest city in Islam, after Mecca and Medina in what is now Saudi Arabia. By the time of the Ottoman conquest, the overwhelming majority of Palestine's population were Arabic-speaking Muslims.

THE OTTOMAN ERA

OTTOMAN ADMINISTRATION

During the Ottoman (Turkish) era, Palestine was not governed as a single or distinctive province but was divided into small administrative districts, part of greater Syria. In 1864 it became part of three newly established Ottoman administrative regions. The central and largest region of Palestine was part of the larger province of Damascus. The northern section was part of the province of Beirut. Because of its special religious status and European interest in the city, Jerusalem and southern Palestine was established as an independent unit or district governed directly from the Ottoman capital, Istanbul.

Historical Overview

By the mid-19th century, the population of Palestine was about 500,000, more than 80% Muslim Arab, 10% Christian (mostly Arab), about 1% Druze (an offshoot of Shi'ite Islam) and about 5% Jewish. The southern half of the country, later called the Negev, was mostly desert, sparsely inhabited by nomadic bedouin tribes. The country was relatively poor, with no mineral or significant resources other than the land. Only one-third of the area was suitable for cultivation. The Muslim-Arab population was mostly engaged in agriculture despite the poor environment—water was scarce and soil rocky in areas where most of the farmers lived.

Prior to the 19th century, Palestine had been a neglected backwater of the Ottoman Empire. Istanbul had lost control over local clan chieftains, who repressed and exploited the local peasantry, or *fellahin*. With the decline of agriculture and commerce, most of the inhabitants had become impoverished.

In response to the European empires' attempts to carve out spheres of influence in the Middle East, the Ottoman rulers initiated a reform program called the Tanzimat, which lasted from 1839 to 1876. One of its goals was to reestablish Istanbul's authority in outlying provinces and to centralize control over the economy and political life of the empire.

Among the reform measures of the Tanzimat were the 1858 Land Law and the 1864 Wilayat (Provincial) Law. Istanbul hoped to regain control over state lands and to register land ownership for tax purposes through the Land Law. However, most *fellahin* evaded the land registration, fearing that it would lead to their conscription in the Ottoman army and to higher taxes. The result was that much of the cultivated area was registered in the name of wealthy urban notables and the *fellahin* became sharecroppers or hired hands. Under the Wilayat Law, responsibility for tax collection passed from rural *sheikhs* (village elders) to urban notables—wealthy and powerful community leaders—further increasing their hold on the economy. The 1858 Land Law also established local administrative councils to help govern the cities and to implement the Tanzimat reforms. But membership in the councils was restricted to candidates who were able to pay a tax that most villagers could not afford, with the result that the notables soon dominated Palestine's economic and social life. By the beginning of World War I, some 250 Palestinian Arab families owned about half of the cultivated area of Palestine, an amount equal to the land owned by the country's *fellahin*.

There was frequent conflict among the notable families for control of local affairs or to gain influence with the Ottoman authorities. Notable families exercised their influence over the villages through extended family or clan relationships; villages would be identified with one or another clan, and larger villages might be divided between two or more clans. These divisions often resulted in internecine clashes among competing extended families. There was little, if any, nationalist sentiment; loyalty was to the clan and its chieftains rather than to any political movement or leader. Individuals identified themselves as Muslims, Christians or Jews rather than as Palestinians or Ottomans. Residents of Palestine often referred to their homeland as southern Syria.

By the latter part of the 19th century, a new class of commercial bourgeoisie representing Palestinian Arabs, Christians, Jews and Europeans played an increasingly important role in integrating the economy into the international economic system. Commodities such as wheat, barley, sesame, olive oil and oranges were cultivated for export. Small-scale industry produced textiles, soap, olive oil and religious items.

Although there were Arab Christians who lived in villages and farmed the land, most of the Christian and Jewish communities were urban, engaged in trade and commerce. Christians were represented by a dozen different denominations and sects; the largest was the Greek Orthodox, followed by the Latin or Roman Catholic church.

Until the end of the 19th century, most Jews were those who had come to Palestine for religious reasons, with the largest number concentrated in the city of Jerusalem. Immigration of Jewish Zionists, those who came to establish a "national home" in Palestine, began during the last quarter of the century. During the 19th century, the Jewish population of Palestine more than tripled, from about 25,000 to over 80,000.

Jerusalem was the cultural, intellectual, religious, social and economic center of life for the Muslim, Christian and Jewish communities of Palestine. The most influential notable families lived there. The principal shrines of all the religious communities were located in or near Jerusalem. It was also the focus of interest of European powers seeking to establish their influence in the region; protection of non-Muslim religious minorities was their frequent excuse for intervention. These interventions in turn provoked squabbles among the European powers. A conflict over "rights" in the Church of the Holy Sepulcher (Christ's tomb) between Catholic and Orthodox clergy, the former the protégés of France and the latter the protégés of Russia, became one of the causes of the Crimean War.

Under the Ottoman *millet* system of governance, each religious community (*millet*) was permitted to run its own internal affairs, and each was headed by its own religious leader—the Christian patriarch, the Jewish Chief Rabbi and the Muslim Sheikh al-Islam. Each *millet* was permitted wide autonomy to develop and regulate its religious, legal, cultural and educational life provided it remained loyal to the Ottoman sultan and produced the taxes levied by Istanbul. Matters of personal status such as marriage, divorce and inheritance were regulated by the religious law of each *millet*. Each *millet* was also entitled to use its own language. In disputes between Muslims and non-Muslims, the former were considered superior, and Islam was recognized as the predominant religion of the empire.

Ottoman patterns of governance and practices in law were to influence the subsequent rulers, the British during the mandate and the state of Israel after the British departed. Many aspects of the *millet* system, such as religious control of personal status, various land regulations and administrative boundaries established by the Ottomans, continue to the present in Israel/Palestine.

BIRTH OF ARAB NATIONALISM

Although the Arabs of Palestine considered themselves a distinctive group, there was no serious conflict between them and the Ottoman Turkish establishment until the 20th century. Many Arabs, including Palestinians, held important positions in the Ottoman government in Istanbul. They became ministers, generals and provincial governors. The leading religious figures in the Islamic establishment, including judges, administrators and the Sheikh al-Islam were usually Arab. The backbone of Ottoman government was the sacred Sharia law, based on the Koran, which could not be mastered without a thorough knowledge of the Arabic language. Most of the Islamic clergy was trained in religious institutions in Cairo, Damascus, Tripoli and Aleppo, all Arab cities. Several Palestinian Arabs served in the Ottoman parliament established in 1876. The Arab city of Nablus, in Palestine, was reputed to be especially favored by Sultan Abdul Hamid II.

Arab nationalism began in the mid-19th century in the form of an Arabic literary revival. By mid-century, the three centers of revived Arab culture were Cairo in Egypt, Beirut in Lebanon and Damascus in Syria. Palestine was considered an adjunct of Syria and was much influenced by intellectual and political trends in Damascus.

Although both Arabs and Turks were mostly Sunni Muslims, they spoke different languages and had decidedly different ethnic roots. With the revival of Arabic, differences between Arabs and Turks became more pronounced. By the end of the century, a number of Arab intellectuals, many of them Christian, demanded greater autonomy for the Arabic-speaking provinces of the Ottoman Empire. Following the Young Turk Revolution in Istanbul during 1908 and the rise of a new Turkish nationalist sentiment, tensions between Arabs and Turks intensified. Arab national societies were formed, and Arab officers formed secret factions in the Ottoman army. Relations between Arabs and Turks deteriorated because of the zealotry of the more fanatic Turkish nationalists. To enhance its power, the Young Turk government in Istanbul began to strip local officials of their authority. Some radicals even wanted to abolish Arabic and translate the Koran into Turkish.

Arab opposition to Turkification engendered at least 10 substantial groups in Damascus, Beirut, Aleppo, Baghdad and other Arab cities, as well as in

Istanbul. Some were secret, others public. The best organized and most widely known was the Ottoman Decentralization party established in Cairo during 1912. It called for a multinational, multiracial empire in which each province would control its own internal affairs through locally elected representative bodies.

An important secret group was the Young Arab Society, al-Fatat, organized in Paris shortly before World War I. Its members sought Arab independence within a biracial Turko-Arab Ottoman Empire and aspired to raise the level of Arab social and technological development to that of the West. Al-Fatat convened the first congress of Arab nationalist groups in Paris during 1913. At the congress, there was no talk of secession but of implementing reforms demanded by the various nationalist organizations. The stated objective was an Ottoman government in which all citizens would have equal rights and obligations, whether they were Arab, Turk, Armenian, Kurd, Muslim, Christian, Jew or Druze.

During World War I, the various Arab nationalist trends converged into a single independence movement. Not all Arab leaders joined the movement. Many were conscience-stricken about deserting their fellow Muslims in the Ottoman establishment and armies. Many supported the Sultan's government when it joined the Central Powers (Germany, Austria-Hungary, Bulgaria) against the Allies during World War I. Palestinians served as officers in the Turkish army during the war.

JEWISH NATIONALISM AND THE RISE OF ZIONISM

The Jewish national movement began in Europe, home of most of the world's Jews, at about the same time that Arab nationalism appeared. Modern Zionism, the movement for a return to Palestine, was inspired by Jewish association with the biblical Hebrews and the ancient land of Israel, but was also a direct product of the economic, political and social conditions of 19th century European Jewry. Jews had resided in Europe since being expelled from Palestine by the Romans in the first century A.D. They either emigrated or were transported to Europe, where they lived in separate communities based on the laws, traditions and customs of the Holy Land as influenced by Jewish religious writings.

Until the modern era, Jews were outsiders in European countries, excluded from the mainstream of national, social and economic life. Not only were they isolated within, but nearly every major European country exiled its Jews at one time or another. Until the French Revolution and the rise of modern secular nationalism, national identity usually meant association with the Christian identity of the rulers. Jews thus did not qualify for citizenship.

Historical Overview

In the wake of the French Revolution, new concepts of the nation-state and citizenship developed. The walls that had isolated Jews in ghettos started coming down, and Jews entered the mainstream of Western European life. They could now own land, practice law, teach in universities, vote, enter parliament and serve as army officers.

The secular reforms of the French Revolution did not reach Eastern Europe where the great majority of Jews lived. In czarist Russia, the Jewish population became the butt of reaction against "radical" reforms from the West. The Russian government imposed new restrictions on Jewish movement, places of habitation and employment. Jews were confined to specified areas of the empire, known as the Pale of Settlement, and were required to obtain special permits for travel or work beyond their ghettos. By the 1880s, government-inspired pogroms broke out in which Jewish settlements were attacked and scores were killed. The pogroms led to the first mass waves of Jewish immigration from the Russian empire (which included Poland) to Western Europe and the United States. These events also produced new social and political movements to ameliorate the plight of the Jews within the empire.

One of the first such movements was Hoveve Zion (Lovers of Zion), founded in Russia during the early 1880s. Its members advocated Jewish settlement in Palestine as a practical relief measure rather than as a religious ideal. Only a "land of our own" could solve the "Jewish problem," they believed. Several hundred young enthusiasts were recruited to support the movement called the Bilu, from the Hebrew acronym of their rallying call taken from the Old Testament: "O House of Jacob, come, let us go forth." The Bilu established one of the first Zionist towns, Rishon le-Zion (First in Zion), in 1882. By the end of the century, a few dozen other small Zionist settlements called colonies were established in Palestine, mostly by Jewish intellectuals from Russia and Poland.

Within 15 years after establishment of Hoveve Zion, a number of other groups coalesced into a single, unified world Zionist organization. Its founder, Theodor Herzl, was an assimilated Western Jew born in Budapest in 1860. As a correspondent for a Viennese newspaper, Herzl attended the 1894 trial in Paris of Captain Alfred Dreyfus, a French Jewish army officer falsely accused of selling military secrets to Germany. Dreyfus' conviction and imprisonment on Devil's Island stirred protest in Western Europe and sparked a wave of anti-Semitism in France. The trial aroused Herzl's memories of the anti-Semitism he had experienced as a youth, and shortly after the trial, he started work on a pamphlet that was to become a basic document of the new Zionist movement. The pamphlet, written in 1896, was called *Der Judenstaat* (The Jewish State). In it, Herzl presented his analysis of the European Jewish problem and his proposal for a solution. Like earlier Zionist authors who never attained Herzl's acclaim, he argued that the Jew was unique, permanently and irrevocably alienated from society, destined to be universally hated. The Jewish problem was therefore not religious or social, but national. Because the Jews were a "nation without a land," the world powers should grant them a territory to fulfill the needs of a nation. In *The Jewish State*, Herzl presented a plan of action calling for mass emigration of Jews from Europe to a territory of their own. Because he did not have the deep emotional and religious ties to the Old Testament of many Eastern European Jews, he was willing to establish his homeland either in Palestine or in Argentina; later he considered other sites as well.

After publication of his pamphlet, Herzl traveled through the Jewish communities of Eastern Europe to propagate his ideas. He was also received by some of the most powerful political figures of the day, including the leaders of Russia, Germany, Turkey and Great Britain. He failed to convince these non-Jewish politicians to support his scheme.

Among the Jewish masses of Russia, Poland, and Rumania, however, enthusiasm for Herzl's ideas was so great that he was lionized as a new Moses and was able to convene the First Zionist Congress in Basel, Switzerland during August 1897. More than 200 delegates came from all over the world, though mostly from Eastern Europe. Participants represented a cross-section of Jewish society—Orthodox and Reform sects, Ashkenazi and Sephardi, liberals and conservatives.

At the congress in Basel, an official World Zionist Movement was established, and a formal credo was adopted that became the foundation of Zionist nationalism and of the future state of Israel: "The aim of Zionism is to create for the Jewish People a home in Palestine secured by public law." All Jewry would be organized as in Herzl's "Jewish State" to promote systematic settlement of Jewish farmers, artisans and craftsmen in Palestine. Jewish consciousness and national identity would be strengthened, and the funds necessary to attain Zionist objectives would be raised. These remained the objectives of the World Zionist Organization, which continued to meet periodically even after the state of Israel was established in 1948.

Shortly after the first congress in 1897, Herzl wrote in his diary:

> If I were to sum up the Basle Congress . . . It would be this: at Basle I founded the Jewish State. If I were to say this today, I would be met by universal laughter. In five years, perhaps, and certainly in fifty, everyone will see it. The State is already founded, in essence, in the will of the people of the State.

Herzl persuaded the British government to offer one of its holdings in Africa for Jewish settlement, but the offer nearly split the Zionist movement.

Most members of the movement would accept no other place than Palestine as the national homeland of the Jewish people. Despite early disputes within the movement, it continued to grow in numbers and influence. Herzl became recognized as the founder of modern Jewish nationalism and the father of modern Israel. His picture adorns Israeli government offices, schools and public places and is found on the country's postage stamps and currency.

Herzl's pamphlet and the Basel Congress planted the seeds that resulted in the Jewish state and the modern Zionist movement. Today most political parties and movements in Israel are descendants of factions that emerged from the First Zionist Congress in 1897. After the congress, Jewish nationalism became identical with Herzlian Zionism. In less than a decade, a wide range of viewpoints representing diverse social, economic and religious perspectives developed. Within the movement itself, views differed concerning the relationship with the indigenous Arab population of Palestine.

CONFLICT BETWEEN JEWISH AND ARAB NATIONALISM IN PALESTINE

In Palestine, close ties between Jews and local Arabs were rare. Few early Zionists recognized the significance of Arab-Jewish contacts. Herzl himself gave scant attention to the indigenous population of Palestine in his writings. Before the 20th century, most Jews in Palestine belonged to the Old Yishuv, or community, that had settled more for religious than political reasons. There was little if any conflict between them and the Arab population.

Tensions began after the first Zionist settlers arrived in the 1880s. Quarrels broke out between the new settlers and neighboring villages over grazing, crop and other land issues. Disputes also arose when Jewish settlers purchased land from absentee Arab owners, leading to dispossession of the peasants who cultivated it. As the number of Jewish settlements increased and as Arabs became aware of the Zionist intention to establish a Jewish homeland, opposition to the movement spread among the *fellahin*, urban notables, intellectuals and the merchant class. The lack of familiarity of the European settlers with traditional Arab customs often stirred conflict. At times, there were armed altercations between Jewish farmers and Arab herdsmen when the former interfered with cattle or flocks that strayed onto Jewish cultivated areas. One of the first clashes occurred at Peta Tikva, the oldest Jewish colony, established in 1878. When the settlers denied grazing rights to the neighboring Arab village, its inhabitants attacked the colony. The fear of peasant dispossession became a central issue in Arab nationalism.

Appeals by Palestinian Arabs to the Ottoman authorities to stop Jewish settlement were of little avail. Despite legislation restricting Jewish immigration to Palestine after 1882, the Zionist movement gained supporters abroad and increased its presence in Palestine. During the first wave of modern Jewish immigration to Palestine between 1881 and 1903, called the first Aliya (ascent), about 20 new agricultural settlements were established, and some 10,000 settlers entered the country. They constituted a small percentage of the total Jewish population in the country, but they were now highly visible. Although one of the goals of Zionism was to establish a Jewish homeland, much of the labor in these settlements was done by hired Arab *fellahin*. One observer noted that there appeared to be hundreds of Arabs for every few dozen Jewish workers.

Growing apprehension about Zionism as well as opposition to the Turkish nationalist ideology of the Young Turks led to the beginnings of a distinctive Palestinian patriotism expressed in the Arabic press and in the writings of Arab nationalists.

Jews in the diaspora were largely unaware of the situation in Palestine. Like Herzl, many perceived it as "a land without a people awaiting a people without a land," in the words of the British Zionist Israel Zangwill. Ahad Ha'am, an early Zionist writer, observed in 1891 that

> we abroad have a way of thinking that Palestine to-day is almost desert, uncultivated wilderness, and that anyone who wishes to buy land there can do so to his heart's content. But that is not in fact the case. It is difficult to find any uncultivated land anywhere in the country . . . We abroad have a way of thinking that the Arabs are all savages, on a level with the animals. The Arabs, especially the townsmen, see through our activities in their country, and our aims, but they keep silence and make no sign, because for the present they anticipate no danger to their own future from what we are about. But if the time should ever come when our people have so far developed their life in Palestine that the indigenous population should feel more or less cramped, then they will not readily make way for us . . .

THE BRITISH MANDATE

PALESTINE AND WORLD WAR I

The Middle East, including Palestine, was one area of diplomatic and military conflict during World War I. When the Ottoman Empire entered the war on the side of Germany in 1914, Great Britain attempted to seek allies among the various national minority groups under Turkish rule. While promising assistance to groups including both Arab nationalists and Zionists, the British also signed several secret pacts with their French, Russian and Italian allies concerning Ottoman territory in the event of an Allied victory.

In the Constantinople Agreement, a series of diplomatic exchanges among Britain, France and Russia in 1915, the czar was promised control over the Turkish Straits and Istanbul. Arabia, including the holy places of Mecca and Medina, would be placed under Arab rule. Iran, or Persia, would be divided into British and Russian spheres of influence. Italy was induced to join the Allies in the Treaty of London signed in 1915, which recognized Rome's interests in the Mediterranean and promised Italy a share of Ottoman territory. French "interests" in Syria were later acknowledged in the Sykes-Picot Agreement.

Arabs were more concerned by the Sykes-Picot Agreement, a series of notes exchanged by the French, British and Russian governments during 1915 and 1916 that became the key to the future of Ottoman Arab lands. The exchange provided for Russia to take over northeastern Anatolia, but that part of the agreement was invalidated when Russia quit the war as a result of the 1917 revolution. France was to obtain outright possession of the Syrian coastal strip north of the city of Tyre, the Ottoman province of Adana and a large part of Cilicia. Syria and northern Iraq, including the rich Mosul oil fields, were to become an independent Arab zone under French protection. Iraq, from Baghdad to the Persian Gulf, the city of Acre in Palestine and a surrounding enclave were to become a British sphere. An autonomous Arab zone between the cities of Kirkuk in Iraq and Aqaba in southern Palestine extending from the Mediterranean to the Persian Gulf would be placed under British protection. Alexandretta (Iskenderun) on the Levant coast of Turkey would become a free port. Russia insisted that Palestine west of the Jordan River between the cities of Gaza and Tyre become internationalized.

The secret agreements concerning partition of the Ottoman Empire among the various Allied powers conflicted with promises made by Great Britain to both Zionist and Arab nationalists. In exchange for assistance against the Turks, the British promised to support Arab aspirations for independence. Early in the war, negotiations were initiated between British officials in Cairo and the Sherif Husayn, keeper of the holy places in Mecca. Even before the war, the British had schemed to entice the nationalists away from their Ottoman rulers. In an exchange of letters between the high commissioner in Egypt, Sir Henry McMahon, and the Sherif Husayn, the British expressed sympathy for aspirations to independence in the Arabic-speaking provinces of the Ottoman Empire. The exchange of correspondence, called the Husayn-McMahon Correspondence, was not a formal treaty but a fairly ambiguous understanding that the British would support Arab independence if the Arabs joined a military alliance against the Turks. Britain would assist an Arab uprising against the Turks; however, to prevent delay, details concerning territory would be ironed out in the future. The territories covered were the Arab provinces south of Anatolia excluding the "two districts of Mersina and Alexandretta and portions of Syria lying to the west of the districts of Damascus, Homs, Hama, and Aleppo [which] cannot be said to be purely Arab . . ." This vague wording was later to cause bitter disagreement between the British and the Arab nationalists; according to the British, the excluded regions covered what was to become mandatory Palestine.

With the assistance of his sons, the Sherif Husayn rallied surrounding bedouin tribes and Arab nationalist secret societies in Syria and Iraq to join the battle against the Turks. Turkish authority was undermined by the end of the war as a result of joint British and Arab military campaigns, the ruthlessness of the Turkish governor and commander-in-chief in Syria and the inability of the Ottoman government to cope with economic disasters in the region, including a plague of locusts and a major famine.

The Zionists also pressed their claims during World War I. From the time of the Zionist Congress in 1897 until 1917, they had had little success in obtaining international recognition of their aspirations in Palestine. To assist the war effort, Jewish leaders had organized special units, like the Zion Mule Corps attached to the British in the battle of Gallipoli against the Turks. Several Jewish battalions were also attached to General Allenby's forces in Palestine.

The major political attempt to gain recognition was in Great Britain. Dr. Chaim Weizmann, a Russian-born British subject, a lecturer in chemistry at Manchester University, became the focus of these efforts. As a result of scientific accomplishments that greatly aided the munitions industry, Weizmann was brought into contact with high-level British officials whom he persuaded to support Zionist goals. Weizmann's persuasion complemented larger British political interests as well, including attempts to influence American Jews to support the British war effort, to win over Jews in Russia, Germany and Austria-Hungary and to get support for British interests in the Middle East. After months of lengthy discussion caused by divisions in the British cabinet, a watered-down version of what Weizmann and his Zionist colleagues desired was presented in the form of a letter from the British foreign secretary to Lord Rothschild, a prominent British Zionist leader. The letter, called the Balfour Declaration, was published on November 2, 1917. It stated that

> His Majesty's Government view with favour the establishment in Palestine of a national home for the Jewish people, and will use their best endeavours to facilitate the achievement of that object, it being clearly understood that nothing shall be done which may prejudice the civil and religious rights of the existing non-Jewish communities in Palestine, or the rights and political status of Jews in any other country.

As a result of the Balfour Declaration, the Husayn-McMahon Correspondence and the various secret agreements among the Allies, Palestine became a focal point of international conflict at the end of World War I. At the peace conference in Paris, there were major disagreements between Zionist and Arab nationalists, between them and the British and between the British and the French over their respective claims.

Rather than dividing the territorial spoils of war into colonies to be distributed among the victors, a new method of dealing with the defeated countries was devised. Conquered territories were now established as "mandates" under the authority of the League of Nations. In the Middle East, France was given the mandate for Syria and Lebanon. Great Britain received mandates for Iraq, Palestine and Transjordan. According to the new theory, the European mandatory powers were to assist the mandated territories to obtain independence rather than to exploit them.

Palestine was a special case because of its ties to Christianity, Islam and Judaism and because of British wartime promises to the Zionists. The mandate for Palestine incorporated the provisions of the Balfour Declaration and emphasized the rights and privileges of the Jewish community. It formally recognized the Zionist movement as the appropriate Jewish agency in matters affecting establishment of a national home and the interests of the country's Jewish population. For example, it provided for Jewish settlement on state lands and Jewish immigration into the country. There was no specific reference to the Arab population by name. Instead they were called the "inhabitants of Palestine." Although Great Britain was vested with "full powers of legislation and administration," special emphasis was placed on British responsibility "for placing the country under such political, administrative and economic conditions as will secure the establishment of the Jewish national home . . ."

BRITISH RULE IN PALESTINE

When the British occupied Palestine in 1917–18, the population had declined by nearly a fifth to about 650,000 as a result of wartime famine, epidemics and deteriorating economic conditions. The Jewish population decreased by about a third to only 55,000. Because many Jewish settlers were subjects of Turkey's enemy Russia, they had been deported or left the country after 1914.

Initially the country was placed under military rule. In 1920, after Great Britain and France agreed on the frontiers of Palestine and the adjoining French mandated area of Syria and Lebanon, a civilian high commissioner was appointed. He was Herbert Samuel, an English Jew who was a Zionist supporter. In theory, Great Britain was responsible to the League of Nations for administration of the country. However, Palestine was governed much like a British colony. The high commissioner was not responsible to the people of Palestine, but to the British government in London. During the period of the mandate from 1920 to 1948, most of the six high commissioners who followed Herbert Samuel were former generals and colonial governors. Since there were no country-wide elections, they had authority to make appointments and to remove officials and to approve or cancel legislation. The high commissioner had the authority and power of a colonial governor or viceroy in India. He delegated authority through his staff or an appointed executive council of mostly British officials. District commissioners who were also British ruled the three principal subdivisions of the country. There were about 10,000 employees in the Palestine civil service. Apart from the police, only some 250 were British. By the end of the mandate, about one-third were Jewish and two-thirds Arab. Major decisions were made by high-ranking British officials, and day-to-day affairs were implemented by their Jewish and Arab subordinates.

The country was governed under the 1922 Palestine Order in Council, in effect a constitution, passed by the British parliament. Most legislation was based on English law; however, the British also incorporated much of the Ottoman legal system in matters pertaining to land and to personal status. Thus jurisdiction relating to marriage, divorce and inheritance was assigned, as during the Ottoman era, to Muslim, Jewish and Christian religious courts. The respective communities in Palestine were recognized as religious rather than as political under the Religious Communities Organization Ordinance. Through continuation of the *millet* system, each community retained control over many aspects of social and religious life, and the British authorities managed matters such as security, economic development and Palestine's relations with the outside world.

During the mandate, there was major progress in economic development. Formerly isolated regions were linked through new roads; the railway and communications networks were extended; health and educational facilities were improved with British assistance in the Arab sector and by the Jews in the Yishuv. Agricultural and industrial productivity increased. Zionist leaders claimed credit not only for development of the Yishuv, but for improvements in the country as a whole. The British credited their administration. Arab nationalists discounted these advances, asserting that they benefited the British and Jewish settlers rather than the great majority of the population.

British officials made several unsuccessful attempts to establish self-governing institutions. In 1922, they presented a plan for a 23-member legislative council with a 12-member elected majority of 8 Muslims, 2 Jews and 2 Christians. Ten members would be appointed by the high commissioner acting as head of the council. The Jews were unenthusiastic because they would have only 2 of the 23 members. Arab nationalists rejected the plan because it was offered by Herbert Samuel, an "ardent Zionist." Finally, Samuel reconstituted the old advisory council, but even that was too much for Arab nationalists, who forced members of their community to resign.

A year later Samuel encouraged the Arabs to establish their own self-governing Arab Agency, parallel to the Jewish Agency representing the Zionists, but he was rebuffed because such a step would be tantamount to recognizing the mandate.

Until 1936 there were several more efforts to develop national self-governing institutions, but they were all aborted due to differences between Jews and Arabs. The Jews, a minority of the population, feared they would always be outvoted. Arab nationalists charged that because they were the majority they would be underrepresented. The most militant Arab nationalists refused to accept any British attempts to establish political institutions because that would mean recognizing the mandate. Consequently there was little local input into major government decisions. Local government fared better. There was a degree of municipal and village self-government through local councils.

British policy fluctuated at all levels according to the prejudices of local officials, some of whom favored the Jewish community, others sympathetic to Arab nationalism. The dilemma of dual obligation often stymied official policy. According to the mandate, the British were obligated to foster development of a Jewish national home, but they were also obligated to prevent discrimination against any group and to ensure "that the rights and position of other [non-Jewish] sectors of the population are not prejudiced . . ." Palestine also presented difficulties in the larger context of British colonial and foreign policy. Many officials believed that obligations to the Zionists under the mandate would jeopardize friendship with other Muslim and Arab nations.

Rise of Palestinian Nationalism

Between World War I and World War II, the Palestinian Arab community was 90% Sunni Muslim living in some 850 rural villages. The largest urban populations were in Jerusalem and Jaffa; Arabs also lived in several cities and towns including Haifa, Bethlehem, Nablus, Hebron and Ramallah. The social and political patterns established during the Ottoman era continued throughout the mandate period. Most Arabs were *fellahin*, the rate of illiteracy was high, and villages were divided into extended families or clans called *hamulas*. In northern Palestine, many landholdings were controlled by absentee owners living in Beirut and Damascus. The southern half of the country, the Negev, was largely barren desert still inhabited by bedouins belonging to tribal confederations extending across the frontier into the Sinai peninsula and

Transjordan. In the central mountainous regions, there were a larger number of small landowners who lived in impoverished conditions. When the mandate was established, most Arabs in Palestine did not think of themselves as Palestinians but as related to the larger administrative regions in Syria or Lebanon.

Ottoman repression and Allied promises of self-determination during World War I sparked a nationalist awakening by 1918, mostly among the middle class. At first, Palestinians identified with the Arab kingdom established in Syria by the Sherif Husayn's son, Faysal. Palestinian delegations were represented in the nationalist congresses held in Damascus during 1919 and 1920. Older politicians representing the traditional elite and notable families formerly associated with the Ottomans established nationalist Muslim-Christian associations (MCAs) in several towns and induced the Syrian congresses to adopt anti-Zionist platforms.

Younger politicians, many of them also from notable families, formed more militant organizations, such as the Literary Club and the Arab Club. Both initially supported unification with Faysal's Syrian kingdom but later moved toward a distinctive Palestine nationalism. With the separation of Palestine from greater Syria and establishment of British rule, Palestinian Arabs developed their own national sentiment in opposition to Great Britain and Zionism.

The Arab community was much less centralized and more loosely organized than the Yishuv. Religious differences existed between Muslim and Christian Arabs, although the latter were among the most active participants in the nationalist movement. There were marked class distinctions among the wealthy elite, the rural *fellahin* and the urban working class. City Arabs tended to look down on those from the villages and the rural areas. Rivalries between villages often erupted into violence. Political life was dominated by leaders of the principal families and their allied clans. The two most influential were the Husaynis and the Nashashibis. The Arab Literary Club was dominated by members of the Nashashibi family, and the Husaynis controlled the Arab Club.

By far the most influential personality was Haj Amin al-Husayni, appointed by the British as mufti (Islamic religious leader) of Jerusalem and president of the country's Supreme Muslim Council. Husayni notables had obtained large tracts of land in southern Palestine during the 19th century; 6 of Jerusalem's 13 mayors in the half-century preceding the war had been from the Husayni family. To maintain a balance of power after 1918, the British appointed a Nashashibi to the post of mayor of Jerusalem and Haj Amin as the highest Islamic authority.

By 1920 the Husaynis shifted the emphasis of the nationalist movement away from unity with Syria to independence for Palestine. Although Haj

Amin was among the most militant nationalists, Herbert Samuel appointed him to the highest religious office in the country, which made him in effect the leader of the Muslim Arab nationalist movement. As president of the Supreme Muslim Council, he was the successor in Palestine to the former Ottoman Sheikh al-Islam with authority to designate judges in the Islamic Sharia courts, administer funds for maintenance of mosques, shrines and religious schools and assign or dismiss officials in this extensive system. The rival Nashashibi family began to organize against the mufti during the 1920s, setting up National Muslim Societies as a counterweight to the Husayni-controlled MCAs. Attempts to unify the nationalist movement at an Arab Congress in Jerusalem during 1928 failed because the two families could not be reconciled; the congress disappeared after the death of its executive chairman, Musa Kazem al-Husayni, in 1934.

Failures at unification aroused dissatisfaction among many of the younger Palestinian Arab intellectuals, and they decided to organize independently of the Husaynis and Nashashibis during the 1930s. Six new nationalist factions were formed during the next few years, the beginning of a new phase in the national movement. Differences among the groups were based largely on personalities rather than on political ideology or plans for dealing with economic and social problems. All were adamantly opposed to the establishment of a Jewish homeland in Palestine, but they varied in the intensity of opposition to the mandatory government. These factions were dominated by men from influential families and the urban intelligentsia. There were no party elections, and conferences were irregular. Most parties were called by the names of their leaders.

The mufti's Palestine Arab party formed in 1935 remained the most influential by virtue of the Husayni family's extensive network of *hamula* contacts and Haj Amin's role as leader of the Muslim establishment. Several prominent Christian Arabs and one of the larger Arab labor unions were affiliated with the mufti. His party also formed an illegal quasi-military youth group called al-Futuwwah (Chivalry), which was to play a role in the fight against Zionist paramilitary organizations. The party's platform, called the National Pact, demanded that Great Britain repudiate the Balfour Declaration and terminate the mandate and that Palestine become an independent Arab state immediately; Jewish immigration to Palestine and the sale of land to Jews would have to cease. An Arab National Fund was established, emulating the Jewish National Fund, to purchase land that might otherwise fall into the hands of the Yishuv. Arabs who sold land to Jews were threatened with punishment as traitors.

The Palestine Arab party's principal rival was the Nashashibi National Defense party formed in 1934. It was supported by most Arab mayors opposed to the mufti's political domination. The party also had its Christian supporters and was backed by another Arab labor union. The Nashashibis were closely allied with the Emir (prince) Abdullah ibn Husayn, ruler of Transjordan, a bitter rival of the Husaynis. Because of Abdullah's close ties with Great Britain, the Nashashibis were less hostile to the British and more willing to seek political compromise, but they were no less hostile to Zionism and attempts to establish a Jewish national home in Palestine.

The Istiqlal (Independence) party had the program with the greatest ideological content. An offshoot of an organization formed in Damascus after the war, it still called for Arab unity but gave priority to independence of each separate Arab nation. The program attracted many younger professionals and Arab government officials.

The common denominator of all the Arab political factions was unqualified opposition to Zionism and rejection of Jewish historical claims to Palestine. They maintained that the Arab population had not benefited from the mandate; on the contrary, they charged that the local peasantry was being displaced from its ancestral home by Jewish settlers. They also claimed that although there were certain material advantages such as improved roads, health facilities and educational services, the gains were offset by exorbitant taxes, high tariffs to protect new Jewish industries and escalating prices paid for products of Jewish commerce. They argued that selection of Palestine by Great Britain and the West as a refuge for persecuted Jews was misguided humanitarianism. Some believed that it was mere window-dressing for a scheme to destroy Palestinian Arab national and cultural aspirations. Continued Jewish immigration would displace more Arabs and undermine the country's economy.

This line of argument was spread through the Arab community by the Arabic press, in mosque sermons and by teachers in the Arab public school system. After 1933, when Jewish immigration increased as a result of persecution in Nazi Germany, Arab anxiety greatly intensified. The influx of Jewish professionals, such as lawyers, accountants and clerks, raised fears of competition in the Arab middle class. Nationalist impatience was aroused by comparison of their position in Palestine with accomplishments of nationalist movements in the surrounding countries where Great Britain and France were extending greater self-rule to the Arab communities in Lebanon, Syria, Iraq and Egypt.

Although the Jewish population of Palestine was less than one-third and Jews owned less than 8% of the land by 1936, the Yishuv was a highly visible presence. Its principal settlement, Tel Aviv, had grown to a major city; the number of Jewish settlements had increased by scores; Jewish industrial establishments were proliferating; it was becoming clear to the country's Arabs that the Jewish national home was well on its way.

Fear increased that Palestine-Arab aspirations for independence were likely to become unattainable. Radical elements in the Arab community demanded a country-wide strike against the government. By November 1935, independent strike committees were organized in several of the largest Arab towns. In November one of the first Palestine guerrilla groups emerged, led by Sheikh Izz al-Din al-Qasim. The Sheikh's revolt was quickly crushed by the British, and he was killed in battle with the army. However he became a legendary hero whose message spread to national committees in towns and villages. Later guerrilla groups glorified him as the founder of modern Palestinian Arab resistance. Within a few weeks, the sporadic local strikes and incidents of armed violence led to formation of an Arab National Committee to back nationalist demands. A nationwide strike was declared against the British mandatory government, and a boycott was placed on the Jewish community. The various competing Arab factions now formed an Arab Higher Committee to direct the resistance. Passive resistance soon degenerated into a full-fledged revolution. Trains were derailed, bridges blown up, and armed bands including volunteers from Syria and Iraq seized parts of the country.

All sectors of Arab society, including those who worked for the mandatory government, supported the initial strike. Several Arab government officers petitioned the British stating that the unrest had occurred because ". . . the Arab population of all classes, creeds and occupations is animated by a profound sense of injustice done to them. They feel that insufficient regard has been paid to them . . . [and to] their legitimate grievances . . . As a result, the Arabs have been driven to a state verging on despair; and the present unrest is no more than an expression of that despair."

During the first phase of the rebellion, from August to October 1936, the Arab Higher Committee succeeded in imposing order and discipline on the community. The guerrilla bands recognized the authority of the Committee, and local villagers provided the fighters with money, arms and hiding places. By the end of 1936, the strike was called off; the first signs of intracommunal strife broke out between the Nashashibis and Husaynis, and the rulers of Iraq, Saudi Arabia and Transjordan attempted to mediate the disputes. When Great Britain agreed to send a royal commission to investigate, some leaders were willing to call off the uprising, but others wanted to continue fighting. The Nashashibis agreed to halt the violence and consider the royal commission recommendations, but the Husaynis refused to compromise. When the Nashashibi leader resigned from the Arab Higher Committee, it was abandoned to the followers of the mufti, who decided to continue the revolt. By 1937 the uprising spread not only against the British, but against "traitors" in the National Defense party who called for moderation. The result was a civil war that forced the Nashashibis to organize their own armed units, the "Peace

Corps," which retaliated against attacks by the Husaynis. In the interclan fighting, several hundred Arabs were executed by fellow countrymen for resisting Husayni leadership.

Organized Arab bands became so successful that they succeeded in taking over substantial parts of the country, including several towns and the Old City of Jerusalem. A number of guerrilla leaders of that era became folk heroes, their exploits part of Palestinian nationalist mythology. An influx of British troops and an all-out effort to suppress the uprising at the end of 1938 greatly weakened the guerrilla effort. Increasing dissension within the movement and its loss of mass popularity resulting from heavy-handed guerrilla measures against suspected traitors further undermined the revolt. National unity like that of early 1936 was not again achieved until the Intifada against Israel that lasted from 1987 to 1994.

After 1938 national disintegration and increasing interfactional quarrels increased. By the beginning of World War II, the Palestine national movement was in complete disarray. Many leaders had fled the country; several were captured and imprisoned by the British. During World War II, Palestine became a major British base in the eastern Mediterranean, ending possibilities of resistance.

Despite the failures of Arab nationalism in the 1920s, 1930s and 1940s, the 1936–39 rebellion forced the British to abandon the partition proposals of the royal (Peel) commission (see below). On the eve of the war, the British convened the London Round Table Conferences, which culminated in the 1939 White Paper sharply limiting Jewish immigration and land purchases in Palestine and guaranteeing an Arab state in Palestine.

RISE OF THE YISHUV

In the period between the two world wars, the Yishuv, or Jewish community, was able to establish the foundations of the future Jewish state in Palestine by transforming Zionism from an abstract ideology into a national political movement with a solid economic base. The number of Jewish settlements increased tenfold; the Jewish population expanded from a tiny minority to nearly one-third; a Jewish economic infrastructure with its own agriculture, industry, trade and commerce took root. Hebrew—a language most Jews had not known—became the official language of the Jewish community; a number of Hebrew-language newspapers and publishing houses were founded; and Hebrew became the medium of instruction in the Yishuv's educational system, capped by the Hebrew University in Jerusalem.

Between 1919 and 1948, the Jewish population grew from 65,000 to 650,000, largely through immigration. The majority of the Yishuv were immigrants from Eastern Europe, mostly from Poland and Russia, with smaller numbers from Romania, Bulgaria and Hungary. A few came from the Middle East, mainly from Yemen. After 1933 a new wave of Jewish refugees from Nazi persecution came from Germany and Central Europe. Each successive wave of migration was called an *aliya* (ascent) because the arrivals were "going up" to the Holy Land. The first Aliya consisted of the small groups of Bilu (see above) who came from Russia during the late 19th century. Only half of the 10,000 Jews in the first Aliya became farmers. The others began new urban settlements; a few abandoned Palestine and moved abroad.

Failure of the 1905 revolution in Russia led to the second Aliya of young workers and socialist Zionists. Many of the Jewish state's founders and Israel's first political leaders such as David Ben-Gurion came in this wave. The third Aliya between 1919 and 1923 arrived from Poland and Eastern and Central Europe, where economic pressures and increased anti-Semitism made life difficult. Those 35,000 were among the founders of the Yishuv's labor organizations and agricultural settlements (*kibbutzim* and *moshavim*). About half of the settlers in the fourth Aliya left Poland between 1925 and 1929 as a result of economic discrimination and the closed-door immigration policy of the United States after 1925.

The largest Aliya was the fifth, made up of German and Austrian Jews who came after Hitler's rise to power. Between 1933 and 1936, 164,000 Jews immigrated to Palestine as a result of Nazi persecution. The German Jewish Aliya changed the social structure of the Yishuv. A large percentage of these immigrants were university-educated professionals and intellectuals with upper middle-class values, often more cosmopolitan Europeans than typical Ghetto Jews. They introduced many of their values, traditions and cultural preferences to the Yishuv. Until arrival of the middle-class Germans, the Yishuv was fairly homogeneous with no great class differences; during the previous half-century, the Jewish community had mostly come from an area of only a few hundred square miles containing the ghettos of Eastern Europe.

It was easy to develop a strong national sentiment in this small, close-knit community. The average individual grew up with little knowledge of the larger surrounding Arab community. Jews were born in Jewish hospitals, educated in Jewish schools, employed in Jewish factories or trades, belonged to Jewish trade unions, social clubs and political parties and were finally buried in Jewish cemeteries.

During the mandate, the Yishuv developed a number of political and communal organizations that later became became integral components of institutional life in the Jewish state. A national council (Va'ad Leumi) chosen by an elected assembly (Asafat ha-Nivharim) was established in 1920 to manage the day-to-day affairs of the Yishuv. It was responsible for matters such as health, education and social services delegated to it by the British mandatory government. Only a small number of ultraorthodox, non-Zionist Jews opted out of membership in the official organizations of the Yishuv.

As the Zionist movement expanded, many different economic and social perspectives developed among its members: conservative, liberal and Marxist; secular and ultrareligious; militantly nationalist and broadly humanistic. These views were represented by a variety of Zionist political parties, most of them transplanted to Palestine from the diaspora. Early Zionist groups were the predecessors of the major political parties now represented in Israel's parliament, or Knesset. These parties were both national and international because they were represented in the national council in Palestine and in the World Zionist Organization and Congress, which until World War II met in Europe.

By 1936 there were 10 main parties, each uniting two or more subgroups. When the mandate ended, there were nearly three dozen Jewish political factions representing four major trends: labor, centrist, nationalist and orthodox-religious. The dominant trend was labor, which controlled institutions like the national council and the Histadrut, or General Federation of Jewish Workers in Palestine. The Histadrut and the labor parties controlled the agricultural sector, most kibbutzim, much of the transportation system, a large part of the publishing industry, including a major newspaper, and the Haganah, or self-defense organization. As its strength increased, it developed its own industries, marketing cooperatives, banks, financial institutions and social service network. The most influential leaders of the Yishuv came from the labor movement and its affiliated institutions.

Interest in and support for the "national home" among Jews in the diaspora was maintained through the World Zionist Organization, which had affiliates in countries throughout the West. Zionists abroad could demonstrate loyalty to the cause through financial contributions, by voting for one of the parties represented in the periodical meetings of the Zionist Congress and by organizing pressure groups to obtain support from their respective governments. In 1929 Chaim Weizmann, then president of the Zionist Organization, called for establishment of the Jewish Agency for Palestine, a non-Zionist organization created to include Jews who were sympathetic to the idea of the national home but not ideologically committed to Zionism. The Jewish Agency took over responsibility for many activities, including fund-raising and liaison with foreign governments. Although a non-Zionist organization, many of the Jewish Agency's important offices, including the presidency and political, finance, labor, trade and industry departments, were headed by Zionists.

Palestinian Jews outnumbered representatives from other countries by the late 1930s in the principal positions of both the Jewish Agency and World Zionist Organization. For all practical purposes, the most important affairs concerning the national home were in the hands of those who lived there by the end of the mandate. Participation in these organizations and in the mandatory government gave thousands of Palestinian Jews a wealth of administrative experience; they provided the cadre of officials who assumed leadership in the new state of Israel when it was established in 1948.

The Israel Defense Force (IDF) was also forged during the mandate period under direction of the Yishuv leadership; it was then called the Haganah (defense). During the era of British rule, the Haganah was an illegal underground organization. In the 1936–39 Arab rebellion, several Haganah members who favored more militant tactics in fighting the uprising broke away to form the National Military Organization (Irgun Zvai Leumi [IZL]), affiliated with the ultranationalist Revisionist Zionist movement.

Conflict between the Yishuv and the Palestine Arab Community

There was little contact between the Palestinian Jewish and Arab communities during the mandate. Each community conducted its own social, political, economic, cultural and commercial affairs independently of the other. Only in mixed cities like Jerusalem or Haifa were there significant intercommunity relations. (One rare exception was the Palestine Citrus Marketing Board where Jews and Arabs cooperated in seeking favorable overseas markets for their produce.) The two communities were separated by language, religion, social customs and, most importantly, by their respective political aspirations for the future of Palestine.

Most leaders in each community regarded the national goals of the other as incompatible with their own. The Arabs sought to establish an independent Palestinian Arab state, to achieve self-government, as in the neighboring Arab countries, Egypt, Syria, Lebanon and Iraq. The Yishuv wanted to make Palestine the Jewish national home, a refuge for Jews from all over the world. Some favored an independent Jewish state, some an entity part of the British Commonwealth; others were not sure what political status the Jewish entity should hold. A small minority of Zionists sought a compromise through establishment of a binational state in which neither Jew nor Arab would dominate. However the idea of an Arab-Jewish or Jewish-Arab state was rejected by the Zionist majority; only a handful of Arab nationalists found the idea acceptable.

The inevitable consequence of these diametrically opposed national goals was the periodic outbreak of violence. The first clashes broke out in 1920 when Arabs attacked Jewish settlements in Galilee in northern Palestine and anti-Jewish riots erupted in Jerusalem. In 1921 there were attacks on other Jewish towns and fighting between British troops and Arab guerrillas. A

British commission headed by Sir Thomas Haycraft, chief justice of Palestine, concluded that although responsible for the disturbances, the Arabs had a legitimate basis for fear because of Jewish immigration and their perception of Zionist influence on the mandatory government. The British responded by temporarily suspending immigration, then lifting the suspension after protests from Jews abroad.

Continued Arab unrest led the British government to issue a new policy statement on Palestine in July 1922 called the Churchill Memorandum or Churchill White Paper. It reaffirmed Britain's commitment to the Balfour Declaration, stating that the Jews were in Palestine as of "right and not on sufferance." There would be a Jewish "home" *in* Palestine, but Jewish immigration should not exceed the country's economic absorptive capacity. Britain, the memorandum stated, never contemplated "the disappearance or the subordination of the Arabic population, language or culture . . . [or] the imposition of a Jewish nationality upon the inhabitants of Palestine as a whole." The meaning of "economic absorptive capacity" and "Jewish home" were crucial questions.

Some British officials believed that Palestine could become a Jewish homeland under British control, without becoming an independent state. Most Zionist leaders, like David Ben Gurion, aspired to make the country a Jewish state, although there were differences over how and when to realize that objective. Some wanted immediate independence; others preferred to wait until there was a Jewish majority in Palestine.

In 1929 there were far more serious riots. The small Jewish community in Hebron was attacked and driven from the city with many casualties. In Jerusalem a major dispute arose over the Wailing Wall, believed to be the last remnant of the Jewish temple destroyed by the Romans. It adjoined the Haram es-Sherif, site of the two holy mosques. Quarrels between Muslims and Jews over access to the wall led to violent altercations.

Another royal commission sent to investigate these "disturbances" reiterated the observations of Lord Haycraft about Arab fears of Jewish immigration. The report observed, "The Arab fellaheen and villagers are . . . probably more politically minded than many of the people of Europe."

A new policy statement followed in 1930. Known as the Passfield White Paper, it declared that British obligations to Jews and Arabs were "of equal weight" but "in no sense irreconcilable." Because of the scarcity of agricultural land for settling new immigrants, the white paper called for stricter control of immigration and of land sales to Jews. After protests by Zionist supporters in England, Prime Minister Ramsay MacDonald denied that the mandatory authorities were considering a ban on land sales to Jews or placing new limitations on Jewish immigration. Arab nationalists called the prime minister's qualifications of the Passfield document "MacDonald's Black Paper."

By the 1930s, events in Europe exacerbated the tension in Palestine. Pressure increased to permit larger Jewish immigration; on the other hand, Hitler and Mussolini began to express sympathy for Arab nationalist goals. In Palestine, Arab anxiety was intensified by fears of the expanding Yishuv and British support for Zionist goals. Resentment of Britain and fears of the Yishuv finally culminated in the Palestine Arab revolt between 1936 and 1939 (see above).

In 1937 still another royal commission was sent to investigate, headed by Earl Peel, a former secretary of state for India. The report again stated Arab grievances about Jewish immigration and land acquisition. The commission believed that mandatory obligations to the Jews regarding immigration and land settlement could not be fulfilled without British repression of an unwilling Arab population. The Palestine Arabs were bound to accentuate their demands for independence as their community developed and the Arabs in surrounding countries attained self-rule. At the same time, the political assertiveness of Palestinian Jews was equally bound to sharpen as their presence expanded and pressure grew to increase Jewish immigration from Europe. Consequently there was no hope of bridging the chasm between the two communities or of establishing representative institutions in the country. The only arrangement consistent with British obligations was to divide Palestine into sovereign Arab and Jewish states and a British mandatory zone.

Under the Peel Commission plan published in 1937, the Jewish state would have included the Galilee, the Jezreel Valley and the coastal plain midway between Gaza and Jaffa, about 20% of the country's area. This tiny state of approximately 2,000 square miles would have a population of 285,000 Jews and 225,000 Arabs. Jaffa would become part of the Arab state, which would include most of the rest of Palestine united with Transjordan. The British zone would include Jerusalem, Bethlehem, and a corridor linking them to the Mediterranean Sea. Arabs and Jews would both have access to the ports of Haifa and Aqaba.

The Zionist movement was divided about acceptance of the plan. Some objected to partition in principle, insisting that the Jews had an "inalienable right" to all of Palestine. The 20th Zionist Congress in 1937 endorsed the principle of partition but called for further negotiations with Britain to increase the area of the proposed Jewish state.

Both Husaynis and Nashashibis opposed partition but differed in methods of responding to the Peel plan. Only four days before the release of the royal commission report in July 1937, the National Defense party quit the Arab Higher Committee, accusing the mufti of arbitrary conduct. In a memorandum to the British government, the Committee expressed "repugnance to the whole of the partition scheme." The National Defense party called for the establishment of a sovereign, democratic state in which the existing ratio between Jews and Arabs would be maintained.

The Palestine Partition (Woodhead) Commission sent to investigate ways of implementing the Peel plan in 1938 unanimously agreed that partition would be unworkable because the proposed Jewish state was too small and the likelihood of Arab resistance too great. Sir Herbert Samuel observed in 1937 that "the Commission seemed to have picked out all the most awkward provisions of the Peace Treaties of Versailles, to have put a Saar, a Polish Corridor and a half dozen Danzigs and Memels into a country the size of Wales."

Just before World War II, Great Britain convened an Anglo-Jewish-Arab conference in London during February and March 1939 to discuss the future of Palestine. The conference failed to break the deadlock; Arab participants refused to meet face-to-face with the Jewish representatives.

In a final prewar white paper issued in 1939, the British government ruled out establishment of Palestine as a Jewish state. Instead, the government intended to develop self-governing institutions leading to a state in which Jews and Arabs would exercise joint authority within 10 years. Jews, Arabs and British would participate in drafting a constitution that would safeguard the holy places, the special position of the Jewish national home and British interests. Great Britain would no longer impose Jewish immigration on the Arab majority. Instead, within the next five years, 75,000 Jews would be permitted to settle in Palestine as a contribution to solving the European Jewish refugee problem. After 1944 further Jewish immigration would depend on Arab consent. In the meantime, illegal Jewish immigrants would be deported from the country. Land sales would be subject to control of the high commissioner, who could prohibit sales in certain areas. Under this arrangement, the sale of land to Jews was prohibited in most parts of the country; Jewish land purchases were restricted to the small areas where Jews had already settled, constituting less than 10% of the total area of Palestine.

In effect, the 1939 White Paper repudiated the Balfour Declaration, for it gave Palestine's Arab majority the final say on Jewish immigration. Since Arab nationalists were united in their opposition to Jewish immigration—even the moderates objected to increasing the ratio of Jews to Arabs—the white paper meant that within five years the country would have a guaranteed Arab majority.

Zionists and the Yishuv saw the white paper as the death warrant of the Jewish national home—or state—and vowed to resist its implementation. A state in which the number of Arabs was fixed at twice the number of Jews would in effect be an Arab state, the Jewish Agency protested. The Yishuv would be relegated to the position of a permanent minority under domination of an Arab government. In Palestine the Yishuv reacted with dismay at what they perceived to be Great Britain's betrayal. One result was an increase of enlistment in the IZL, the dissident faction that had broken earlier with the Haganah. The leaders of the Va'ad Leumi and the Jewish Agency proclaimed their intention to continue Jewish immigration despite British efforts to restrict it.

Palestinian Arab leadership, already factionalized between Husaynis and Nashashibis, failed to come forward with any unified reaction to the white paper. By mid-1939 the Arab rebellion was crushed by the British army and the mufti and many of his colleagues were in exile, forbidden to return to Palestine. British censorship even prevented the mention of the Mufti's name in the local press. The Nashashibi National Defense party did attempt to rally support for the white paper, and several Arab commando leaders issued a statement declaring it "an acceptable basis for the furtherance of Arab aspirations."

After World War II broke out in September 1939, the conflict between Jews and Arabs in Palestine entered a new phase. The Arab rebellion ended, Jewish attention shifted from the white paper to the struggle against Hitler, and British policy regarding Palestine was overshadowed by larger global concerns. Once the war started, Ben-Gurion stated: "We shall fight the war as if there were no White Paper; we shall fight the White Paper as if there were no war."

TERMINATION OF THE MANDATE AND ESTABLISHMENT OF ISRAEL

PALESTINE AND WORLD WAR II

Despite bitterness caused by the 1939 White Paper, the Yishuv and world Zionist leaders had no alternative but to support Allied war efforts against the Nazis. At the conclusion of the 1939 Zionist Congress a few weeks before war broke out, Chaim Weizmann informed British Prime Minister Neville Chamberlain that the Jews "stand by Great Britain and will fight on the side of the democracies."

During the war, the Yishuv imposed full mobilization on the Jewish community, enlisting some 135,000 men and women volunteers for military and other service. Several companies of volunteers from Palestine were attached to the British army, and a Jewish Brigade was formed in 1942 to fight in North Africa, Italy and the Mediterranean. In Palestine a Jewish Rural Special Police unit was organized as a kind of home guard under British command. The country became one of the most important Allied bases during the war.

The economic contributions of Palestine and the Yishuv to the war effort were also significant. Jewish-owned factories began to produce goods that were formerly imported from Europe but could no longer reach the eastern Mediterranean because of the Axis blockade. Food, clothing, pharmaceuticals, metal, electrical equipment, timber, cement and other industrial products were shipped from Palestine to the surrounding countries, and Jewish contractors were used to build military camps and roads throughout the Levant.

Within Palestine the political climate was considerably calmer that it had been in decades. The most militant Arab nationalists were in prison or in exile, and most of the Yishuv called off its confrontation with the mandatory authorities to help the war effort. Only one small paramilitary faction called Fighters for the Freedom of Israel (Hebrew acronym Lehi), led by Abraham Stern, resolved to continue the struggle against the British. Lehi broke away from IZL when the parent group decided to suspend hostilities against the British for the duration of the war. The Stern gang continued to attack British installations; one of its most reprehensible actions was the assassination of Lord Moyne, British minister resident in the Middle East, in November 1944. The assassination threatened to undermine relations between the Yishuv and Great Britain, leading Weizmann to write Winston Churchill of his "deep moral indignation and horror." Weizmann pledged that the Yishuv would "go to the utmost limit of its power to cut out, root and branch, this evil from its midst."

Throughout the war, the Yishuv continued one form of resistance to the British: the community flouted restrictions on immigration imposed by the 1939 White Paper. Despite the immigration quotas established by the mandatory government, the Yishuv, collaborating with Zionists abroad, organized an illegal underground migration to Palestine called *aliya bet*. A number of small ships, many of them barely seaworthy, were sent with Jewish immigrants from European ports across the Mediterranean to Palestine. Some of these ships were intercepted by the British navy, and the immigrant cargo was dispatched to special camps in Palestine. When the number of illegal immigrants overburdened the camps in Palestine, they were deported to remote British outposts in Africa or to the island of Mauritius.

Many Zionist leaders saw the war as an opportunity to gain international support for their goals and to clarify the concept of Jewish national home. The intensification of Jewish persecution in Europe, the 1939 White Paper and demands for establishment of a Jewish army were all stimulants to a more militant activism. Nearly all Zionist factions could agree on policy concerning these issues. The mainstream parties held an emergency meeting at the Biltmore Hotel in New York City during May 1942 to reevaluate the Zionist program and to decide on a unified course of action in the face of these events.

The restatement of the Zionist program resulting from these meetings was called the Biltmore Program. It urged "that the gates of Palestine be opened" and demanded that the Jewish Agency be given control over immigration into Palestine. Palestine should be established as a "Jewish Commonwealth" integrated into the structure of the new democratic world. The Biltmore Program was adopted by the Yishuv, and it became the basis of mainstream Zionism until establishment of the state of Israel in 1948.

By the end of the war, the Yishuv and the international community realized the full extent of Nazi persecution of Jews in Europe. Under Hitler a Holocaust had devoured some six million Jews, nearly 90% of European Jews or about one in three Jews in the world. The Nazis had made clear their intention to destroy all the Jews who fell under their domination. After Germany's surrender in May 1945, the Allies found that they were faced with the problem of seven million displaced persons, including hundreds of thousands who refused to return to their former homes. By 1946, there were 250,000 Jewish displaced persons, most of whom sought refuge outside their homelands.

Despite the war and the Holocaust, British policy in Palestine was still based on enforcing the provisions of the 1939 White Paper that set a limited quota on Jewish immigration. In the United States, President Harry Truman urged Great Britain to admit 100,000 Jewish survivors to Palestine immediately; in response to his appeals, the U.S. Congress agreed to allow 20,000 to enter the United States.

The World Zionist Organization and the Yishuv in Palestine demanded that all restrictions on Jewish immigration be removed and the provisions of the white paper be totally rescinded. Both the Yishuv and Zionist supporters abroad declared that they would openly flout any British restrictions on development of the Jewish national home.

REVOLT OF THE YISHUV

Even before the war ended, the Yishuv initiated a campaign to resist the British. The Haganah and its strike force, the Palmah, joined the two dissident Jewish factions, IZL and Lehi, in attacks on British installations used to control illegal immigration. A radar post, police stations and military airfields were hit; railways and the British-owned Iraq Petroleum Company pipeline were sabotaged. Despite collaborating in several operations, the three Jewish paramilitary groups remained politically divided. The Haganah ordered its members to limit their actions to attacks on military installations and to avoid, where possible, injuring those manning them. Lehi and IZL were not so scrupulous, often deliberately killing British soldiers or civilian employees of the government. To finance their operations, the two dissident organizations also held up banks and threatened businesses. As a result, both Lehi and IZL became known as terrorist organizations, and many in the Yishuv and among Zionists abroad denounced them for their ruthlessness. Even the leaders of the Yishuv disclaimed responsibility for Lehi and IZL; members of the two groups accused the Jewish Agency and the Haganah of helping the British in tracking down those who participated in actions denounced by the Yishuv leadership.

After the war, Jewish illegal immigration was stepped up, and the number of ships crossing the Mediterranean with refugees from the displaced persons camps in Europe increased. One of the most publicized ventures was the trip of the *Exodus 1947* which, after being intercepted by the British navy, arrived in Haifa from France during July 1947, with some 4,500 refugees. When the British refused to permit the passengers to disembark, fighting broke out, and several refugees were killed or wounded. The British ultimately forced the ship with its refugee cargo to return to its port of origin in France. In most instances, when ships were intercepted or refugees arrested after landing, they were interned in camps near Haifa or sent to large detention centers set up by the British military in Cyprus.

British attempts to contain violence in Palestine were increasingly frustrated. Several thousand additional troops were sent, and the number of British police officers increased, but to no avail. In June 1946, the Haganah severed transport between Palestine and neighboring countries by blowing up the principal rail and highway bridges along the borders. The IZL struck at the heart of British mandatory officialdom in July when it bombed government offices in Jerusalem's King David Hotel, killing some 80 British, Arab and Jewish government workers. Although the attack was denounced by the Jewish Agency and the leadership of the Yishuv, the British decided to take drastic measures. A curfew was imposed on the entire Yishuv and house-to-house searches for arms were made. All Jewish homes and businesses were placed out of bounds for British soldiers; they were ordered not "to have any social intercourse with any Jew."

By the end of the war, the Arab community also again became politically active. The Palestine problem arose as one of the principal concerns of the newly formed League of Arab States (also known as the Arab League) and of the five Arab members of the United Nations: Egypt, Syria, Lebanon, Iraq and Saudi Arabia. The Arab League pact contained a special annex on Palestine that stated, "Her international existence and independence in the legal sense cannot . . . be questioned, any more than could the independence of the other Arab countries." Provision was made for Palestine Arab participation in the league as though it were a member state.

Within Palestine the Arab community was still politically divided between the Husaynis and Nashashibis. The Husaynis reorganized the Arab Higher

Committee in 1945, but the opposition countered with an Arab Higher Front. After intervention by the Arab League in 1946, another Arab Higher Committee was set up to represent all elements of the community. A major problem confronting the Palestinian Arab community was that its most widely accepted leader, Haj Amin al-Husayni, was still not permitted to return. He was even less acceptable to the British by 1945 because of his wartime collaboration with Germany.

The involvement of the surrounding Arab states in the Palestine problem put pressure on the British government to stand fast in its prewar policies limiting expansion of the Jewish national home. However, the rising tide of Jewish terrorism and international pressure to admit more refugees placed Great Britain on the horns of a dilemma. Furthermore, the British were exhausted by the war, and their economy was in dire straits. When the new Labor government took over in 1945, it sought to spread responsibility for Palestine by calling for an Anglo-American Committee of Inquiry to investigate the refugee problem in Europe and to make recommendations about the future of Palestine. The new policy was a complete about-face from Labor's former approach to the problem. As recently as 1945, the Labor party had called for revoking restrictions on Jewish immigration and even passed a resolution recommending transfer of Palestinian Arabs to the neighboring countries.

After visiting refugee camps in Europe and holding hearings in Jerusalem, the Anglo-American Commission concluded that even though most European Jews desired to go to Palestine, the country did not have room for all of them. The United States and other Western nations were urged to open their doors to the displaced persons. During 1946, however, 100,000 refugees from the displaced persons camps should be issued permits to enter Palestine. Future immigration would be based on agreement between Jews and Arabs. The land transfer regulations of the 1939 White Paper should be terminated at the same time as limitations placed by Jewish institutions on Arab labor working Jewish-owned land should be ended. Because of Palestine's historical significance to three religions, it should be neither a Jewish nor an Arab land, but binational with equal representation for both groups in a democratic government. The deep animosity between Jews and Arabs prevented independence achieved by peaceful means, therefore Palestine should become a trust area under the United Nations, which would prepare the inhabitants for ultimate independence on a binational basis. The Jewish Agency should assist the mandatory government in suppressing both terrorism and illegal immigration.

President Truman accepted the recommendations providing for admission to Palestine of 100,000 refugees but did not respond to the other parts of the commission's report. Great Britain insisted that if the recommendations on immigration were fulfilled, the report had to be implemented in all its parts. The mainstream Zionist organizations rejected the recommendations, insisting on immediate statehood. Ben-Gurion asserted that "statehood was now more necessary than the 100,000 refugees."

The Palestinian Arab response to the Anglo-American Commission was continued insistence on a unitary Arab state with a permanent Arab majority. At an extraordinary session during June 1946 held in Bludan, Syria, the Arab League angrily denounced the report, complaining that the United States had no legal right to intervene in Palestine. It asserted that "a clamorous and noisy band of Jews" was trying to control American public opinion and undermine U.S. interests in the Arab world. The response to London was that approval of the recommendations would constitute "an unfriendly action" and that Britain and the United States would be responsible for further disturbances, not only in Palestine but throughout the whole Arab East. The Arab League demanded that Great Britain negotiate with the Arabs in accordance with the U.N. Charter, immediately halt Jewish immigration to Palestine and deport all illegal immigrants. A number of secret resolutions were adopted providing for military and other aid to the Palestine Arabs and for sanctions against Britain and the United States should events adversely affect the right of Palestine to become independent.

The Arab League also intervened on behalf of the mufti, Haj Amin al-Husayni, whose return to Palestine had been blocked by mandatory authorities. His followers asserted that Haj Amin was the leader of Palestine's Arabs "for whom they can accept no substitute." He was not really a collaborator with the Nazis but had fled to Germany because of fear for his life, they claimed. In May 1946, the mufti escaped from his refuge in Lebanon and fled to Cairo from where he openly assumed direction of the Palestine Arab Party activities. After the Arab League ordered the reconstitution of the Arab Higher Committee, he also controlled it from Cairo. Within a few weeks, his reputation among the majority of Palestine Arabs was restored, and he was again seen as the leader in the struggle against Zionism and Great Britain.

During July 1946, in an attempt to patch up their differences over Palestine, Great Britain and the United States designated a joint cabinet committee of experts to work out mutually acceptable plans for implementation of the Anglo-American Commission recommendations. Henry F. Grady, representative of the U.S. secretary of state, and Herbert S. Morrison, lord president of the council and later leader of the House of Commons, agreed on a plan to convert the mandate into a British trusteeship. Under the trusteeship, Palestine would be divided into an Arab province, a Jewish province and a British-administered area comprising the districts of Jerusalem and the Negev. Ultimately the scheme would lead to a unitary or a binational state or to partition. In the interim, Great Britain would control defense, foreign affairs, customs and other important functions. Each province would elect a legislature whose president would be appointed by the British high commissioner during the initial five-year period. During the first year, 100,000 Jews would be admitted into Palestine. Thereafter the British would control immigration, determining quotas based on economic absorptive capacity.

President Truman rejected the Morrison-Grady Plan; the Zionists turned it down because it failed to give them control over immigration. Meanwhile the Jewish Agency adopted a secret resolution favoring partition, provided it included enough territory for a viable Jewish state.

Britain decided to convene a conference in London to consider the Morrison-Grady Plan but stated that participants could also make their own proposals. The Arab governments agreed to participate in the conference, but the Palestinian Arabs refused because the British would not permit the mufti to attend. The Jewish Agency turned down the invitation because they could not include in their delegation several leaders who were being held in custody in Palestine. Without the participation of the United States, the Zionists and the Palestine Arabs, the London conference could not make any progress and was adjourned in October 1946.

A second and final phase of the London conference opened in January 1947 attended by representatives of the Arab League and the Palestine Arab Higher Committee. The Jewish Agency continued to boycott the conference, insisting that partition was the only solution to the problem; however agency representatives did meet informally with the British. The British submitted a final proposal, which was a modified version of the Morrison-Grady Plan. It did not consider partition but proposed instead division of the country into cantons rather than provinces. Palestine would remain a unified British trusteeship for a maximum of five years, during which the high commissioner would exercise supreme authority. During the five-year transition period, the country would be prepared to become a unitary Arab-Jewish state. The 100,000 Jewish immigrants would be admitted over a two-year period rather than in a single year. The Arabs would be given a voice in determining immigration policy in the last three years of trusteeship. At the end of four years, a constituent assembly of the proposed unitary state would be elected. In case of disagreement over the constitution, the matter would be referred to the new U.N. Trusteeship Council.

Both Jews and Arabs rejected this final offer, the Zionists insisting on partition and the Arabs continuing to demand a unitary, independent, Palestinian Arab state. The most the Arabs were willing to offer the Jews was equal citizenship in the Palestinian state, provided Jewish immigration was terminated and Zionist state-building activities discontinued. The London conference came to an abrupt halt on February 14, 1947, with the announcement that "His Majesty's Government had decided to refer the whole problem to the United Nations."

PALESTINE BECOMES A UNITED NATIONS CONCERN

On April 2, 1947, Great Britain requested the U.N. secretary-general to call a special session of the General Assembly to constitute a committee to prepare for consideration of the Palestine question at the next regular session of the assembly. The British were in effect abandoning Palestine because of the complications it had created for both domestic and foreign policy.

With a floundering British economy, the cost of maintaining security in Palestine had become prohibitive. The dispute between Zionist and Arab nationalists was creating acrimonious divisiveness on the home front, and attempts to repress resistance in the Yishuv caused an international embarrassment. The search for a compromise between Arab and Jewish demands only seemed to antagonize both sides. British policy in the Middle East, the source of vital oil supplies and valuable foreign currency earnings, was jeopardized by attempts to maintain a balance. Beyond the Middle East, there was a danger that relations with the entire Muslim world would be undermined by events in Palestine. It appeared that after 30 years the British had failed, and it was time to return the mandate to the international community.

The first special session of the U.N. General Assembly was convened in May 1947 to deal with the Palestine question. The five Arab members of the United Nations failed in their attempt to include on the agenda immediate abrogation of the mandate and proclamation of Palestine's independence. Despite their objections, which were supported by Turkey and Afghanistan, the assembly authorized a Special Committee on Palestine (UNSCOP) to investigate and make recommendations to the United Nations by September. The 11 members of UNSCOP were Australia, Canada, Czechoslovakia, Guatemala, India, Iran, the Netherlands, Peru, Sweden, Uruguay and Yugoslavia. They were a fairly balanced representation of U.N. membership at the time, including countries from the East, the West, Europe, Latin America, Asia and the Christian and the Islamic world.

Between May and the end of August 1947, UNSCOP conducted hearings in New York, Jerusalem, Beirut and Geneva. They met with representatives of the Jewish Agency, the Arab League and Jewish displaced persons camps in Germany and Austria. The Palestine Arab Higher Committee boycotted the proceedings, charging that UNSCOP membership was weighted in favor of the Zionists.

Among the principles UNSCOP unanimously adopted were the termination of the mandate and granting of independence to Palestine at the earliest practicable date; the new state or states to be established should be democratic and representative in character; the economic unity of Palestine should be maintained; the sacred character of the holy places and access to them should be safeguarded; and the General Assembly should immediately initiate measures to solve the plight of the 250,000 Jewish displaced persons in Europe. Two UNSCOP members dissented on accepting as a basic principle that "any solution for Palestine cannot be considered as a solution of the Jewish problem in general."

The committee divided into a majority and minority in its recommendations regarding the political future of Palestine. The majority proposed to partition the country and to establish an economic union. According to this plan, the Arab sector would consist of 4,300 of Palestine's 10,000 square miles. The Jews, constituting one-third of the country's 1,269,000 inhabitants, were allotted 5,700 square miles. The proposed Jewish state contained most of the Jewish-owned land at the time, between 6% and 8% of the total or about a fifth of the arable area. This included the fertile coastal plain south of Acre, eastern Galilee and the Negev, which was mostly desert. Arab territory was in the less fertile highlands of central Palestine and northern Galilee. The large Arab city of Jaffa was included in the Jewish state. Jerusalem and its environs would be placed under an international trusteeship.

According to this arrangement, the proposed Jewish state would have nearly as many Jews as Arabs, approximately 497,000 Arabs and 498,000 Jews. It was expected that the Jewish population would greatly increase with immigration of several hundred thousand displaced persons from Europe. The population of the Arab state would be divided between 725,000 Arabs and 10,000 Jews, and in Jerusalem there would be 100,000 Jews and 105,000 non-Jews. Jerusalem residents would be entitled to vote in either the Jewish or Arab state. The two states would become independent after a two-year transitional period during which Great Britain would retain control subject to U.N. supervision. During the first two years, 150,000 Jewish immigrants would be permitted to enter; subsequently the number would decrease to 60,000 a year. Economic unity of Palestine would be maintained by a ten-year treaty between Arab and Jewish states providing for common customs, currency, communications and development plans.

The UNSCOP minority of India, Iran and Yugoslavia considered partition unworkable and anti-Arab. They proposed to keep the country intact under a federal union of autonomous Arab and Jewish states with Jerusalem as the capital. Each state government would be responsible for education, local taxation, health, roads, agriculture, local industry and other similar functions. Immigration, foreign relations and national defense would be controlled by the central government. There would be a two-chamber national legislature, with equal representation in one and proportional representation in the other. A majority of both bodies would be required to pass legislation. In case of a deadlock, the issue in dispute would be submitted to an arbitral body of no fewer than two Arabs and two Jews. Jewish immigration would be permitted for two years, not to exceed absorptive capacity.

The Arabs rejected both majority and minority proposals. The Arab League warned that implementation of either would precipitate a Middle East war that would probably lead to a world war. The Palestine Arab Higher Committee labeled both plans "absurd, impracticable and unjust," threatening that not a single Jew would be permitted to immigrate to Palestine. "The Arabs will fight to the last man to defend their country, to defend its integrity and to preserve it as an Arab country." Strikes and demonstrations against the UNSCOP proposals were organized in Palestine and in various Arab capitals.

The Zionist leadership found the UNSCOP minority plan "wholly unacceptable" but approved partition provided it allocated more territory to the proposed Jewish state. Great Britain stated that it would accept the recommendation to end the mandate but would remain neutral on proposals to divide Palestine. The British would only give their support to a plan approved by both Jews and Arabs; they would not participate in implementation of any scheme not acceptable to both parties.

After receiving the UNSCOP report, the General Assembly debated the issue and heard presentations from both the Jewish Agency and the Arab Higher Committee, which now realized its error in not cooperating with the U.N. commission. In the U.N. debates, the Arabs reiterated their protests, emphasizing that the Jews, representing only a minority of Palestine's population, would receive the best parts of the land and that partition would leave nearly as many Arabs as Jews in the proposed Jewish state. They denied the legal and moral right of the United Nations to partition Palestine against the wishes of the country's majority. If necessary, they warned, they would resist by force under the right of self-defense.

Before submitting the UNSCOP majority proposal to a final vote in the General Assembly, it was amended to increase the powers of the joint economic board that was to implement economic union; the borders were altered to reduce the number of Arabs left in the Jewish state, and Jaffa was allocated to the Arab state. Under the revised plan, the Jewish state would constitute about 55% of the territory of Palestine and contain 500,000 Jews and 400,000 Arabs. The U.N. Security Council was given greater authority to implement partition through a commission set up to administer Palestine during the transition period.

After several days of acrimonious debate, on November 29, 1947, the General Assembly voted for partition (U.N. Resolution 181[II]) with 33 in favor, 13 against and 10 abstentions. The Arab members were joined in opposition by other Muslim countries and India, Cuba, Yugoslavia and Greece. Great Britain abstained because the plan was not supported by both parties to the conflict. The vote was unusual because both the United States and the Soviet bloc joined to back a major political issue. Their mutual support for partition influenced several countries that previously had doubts about the plan. There was considerable controversy about the role played by the United States in whipping up votes for partition. Charges were later made that members of the Jewish Agency and of the American U.N. delegation exerted heavy pressure on representatives of smaller nations to gain their votes.

Approval of the partition plan by the General Assembly did not assure its implementation. The Arabs questioned the validity of the assembly's authority, pointing out that its resolutions did not have the force of law; General Assembly resolutions were merely recommendations, unlike those of the Security Council, which were required to be implemented. Universal condemnation of the plan by the Arab states and the Arab majority in Palestine raised doubts about both the practicality and morality of partition. Great Britain, the country most responsible for law and order in Palestine, was overtly hostile to U.N. intervention despite the fact that the British government had brought the issue before the international body. Who, then, would take responsibility for carrying out the General Assembly's recommendations? Although willing to contribute small amounts of money to resolve the issue, the United States was unwilling to provide any military force to maintain the peace; nor would the Western powers sanction the use of Soviet troops in the Middle East.

The U.N. Palestine Commission, which was designated to implement the partition plan, proved to be almost totally ineffective. The British mandatory government announced that it would refuse to turn over any authority to the United Nations before May 15, 1948, the date the Colonial Office designated for terminating the mandate. Nor would the British permit the commission to enter Palestine before May 1. By February the commission reported that it would be unable to carry out its responsibilities without armed assistance. Only the Jewish Agency was willing to cooperate with the commission; thus it did succeed in starting plans for a Jewish provisional council to take over the areas designated for the Jewish state. With departure of the British on May 15 and proclamation by the Yishuv leadership of the state of Israel, the commission ceased to exist.

The day after the partition resolution was passed, civil unrest erupted in Palestine. The Arabs declared a general strike and organized angry protest demonstrations throughout the country. Simultaneously the Yishuv broke into joyous celebration; it appeared that the long-sought goal of a Jewish state was realized. For the first time since the end of World War II, there was spontaneous fraternization between Jewish youths and British soldiers.

Within hours there were clashes between the celebrating Jews and embittered Arab inhabitants in areas such as Jerusalem, Haifa, and Tel Aviv–Jaffa where the two communities lived cheek-by-jowl. In a few days, these demonstrations grew into armed conflict between the Yishuv and the Arab community, becoming a full-scale civil war. Each side accused the other of precipitating the hostilities, and each accused the British of helping its enemy.

Although official British policy was not to intervene on either side but to withdraw in stages to Haifa, the final point of departure on May 15, there were numerous instances of officers assisting either Arabs or Jews, according to personal predilections. When the British vacated army camps, depots, police stations and government offices, fighting would occur as Jewish and Arab units sought to gain control of the evacuated areas. Some officials were highly critical of the way in which Great Britain abandoned Palestine, charging that the helter-skelter, disorganized departure almost guaranteed armed conflict between the Jews and Arabs left behind.

By January 1948, the civil war began to be internationalized. Hundreds of armed Arabs were crossing the border into Palestine, some of them individual guerrilla fighters, others in organized military units. The Arab Liberation Army, formed in December 1947 for the Arab League, occupied Arab areas in northern Palestine and laid siege to several Jewish settlements. In the south, armed bands from Egypt organized by the Muslim Brotherhood were assembled. At first the Arab units succeeded in blocking the road between Jerusalem and Tel Aviv to Jewish traffic, but within a month the siege was broken by the Haganah.

By April the Haganah turned the tide of battle, seizing several important cities and towns, including Tiberias, Haifa, Safad, Jaffa, Acre and the western sections of Jerusalem. Haganah strategy was to gain control of as much territory allocated to the Jewish state in the partition plan as possible to assure that it would remain in Jewish hands. During these field operations, Arabs were frequently forced to evacuate their towns and villages, leaving behind large abandoned areas of agricultural land, orchards and urban centers.

Atrocities committed by each side against the other became more frequent. In Jerusalem Arabs blew up the *Palestine Post*, the country's English-language daily newspaper, and the offices of the Jewish Agency. In Haifa, after Arabs attacked Jewish employees at the oil refinery, members of the Irgun Zvai Leumi and Lehi threw bombs at a group of Arab workers, killing 6 and wounding over 40. A few days later, Haganah members disguised as Arabs killed 60 villagers, including women and children, in retaliation for Jewish deaths in Haifa. In Jerusalem, Arabs ambushed and killed over 70 Jewish physicians and medical workers in a convoy attempting to reach the Hadassah Hospital besieged on Mount Scopus.

One of the most fateful incidents was the attack by the Irgun and Lehi on Dayr Yasin, an Arab village on the outskirts of Jerusalem, on April 4, 1948. Although the village had not been involved in any significant hostilities against the Yishuv, the leaders of the Irgun and Lehi justified their surprise attack, charging that the village was a guerrilla base. During the attack, some 200 to 250 men, women and children were massacred; many bodies were mutilated and thrown into a well.

The leaders of the Yishuv, including Ben-Gurion, strenuously denounced the attack and disclaimed any responsibility for it. However, commanders of the two dissident factions maintained that the Haganah had been informed of their plan in advance and provided covering fire for the attack. Dayr Yasin was important because it symbolized the extent to which the struggle between the two communities was becoming an all-out civil war; it was a major factor contributing to the panic that soon led to the collapse and mass flight of the Palestine Arab community.

As the fighting escalated, U.N. attempts to deal with the crisis in Palestine intensified. The Security Council issued repeated calls for a cease-fire to Palestinian Arabs and Jews and to the neighboring countries and requested the U.N. Trusteeship Council to examine measures for the protection of Jerusalem and its inhabitants. Two days before the end of the mandate, an American Quaker, Harold Evans, was named special municipal commissioner for Jerusalem, but by mid-June he resigned the office without having left for Palestine. Within hours after the end of the mandate, the General Assembly appointed a mediator to promote a peaceful resolution of the conflict.

The turmoil in Palestine and the angry reaction of the entire Arab world to the partition scheme appeared to threaten Western interests in the Middle East, especially the Western-operated oil sources that had become vital to the postwar economic recuperation of Europe. President Truman's advisors warned that partition could not be implemented without outside military intervention. They estimated that as many as 160,000 troops might be required to carry out the task. If an international force were organized, it might require the use of Soviet troops, an unwelcome prospect in the light of tensions growing between the Soviet Union and the West.

The United States now began to have second thoughts about partition, and its representative at the United Nations observed that the General Assembly resolution was merely a recommendation. Since the Security Council was not prepared to enforce partition, the United States now proposed establishment of a temporary trusteeship to maintain the peace until Jews and Arabs could reach agreement. On April 1, the Security Council called for another special session of the General Assembly to reconsider the question of the future government of Palestine. Later in April, the United Nations set up a special truce commission of the American, Belgian and French consuls in Jerusalem to observe any truce that might be arranged. The Zionists and their friends in the United States adamantly opposed any retreat from partition but agreed to accept a truce provided that it did not interfere with Jewish immigration or delay independence. By May 15 the trusteeship proposal was abandoned, and attention shifted to appointment of a mediator to carry out the Security Council's truce resolutions.

FIRST ARAB-ISRAEL WAR AND ISRAEL'S INDEPENDENCE

On May 14, 1948, hours before the British departure from Haifa and the official termination of the mandate, Israel declared its independence. A new provisional national council replaced the Jewish Agency, the elected assembly's national council and the British mandatory government as the highest authority in territory under its control. The next day Egypt, Transjordan, Syria, Lebanon and Iraq dispatched their regular armies, between 20,000 and 25,000 troops, to assist the Arab Liberation Army and the Palestine Arabs. Saudi Arabia sent a token unit, and Yemen was only nominally involved. The civil struggle between Palestinian Jews and Arabs now became an international conflict, the first Arab-Israel War, called by Israelis the War of Independence.

In an attempt to gain Jordan's full cooperation, the other Arab combatants agreed to appoint the Emir Abdullah as commander-in-chief of the invading forces. They were concerned about Jordan because it was reportedly involved in secret negotiations with Israel to divide Palestine. One motive for Arab intervention was to preempt Abdullah's scheme to take over the largely Arab-inhabited parts of the country. At first the Arab states took the initiative; Egyptian forces moved northward, up the Mediterranean coast toward Tel Aviv. Plans called for Syria, Lebanon and Iraq to attack Haifa after taking over Galilee; Transjordan's British-commanded Arab Legion was to head for the coast after occupying central Palestine. However the Arab Legion did not cross the U.N. partition line, separating the Arab sector from the proposed Jewish state, and the other Arab forces were blocked before they could reach their objectives.

Despite appointment of a commander-in-chief, the Arab states failed to coordinate their battle plans, each army operating under its own generals without integrating its actions with those of its allies. Except for the Arab Legion, the Arab armies were poorly trained, badly equipped and rife with corruption among their civilian arms suppliers. Consequently morale was low. By June the Arab invasion of Palestine lost its momentum. The only really credible military successes were those of the Arab Legion, which isolated Jerusalem, holding the Jewish sector under siege.

Two weeks after the war began, the U.N. Security Council ordered a four-week cease-fire. The truce was supervised by a newly appointed U.N. mediator, Count Folke Bernadotte, president of the Swedish Red Cross, who had been an intermediary between Germany and the Allies in the closing days of World War II. Bernadotte arranged for the truce to begin on June 11. He was backed by the Security Council's threat of sanctions for violation of the cease-fire. Nevertheless, both sides ignored the restrictions on introduction of additional military equipment and manpower during the truce. With financial assistance from abroad, Israel established a regular supply route with weapons airlifted from Czechoslovakia. Young men recruited in Europe and America, many of them World War II veterans, also arrived in the country. By the end of June, Israeli forces were reasonably well equipped. The Arab forces also added to their strength but were less successful than Israel in preparing for the next round of battle.

During the break in fighting, Bernadotte proposed a new political compromise calling for a Palestine Union based on autonomous Arab and Jewish units, each to control its own domestic affairs, and to include Transjordan. The partition borders would be altered in favor of the Arabs; Jerusalem would be placed under Arab control but with a U.N. guarantee of access to the holy places. Both Israel and the Arab states rejected the offer. When the Security Council called for the prolongation of the four-week June cease-fire, Israel was willing to continue, but the Arab states rejected the proposal.

With resumption of fighting on July 8, Israeli forces, now consolidated and equipped with heavy weapons purchased in Europe before May, took the offensive, rounding out the territory controlled before the truce. They seized Arab areas, including Nazareth, in Galilee but failed to capture the Old City of Jerusalem or to break through Egyptian lines and reach Jewish settlements in the Negev.

After six days of renewed fighting, the Security Council ordered a new cease-fire to begin on July 19. The second truce was broken several times when Israeli forces tried to breach the Egyptian blockade of the Negev. Israel did capture Beersheba in October and isolated most Egyptian units south of Jerusalem. By the end of the year, Egyptian forces were either driven from Palestine or besieged in the south. In the north, Israel extended the area under its control, seizing most of Galilee and crossing the border into southern Lebanon. Between May and December 1948, the U.N. Security Council tried without success to halt the fighting in Palestine; neither Israel nor the Arab states appeared interested in ending the conflict. The Arabs, with the exception of Transjordan, were determined to defeat Israel and to establish an Arab state in the country. The Emir Abdullah still wanted to annex those sectors allocated to an Arab state in the partition resolution and conducted secret negotiations with Israel. After initial setbacks, Israel emerged as a powerful military force, reluctant to stop the fighting before it consolidated all territory assigned to it by the U.N. resolution.

The U.N. mediator, Count Bernadotte, continued his efforts but was unable to find any accommodation between Jews and Arabs. He reported to the General Assembly that both sides had assumed uncompromising positions. Although the Arabs were willing to continue the truce, they were unalterably opposed to any suggestion of recognizing the Jewish state. They feared that because of unrestricted immigration, the Jewish state would attempt to expand. As a consequence of its recent victories, Israel became less receptive to mediation and insisted on implementing those parts of the partition resolution favorable to it while rejecting the parts it no longer wanted. As a result of its new strength, Israel now preferred to bypass the mediator and demanded direct peace negotiations with the Arabs. Furthermore, Israel was refusing to permit return of the Arab refugees until peace was attained.

Bernadotte also submitted a revised version of his earlier proposal for a political settlement. The new plan called for an exchange of territory in which Israel would take over Galilee and the Arabs would get the Negev. The Arab sections of Palestine would be annexed by Transjordan, Haifa would be a free port for both nations, and Jerusalem would become a U.N. trusteeship. The Arab refugees would be permitted to return to their homes in Israel. A new U.N. conciliation commission would be formed to help replace the existing cease-fire with an armistice or a peace agreement.

Recently established as an independent state in control of most territory allocated to it, Israel totally rejected Bernadotte's proposals as anti-Israel. In retaliation for what they believed to be Bernadotte's animosity to the Jewish state, he was shot by members of Lehi in Jerusalem on September 17, 1948.

Among the Arabs, only Jordan viewed the plan favorably, since it assigned the Arab section of Palestine to Abdullah. Great Britain, Transjordan's principal ally at the United Nations and its chief supplier of military and economic aid, also backed the proposals. U.S. Secretary of State George Marshall endorsed the Bernadotte proposals, but after strenuous objections from American Zionists, President Truman promised not to endorse any change in the partition scheme unacceptable to Israel. The Soviet Union, at the time Israel's chief supporter at the United Nations, also stood by partition and denounced the Bernadotte scheme as a British plot to entrench its foothold in the Middle East.

By the end of 1948, Israel had seized nearly all territory allocated to it by the partition plan in addition to nearly 2,000 square miles beyond the partition borders. In the south, Israeli forces crossed the borders of Palestine and moved into Egypt's Sinai peninsula. Egypt's leaders were among the first in the Arab world to realize that they could not win this first encounter with Israel and in January 1949 decided to enter armistice negotiations.

ARMISTICE AGREEMENTS

After the United Nations declared another cease-fire, armistice talks began on January 12 on the Greek Mediterranean island of Rhodes. Dr. Ralph Bunche, a high-ranking U.N. officer, an African American who was a former U.S. State Department official, replaced Bernadotte as acting mediator. Bunche succeeded in organizing informal meetings between Israeli and Egyptian delegations, the first direct, public, official contacts between the combatants. By the end of February, the two countries concluded a permanent armistice agreement fixing the boundaries between Egypt and Israel. Except for the Gaza Strip in southern Palestine, which remained in Egyptian hands, the frontiers were drawn along the old borders between Palestine and Egypt. An Israel-Egypt Mixed Armistice Commission composed of officers from the two countries and a third neutral representing the United Nations was charged with implementing the agreement.

By July 20 three additional armistice agreements were negotiated on Rhodes under U.N. sponsorship with Dr. Bunche as the intermediary. Mixed Armistice commissions (MACs) were also established between Israel and Transjordan, Lebanon, and Syria. Iraq refused to participate in the negotiations.

On August 12, the U.N. Security Council formally recognized the end of this phase of the war by terminating the office of acting mediator. Dr. Bunche was later honored with the Nobel Peace Prize for his peacemaking success. As a result of the armistice agreements, Israel retained nearly all the land it occupied when the fighting ended. This included the territory allocated to the Jewish state in the U.N. Partition Resolution and the 2,000 square miles in the U.N.-designated Arab state that Israel captured during the war. Palestine was now divided between Egypt in the Gaza Strip (140 square miles), Transjordan in East Jerusalem and eastern Palestine (later called the West Bank; about 2,270 square miles), and the state of Israel (about 8,300 square miles).

Jerusalem was divided between Israel and Transjordan; both countries opposed placing the city under international control. Four areas along the armistice frontiers were designated as demilitarized zones (DMZs). They included one in the north between Israel and Syria; another in Jerusalem surrounding the Hadassah Hospital and Hebrew University on Mount Scopus, which were beseiged by Jordanian forces; a third, also in Jerusalem, enclosing the former headquarters of the Palestine high commissioner; and a fourth at al-Auja on the border between Egypt and Israel. These DMZs were to become the source of continued dispute between Israel and the Arab armistice signatories; they frequently sparked frontier incidents that flared into renewed conflicts.

Although the armistices called for transition to peace agreements, it was to take almost another 30 years before the first peace treaty would be signed between Israel and Egypt. In the interval, the Arab states continued hostile activities such as the economic boycott and blockade of Israel and closure of the Suez Canal to Israeli shipping. The Arabs argued that these sanctions were not banned by the armistice agreements. (In 1967 Israel unilaterally disavowed the armistice agreements, charging that they had been violated by Arab aggression.)

At the time Dr. Bunche was conducting the armistice parleys on Rhodes, the United Nations established the Conciliation Commission for Palestine (CCP) originally proposed by Count Bernadotte. The CCP was to continue from the point at which Dr. Bunche concluded his task. Its three members, the United States, France and Turkey, were charged with organizing peace negotiations. During most of 1949, the CCP carried on its work in Lausanne, Switzerland; but it was never able to bring Arab and Israeli representatives together, and within a few months abandoned the goal of attaining peace treaties. Instead, the CCP shifted emphasis to establishment of an economic survey mission whose task was to devise development schemes for the region as a whole and to integrate the Arab refugees into the economies of the Middle East.

THE PALESTINE ARAB REFUGEES

One of the most tragic results of the war was the flight of over 700,000 Palestinian Arabs from their homes in territory conquered by Israel (the U.N. Figure was 726,000). The Palestine refugee problem was to plague the United Nations and the international community for the next half century and become another source of continued tension between Israel and its neighbors. The flight began shortly after the announcement of the U.N. partition resolution and the eruption of fighting between Palestinian Arabs and Jews. At first some 30,000 middle- and upper-middle-class Arabs left for neighboring countries in the hope of returning after the "troubles" died down. In April 1948 the exodus was accelerated after word of the Dayr Yassin massacre spread and several successful Haganah operations led to Jewish capture of Arab villages. By May 15, when the invasion of neighboring states began, over 200,000 Arabs had become refugees. After the fighting ended in 1949, the number had increased more than threefold.

Israel disclaimed all responsibility for the flight of the refugees and for their care. It maintained that the Arab states had urged the Palestine Arabs to depart and to return after victory over the Jewish state. The Arabs charged that the refugees were driven from their homes by Israeli military forces and that they should be permitted to return before negotiations with Israel for a peace settlement. Recently Israeli scholars, examining newly-opened Israeli documentary sources, have substantiated evidence that there were numerous instances in which Arabs were driven from their villages by the Haganah and later by the IDF. There is little reliable evidence indicating that the refugees were urged to depart by their own leaders or by the surrounding Arab states or that they did not intend to return.

A major contributory cause of the flight was the total breakdown of Palestinian Arab society due to the civil war and the invasion that followed. As a result of the upheaval, the traditional organizations, institutions and social structures of the Arab community were shattered. Most of its leaders were either in exile or had departed early in the conflict. During the mandate, many vital functions of the Arab community were directed by mandatory authorities; thus with departure of the British, services such as water supply, health, education, mail and security collapsed. In the Yishuv, many of these functions had already been organized, and the Jewish community was ready to replace mandatory administration months before May 15. It even had its own postal system and stamps prepared for the British departure.

There was never an accurate count of the original number of refugees; the United Nations estimated that over 700,000 left during the period from November 1947 until the armistice agreements were signed in 1949. When the problem arose, three international voluntary agencies were assigned to care for the refugees under U.N. auspices. After it became clear that this was not a passing problem and that the refugees would not return to their homes soon, the General Assembly established the U.N. Relief and Works Agency for Palestine Refugees in the Middle East (UNRWA), which continues to care for the refugees to the present day.

The agency provides food rations, housing, education, health care and social services for the refugees in Lebanon, Syria, Jordan, the Gaza Strip and the West Bank occupied by Israel in the 1967 war. At first most assistance provided by UNRWA was for food and shelter. As the refugees became increasingly self-sufficient, most UNRWA aid shifted to education and technical training.

Not all Palestinians who fled or were driven from their homes in 1947–48 remained refugees. Many became integrated into the economic, political, and social life of the host countries. Hundreds of thousands emigrated to the Persian Gulf, Europe and North America, becoming successful in business, academic and professional activity. UNRWA has defined a Palestine refugee as a person whose normal residence was in Palestine for a minimum of two years preceding the 1948 conflict and who, as a result of the conflict, lost both home and means of livelihood and took refuge in one of the countries where UNRWA provides relief. Refugees according to this definition, and their direct descendants, are eligible for UNRWA assistance. By early 1996, there were over three million Palestinians receiving some form of UNRWA assistance. They constituted about half the total number of Palestinians living throughout the Middle East and in the rest of the world.

Originally most refugees were accommodated in tent camps organized by the voluntary agencies. By 1996 nearly a third of the refugees lived in the 59 camps provided by UNRWA. The other two-thirds lived in villages, towns and the large cities of the host countries. At first the refugees refused to move into permanent shelters, preferring to stay in their tents; moving to permanent structures meant that they would be unable to return to their homes in Palestine. As it became evident that return would not be soon, they accepted more permanent quarters made of cement blocks, adobe brick, and the like. Over the years, many of these camps became slumlike extensions of the large cities they adjoined.

Palestinians living outside Israel, especially those who were refugees, developed an intense national consciousness. Even those who fared well economically retained strong ties to their homeland, insisting on their right to return. This became a fundamental credo, the principal demand of most Palestinians and nearly all refugees living in the diaspora. Where Palestinians found employment and were permitted to remain in the host countries, the local governments regarded them as temporary residents rather than permanent settlers. There was often tension between host populations and the refugees, who were perceived as a disruptive element, likely to stir up political unrest and antigovernment activity. In some countries, Palestinians were oppressed by security authorities and subjected to harassment by the police and secret services.

Although the Arab governments were unanimous in their demand that the refugees be permitted to return to their homes in Israel (by 1990 the concept of "right of return" meant return to Palestine, not necessarily to original homes), treatment of the refugees varied.

Syria extended many of the benefits of citizenship but kept Palestinians under strict security control. Although there was no discrimination in employment, Palestinians could not acquire land except under special circumstances. The Syrian government established a special agency, the General Authority for Palestine Refugees, to assist and to keep track of the refugees. Palestinians in Syria were more integrated into the country's economic, social and political life than in any other country apart from Jordan (see below). In Syria they have been prominent in the military and in the country's dominant political party, the Ba'ath. With assistance from Syrian authorities, Palestinians formed their own paramilitary and other organizations, most notably, the Sa'iqah commando group. However, there have been frequent quarrels between Syrian President Hafez al-Assad and the leader of the Palestine Liberation Organization (PLO), Yasir Arafat, caused by Syrian attempts to take over the Palestinian political movements.

Lebanon was the host country least hospitable to the Palestinians. From their arrival in 1947–48, they constituted about 10 % of the population and were regarded by the ruling establishment as a threat to internal political and social stability. Nevertheless, the refugees were often exploited as a source of cheap labor when the economy was booming and there was a shortage of unskilled workers. Lebanon's supply-side economy and free-market government policies attracted hundreds of middle-class Palestinian investors and venture capitalists; many played a pivotal role in developing the country's economy between the 1950s and 1970s. After 1975 the 15-year-long Lebanese civil war undermined business confidence and physically destroyed most enterprises in the country.

Because most Palestinians are Muslims, the Lebanese government has opposed their continued stay in the country, fearful that they would upset the delicate balance between Muslims and Christians that was the basis of the Lebanese political system. Palestinians played an important role in the civil war when their militias sided with antiestablishment forces. After 1970 Israel began large-scale attacks on Palestinian guerrilla bases in south Lebanon, which were one of the main targets of the Israeli invasion in 1982. For these reasons, many Lebanese insist that the only solution to the refugee problem is Palestinian departure from Lebanon, preferably back to Palestine.

Following the exodus from Israel in 1948, large numbers of Palestinians began to arrive in Kuwait, especially after the oil boom of the 1960s and 1970s. They provided many of the professional and technical workers required to transform Kuwait from an undeveloped, desert hinterland to a modern nation. Palestinians prospered in Kuwait, ascending to influential posts in government and industry, and many became wealthy. But Kuwait's nationality law placed such severe restrictions on acquisition of citizenship that very few Palestinians could become Kuwaitis.

The rulers of the country contributed large amounts of money to the PLO and Palestinian causes, and relations between Kuwaitis and Palestinians were cordial until Iraq invaded the country in 1991. Because many Palestinians were enthusiastic supporters of Iraq's President Saddam Husayn, relations between Kuwaitis and Palestinians soured almost over night. The great majority were forced to leave; most fled to Jordan where they had family and financial investments. However, thousands of Palestinians departed in such haste that they abandoned homes, property and lifetime savings acquired in the past generation or two.

Jordan was the only Arab country that offered Palestinians automatic citizenship. When King Abdullah annexed the West Bank and Jerusalem in 1950, the Emirate of Transjordan became the Hashemite Kingdom of Jordan; the Palestinian Arabs who were refugees on both sides of the Jordan River and those with homes in the West Bank became Jordanian subjects, nearly tripling the sparse population of Abdullah's former desert principality. By the 1990s, most Palestinians, including refugees, lived in Jordan.

Within the past 50 years, there were three waves of refugee migration to Jordan: those who fled from Israeli territory in 1948, refugees and displaced persons who came during the 1967 war and those who came from Kuwait and the Persian Gulf as a result of the 1991 Gulf War. Among the 320,000 who came from the West Bank and Gaza in 1967, 120,000 were refugees for a second time, that is, they left their original homes in Israel during 1947–48 for the West Bank, then fled again in 1967.

After the West Bank was annexed in 1950, Jordan's rulers attempted to "Jordanize" their new subjects and made strenuous efforts to obliterate Palestinian consciousness within the kingdom. Palestinians attained the highest ranks in Jordanian society. They became officers in the army, cabinet officials and even prime ministers. Palestinian businessmen prospered, investing in agriculture, industry and finance. The Arab Bank, Jordan's largest financial institution, was owned and managed by Palestinians. However there was always a certain reserve between Palestinians and indigenous East Bank Jordanians. Most of the king's closest advisors and the chiefs of his select security services were from traditional East Bank families. Although many Palestinians flourished in Jordan, by the 1990s there were still over one million refugees in the East Bank and more than 500,000 in the West Bank.

After Arab defeat in the 1948 war and the Palestinian dispersion, most Palestinian political leadership was discredited. Many Palestinians established relationships with opposition factions in the host countries. Groups such as the Arab Nationalist Movement, the Syrian Social Nationalist Movement, the Ba'ath Party, the Communists and the Muslim Brotherhood succeeded in attracting younger Palestinians searching for answers to their plight. During the late 1950s and 1960s, Egyptian President Gamal Abd al-Nasser had a great appeal to many because of the political successes he achieved in Egypt and on the international scene. Many regarded him as a messiah who would redeem Palestine and lead them back to their homeland. The defeat of Egypt, Syria and Jordan in the 1967 war alienated most Palestinians who then turned away from Nasserism and the other political movements in which they had placed their faith.

By the early 1960s, distinctive Palestinian organizations began to form, many with paramilitary guerrilla or commando militias seeking to engage Israel in armed struggle. Estimates are that following Arab defeat in the June

1967 war, there were several dozen of these armed bands, some with fewer than 100 members. The most important was Fatah (Palestine Liberation Movement), created in the late 1950s, and led by Yassir Arafat, who later became chairman of the PLO. The PLO was established in 1964 with Arab League backing, but initially groups like Fatah regarded it as a tool of the Arab regimes to control the Palestinians. It was not until after the June 1967 Six-Day War (see below), when members of the commando organizations took over the PLO and made Arafat chairman, that the PLO acquired wide credibility among most Palestinians. The United Nations and most other countries eventually recognized the PLO as the representative body of the Palestinian people.

After the 1967 Six-Day War, attention shifted from the Palestine Arab refugee problem to the political issue of establishing a Palestinian state. When the PLO and its affiliated groups such as Fatah, the Popular Front for the Liberation of Palestine (PFLP) and the Democratic Popular Front (DPF) were founded, nearly all of them sought to eliminate Israel by armed struggle and to replace it with a Palestinian Arab state. By the 1970s, divisions began to appear over strategy and tactics. A moderate wing emerged that began to consider political compromise. Some discussed setting up a Palestinian entity in part of the country, others began to talk about a two-state (Israel and Palestine) solution. These internal discussions eventually led to the PLO decision in 1988 to abandon the use of terrorism, recognize Israel and comply with the U.N. resolutions that called for peaceful settlement of the Arab-Israel conflict.

International Peace Efforts

At the Lausanne Conference in 1949, the Arab states insisted that they would not begin direct negotiations with Israel until the refugees were permitted to return to their homes. They also demanded that Israel leave the territory it conquered beyond the U.N. partition boundaries and that Jerusalem be internationalized. The three members of the CCP (United States, France and Turkey), who convened the conference, succeeded in getting the Arabs and Israel to sign a protocol stating that they would accept the partition plan as the starting point for negotiation and the framework for discussion of peace. But each side interpreted the protocol to suit its own requirements. The Arabs insisted that Israel's signature meant that it would return to the 1947 U.N. partition borders; Israel insisted that the plan was merely the basis from which discussions would begin.

Although Egypt, Syria, Lebanon and Jordan refused face-to-face meetings with Israel to discuss a peace settlement, Israeli and Arab military officers met in the mixed armistice commissions (MACs) to iron out practical problems relating to the armistice frontiers. Periodically they would take up questions such as farm animals that strayed across the border, violations of the DMZs, permission for Israeli Christian Arabs to visit the holy places in Jordan's sector of Jerusalem, cross-border shooting and other incidents that threatened to escalate into full-scale warfare. In the Israel-Jordan MAC, the parties also discussed problems such as malaria control along their mutual armistice line and other nonmilitary matters that were not politically sensitive.

Neither Israel nor the Arab states were willing to make major concessions for peace. Israel's defeat of five Arab armies was a severe blow to Arab self-esteem. When the 1948 war began, few expected Israel, with its small population and area, to survive the onslaught of the combined Arab forces. Arab failure in the battlefield meant the loss of Palestine, an area of historic importance to the Islamic world. The Palestinian Arabs who fled to the surrounding countries were not only an economic burden but a constant reminder of Arab humiliation. Popular opinion throughout the Arab world turned not only against Israel and the West, perceived as Israel's ally, but against Arab leaders held accountable for the disaster.

Within the decade following the defeat, one Arab country after another was wracked by revolutionary upheaval. True, a major cause of the turbulence was the economic and social condition of the Arab world. But the defeat in Palestine was a catalyst that started a chain reaction of rebellion against established authority.

The first major revolution was against the corrupt monarchy in Egypt and was led by Nasser during 1952. One cause of the revolt by young Egyptian army officers was the failure of the government to provide reliable arms, equipment and leadership in the 1948 war. In Syria and Lebanon, political leaders regarded as corrupt and incapable of dealing with the Palestine problem were assassinated. King Abdullah of Jordan was shot while entering the al-Aqsa Mosque in Jerusalem in July 1951 by a Palestinian who accused the king of betraying the Arab cause. In the revolutions that occurred in Iraq and Lebanon during 1958, antiestablishment forces also accused their governments of conspiring with Zionists and the West against the Arab cause.

During the 1950s and 1960s, the number of nations that gained independence and joined the Arab League grew from 7 to 21; nations belonging to the Islamic Conference increased to over 40, greatly intensifying international opposition to Israel. More than 60 countries regarded the Palestine conflict as an issue of injustice done to the Palestinians by Western imposition of Israel on the Arab/Islamic world.

The stronger the opposition to Israel, the more determined Israel's resistance to any concessions that appeared to undermine national security. Although Israel's leaders had initially accepted the U.N. partition plan as the best compromise available, they now considered surrender of territory and return to the partition resolution suicidal. The 1947 partition boundaries were indefensible; Israel would never give up its hold on West Jerusalem, they insisted. They flouted international opinion by moving the capital from Tel Aviv to Israeli-held Jerusalem in 1950 even though the most sacred parts were still in the Jordanian-held Old City. Jordan also opposed internationalization; both Israel and Jordan wanted to maintain the post-1948 status quo in the Holy City.

Between 1949 and 1967, international attempts to find a peaceful resolution to the Arab-Israel conflict focused on the refugees. The United States and its allies in the West believed that if they were repatriated or resettled, a major obstacle to peace would be removed. Therefore most attempts at mediation, efforts through the United Nations and bilateral negotiations emphasized the refugee problem.

The longer the refugee question remained unresolved, the more Israel resisted repatriation. In response to the General Assembly's call for return of the refugees in 1948–49, Israeli officials claimed that an immediate refugee return would be militarily advantageous to the Arab states, still at war with Israel. A mass refugee return, they argued, would engage large security forces and might even lead to epidemics. Thousands of Palestinians returning from enemy territory could create a "fifth column" that would threaten the country. Rehabilitation and care of so many returnees would engage the services of many personnel from the armed forces.

A limited number of Palestinians were permitted to return to relatives in Israel through negotiations conducted with the CCP for reunion of broken families that included wives and minor children of "Arab bread-winners lawfully resident in Israel." Family reunions were permitted on an individual, case-by-case basis, totaling some 50,000 persons by the 1960s. After the 1967 war, another 60,000 Palestinians were permitted to return to the West Bank and 10,000 to East Jerusalem. Return of Palestinians under the family reunion scheme was seen by Israel as a humanitarian gesture on its part, not as a refugee right.

Israeli officials called for resettlement of the refugees in the Arab world instead of repatriation. They argued that Israel, with only one-hundredth of the land in the Middle East, was burdened with one-sixtieth of the population. Despite this disproportion, it was willing to take hundreds of thousands of displaced Jews from Europe, whereas the Arab states, with their vast territories, had done little if anything for the Palestinian refugees.

Under pressure from the United States, Israel offered to accept approximately 200,000 Arab refugees and 70,000 indigenous inhabitants of the Gaza Strip as citizens provided that Egypt turned the region over to Israel and that refugee resettlement would be facilitated by international aid. When this proposal was rejected, Israel offered, also under U.S. pressure, to permit the return of 100,000 Palestinian refugees as part of an overall settlement plan to be implemented by a special U.N. body. But this also was turned down by both the Arab states and the CCP. After 1949 Israel's attitude toward repatriation hardened. It feared that large numbers of Arabs would become a security risk. Because of the higher Arab birth rate, the ratio between Jews and Arabs within Israel would shift in favor of the latter. Nearly all Israeli political parties rejected the Palestinian Arabs' "right of return" as tantamount to the destruction of the Jewish state. Following arrival of hundreds of thousands of Jewish immigrants from several Arab countries in the 1950s and 1960s, some Israelis asserted that a de facto population exchange had taken place—approximately 700,000 Palestinians to the Arab world in exchange for about 700,000 Jews from Arab countries.

REFUGEE COMPENSATION

Economic factors were an important consideration in Israel's policies toward the refugees. Expropriated Arab fields, orchards, vineyards, homes, shops, factories and businesses were major contributors to the economic viability of the Jewish state in its early years. These assets helped provide sustenance and employment to the tidal wave of Jewish immigrants who arrived between 1948 and 1951.

From 1948 to 1953, 350 of the 370 new Jewish settlements were located on formerly Arab property. By 1954, more than one-third of Israel's Jewish population lived on formerly Palestinian-owned land. An additional 250,000 Israeli Jews, including a third of the new immigrants, lived in abandoned Arab urban property. Whole cities, such as Jaffa, Acre, Lydda, Ramleh, Beit Shan and Migdal-Gad, plus some 400 towns and villages and large parts of 94 others, had belonged to the Palestinian Arabs, now refugees, and were taken over by Jewish settlers. These areas contained nearly a quarter of all buildings in Israel at the time. Most of the 120,000 *dunums* (about 30,000 acres) of Arab orange groves, about half the citrus land in Palestine at the end of the mandate, were seized by the Israeli government. In addition some 40,000 *dunums* of vineyards, at least 10,000 *dunums* of other orchards and nearly 95% of Israel's olive groves had formerly belonged to those who were now refugees. Abandoned Arab land was about two and one-half times the total area of Jewish-owned property in 1947–48.

Most of this abandoned property was originally taken over by the Israel custodian of absentee property and later distributed through a variety of agencies to Israeli Jewish individuals and institutions such as development companies, kibbutzim and moshavim. According to the Israeli Absentee Property Law, the departed Palestinians were declared absentees. Many Israeli Arab citizens as well as refugees in the surrounding countries were classified as absentees under this law. In effect, the Absentee Property Law legalized the de facto seizure of property acquired from the 1948 war.

The Israeli custodian had arbitrary power to make decisions defining absentees, their property and its use. Many of the government's policy decisions concerning absentee property were made in secret. Jewish critics of the law as well as Israel's Supreme Court raised questions about what it called arbitrary and excessive abuse of the civil law by the custodian.

Compensation for abandoned Arab property in Israel was one of the matters discussed in early attempts to resolve the conflict. U.N. Resolution 194(III) called for payment to refugees "choosing not to return" to Israel and "for loss of or damage to property which under principles of international law or equity should be made good by the Governments or authorities responsible." The CCP became actively involved after the General Assembly passed a resolution in 1950 noting "with concern" that compensation had not yet been paid. The assembly called on the CCP to establish a refugee office to identify and determine the extent of absentee property, evaluate it and attempt to open negotiations for equitable payment. These aspects of the problem were controversial, and, after several years, settlement of compensation was side-lined.

The CCP's committee of experts attached to the Refugee Office estimated that more than 80% of Israel's total area represented abandoned Arab lands, although only a little more than one-quarter was considered cultivable. Most of the Negev, constituting about half the area of Israel, was occupied by bedouin tribes whose ownership was never clearly defined. It was not possible to assume with certainty that these lands were not state domain, therefore legally transformed from mandatory to Israeli government property. The CCP estimate of abandoned property in addition to land and real estate included industrial equipment, commercial stocks, motor vehicles, household effects, agricultural equipment and livestock. After several months, the CCP gave an estimate for abandoned property of 120 million pounds sterling, or approximately $1.85 billion in 1990 U.S. dollars.

Arab economists disputed the CCP evaluation. They maintained that it was much too low and failed to consider several critical items such as psychological and human suffering, lost opportunity and public property. The CCP's evaluation, they charged, did not account for the potential development value of land and placed no value on uncultivable areas. When human capital losses were added to the Arab estimates, they ranged up to 20 times the CCP estimate.

Israel agreed in principle to pay compensation in 1949–50 with several qualifications. Compensation had to be part of an overall peace settlement paid as a global sum rather than to individuals; payments would have to be used to resettle Arab refugees outside Israel; and Jewish property losses in areas of Palestine occupied by Arab forces would have to be taken into account. Israeli claims against the Arab states would also have to be considered. With the exodus of Jews from Arab countries that began on a large scale after 1951, counterclaims were made for Jewish property abandoned in Iraq, Syria, Lebanon, Egypt and other Arab countries. By 1957 Israel linked the problem of compensation to the Arab blockade and boycott of Israeli goods. "It could hardly be practicable for Israel to pump vast sums of money into the economies of neighboring countries, while those countries were trying to bring about Israel's collapse through economic strangulation," Israel's U.N. ambassador asserted in 1957. He accused the Arab countries of policies that blocked compensation for the refugees.

By the end of the 1956 Suez-Sinai War, which resulted in the exodus of up to 50,000 Jews from Egypt, there was strong public sentiment in Israel against payment of compensation. Counterclaims by Jews from Middle East countries were strengthened in 1974 with formation of the World Organization of Jews from Arab Countries (WOJAC) backed by the Jewish Agency and the Israeli government. WOJAC claimed that more than 800,000 Jews were refugees from Arab countries. They and their descendants, according to WOJAC, constituted nearly half the Jewish population of Israel. One of their organizers asserted that Jewish refugees from Arab countries left five times more property than the Arabs left in Israel.

The Arab position on compensation has been consistent. Because Israel bears primary responsibility for the refugees, it must pay compensation to the individuals affected. Compensation is "an individual right of the refugees personally or of their benefactors," which they should be able to exercise "without any limitations of time or space." Establishment of any relationship between Israel's financial capabilities and its financial obligations would result in "pure and simple confiscation of the property of the Arab refugee." Because of the U.N. role in the establishment of Israel, it should take up the obligation to pay compensation if the principal debtor is insolvent. When the Federal Republic of Germany agreed to pay reparations to Israel on account of the Holocaust, the Arab League unsuccessfully attempted to force payment of Arab refugee compensation from the funds Israel was to receive.

The problem of compensation has become increasingly complicated since the refugee flight in 1947–48. There was a substantial increase in property values. Many former Arab homes, offices and buildings that still exist have been reconstructed so that their worth today has little relationship to market costs in 1947–48. Persons who owned property half a century ago in mandatory Palestine would now be often difficult to locate. Much land that was once agricultural became urban. Scores of former Palestinian Arab villages have disappeared. In many cases where there were Palestinian Arab farms, orchards or groves, there are now high-rise apartment or office buildings. Movable property such as vehicles, factory machinery, household goods, farm animals and personal possessions, long ago disappeared without any record.

Among other problems surrounding the compensation issue is the fact that most of the original land registration records in Palestine were destroyed during the 1947–48 war or are missing for other reasons. Many microfilmed records brought to England were found to be illegible. Some land transactions were concluded privately outside the official land registry offices, and their title deeds were never recorded. In many areas, land ownership was already disputed in the 1940s, some holdings with as many as 30 claims per parcel.

Although the United Nations never resolved the compensation issue and the CCP maintained only a shadowy existence after 1957, the CCP's records are still intact at headquarters in New York. The CCP did accomplish three steps toward payment of compensation: (1) it completed a global estimate of the value of Arab property; (2) it obtained the release of some refugee bank accounts frozen in Israeli banks, worth about 4 million Palestine pounds; and (3) it identified a substantial number of individual refugee property holdings of considerable worth in Israel. The compensation issue will sooner or later be involved in the peace negotiations between Israel and the PLO as part of the refugee question. There has been some discussion of using Jewish settlements established since 1967 in the West Bank and Gaza in partial payment of compensation. Israeli government investment in the occupied areas is worth several billion dollars, and evacuated Jewish housing might be turned over for the use of Arab refugees in lieu of compensation payments.

THE 1956 SUEZ/SINAI WAR

In the years following the 1948 war, Israel was established on firm foundations. On the home front, it successfully absorbed several hundred thousand Jewish immigrants from Europe (Ashkenazi Jews), and a mass immigration of Jews from Asia and North Africa (Oriental or Sephardi Jews) began. It was to take a decade or more to actually integrate many of these new immigrants, especially those from Islamic countries. Thousands of them continued to live in transition camps (*ma'abarot*) for years after coming to Israel. The huge influx placed severe strains on the economy, and during the 1950s, the country passed through a period of great austerity. As noted above, government acquisition of property abandoned by the Arab refugees was important in hastening the economic integration of hundreds of thousands.

One reason for the economic crisis of the early 1950s was Israel's defense burden. A major part of national income was devoted to the purchase and manufacture of arms and to maintaining a large army. The continued hostility between Israel and its Arab neighbors made national security the top priority—in money, manpower, industry and overall national effort. Under Ben-Gurion's leadership—he was both prime minister and minister of defense—Israel built the Israel Defense Forces (IDF) into one of the most powerful military machines in the region.

Ben-Gurion also conducted shrewd foreign policies. One of his most important achievements was the close alliance with France, angered by Egypt's assistance to the Algerian rebels fighting for independence. Israel feared Nasser's growing political influence throughout the Arab world and the spread of militant pan-Arabism, which appeared to threaten the existence of the Jewish state. As a result of their mutual antagonism to Egypt, Israel acquired a fleet of the latest war planes from France and assistance in developing its first nuclear reactor, which later was used to produce an arsenal of atomic weapons. France also became an intermediary between Israel and Great Britain, concerned about Nasser's nationalization of the Suez Canal in 1956.

Although the dispute between Egypt and Great Britain and France over the Suez Canal was the central focus of the 1956 war, several other issues contributed to the conflict. Hostility to Israel, exacerbated by the humiliation of defeat in 1948 and underscored by the continued presence of several hundred thousand Arab refugees in Lebanon, Syria, Jordan and Egypt, resulted in the Arab states' continuing refusal to negotiate directly with, or to recognize, Israel and in other antagonistic measures, including a total economic boycott, a blockade and closure of the Suez Canal to Israeli commerce.

Following the failure of the CCP to broker a peace settlement in 1949, the United States attempted to shift the emphasis to an economic approach. The CCP formed a Middle East economic survey mission headed by Gordon Clapp, former director of the U.S. government's Tennessee Valley Authority (TVA), to devise a major development plan for the region. The Americans expected that cooperative efforts in development and expansion of Middle East resources would help resettle the refugees, make them economically self-sufficient and integrate them into the economies of the Arab countries surrounding Israel. It was believed that by ameliorating the plight of the refugees, the major obstacle to a peace settlement would be removed.

The Clapp mission's final report in 1949 included a warning:

> The region is not ready, the projects are not ready, the people and Governments are not ready, for large-scale development of the region's basic river systems or major undeveloped land areas. To press forward on such a course is to pursue folly and frustration and thereby delay sound economic growth.

Despite the warning, wholesale adoption of large-scale development projects was encouraged by the Western powers. In the next few years, several hundred million dollars were earmarked for major irrigation and land development schemes. But by the end of the 1950s, most Arab governments hesitated to take advantage of the available funds, and only a few small projects were initiated, not enough to employ more than a few hundred refugees.

One component of the economic approach was the Johnston Plan to develop the Jordan River Valley. The plan envisaged use of Yarmuk and Jordan River waters to irrigate several hundred thousand acres of land along the river banks and creation of new electric power sources. More than 300,000 workers and their families would find employment in the Jordan Valley by the end of the 1950s, according to the plan. President Dwight Eisenhower delegated Eric Johnston as his special representative to the region to convince the riparian states—Israel, Jordan, Syria and Lebanon—of the importance of the project. Between 1953 and 1955, Johnston made five trips to the Middle East. He succeeded in bridging the gap between Israelis and Arabs over division of the Jordan waters and in getting approval for technical implementation. But progress was stalled by opposition from the Syrian government, reluctant to take the political risks of cooperation with Israel. Failure to secure agreement meant that the river would continue to be a source of conflict, especially when Israel later unilaterally decided to develop its own diversion scheme.

Tension along the borders between Israel and Egypt, Syria and Jordan escalated between 1949 and 1956 (there were few significant incidents between Israel and Lebanon during this period). Most border clashes were caused by infiltration of Palestinians, some as guerrilla bands, most as individuals attempting to return to their property in Israel. Infiltration sometimes led to murder of Israeli civilians and sabotage, although most attacks were directed against military objectives. These guerrilla, or *fedayeen*, raids reached a peak between 1955 and 1956, leading to more frequent Israeli retaliation. At first infiltration appeared to be haphazard, but as the seriousness and organization increased, Israel accused the Arab governments of planning them. When Israel's complaints were discussed in the MACs, the Arab states denied responsibility, blaming the incidents on the unsolved refugee situation.

Israel responded with major retaliatory raids across the armistice lines. The first major retaliation was against the West Bank Jordanian village of Qibya in October 1953, when more than 50 Jordanians were killed. One of the most critical raids was the IDF attack on Gaza in February 1955. President Nasser asserted that the Gaza incident was the turning point in Israel-Egyptian relations and in Egyptian foreign policy. The raid found the Egyptian army unprepared and ill-equipped to cope with the IDF. Nasser maintained that the attack was a primary reason for his turning to the Soviet bloc for modern weapons. Between January 1955 and September 1956, the U.N. Truce

Supervision Organization (UNTSO) reported that nearly 500 Arabs and over 120 Israelis were killed, and over 400 Arabs and 330 Israelis injured, in border incidents.

Relations between Egypt and the West began to deteriorate after the United States, Great Britain and France refused to sell Nasser the modern military equipment he believed was required to protect his country. Since 1950 the three Western governments had attempted to keep a balance of power and prevent an arms race by controlling the flow of weapons to the Middle East. But this did not keep Britain and the United States from sending military assistance to Iraq, Iran, Pakistan and Turkey as part of a worldwide strategy to "contain" the Soviet Union through a series of so-called defensive alliances, the most important being the North Atlantic Treaty Organization (NATO). During the Eisenhower Administration, plans were devised to link the Middle East to NATO through agreements including the above-mentioned Arab and Muslim states and Great Britain. By 1955 all were signatories of the Baghdad Pact; some Americans hoped to persuade Egypt to join as well. Nasser's refusal to become a member was one of the major reasons why his request to purchase Western arms was rejected; as a result, he turned to the Soviet Union instead.

By breaking the Western arms monopoly in the Middle East, Nasser greatly enhanced his reputation as a leader and patriot among Arab nationalists who were hostile to the United States, France and Great Britain. Because of his growing ties with the Soviet Union, Nasser aroused the ire of the Western powers and apprehensions in Israel about his ultimate ambitions. Many in the West and in Israel now believed that Egypt was on the way to becoming a Soviet satellite and the dominant regional power.

When Nasser again asked the West for financial assistance in construction of the Aswan High Dam on the Nile River, a project perceived as the key to Egypt's future economic progress, he was turned down, and he requested Soviet support again. In an angry speech on July 26, 1956, Nasser declared that Egypt would nationalize the Suez Canal and use the revenues collected from transit fees to help pay the costs of the new dam.

Nationalization of the canal precipitated an international crisis. Great Britain and France, principal beneficiaries of Suez Canal Company profits, were infuriated. The canal was a major strategic asset for Britain because so much of its shipping, especially oil tankers, passed through the waterway. The canal was often called the lifeline of the British Empire.

The United States attempted to defuse the crisis through diplomacy and negotiations by convening a conference of canal "user states" to prepare guidelines and establish an international body to administer the canal. Egypt rejected this proposal and a later American plan to create a Canal Users' Association. Attempts to find a compromise in the U.N. Security Council also failed because of disagreement among the major powers. Britain and France refused to recognize Egyptian sovereignty over the canal, but the Soviet Union backed Egypt's rejection of an international authority, asserting that Cairo was within its rights to nationalize the waterway.

By the summer of 1956, both Britain and France were convinced that Nasser was a threat to their interests in the Middle East and that the only solution was to overthrow him, by war if necessary. Israel was prepared to join the French and the British because it regarded Nasser as the leader of a hostile Arab coalition that was rapidly gaining strength.

Nasser's reputation as an international figure was enhanced when he participated in the first conference of nonaligned states at Bandung, Indonesia in 1955 where he joined with other Third World leaders, including India's Jawaharlal Nehru, Indonesia's Sukarno and Ghana's Kwame Nkrumah, in denouncing Western colonialism and imperialism. As a result of the Soviet arms deal, nationalization of the Suez Canal and his fierce rhetoric against the Western imperialist powers and Israel, it appeared that Nasser was about to galvanize radical forces in the Arab world into a cohesive bloc. He had already concluded a military pact with Syria and in October 1956 persuaded Jordan to join the alliance. These factors, added to escalating border incidents, convinced Israeli leaders that the best defense was an aggressive offense. Thus, in September 1956, Israel accepted France's invitation to join in a tripartite attack on Egypt. Israeli and French military officials met to plan a secret meeting in Paris between Prime Minister Ben-Gurion and British and French representatives. Timing of the projected attack coincided with a U.S. presidential election campaign and, as it happened, an anti-Soviet revolution that was about to erupt in Hungary.

Israel launched its Sinai campaign on October 29, 1956, coordinating the attack with the British and French. A day later (after the IDF reached the vicinity of the Canal), as if in response, but actually by prearrangement, France and Britain issued an ultimatum to both Israel and Egypt to withdraw from the banks of the canal. Israel, as planned, accepted the ultimatum before its forces reached the canal; Egypt, as anticipated, rejected it. Twelve hours after Egypt refused to give in to their demands, the British and French started to bomb Egyptian airfields.

Nasser responded by sinking more than 40 ships filled with concrete to block the canal. Most fighting was over, and nearly all of the Sinai peninsula was captured by Israel within 100 hours. British and French paratroopers did not arrive until after most Egyptian forces were defeated. They seized Port Said at the northern end of the canal with little fighting, and the town quickly surrendered.

Although the war ended in a disastrous military defeat, Nasser recuperated politically and further enhanced his reputation as an Arab patriot. During the war, Egypt nationalized British and French holdings and took over much property belonging to native Egyptian Jews. Approximately 90% of the country's Jewish population left, for all practical purposes ending the existence of the Egyptian Jewish community. Tens of thousands of British, French, Italian and Greek citizens also departed as hostility to Westerners escalated because of the invasion. Nationalization, or "Egyptianization" of hundreds of "foreign" banks, trading companies, factories, stores, shops and other businesses became the basis for the future attempt by Nasser to socialize Egypt's economy.

International efforts to deal with the war in the U.N. Security Council were paralyzed because of differences between the United States and the Soviet Union and because of the worldwide crisis created by the Soviet invasion of Hungary. When action was stymied in the Security Council, the Middle East dispute was turned over to the General Assembly, early in November. With rare unanimity, the United States and the Soviet Union called for immediate withdrawal of the invasion forces. Israel was to move back to the armistice frontiers, and Britain and France were to withdraw from the Suez Canal Zone. The Eisenhower administration was angered by the tripartite invasion because its European allies failed to consult it and because the war was poorly timed. It was opportune for the Soviet Union since it drew attention away from Russian actions in Eastern Europe and gave Moscow another chance to prove its support for Arab nationalism. When Britain and France stalled in accepting the General Assembly order to withdraw, the Soviet Union threatened military intervention and broadcast hints about the atomic destruction of London and Paris.

The United Nations established the new United Nations Emergency Force (UNEF) to replace British, French and Israeli forces and to oversee implementation of the order calling for evacuation of foreign troops from Egypt. Although UNEF was established as a temporary force, Nasser allowed it to remain on the Egyptian side of the armistice line until 1967 (the option to demand withdrawal was the condition for Nasser's approval of UNEF in 1956).

Israel agreed to leave Egypt provided UNEF guaranteed freedom of navigation in the Gulf of Aqaba. British and French forces withdrew by the end of 1956, but Israel delayed its departure from Sharm al-Sheikh at the entrance to the gulf until January 1957 and from Gaza until March 1957. Israel's major accomplishment in the 1956 War was to attain free passage through the Gulf of Aqaba and the prestige of a major military victory over the strongest Arab nation.

The Suez War constituted a major diplomatic defeat for Great Britain and France. Egypt remained in total control of the Suez Canal, and both Western nations lost much of their influence in the Middle East and throughout the

Third World. Many observers considered Suez the last nail in the coffin of the British Empire. Neither Britain nor France ever regained their diplomatic prestige following the forced withdrawal from Suez. As a result of intervention on behalf of Egypt, the United States and the Soviet Union became the most influential foreign actors in the region with the result that after 1956 the Arab-Israel conflict became one of the most important frontiers in the Cold War.

THE JUNE 1967 SIX-DAY WAR

Nasser's prestige reached its peak during the decade following the 1956 Suez/Sinai War, and revolutionary Egypt became the model for and leader of radical forces throughout the Arab world, in every country from the Mediterranean to the Persian Gulf. Cairo provided material assistance and advice to antiestablishment groups in countries with conservative regimes. Nasser's influence was evident in the civil wars and revolutions that shook Lebanon and Iraq in 1958 and Yemen in 1962 and in the political unrest in Jordan and Saudi Arabia. The new radical Nasserite political groups were no more willing to establish peaceful relations with Israel than were their conservative predecessors.

After 1956 the Middle East was no longer exclusively a Western sphere of influence. In the competition to win clients and allies, both superpowers were responsible for escalating the arms race; the Soviet Union provided massive weapons shipments to Egypt, to Syria and to Iraq after its 1958 revolution. The United States became the major supplier to Saudi Arabia and Iran (not an Arab country) and a secondary source of arms for other conservative regimes. The first major American arms agreement with Israel was in 1962 when the Kennedy administration provided it with Hawk antiaircraft missiles, although most Israeli weapons imports during the 1960s until the Six-Day War came from France.

New elements adding to tensions in the region were the emergence of Palestinian guerrilla organizations, formation of the PLO in 1964, disputes over diversion of the Jordan River and the first Arab summit meeting in Cairo during 1964.

One of the first and the most important Palestinian guerrilla organizations was Fatah, the Palestine Liberation Movement, founded during the late 1950s by Yassir Arafat and several colleagues. Initially Fatah's objective was to destroy the Jewish state through the use of force. Fatah's first guerrilla operation against Israel was in January 1965.

The PLO was founded under Arab League auspices, largely on Nasser's initiative, at a congress in Jerusalem during May and June of 1964. The PLO charter called liberation of Palestine "a national duty" and demanded the "purge of the Zionist presence." It stated that "the Palestine Arab people . . . through the armed Palestine revolution, rejects any solution that would substitute for the complete liberation of Palestine." The Balfour Declaration, the mandate for Palestine, the U.N. partition plan and the establishment of Israel were all declared null and void. The charter denied Jewish claims to historical and spiritual ties with Palestine because "Judaism . . . is not a nationality . . . [and] the Jews are not one people." Armed struggle, with guerrilla groups forming the nucleus of the popular forces of liberation, would redeem Palestine.

The charter was amended to include a possible confederation of Palestine and Jordan. Some PLO members later agreed to accept Jews in Israel as citizens of a Palestinian state. By 1990 most provisions in the charter hostile to Israel were, for all practical purposes, disregarded. Israel, however, considered the charter proof of the mortal enmity between Zionism and Palestinian nationalism and demanded that it be revoked before concluding a peace settlement with the PLO.

After the PLO was established, its military arm, the Palestine Liberation Army (PLA), was formed with units attached to the various Arab armies because the Palestinians had no territorial base of their own. The PLO lost control of most PLA units after they were integrated into the Egyptian, Syria, Iraqi and Jordanian armies. Before 1967 there was little coordination between the activities of the independent Palestinian guerrilla factions and the activities of the PLO and PLA.

The 1964 Cairo summit was convened by Nasser to overcome serious inter-Arab rifts, such as the tensions between Egypt and Saudi Arabia over the civil war in Yemen and the uprising of Kurds in Iraq, and to create a united front against Israel. Decisions taken at the meetings included (1) creation of a unified military command to coordinate Arab strategy, (2) agreement to reduce inter-Arab tensions and to increase cooperation among the Arab states, (3) a request to Ahmad Shukairi, the Palestine Arab League representative, to organize a Palestine entity and (4) an appeal to Arab governments for financial assistance for a Jordan River diversion project.

After failure of the Johnston Plan (see above), Israel decided to initiate its own unilateral scheme to use the Jordan River and its tributaries, the principal source of water for both Jordan and Israel. The plan included drainage of the Hula swamps in northern Israel and use of the Sea of Galilee (Lake Tiberias) to store water for diversion to a national water carrier providing irrigations in southern Israel. Much work in these projects occurred in the demilitarized zone between Israel and Syria. Syria maintained that Israel's project violated the armistice agreement because it would result in changes of the terrain militarily favorable to Israel and because it included confiscation of Arab-owned land. Israel countered that the project was not a violation since it was a purely civilian operation intended to improve economic productivity.

Jordan also began to implement its own unilateral plan involving construction of a large dam on the Yarmuk River, which flows into the Jordan River. According to Israel, Jordan's program would greatly diminish the amount of available water. Although the two countries reached an understanding to keep the water quotas assigned in the Johnston plan, the Arab League opposed any project to divert the river.

At the 1964 Cairo summit, the Arabs decided to deny the use of any Jordan sources to Israel by diverting the Hasbani and Baniyas rivers. When Lebanon and Syria began work on the project, Israel started military operations against the diversion by bombarding and seriously damaging the construction work, using incidents of infiltration from Syria as an excuse. When the Arab states refused to guarantee military assistance to Lebanon should the fighting escalate, the diversion scheme was abandoned. But hostilities continued along the armistice frontier because Israel still regarded the possibility of Arab diversion as a major threat to its own development plans.

By the mid-1960s, border tensions between Israel and its neighbors, except Lebanon, had escalated to an all-time high. Israel's feeling of encirclement was intensified when Egypt formed new military pacts, with Syria in November 1966 and with Jordan in May 1967. Failure to resolve the Arab refugee problem and the loss of the 1948 and 1956 wars still rankled the Arab world. However, a belief that an all-powerful coalition was now ready to take on Israel and avenge the defeats of 1948 and 1956 changed the mood to one of exuberant confidence. Nasser was looked up to as the leader who would unite all Arab forces in the final battle.

On April 7, Israel attacked Syrian artillery positions in the Golan Heights that were shelling northern Israeli settlements. An air battle ensued, and Israeli planes shot down six Syrian MIG fighters. When Syria complained that Egypt failed to come to its rescue, Nasser announced that he would no longer tolerate Israeli aggression and moved his army into the Sinai Penninsula up to the border with Israel. One of the most controversial prewar incidents was a message from Moscow to Egypt asserting that Israeli forces were massed along the Syrian border, a claim that proved to be untrue.

The Soviet "warning" led to the final escalation; Nasser responded by ordering the U.N. emergency force (UNEF) moved from the border with Israel, leaving Egyptian troops face-to-face with the IDF. He also renewed the blockade of the Straits of Tiran, the gateway to the Gulf of Aqaba, by closing the waterway to Israel for the first time since 1956. International efforts to defuse the tension were of no avail. Nasser asserted that his actions were only to prevent an Israeli attack on Syria. He claimed it was necessary to remove UNEF from the border so Egyptian forces would be prepared in case of an Israeli attack.

Israel interpreted Nasser's moves, the Syrian bombardment of Israeli settlements and the war hysteria that spread through the Arab world as harbingers of a mass onslaught. Although Israeli military strength was superior to that of any Arab combination, there was talk of another Holocaust. Lack of confidence in the government led to a major shake-up and formation of a new national coalition cabinet including all but the Israeli Arab parties and the Communists.

Early in June, the cabinet decided on a preemptive strike to forestall any Arab attack. On June 5, 1967, the Israel air force staged a massive raid on Egyptian airfields and later in the day also destroyed air bases in Syria, Jordan and Iraq. In one day, most of the Arab air forces, over 400 planes, were destroyed, with the loss of only 19 Israeli planes. The IDF simultaneously attacked Egyptian ground forces in Gaza and Sinai. Egypt's retreat soon became a rout, and by the third day of the war, Israel had captured Gaza and all of Sinai up to the banks of the Suez Canal.

Israel warned Jordan's King Husayn to keep out of the war, but mass excitement in Amman and Jerusalem and false reports about Egyptian success, raised unrealistic expectations that Jordan could join in easily defeating Israel. Shortly after Jordanian artillery opened fire on Jewish Jerusalem, the IDF began an offensive that ended in two days with Israel occupying Arab East Jerusalem and most of the West Bank.

The Syrian front was relatively quiet during the first few days of the war, with only intermittent shelling of Israeli settlements from the Golan Heights. However when Syria refused to accept a Security Council cease-fire on June 8, Israel attacked with full force. In less than a day of intensive fighting Israel captured the Golan Heights, and on June 10, Syria too accepted the cease-fire.

Israel had overturned the balance of power in the Middle East. Its principal Arab foes were militarily crushed, and any hope of destroying Israel by force was now out of the question. Israel's strategic position was, for the moment, greatly enhanced with control of Gaza and the Sinai peninsula, all of Jerusalem and the West Bank and the Golan Heights. The size of territories acquired in the war was about four times the total area of Israel inside the 1949 armistice frontiers.

The former Jordanian West Bank included most major towns in the Hashemite Kingdom. In addition to Jerusalem, there were important cultural and economic centers in Hebron, Nablus, Jenin, Jericho, Tulkarm, Ramallah, Kalkilya and Bethlehem. The Jerusalem-Bethlehem tourist region had been a mainstay of Jordan's economy, providing about a quarter of the country's foreign currency earnings. The West Bank had contributed 40% of Jordan's gross domestic product. Investment in the West Bank represented about 95%

of total Jordanian investment in tourism, 60% in private construction, 52% in government buildings, 48% in municipal and rural development plans and 44% in highways and roads. Although less than a third of Jordan's cultivated lands were on the West Bank, it produced nearly half the vegetables and 80 percent of the fruits. More than half the government-financed cooperative societies were in the West Bank.

Jordan was flooded with more than 300,000 new refugees, while losing one-third to one-half of its economic productivity; 120,000 of the Palestinians were second-time refugees, having left their original homes for the West Bank in 1947–48. The more remote the likelihood of peace, the less inclined Israel was to permit the refugees to return to the West Bank, now under military occupation. Official policy was to permit repatriation of only a limited number in special family-reunion cases. Eventually some 70,000 Palestinians returned to occupied Jerusalem and the West Bank under the family-reunion concession.

An incipient economic recovery in Gaza was shattered by the war and the occupation that followed. Israel announced that Gaza had never been part of Egypt and would not be returned. The government made similar statements about the Sinai, and Israeli scientists began to take inventory of the peninsula's resources.

Syria suffered the least as a result of the war. However, between 80,000 and 100,000 Syrian Arabs fled from the Golan Heights, leaving behind fewer than 7,000 inhabitants, mostly Druze villagers. Loss of the Jordan Valley headwaters by Syria was a serious blow to Arab plans to disrupt Israel's Jordan Valley development program.

The dominant factor shaping Israel's policy toward the newly occupied territories was military strategy. For the first time, only a handful of Jewish settlements could be directly threatened by organized Arab armed forces. Territorial expansion shortened the borders between Israel and its Arab neighbors. The Gaza Strip was eliminated as a military threat to central Israel and the military frontier with Egypt was shortened by several hundred kilometers. Before 1967 the border with Jordan had been the most sensitive. Until Israel occupied the West Bank and East Jerusalem, Jordanian tanks were only a few minutes from Natanya, midway between Haifa and Tel Aviv, the two largest cities on the Mediterranean coast. Jewish Jerusalem was within the range of Jordanian guns until June 1967 when the frontier was pushed back across the Jordan River.

In the north, Syrian guns on the Golan Heights were spiked, and the labyrinth of Syrian fortresses and tunnels was captured by Israel. Syria also lost Kuneitra, its principle town on the Golan, once a city of 20,000 and the command post of its southern armies. Jewish settlements from Lake Tiberias to Lebanon appeared to be secure for the first time since 1948.

In 1967, Israel was prepared to restore all the occupied territories except for East Jerusalem in return for a final and complete peace settlement. But the longer the occupied territories remained in Israeli hands, the more difficult it became to contemplate their return. The petroleum from Egypt's Sinai oil fields soon became a mainstay of Israel's economy. Jewish tourists soon became accustomed to visit Rachel's tomb in Bethlehem, the Tomb of the Patriarchs in Hebron and the Western Wall of the second temple in the Old City of Jerusalem. Many orthodox Jews and territorial nationalists believed that these and other Biblical sites should never again be abandoned. The territorial question dominated Israeli politics for the next quarter of a century.

Before June 4, 1967, only the Herut (Freedom) party, successor to the Irgun and ideological descendants of Vladimir Jabotinsky's Revisionist Zionist Movement, made acquisition of territory beyond the 1949 armistice frontiers an integral part of its dogma. After the June war, a growing number of militantly nationalist religious Zionists also espoused the concept of territorial Zionism. No party except the Arab Communists and small left-wing factions was willing to return all the conquered territories. Even the Labor movement was divided over the future of the occupied lands. Few Israelis wanted to return Jerusalem and the Golan Heights, although some were willing to make territorial concessions for peace in Sinai and in the West Bank.

In the Arab world, the 1967 defeat was perceived as a disaster equal to the 1948 war. Israel now appeared to be entrenched more securely than ever, with control over an additional one million Arabs. Although elimination of the Jewish state by force was only remotely possible, the defeated Arab states were still unwilling to enter direct negotiations unless Israel withdrew from the territories occupied in June. An Arab League summit meeting during September 1967 in Khartoum, Sudan to find a "political solution," declared that there could no peace with Israel, no negotiations and no recognition. The league called on the international community to support the U.N. charter's principle of the "inadmissibility of the acquisition of territory by war."

The war further polarized relations between the Soviet bloc and the West. Russia and several East bloc countries cut diplomatic ties with Israel; Egypt, Syria, Iraq, Sudan, Algeria and Yemen broke relations with the United States. Most Arab states believed that the United States had colluded with Israel; unconfirmed rumors circulated that American soldiers flew Israeli planes during the war and provided the IDF with intelligence information. The Middle East arms race escalated to a new high when the Soviets restored the weapons lost by Egypt and Syria. The United States now replaced France as Israel's weapons supplier and American military planners began to consider Israel as a strategic asset. President Charles de Gaulle, on the other hand, chagrined at Israel's refusal to accept his advice to refrain from war, withdrew

French assistance and severed his close diplomatic and military ties with the Jewish state.

With Soviet support, the Arab states tried to persuade the United Nations to order Israeli withdrawal from the occupied territories. When this failed, the United States and the Soviet Union sought to reach an agreement and settle the conflict. After protracted debate and intensive bargaining, the Security Council adopted Resolution 242 on November 22, 1967. This compromise resolution became the basis for future attempts to resolve the conflict.

Resolution 242 emphasized the need to work for a "just and lasting peace" and the "inadmissibility of the acquisition of territory by war." It called for "withdrawal of Israeli armed forces from territories occupied in the recent conflict"; the "termination of all claims or states of belligerency and respect for and acknowledgment of the sovereignty, territorial integrity and political independence of every state in the area"; guarantees for freedom of navigation through international waterways in the area; and "a just settlement of the refugee problem."

The call for withdrawal "from territories" was to cause continued future disagreement. Israel and its supporters argued that "withdrawal from territories" rather than "from *the* territories" meant that it was not required to leave all areas seized during the war. The Arab states and their backers asserted that the resolution did mean total withdrawal.

Resolution 242 soon replaced General Assembly Resolution 194 of December 1948 as the unofficial basis for future attempts to resolve the Arab-Israel conflict. Although Resolution 194 was reaffirmed at annual meetings of the General Assembly, most post-1967 peace proposals were established on the principles in Resolution 242, calling on Israel to return to the pre-June 1967 armistice frontiers. Attempts to find a solution were no longer based on return to the 1947 U.N. partition borders. Most proposals after 1967 called for a "just solution" of the refugee problem rather than for their return to their homes in Israel. Even the Arab states appeared to abandon expectations that Israel would return to the partition plan and now demanded that it withdraw to the 1949 armistice borders.

Resolution 242 also requested the U.N. secretary-general to appoint a special representative to promote agreement and assist efforts for a peaceful settlement. The special envoy was Gunnar Jarring, Sweden's ambassador to the Soviet Union. Jarring found that Syria would not accept Resolution 242 and therefore bypassed Damascus in the negotiations. Israel continued to insist that progress could only be made through direct negotiations with the Arab states. Egypt demanded that Israel withdraw from Sinai and Gaza as a prerequisite for negotiations. Differences between the parties finally brought

Jarring's efforts to a halt, and fighting was renewed between Israel and Egypt along the banks of the Suez Canal.

THE WAR OF ATTRITION

The War of Attrition in 1969–70 was really a continuation of the 1967 war with artillery and air attacks. Friction across the Suez Canal between Egypt and Israel began soon after the 1967 war and escalated to alarming proportions during 1968 and 1969. In the spring of 1969, Nasser announced that the June 1967 cease-fire was no longer valid, and Egyptian artillery began to pound Israeli outposts along the canal banks. Nasser's principal objective was to keep superpower interest alive; he feared that without their involvement, Egypt would never be able to reclaim its lost territory. In March he officially announced that the "War of Attrition" was underway. Nasser sought to inflict such a heavy toll on Israel that it would withdraw from the canal and, under pressure from the United States and the Soviet Union, become more amenable to a political solution favorable to Cairo.

Israel retaliated by bombarding heavily populated cities and towns in the Suez Canal Zone, forcing evacuation of the civilian populations. More than 1,000 Israeli soldiers were killed between June 1967 and July 1970 along Israel's Bar-Lev Line, a network of fortifications and bunkers on the eastern shore of the canal. These were casualties heavier than Israel sustained in the Six-Day War. Israeli commandos destroyed a key radar installation, an essential part of Egypt's air defense system, in response to an Egyptian raid across the canal. This was followed by massive air attacks on Egyptian artillery, airfields and deep-penetration raids striking at industrial and civilian targets hundreds of miles into upper Egypt with hundreds of civilian casualties. Nasser responded by turning to the Soviet Union, which sent personnel to help operate the air defense system and to pilot Egyptian aircraft in the battles with Israel.

Soviet intervention aroused American concern that the canal conflict might escalate into a larger war leading to superpower confrontation. To defuse the tension, U.S. Secretary of State William Rogers proclaimed that American policy would be more "evenhanded" and in October 1969 announced a plan to prevent further escalation. It called on Israel to withdraw behind the international border with Egypt—that is, the 1949 border—and from the Gaza Strip, with Gaza's future subject to negotiations. Rogers also called for free navigation in the Suez Canal and the Gulf of Aqaba. Both Israel and Egypt (backed by the Soviet Union) rejected the Rogers plan.

In December 1969 a parallel plan was addressed to Israel and Jordan calling for Israel's withdrawal, with slight revisions, to the 1949 armistice frontiers;

equal rights for both Israel and Jordan in a united Jerusalem whose political status would be determined by mutual agreement; and settlement of the refugee problem. Jordan accepted this proposal, but Israel rejected it.

Another plan, called Rogers II, was proposed in June 1970 appealing for an immediate Egypt-Israel cease-fire and reactivation of the Jarring mission, suspended since 1969. Rogers II reemphasized the principles of Resolution 242. Both Egypt and Jordan accepted it, but Israel demanded detailed "clarifications." After President Nixon explained that withdrawal would take place only within the framework of a binding peace agreement and that it did not necessarily mean return to the pre-1967 borders, that the refugee problem would be solved in a way that would not threaten Israel's security or Jewish character and that the United States would ensure Israeli security and the existing balance of arms, Israel accepted the proposals. Agreement by the majority of the Israeli cabinet caused a crisis that led the right-wing Gahal (Herut and General Zionist parties) and its leader Menachem Begin to withdraw from the government.

On August 7, 1970, after Egypt and Israel accepted Rogers II, a cease-fire came into effect. It was threatened when Nasser moved new missiles close to the canal, assuring Egypt's military advantage. Israel protested and refused to renew the Jarring talks until December when the United States promised to restore the balance. Jarring's renewed efforts proved to be abortive and were finally terminated.

With Nasser's death in September 1970 and the succession of Anwar Sadat as the second president of Egypt, a fresh chapter began in the Arab-Israel conflict.

PALESTINIAN NATIONAL REVIVAL

Disenchantment over political and military failures of Arab political leaders led to the rise of the Palestinian national movement after 1967. Before the Arab defeat in the Six-Day War, many Palestinians looked for assistance in redeeming their homeland to a variety of political movements in the Arab world, from Communists and Ba'athists to religious fundamentalists such as the Muslim Brotherhood. Egypt's President Nasser was perhaps the most revered figure; many regarded him almost as a messiah who would lead the Palestinians back to their homes.

Following defeat in the Six-Day War, Palestinians turned to a new generation of their own leaders and nationalist-guerrilla organizations. In the months following the war, over a score of these new groups were formed, most with the objective of liberating Palestine through armed struggle. Attention began to shift from the refugee problem to establishing a Palestinian state. Initially, nearly all factions focused on armed struggle, believing that guerrilla action could undermine the Jewish state.

The PLO's orientation became much less rejectionist after 1974 when the PNC decided to include "political, popular, and democratic struggle" as well as armed struggle in its program to liberate Palestine. The PNC also took the first steps toward a two-state solution (a Palestinian state coexisting with Israel) by abandoning the goal of a "democratic secular state" in all of Palestine.

By 1968 the PLO had been widely accepted as the representative of the Palestinians. It included several groups that disagreed about Palestinian relationships with the Jewish people, with the Zionists and with the state of Israel. Arafat's Fatah was by far the largest. Suspicions and tensions between the PLO and most other guerrilla groups were overcome with the election of Arafat as president. The PLO became an umbrella organization for the major guerrilla factions and its Palestine National Council (PNC) became the Palestinian parliament-in-exile.

As the PLO gained recognition in the Arab world and among most Third World countries, it acquired respectability and political influence. In October 1974 the U.N. General Assembly voted 105 to 4 with 20 abstentions to recognize the PLO officially as the representative of the Palestinians and to grant it observer status in the various U.N.-affiliated bodies. Arafat was honored in November 1974 when he was invited to address the General Assembly. The organization also became a full member of the Arab League with the status of a nation-state in 1976. By the 1980s, the PLO was legitimized internationally by the recognition of many states, including the Vatican and the Soviet Union. Israel and the United States, however, continued to refuse recognition of or negotiations with the PLO; both countries classified it as a "terrorist" organization because of attacks on civilians by PLO guerrilla factions.

Relations between the Arab states and the PLO leadership were far from smooth. Several leaders, both Palestinians and others, considered too moderate in their approach to the Palestine problem were assassinated. The most militant factions, such as the Fatah Revolutionary Command (Black June, Black March) of Abu Nidal (Sabri al Banna), broke away and carried out their own unauthorized terrorist activities against civilians in Europe, Israel and in Arab countries; some threatened the lives of PLO leaders they considered too compromising.

Relations with Arab states deteriorated when the PLO attempted to carry out commando attacks against Israel contrary to policies of Arab leaders. Syria kept its Palestinians under tight control, preventing any independent action from its soil, but it encouraged guerrilla raids from Lebanon into Israel. Relations with Jordan deteriorated in 1970–71 when the PLO attempted to take over parts of the country and establish quasi-independent Palestinian enclaves as bases for operations against Israel. Clashes between PLO factions and the Jordanian Arab Legion ignited a civil war that ended when the guerrillas and PLO offices were driven from the country. Most found refuge in Lebanon, which was turned into the principal base of Palestinian operations until the 1982 war. After 1982, Tunis, the capital of Tunisia, became PLO central headquarters but PLO military units were dispersed in several Arab countries (see below).

The PLO was organized like a government-in-exile; as noted above, it received diplomatic status and had embassies in several countries. In addition to political, diplomatic and paramilitary activities, it had an extensive network of economic and social functions. This infrastructure included health care, welfare, cultural, educational and recreational institutions, as well as several businesses generating hundreds of millions of dollars a year. The Palestine National Fund was established to raise monies and to deal with fiscal matters. These activities were carried out by the General Union of Palestinian Women and several other unions for workers, engineers, writers and students. The unions and the guerrilla organizations elected the representatives to the PNC.

The PNC usually met once every year or so to develop broad policy outlines for the national movement. The council represented diverse views on issues relating to the Palestinian people, including those outside the Middle East, mostly in Europe and the United States. Members of the PNC were drawn from all walks of life, including personalities well known in the arts and sciences and the business world. Professors and scholars were included; among the more prominent was Edward Said of Columbia University. The PNC played an important role during 1988 when it issued the Palestinian Declaration of Independence and its accompanying political communiqué at Algiers (see below).

THE 1973 OCTOBER WAR

Nasser's sudden death in September 1970 took the Middle East by surprise. His successor, former vice-president Anwar Sadat, was at first seen as a transition figure and not as a strong personality. Sadat soon proved to be forceful, outwitting his opponents and gaining full control of the government, including policy in the Arab-Israel conflict. He believed that for Egypt's political, military and economic well-being, to regain self-confidence at home as well as respect in the world community, it was crucial to wipe out the disgrace and humiliation of the 1967 defeat. At first Sadat tried diplomacy, extending the Rogers plan and offering to reopen the Suez Canal if Israel withdrew to the Mitla and Gidi passes in the Sinai peninsula. He also offered to restore diplomatic relations with the United States, declare a cease-fire and sign a peace with Israel based on full implementation of Resolution 242.

Sadat's offers encouraged the United States and the Soviet Union to reactivate the Jarring mediation mission between Egypt and Israel. Israel bluntly stated that it would not withdraw to the pre-June 5, 1967, armistice lines, bringing the Jarring mission to a halt again. By the end of 1971, Sadat began to lose faith in diplomacy, and he warned that 1971 would be the "year of decision" in the conflict, implying that war might be necessary to regain the lands lost in 1967. He repeated warnings about the year of decision in 1972 but took no radical action. By the end of 1972, Israelis, Americans and even many Arabs considered Sadat's pronouncements empty threats, not to be taken seriously.

While calling for diplomatic approaches to the conflict, Sadat was also preparing for a two-front war against Israel with Syrian President Hafez al-Assad. Under cover of talks about a Libyan scheme for a Federation of Arab Republics (Egypt, Syria, Libya and Sudan), military staffs held several planning sessions. Egypt was still dependent on the Soviet Union for modern weapons; an assured supply was necessary if war were to be waged. But Sadat suspected that Moscow was deliberately slowing down the arms flow as part of the Soviet-American detente. Angered by Russia's failure to respond to his demands, Sadat surprised the international community in July 1972 by expelling all 21,000 Soviet military advisors and personnel serving in Egypt. Many in the West believed this would delay the war. Instead the Soviet Union stepped up arms deliveries to both Egypt and Syria to regain Sadat's favor.

In a last attempt at a political settlement during July 1973, Sadat persuaded eight members of the U.N. Security Council to introduce a resolution reiterating the call for territorial withdrawal by Israel and underscoring Palestinian rights. The resolution was vetoed by the United States because it undermined Resolution 242, "the one and only agreed basis" for a settlement. The U.S. veto and failure of Presidents Nixon and Brezhnev to mention the Middle East in their June summit meeting convinced the Arab states that only war could resolve the conflict.

In Israel positions had hardened since the 1967 victory. The country emerged from the war as the strongest military power in the region, stronger than any combination of Arab states. The new boundaries appeared to guarantee national security for the foreseeable future. Differences among political parties over the future of the occupied territories concerned their political status rather than whether or not to return them. The Likud bloc (a coalition of right-wing parties led by Menachem Begin and successor to the Gahal party) opposed withdrawal from any occupied territories for both security and ideological reasons; many in Likud and among other militant nationalists called for annexation. The glue that held Likud together was the belief that all of mandatory Palestine belonged by right to the Jewish people; Sinai and the Golan could not be returned because of security.

The governing Labor Party generally accepted the principle of "territory in exchange for peace," although it adamantly opposed return of all the occupied lands, asserting that for security reasons, Israel would have to remain in substantial areas. Sadat's failure to follow through after his proclamations about the "year of decision" in 1971 and again in 1972, led the Israeli general staff to conclude that the country was safe from an Arab attack. This "conception," founded on the assumption that the IDF was invulnerable and that the Bar-Lev line along the banks of the Suez Canal was impenetrable, threw Israel's army commanders off guard. Israeli intelligence misinterpreted the buildup of forces along the canal in the days before the war as part of military exercises, unlikely to escalate into an actual attack.

The two-front war began on October 6, 1973, the Jewish Day of Atonement, so in Israel it was called the Yom Kippur War. It also was the Muslim month of fasting; thus the conflict was called the Ramadan War by the Arabs. Egyptian forces quickly crossed the canal and overran the Bar-Lev line. In the north, Syria moved into the Golan Heights nearly reaching the pre-1967 border with Israel. The IDF was outnumbered almost 12 to 1 when the fighting began because it had not yet fully mobilized, but within the next few days rapid call-up of reserves redressed the balance.

The fighting was the heaviest since 1948, with major losses of manpower and material on both sides. The numbers of tanks, planes and artillery destroyed was larger than in any battle fought between World War II and 1973. Losses were so great that each side had to be rearmed in the midst of the fighting. Huge U.S. Galaxie transport planes rushed tons of spare parts and equipment to the IDF; when reaching Israel, supplies were immediately unloaded and brought directly to the front lines. The Soviet Union provided similar assistance to Syria and Egypt.

During the first days of the war, the Israelis feared that Arab forces, especially the Syrians in the north, might penetrate the pre-June 1967 borders. Within a week, however, Israeli counter-offensives had turned the tide of battle. The Syrians were beaten back on the Golan Heights, and Israeli forces crossed the Suez Canal and began a push toward Cairo.

The war precipitated a tense international crisis when the Soviet Union responded to an urgent appeal from Cairo to save the Egyptian Third Army surrounded by the IDF in Sinai. Despite Security Council cease-fire orders, Israeli troops continued to attack, in an attempt to destroy the Egyptian forces remaining in Sinai. When Moscow threatened to send troops to assist the Egyptians, the United States declared a worldwide military alert. The crisis ended when all parties agreed to negotiate a safe retreat for the Egyptians.

By the time the combatants accepted a cease-fire on October 22, Israeli forces had regained control of Sinai and crossed to the west side of the Suez Canal. Israel recaptured most of the Golan and occupied some 600 square kilometers of Syrian territory beyond. Both Egypt and Israel claimed success, Egypt because it crossed the Canal into Sinai and Israel because it finally scored a military victory. The price, however was steep. Nearly 3,000 Israeli and more than 8,500 Egyptian and Syrian soldiers were killed, and 8,800 Israelis and almost 20,000 Egyptians and Syrians were wounded. Israel lost 840 tanks; the Egyptians and Syrians, 2,550. The cost of the war equaled approximately one year's gross national product for each of the combatants. Expenditures for the October War drained funds for development programs in Egypt and Syria, despite massive financing from Saudi Arabia, and began a serious downturn in Israel's economy, making it more dependent on U.S. military and economic aid. Egypt and Syria now had to turn to the Soviet Union to restock their arsenals.

The October War also had severe international economic repercussions. It emboldened the Organization of Petroleum Exporting Countries (OPEC) to double prices for oil. The Arab members now insisted on tying the sale of oil to support from its customers in the war against Israel. The Arabs also called for a reduction of 5% in oil production each month until Israel restored the territory it captured in 1967 and respected the rights of the Palestinians. Saudi Arabia cut production by 10% and placed an embargo on shipments to the United States in retaliation for American arms supplied to Israel. Fear of oil shortages in the West drove oil prices to unprecedented levels, about three times the pre-war price. Gasoline shortages in the United States resulting from the Arab embargo, combined with the rise in oil prices, began a spiral of world-wide inflation and a recession in 1974–75.

Attempts to restart the peace process began with Security Council Resolution 338, passed when the cease-fire was ordered on October 22, 1973. The resolution called for immediate termination of all military activity, implementation of Resolution 242 and the start of negotiations "aimed at establishing a just and durable peace in the Middle East." Resolution 338 subsequently became a companion piece to 242 as the basis of future proposals for a peace settlement. In December a Middle East Peace Conference convened in Geneva under the cochairmanship of the Soviet and American foreign ministers and the U.N. secretary-general. Egypt, Jordan and Israel attended, but Syria refused to participate. After opening speeches and two days of wrangling over procedure, meetings were suspended, and the conference failed to reconvene. An Egyptian-Israeli Military Committee also met in Geneva to discuss separation of forces in Sinai, but it too accomplished little.

The most important diplomatic achievements resulting from the war were a series of disengagement agreements between Israel and Egypt and Syria brokered by U.S. Secretary of State Henry Kissinger. Collapse of the Geneva Conference provided Kissinger with an excuse to bypass the U.N. and the Soviet Union. Initially, Kissinger sought a comprehensive agreement, but it was soon evident that the conflict could not be resolved quickly. Instead, U.S. policy turned to a "step-by-step" approach.

The initial step was a cease-fire agreement providing relief for Egypt's besieged Third Army and the return by Israeli forces to the lines of October 22. This was the first bilateral accord signed between Israel and Egypt since the 1949 armistice. Kissinger began another round of shuttle diplomacy in January 1974. He persuaded Israel to withdraw its forces in the Sinai to some 20 miles east of the Suez Canal. Egypt agreed to reduce the number of its troops east of the Canal, not to place missiles east of Suez, to establish a buffer zone in Sinai patrolled by a U.N. Disengagement Observer Force (UNDOF) and to reopen the canal to non-Israeli shipping. The agreement led to renewal of full diplomatic relations between the United States and Egypt after a seven-year hiatus.

It was much more difficult to persuade Syria to sign a disengagement agreement with Israel. Damascus maintained a hard line, and border clashes with Israel continued for months after the October 1973 cease-fire. After several shuttle trips between Damascus and Jerusalem, Kissinger finally obtained an agreement in May 1974. Israel agreed to leave territory it had seized in Syria during October 1973 and to withdraw from the town of Kuneitra in the Golan region. A buffer zone patrolled by UNDOF was established between Israeli and Syrian forces in the Golan Heights, and President Assad agreed to prevent Palestinian guerrillas from using Syria as a base for attacks on Israel. This agreement was also followed by renewal of U.S.-Syrian diplomatic relations.

Attempts to extend the disengagement agreements with Syria were unsuccessful. However, Kissinger negotiated another Israeli-Egyptian agreement in September 1975 providing for further withdrawal of Israeli forces into Sinai and a new U.N. buffer zone. Surveillance and early-warning stations were set up, one manned by American civilian technicians. Oil installations on the Red Sea coast occupied by Israel were restored to Egypt and demilitarized under U.N. supervision. Egypt agreed to permit cargoes bound for Israel to pass through the Suez Canal provided they were not on Israeli ships.

The disengagement agreements were the diplomatic climax of the 1973 war; they were the major accomplishment in peace negotiations until Sadat's 1977 iniative. Sadat's popularity and Egypt's standing in the Arab world improved as a result of the war. Egyptian forces had performed better during October 1973 than in the three previous wars with Israel. In Egypt the October War was regarded as a great victory and the "crossing" (of the canal) was commemorated annually as a national holiday. Postage stamps and other memorabilia were produced to honor the "victory." Egypt's 1973 military accomplishments opened the way for Kissigner's diplomacy and were a prelude to Sadat's 1977 startling peace initiative (see below).

Relations between Egypt and Syria deteriorated after the war. Sadat's concessions in the second disengagement agreement between Egypt and Israel angered Assad. He feared that Egypt's compromise would undermine his own efforts to regain the Golan. Assad refused to participate in further peacemaking efforts and joined a new anti-Israel Rejectionist Front that included Iraq, Algeria, Libya, South Yemen and the PLO.

For Israel the long-term consequences were disastrous, despite its military recovery after the first few days of the war and occupation of additional Egyptian and Syrian territory. Casualties exceeded those in the two previous conflicts, and military intelligence was discredited because it failed to predict the attack. It would take more than a decade to recover from the economic consequences of the war. The setback broke through a psychological barrier to territorial concessions and raised doubts about Israel's invincibility. Although the war enhanced Arab self-confidence, it shook Israeli belief in the idea ("conception") that no concessions were needed and that the territories could be kept indefinitely. The war led to closer relations with, and greater dependence on, the United States, but it caused a break in relations with most Third World nations, which severed their diplomatic ties with Israel.

An inquiry board, the Agranat Commission, established in November 1973 to probe the reasons for the disaster, blamed the IDF's mistaken "conception" of Egypt's war prowess and recommended removal of the chief of staff and other high-ranking officers. The Agranat report led to a major shakeup in the Labor government, the resignation of Prime Minister Golda Meir and a new cabinet led by Yitzhak Rabin in June 1974. The 1973 setback and the Agranat report were among the major factors leading to Labor's defeat in the 1977 Knesset elections.

SADAT'S PEACE INITIATIVE

The policies of Israel's Labor government in the occupied territories and in Arab-Israel relations following the 1967 war were ambivalent. On one hand, Labor called for "peace in exchange for territory," meaning territory taken in the 1967 war; Prime Minister Golda Meir asserted that "everything is negotiable," but only within the framework of direct peace negotiations. On the other hand, Labor encouraged Jewish settlement in strategic areas of the West Bank, in Golan and in Sinai. Defense Minister Moshe Dayan stated that Israel would create "new facts" in the occupied territories and that Israel's presence in the West Bank was "of right and not on sufferance, to visit, live and to settle . . . we must be able to maintain military bases there . . . we must of course, be able to prevent the entry of any Arab army into the West Bank." "New facts" meant establishing some 25 Jewish settlements in the occupied territories; incorporation into Israel of East Jerusalem; greatly extending the West Bank road network and linking it with highways in Israel; connecting the West Bank electricity grid with Israel; organizing Israeli business and commercial operations in the occupied areas; and offering large subsidies to Jewish investors in the territories. A major difference between Labor and the opposition Likud during the 1977 election was that Likud opposed any territorial concessions for peace, while Labor considered the possibility of a "Jordan option," that is, concessions in the West Bank placing its Arab population under Jordanian civil administration.

The outcome of the election was a shock and a major setback for Labor that some called an "earthquake." When Likud leader Menachem Begin became prime minister in June 1977, most observers expected that he would harden Israel's position toward concessions in a peace settlement. Begin immediately stepped up Jewish settlement in the West Bank, and the members of his coalition favoring the creation of "Greater Israel"—all of mandatory Palestine, including the West Bank, which they referred to as "Judea and Samaria"—called for annexation of the territories. President Sadat, however, believed that the time was ripe for a new peace initiative.

In the months before Begin assumed office, Sadat was taken aback by President Jimmy Carter's attempt to reconvened the Geneva Middle East Peace Conference in cooperation with the Soviet Union. On October 1, the two superpowers issued a joint statement calling for a comprehensive settlement, including Israeli withdrawal from the 1967 occupied territories and a guarantee of the "legitimate rights of the Palestinian people." Israel found the Soviet-American declaration unacceptable although it was willing to join a reconvened Geneva conference provided the PLO did not participate. Sadat, who had expelled his Russian advisors in 1972 and was suspicious of Moscow, decided to undertake his own initiative, to preempt the Soviet-U.S. plan and to seize the chance to negotiate with a militantly nationalist government in Israel. Too long a delay might give Begin the opportunity to consolidate Israel's occupation and end any chance of getting the Sinai back.

The deadlock was broken in November 1977 when Sadat surprised Israel, the Arab states, the United States and the rest of the world in a speech to the Egyptian National Assembly announcing that he was prepared to fly to Israel, address its parliament (Knesset) and discuss peace. Prime Minister Begin had no alternative but to accept. Advance preparations for the negotiations had been made in secret talks between Egypt and Israel in Morocco, with King Hassan and President Ceausescu of Romania acting as intermediaries.

Sadat arrived in Jerusalem on November 19 to meet with Israel's leaders and to address the Knesset, a move that immediately raised hopes for an end to the conflict. In his Knesset address, Sadat told Israel, "I declare to the whole world that we accept to live with you in permanent peace based on justice." However, he also laid down a number of demands that Begin was unlikely to accept, such as withdrawal from all territories occupied in 1967 and recognition of the Palestinian right to self-determination. These conditions were to stall further progress for several months. The visit was important because it broke the 30-year-old psychological barrier that prevented public face-to-face negotiations and because it signaled Egypt's willingness to recognize the Jewish state. It concluded with agreement to begin peace negotiations but also led to moves by Arab states to ostracize Egypt. Later when Sadat continued to defy Arab opposition to the negotiations, Egypt was suspended from membership in the Arab League and most other inter-Arab organizations.

Talks between Israel and Egypt continued for several months, at times threatening to collapse because of disagreements over the future status of the occupied territories. Egypt demanded total withdrawal and self-government for the Palestinians in the West Bank and Gaza. Begin was only willing to concede administrative autonomy permitting the Palestinians to hold municipal elections and control local affairs such as education, health and welfare. His scheme did not foresee territorial autonomy but self-governing institutions in an arrangement similar to the Ottoman *millet* system.

When a stalemate was reached and the negotiations were about to come to an abrupt halt, President Carter summoned Begin and Sadat to meet him at the presidential retreat in Camp David, Maryland during September 1978. The Camp David talks lasted 13 days, with hard bargaining by all parties. Only President Carter's personal intervention prevented the negotiations from collapsing. During the talks, there were tense moments when either Sadat or Begin threatened to walk out. However, hours before the conference was about to break up, Carter convinced Egypt and Israel to sign two accords—"Framework for Peace in the Middle East" and "Framework for the Conclusion of a Peace Treaty between Egypt and Israel."

The "Framework for Peace in the Middle East" committed Egypt and Israel to seek "a just, comprehensive and durable settlement of the Middle East conflict through the conclusion of peace treaties based on Security Council Resolutions 242 and 338"; to resolve the "Palestinian problem in all its aspects"; to provide for establishment of normal diplomatic, economic and other "good neighborly relations"; and to provide "full autonomy" for the inhabitants of the West Bank and Gaza by allowing them to elect a self-governing authority whose powers and functions would be determined in negotiations between Israel, Egypt, Jordan, and representatives of the inhabitants. This elected authority would replace the Israeli military government for a five-year transitional period. Within three years after beginning the transition period, Egypt, Israel, Jordan and representatives of the territories would negotiate the final status of the West Bank and Gaza. The agreement on final status would be submitted to a vote by the elected representatives of the territories. Israel insisted that the autonomy regime in the West Bank and Gaza was not based on territory but applied only to "the inhabitants." The agreement made no reference to either Jerusalem or the Golan Heights, but separate letters were exchanged between Egypt and the United States and Israel and the United States presenting their respective positions on these issues.

The "Framework for the Conclusion of a Peace Treaty between Egypt and Israel" called for a phased Israeli withdrawal from all of Sinai. Israeli negotiators were unable to obtain Sadat's assent to an Israeli presence at Sharm al-Sheikh and on the Sinai east coast or to retention of Jewish settlements in northeastern Sinai. Three major airfields constructed in Sinai by Israel were to be turned over to Egypt, restricted to civilian use only. Free passage was assured for Israeli ships through the Suez Canal, the Gulf of Suez, the Straits of Tiran and the Gulf of Aqaba. Limitations were placed on military forces in Sinai, and a multinational observation force under U.S., not U.N. direction, was stationed in the peninsula. "Complete, normal relations" between Egypt and Israel were to be established after they signed a peace treaty, and "economic boycotts and barriers to the free movement of goods and people" would be terminated.

Attempts to include other Arab countries in the peace settlement failed. When in November 1978 Sadat invited Jordan, Syria, Lebanon and the Soviet Union to participate in a Cairo meeting scheduled to revive the dormant Geneva Middle East Peace Conference, they rejected his bid. Only the United States, Israel and Egypt attended. Negotiations over a draft peace treaty dragged on for several months until in March 1979 agreement was reached through U.S. mediation. The Egyptian-Israeli Peace Treaty signed in Washington, D.C. on March 26, 1979, included provisions of the 1978 Camp David framework for Egyptian-Israeli peace. Several accompanying documents and minutes elaborated on the contents of the agreement. The treaty was ratified and went into effect on April 25, 1979, and Israel began a phased withdrawal from Sinai, concluded in April 1982 except for the small area of Taba adjacent to the southern port of Eilat. The Taba dispute was submitted to international arbitration and finally settled in Egypt's favor.

The treaty opened a new phase in Israeli-Egyptian relations. Ships flying the Israeli flag could now pass through the Suez Canal. The two countries exchanged ambassadors and opened embassies in each other's respective capitals in February 1980. The Arab boycott laws were repealed by the

Egyptian National Assembly and trade, on a small scale, began. In March 1980, regular airline flights started between Cairo and Tel-Aviv, and Egypt began selling large quantities of oil to Israel. Although few Egyptians came to Israel, thousands of Israeli tourists visited Egypt annually. Many Israelis complained that the agreement was one-sided, that Egypt discouraged its tourists, academicians and scientists from visiting Israel and that trade between the two countries was minuscule.

In Egypt, after initial enthusiasm for peace and a warm welcome for Israeli tourists, relations began to cool. Left opposition parties and Islamic fundamentalists strongly opposed the treaty, and much of the Egyptian press consistently attacked Israel. Many Egyptians were disenchanted when they found Sadat's predictions that peace would bring prosperity unfulfilled. Egypt's isolation from the rest of the Arab world as a result of the treaty also alienated pan-Arabists or those who sought employment in other Arab countries.

Relations between Israel and Egypt were also strained by Begin's activist foreign policy and his heavy-handed approach to the occupied territories. Israel's invasion of south Lebanon in March 1978 following a terrorist attack on civilians was intended to dislodge the PLO from its bases (see below). Although Israel withdrew from Lebanon, the invasion aroused anger throughout the Arab world. Such Israeli acts as the air raid on Iraq's nuclear reactor in June 1981, a second invasion of Lebanon in 1982 (see below) and legislation annexing East Jerusalem in 1980 and the Golan in 1981 embarrassed the Egyptian government and fueled the anger of militant nationalists and Islamic fundamentalists.

Attempts to continue negotiations to implement the Camp David framework agreement on Middle East peace ran into continuing obstacles. Egypt maintained that the final objective was Palestinian self-determination and an end to Israeli rule in the West Bank and Gaza. But Begin's Likud bloc continued to oppose further territorial concessions. Begin argued that Israel had fulfilled its obligations to withdraw "from territories" according to Resolution 242 by returning Sinai to Egypt and that additional concessions were out of the question. Israel's obligations under the framework agreement could only be realized by granting limited autonomy to the Palestinians. Begin was pressured by the most militant territorialists in his party, several of whom defected to form a new right-wing faction, Tehiya, in opposition to the Camp David agreements.

Quarrels between Egypt and Israel over procedure as well as substance were caused by Israel's insistence that negotiating sessions be held in Jerusalem and not only in Cairo, a demand that Egypt rejected. The disagreement over the occupied territories was inflamed even more by Likud's policy of greatly expanding Jewish settlement in the West Bank and Gaza. Talks with Egypt on the future of the territories dissipated by the end of 1979 and were finally suspended.

Despite the unhappiness of many Israelis, Egyptians and most other Arabs with the peace accord, it nevertheless stabilized the political situation in the Arab-Israel conflict for several years. Thousands of Israelis now gained an opportunity for a first-hand look at an Arab country, and the Israeli government acquired a direct channel of communication with its neighbors. Peace with Egypt, the Arab country with the largest military force, precluded the chance of a general war. Before, an Israel-Arab conflict would have been a two-front war; now the prospects for conflict were greatly diminished. Although Egypt was ostracized at first, it gradually became a mediator between Israel and other Arab countries. Sadat and Begin were jointly awarded the Nobel Peace Prize in 1978. Sadat, however, was forced to crack down hard on his domestic political opponents. He was assasinated in 1981.

The Palestinians, however, believed they had gained little if anything from the peace settlement. They had not been a party to it, and saw that the agreement freed Begin to pursue more rapidly his policy of establishing Jewish settlements in the occupied territories and to integrate them into Israel. Palestinians regarded the proposed autonomy arrangements as a blow to their goal of establishing an independent state in the West Bank and Gaza.

THE 1982 WAR IN LEBANON

The pace of Jewish settlement and fear that the Likud government would eventually annex the West Bank sparked increased resistance to the occupation, and the military government authorities responded with severe countermeasures. In the early 1980s, Begin decided to impose his autonomy plan unilaterally and to establish a "civilian administration" in the West Bank. A major objective was to undermine the influence of the PLO, which Israel held accountable for Palestinian resistance in the territories. To counteract the PLO, believed to be most influential in the larger Arab towns and cities, the government organized a system of village leagues exploiting traditional animosity between rural and urban populations. Israel rewarded villagers with monetary patronage and priority in employment and housing. Those unwilling to "play the game" were subjected to harsh penalties and cut off from outside financial assistance. Pro-PLO mayors in the larger cities were dismissed, and the number of deportations, curfews, house demolitions, property seizures and imprisonments without trial increased.

These measures caused a new wave of opposition to the military government culminating in the greatest unrest since the occupation had begun.

Many Palestinians, and Israelis as well, regarded the new "reforms" as a prelude to annexation. When Palestinian municipal councils refused to cooperate with the new Israeli "civil authorities," Arab officials were replaced by Israeli army officers and punitive curfews were imposed. The Palestinian National Guidance Council (NGC), established by West Bank nationalist personalities and local leaders in 1978 to coordinate protests against the occupation, was disbanded. Israeli military government authorities described the NGC as an "arm of the PLO" responsible for "subversive activity." By March bloody clashes with the Israeli authorities were frequent, and civil unrest led to increased personal and collective punishments. Protesters chanted slogans such as "Palestine is Arab!" and "Get out of Palestine!" Jewish settlers added to the unrest, causing incidents in which several Arabs were killed and wounded.

Palestinian unity was demonstrated in a statement issued by 25 West Bank municipalities threatening to shut down all services unless the IDF's civil administration was abolished and the Arab mayors reinstated. The statement also reaffirmed allegiance to the PLO.

For the first time since the occupation began, there was widespread public criticism within Israel of the tactics used by the military to deal with Palestinian resistance. Several former high-ranking Israeli commanders believed that the government's hard line was counterprodutive, and they accused the army of overreacting to the unrest.

The outbreak of civil resistance only reinforced the Begin government's determination to weed out Palestinian nationalism and to uproot PLO influences blamed for the unrest. The defense minister, Ariel Sharon, a former general and hero of the 1967 war, believed that if the PLO were eliminated, the government could implement its autonomy plan and civil administration. As long as the PLO retained political and military bases in Lebanon, Sharon believed, no alternative leadership could be fostered in the West Bank and Gaza. He told the U.S. ambassador to Israel that destruction of the PLO in Lebanon would help "solve the problem of the West Bank and Gaza."

Following defeat of Palestinian guerrilla forces in Jordan and their exodus to Lebanon during 1970–71 (see above), the PLO had established political headquarters in Beirut and organized military bases in south Lebanon. Refugee camps in the south were, for all practical purposes, run by commando groups free of control by Lebanese authorities. By the late 1970s, raids across the border increased, and Israel began to retaliate more fiercely.

The Palestinian political situation in Lebanon was complicated by their sympathies for and participation with the antigovernment forces in the Lebanese civil war that began in 1975. Palestinian commando groups collaborated with the alliance of leftist, Muslim and pan-Arab factions fighting against the largely Maronite Christian groups dominating the government. Because they too were an underprivileged out-group, Palestinians joined with the various Shi'ite, Sunni, Socialist, Communist and other factions seeking a more equitable distribution of power and resources.

Palestinian alliance with antigovernment groups in Lebanon only strengthened Israel's determination to reinforce ties with the Maronites, especially with their paramilitary organization, the Lebanese Forces. Negotiations between Zionists and Maronite leaders had occurred for decades in the pre-Israel era, based on their mutual fear of pan-Arab nationalism. A quasi-alliance between Israel and the Maronite-dominated Lebanese Forces against the Palestinians was formed in the late 1970s and early 1980s. The Lebanese Forces were a coalition of mostly Christian militias representing the most powerful Maronite families; the strongest was the Phalange headed by the Jemayels, the most influential of the Maronites. Pierre Jemayel, founder of the Phalange, and his sons wanted to maintain the political status quo, while the anti-Phalange groups demanded more equitable representation for the Sunni and Shi'ite Muslims.

After a commando attack by Fatah on the beach between Haifa and Tel Aviv in March 1978, Israel invaded Lebanon with 20,000 troops. The announced purpose was to clear an area about 10 kilometers wide on the Lebanese side of the border and convert it to a security zone patrolled by the Lebanese militia allied with the IDF. The PLO was pushed back some 18 miles to the north, across the Litani River. The U.N. Security Council called on Israel to withdraw and posted in the area a new peacekeeping unit, the U.N. Interim Force in Lebanon (UNIFIL), of several thousand troops. Despite UNIFIL's presence, Palestinian commandos again infiltrated south Lebanon to set up installations that the Israelis regarded as menacing.

By 1980 these incidents in south Lebanon turned into a border war between the PLO and the IDF. Israeli counterattacks and air raids against the PLO inevitably endangered Lebanese villagers and Palestinian civilians in the refugee camps. The clashes also led to air battles with Syrian troops located in eastern Lebanon and threatened to erupt into a full-scale war between Israel and Syria. By 1981 it was clear to most observers that the Begin government was about to launch another full-scale invasion of Lebanon.

The invasion was forestalled through mediation by the United States, and a cease-fire was arranged, halting Palestinian attacks on Israel and Israeli reprisals into Lebanon for almost a year, until a Palestinian terrorist shot and severely wounded Israel's ambassador in London on June 3, 1982. Israel immediately blamed the PLO, although it was later determined that a dissident Palestinian faction was responsible. Israel responded by shelling Palestinian bases in south Lebanon, and the Palestinians fired back. On June

6, Israel launched a major campaign called "Peace for Galilee," intending to wipe out Palestinian military capabilities.

When the operation began, Defense Minister Sharon announced that his goal was to eliminate the PLO in south Lebanon, but Israeli forces moved rapidly northward with little resistance, reaching the outskirts of Beirut in less than a week. When a cease-fire took hold on June 25, the IDF linked up with Maronite Phalange units and encircled the capital. Maronite East Beirut now served as a base for Israel's siege of Muslim West Beirut. Attempts to avoid confrontation with Damascus failed when ground and air battles also broke out between the Syrians and the IDF in northeastern Lebanon.

In Israel "Peace for Galilee" sparked a bitter debate over the management and goals of the war. Although most groups, including the opposition Labor party, backed the original objective of removing the PLO from south Lebanon, when Sharon ordered the IDF to move northward and lay siege to West Beirut, he met with open criticism. Both Israeli critics and the international community were taken aback by the large number of Lebanese and Palestinian civilian casualties and the destruction wrought in the bombardment of Beirut—thousands of civilians dead and wounded, tens of thousands of refugees and massive destruction to the capital. For the first time, a number of Israelis became conscientious objectors, refusing to participate in the invasion; they included one full colonel who asked to be relieved of his command in the siege of Beirut.

Some Israelis believed that Sharon had deceived both the government and the public by failing to disclose his true objectives. As the war progressed, it became clear that Sharon had planned to eliminate not only the PLO but Syrian influence as well, and to intervene in Lebanese politics by helping the Phalange to obtain a dominant role in government. Sharon's intention was to forge a permanent alliance with a Christian-controlled Lebanon and to persuade the Phalange to sign a peace treaty. The goal was almost achieved in August 1982 when the term of President Elias Sarkis expired. The Lebanese parliament, under protection of Israeli guns, elected as his successor Bashir Jemayel, a Phalange leader, head of the Lebanese Forces and a close ally of Israel.

Pressured to lift the siege of Beirut, Israel refused unless the PLO left the country. When PLO leaders agreed to be evacuated from Beirut and south Lebanon, the United States sent a detachment of Marines to supervise and assist in the operation. By mid-August, an international force of U.S. French and Italian troops arrived to take charge of the PLO evacuation and the withdrawal of Israeli troops from West Beirut. About 11,000 Palestinian fighters departed to Tunisia, Algeria, Yemen, South Yemen and Syria, and PLO headquarters were moved to Tunis.

The withdrawal of Israeli forces was halted on September 14 when President-elect Jemayel was killed in an attack on Phalange headquarters. The same night the IDF returned to West Beirut; two days later Phalange militia allied with Israel entered the Sabra and Shatilla Palestinian refugee camps and slaughtered hundreds of men, women and children. Israel bore a major share of responsibility for the attack because of the alliance with the Phalange and the IDF's failure to intervene. Shocked by the massacre, thousands of Israelis organized one of the largest protest demonstrations ever against their government. Later a high-level Israeli inquiry commission blamed the IDF for failing to prevent the Phalange revenge attack. The commission criticized both Sharon and Begin. The findings caused Sharon's dismissal as defense minister. Begin felt betrayed by Sharon; this and the commission's findings were factors in his resignation as prime minister and retirement from public life in 1983.

After protracted and difficult negotiations, a peace agreement was signed between Israel and Lebanon in May 1983, ending the state of war. The treaty confirmed the existing international border between the two countries, banned the incursions of irregular forces or armed bands into each other's territory, established an Israeli liaison office in Lebanon and a Lebanese office in Jerusalem and provided security arrangements for Israel in south Lebanon, including a zone to be policed by a local force allied with Israel. Syria adamantly opposed the agreement, and the Lebanese parliament refused to ratify it; therefore it never came into effect. In July 1983, the Israeli liaison office in Beirut was ordered to close, and a new Lebanese National Unity government formally annulled the peace treaty in March 1984.

Increased Palestinian and Shi'ite guerrilla attacks led to a phased withdrawal southward by Israeli occupation forces. The war failures and the continued occupation were controversial issues in the 1984 Israel election when Labor called for withdrawal further south to the "security zone." After a National Unity government was formed in 1984, Labor party leader Yitzhak Rabin became minister of defense and was responsible for the decision to pull out of Lebanon. Withdrawal was completed in June 1985, leaving Israel in control of a southern security zone along the border three to six miles wide, inhabited by some 150,000 mostly Shi'ite Lebanese. The zone was policed by the Israeli-trained and supplied South Lebanese Army (SLA), led by a former Lebanese general and made up of mostly Christian troops. Sporadic fighting continued between the SLA and Shi'ite guerrillas, largely members of Hizbullah (Party of God), affiliated with Iranian fundamentalists.

The 1982 invasion of Lebanon was a major Israeli political failure. None of Sharon's objectives was realized. Although the PLO was temporarily dislodged from Beirut and south Lebanon, it soon began to reestablish its offices and militias there. Syria not only remained but greatly increased its influence in Lebanon. Peace arrangements with the Lebanese government were never ratified, and even Maronite hostility toward Israel increased. The war was an economic disaster, costing Israel about one million dollars a day. Relations with the Third World and with Egypt, the only Arab country to make peace with Israel, were severely strained. The security situation in south Lebanon remained unstable, and Israel continued to make periodic incursions in unsuccessful attempts to root out hostile elements. Finally, Palestinian national sentiment in the West Bank and Gaza intensified, becoming more firmly identified with the PLO than ever before.

THE INTIFADA

The United States had tacitly approved Israel's invasion, hoping that demise of the PLO would weaken Arab militant opposition to a peace settlement. However, Israel's forceful measures in Lebanon, especially the prolonged siege of Beirut, caused many in the Reagan administration to have second thoughts about the wisdom of "Peace for Galilee."

Many officials regarded the Palestine problem as the key to an overall peace settlement and accordingly sought to revive the autonomy arrangements in the Camp David protocols. These ideas were presented on September 1, 1982, in the Reagan plan for Middle East peace. The plan called for a five-year transitional regime in the West Bank and Gaza under an elected self-governing Palestinian authority. The United States would not support an independent Palestinian state or permanent Israeli rule over the occupied territories, nor would it approve further Jewish settlement in the West Bank and Gaza. According to Reagan's plan, "self-government . . . in association with Jordan" offered the best chance for a "just and lasting peace." Jerusalem should remain undivided, its final status to be decided through negotiations. The Arab-Israel conflict would be resolved through negotiations leading to an exchange of land for peace as called for in Resolution 242.

Israel, the PLO and rejectionist Arab states immediately turned down the plan. Arafat, however found in it some positive elements. Its most serious flaw, he believed, was that it opposed establishment of a Palestinian state and did not refer to his people's national rights. The Soviet Union called the plan a "farce," a scheme by which the United States alone intended to arrogate the prerogative of controlling the future of the Middle East.

In response to the Reagan proposal, an Arab summit met in Fez, Morocco, on September 8. The Arabs proposed an eight-point plan that included total Israeli withdrawal from the occupied territories, including East Jerusalem; dismantling of Jewish settlements in the territories; establishment of a PLO-governed Palestinian state; compensation to nonrepatriated refugees; the guaranteed right of worship for all religions in Jerusalem; and U.N. Security Council guarantees for peace and security of all states in the region.

Peace negotiations between Israel and Jordan appeared about to bear fruit in 1987 when Shimon Peres of the Labor Party became Israel's foreign minister. Through U.S. mediation, he reached a secret understanding with King Husayn to proceed with plans for an international conference based on Resolutions 242 and 338. Peres and Husayn publicly commended each other's efforts; the king even referred to Peres as "a man of peace" in a speech at the United Nations. But Prime Minister Yitzhak Shamir, leader of the Likud bloc, undermined the conference, labeling it a "Soviet-inspired invention."

Relations between Jordan and Israel had long been ambiguous. During the 1948 war, the IDF and the Arab Legion had fought fierce battles at the same time King Abdullah and Israel conducted secret negotiations to divide Palestine between them, preventing its nationalists from taking over the country. Although Israel agreed to Abdullah's acquisition of the West Bank, it refused to recognize formal Jordanian annexation. There were scores of secret meetings between Abdullah, his grandson and successor Husayn and the Israelis, several of which almost led to a settlement. But each time, at the last moment, success was aborted because of disagreement over details and Husayn's reluctance to finalize an agreement without the concurrence of other Arab governments.

In November 1987, Husayn convened an Arab summit in Amman to endorse the concept of an international peace conference. One indication of the changing atmosphere was the decision permitting Arab countries to restore relations with Egypt, severed since Sadat's 1977 peace initiative. The summit also endorsed Iraq's position in the war with Iran. To Palestinian chagrin, however, their concerns received secondary place on the agenda.

The Palestinians were sorely disappointed by the "conspiracy of silence" during the 1982 war in Lebanon when other Arab leaders failed to come to their assistance. Although Sharon's hope of eliminating the PLO and imposing a new regime on the West Bank and Gaza failed, the harshness of the military occupation did not diminish. The IDF still broke up protest demonstrations, arrested and imprisoned hundreds of Palestinians without trial, deported scores accused of subversive political activity, demolished the homes of suspected terrorists and controlled nearly all aspects of civil life from the school system to trade and commerce (by requiring permits for business activity).

In the 20 years since the occupation had begun, Israeli commanders in the occupied territories had modified previous Jordanian legislation through some 1,500 military orders governing education, agriculture, land and water rights, taxation and social welfare, in addition to security and military matters. Nearly half the land in the West Bank and a third in Gaza was taken over by Israeli authorities for Jewish use, including settlement. Loss of land was accompanied by a sharp decline in the number of Palestinians in agriculture. Most peasants displaced from farming found work in a variety of unskilled jobs at the bottom of the wage scale in Israel; several tens of thousands left the occupied territories to seek employment in neighboring Arab countries. By the end of the 1980s, nearly a third of the Palestinian work force in the West Bank and Gaza earned their livelihood in Israel, mostly in agriculture, construction and services.

A major constraint against expansion of Arab agriculture in the West Bank and Gaza was the limited water supply. With Israelis in charge of water distribution, Jewish settlers received several times per capita the amount allocated to the indigenous population. As noted, the electricity grid in the West Bank and Gaza was integrated into the Israeli system despite attempts by the Palestinian population to control their own supply.

Israel's plans for economic integration of the occupied territories into its own "common market" began in the late 1960s. Defense Minister Moshe Dayan's policy of creating "new facts" asserted Israel's right to be in the territories despite his Labor Party's opposition to annexation. Dayan introduced a policy of "Open Bridges," facilitating Palestinian visits and commercial relations with Jordan. Palestinians could also travel to other Arab countries from Jordan, using the bridges to return. This policy was intended to prevent total collapse of the West Bank economy, which had been integrated with Jordan's before 1967. It also helped inhabitants of the territories maintain family contacts with relatives from whom they were separated by the occupation.

When Likud assumed power in 1977, policies grew less ambiguous and more severe. Likud openly encouraged Jewish settlement and strongly opposed the idea of "land for peace." Ten years after Begin became prime minister, the number of Jewish settlers in the territories increased from just under 5,000 to more than 60,000 and the number of settlements from 36 to nearly 100. Twenty years later some observers asserted that the West Bank was already annexed, that Israel had attained its objectives and that Jewish interests were well entrenched.

In the final months of 1987, there was a burst of vigilantism by Jewish settlers, with increased violence against Arab towns and refugee camps. Israeli public opinion appeared to gather momentum against the growing Palestinian unrest and defiance of the occupation authorities. Discussion of "transfer" (deportation of Palestinians from the territories to the surrounding countries) was more open in many Israeli political circles.

Two decades of close contact produced changing Palestinian views of Israel and of Israelis. Although many admired the relative political and social democracy and press freedom in Israel, they felt insecure in their own homes because Israeli domestic law did not apply in the territories. Nevertheless young Palestinians were no longer cowed by the Israeli presence. Youths began to rebel, not only against their parents and Palestinian authorities, but against Israeli authority. One Israeli observer concluded: "Palestinian perceptions of Israeli society cannot be separated from the pervasive political and military reality of occupation. Palestinians say it poisons the atmosphere, filling it with mistrust, severely limiting opportunities for natural contact between cultures very different from each other."

Palestinian youth had become more politically active by the early 1980s, in student organizations, refugee camps and village and town associations of various types. There already was a vibrant civil society, a network of educational, health and social welfare institutions, many with decided political overtones. Each of the various Palestinian political factions, the Communists, Fatah, Popular Front for the Liberation of Palestine (PFLP), Democratic Front for the Liberation of Palestine (DFLP) and various Islamic groups had their own women's, youth and social service activities.

By December 1987, tension within the territories was palpable. Only a spark was needed to set off an explosion. The spark came on December 8 in a road accident in which four Palestinian workers returning from Israel were killed and seven seriously injured by an Israeli army transport. Three of the dead were from the large Jabalya refugee camp adjoining Gaza; their funerals on December 8 and 9 became the occasion for a massive demonstration against the occupation and its policies. On previous occasions, the IDF had entered Jabalya and other refugee camps to quell demonstrators with little danger, but this time the grief and anger were fiercer and more intense than before. Instead of ending the demonstration after an initial outburst, the unrest increased and spread like a brush fire. The Intifada (resistance) had started.

Within the next few days, the rioting spread through Gaza and to the West Bank in a spontaneous upsurge of anger. Although IDF spokesmen asserted that these "incidents," or "troubles," would, as on previous occasions, pass in due course, it was soon evident that this was a new situation. The press reported that the unrest was the worst since protests broke out again Sharon's civil administration in 1981. Israelis began to debate whether this was a spontaneous rebellion caused by "genuine despair" or merely another outburst inspired by PLO agitators, enforced by a minority, as the Israelis saw it, on the law-abiding Palestinian majority.

It took about a month for Israelis to realize that these "disturbances" were not a flash in the pan, a passing series of incidents that could be suppressed in routine fashion. The authorities admitted that the uprising was spontaneous, politically inspired, its origins within the territories, unprovoked by outside forces. Defense Minister Rabin concluded that tough new measures were required and openly proclaimed a policy of using "might, power, and beatings" to quell the unrest. This policy, he argued, would save lives and was preferable to using live ammunition against a civilian population.

The use of "might, power, and beatings" accompanied by mass arrests, deportations, punitive economic measures, frequent curfews and introduction of thousands of Israeli troops to police the territories, failed to end the uprising. Instead, the more harsh the methods used, the stronger and better organized civil resistance became. What began as spontaneous demonstrations of youths throwing rocks, iron bars and occasional Molotov cocktails, soon became a well-organized civil resistance movement. Young children throwing stones at Israeli soldiers became the world's image of the Intifada. Poems and songs were written about the uprising using the stone as a metaphor.

Leaflets began to appear throughout the West Bank and Gaza spread by an anonymous "popular committee" with a program to expand the scope of resistance. The committee called on Palestinians to sever all connections with the occupiers by refusing to work for Israelis, by boycotting Israeli-made goods and by refusing to pay taxes or fees. A form of nonviolent activism was recommended: When security forces seized a villager, all villagers would come to the police station; if curfews were imposed, villagers were urged to disobey and raise the prohibited Palestinian flag. Many measures against the occupation urged by the leadership called for civil disobedience rather than violent physical confrontation.

An organized underground soon took control of the uprising. The infrastructure for leadership already existed in the scores of committees, self-help groups and organizations established long before the Intifada. Some were organized along geographic lines at the village, town and district levels, others functionally in groups of women, physicians, lawyers, students, teachers, trade-union and various professional groups. In contrast to the traditional old-guard leadership with close links to Jordan, members of the self-help organizations were younger and less identified with the notable families of Palestinian society. Many in the new leadership represented the refugee camps and the urban working class.

The principal underground leadership group was the Unified National Command (UNC), with representatives from Fatah, PFLP, DFLP and the Palestine Communist Party (PCP). Next in influence was Hamas, the Islamic Resistance Movement, organized shortly after the Intifada started by fundamentalist activists associated with the Muslim Brotherhood and the Islamic Association in Gaza. Islamic Jihad, another fundamentalist group, also played an active role. (Before the Intifada, occupation authorities had encouraged and even assisted Islamic factions in Gaza as an alternative to the PLO, which the Israelis considered more dangerous. Many members of these Islamic groups later joined Hamas, which called for the destruction of Israel and opposed any negotiations with Israeli authorities.)

The Intifada galvanized the Palestinian community and unified it as never before. Unlike the situation in the 1936–39 Arab revolt against the British (see above), traditional clan rivalries were repressed. A major reason for failure of the 1936 revolt was internecine struggle among Palestinian factions, notable families and different regions and classes. In the Intifada, the various groups overcame their differences, at least temporarily. Both the Islamic fundamentalists and the leftists supported the uprising and, initially, refrained from undermining each other. The new leadership also demonstrated that traditional Muslim-Christian tensions could be suspended in the national interest. Christians had sometimes found their religion a liability in the predominantly Muslim society of Palestine; now it appeared that interfaith tensions greatly dissipated.

Women played a key role in the uprising, often assuming leadership positions. Many were skilled professionals in medicine, education and law. Women's groups sent emergency teams to treat the wounded or organize child care and to deal with pupils at the time of strikes or school closings. During strikes declared by the UNC or in curfews imposed by the military, women organized provisions for people unable to shop at the designated hours, those whose funds were drained as a result of the economic crisis or those whose family breadwinners had been arrested or killed. Women's activism reached the traditional villages as well as the more sophisticated urban centers, and even in the most conservative rural communities, even those controlled by Islamic fundamentalists, women's groups were organized.

Another blow to Israeli strategy for dealing with the West Bank was the easing of traditional urban-rural tensions within Palestinian society. During the early 1980s, Defense Minister Sharon attempted to exploit these tensions and devise an alternative leadership to the PLO by organizing village leagues (see above). This tactic failed then and later, when many former village league chieftains supported the Intifada.

The IDF was unable to occupy all of the approximately 500 Arab villages simultaneously. Many were effectively left to their own devices, and became semiautonomous "little Palestines" or "liberated zones" while the larger cities and towns lay incapacitated under military occupation. Often these fervently nationalist enclaves organized their own local committees, issued their own leaflets, flew the prohibited Palestinian flag and plastered walls with slogans and symbols of the Intifada—all to spite the military regime that outlawed these actions.

During the first two or three years of the uprising, Palestinian society experienced greater social and psychological change than in many decades. Inhabitants of the territories no longer waited for salvation to come from abroad but insisted on taking matters concerning their future into their own hands. They realized that they could not rely on the United States, the Arab states or the PLO leaders in Tunis to "shake off" the occupation. This self-reliance and spirit of solidarity helped create new leaders who it was hoped would take over from the occupation authorities.

The uprising restored the Green Line, the armistice demarcation line between Israel's pre-1967 border and the occupied territories, which five years earlier Prime Minister Begin had declared "vanished forever." The Intifada reinforced the separation of Arab Palestine from the Jewish state despite the large number of Jewish settlements established by the Likud government to underscore Israel's "historic" claims in the West Bank and Gaza.

The economic burden of the Intifada was heavy. As many Palestinians lost their jobs in Israel, unemployment increased, at times reaching over 50%. Frequent curfews and strikes closed down many businesses, shops and small industries. Often farmers were cut off from their fields and markets because of military restrictions. The new atmosphere created a sense of euphoria and nationalist fervor among youth, but it also led to incidents when militants took the law into their own hands, imposing drumhead justice on fellow Palestinians suspected of collaborating with Israel or violating community moral standards. By the early 1990s, self-appointed vigilantes had "executed" several hundred fellow Palestinians, nearly half the number killed in altercations with the IDF.

After three or four years living under these difficult conditions, Palestinians became impatient with the UNC's inability to achieve its objectives or to end the occupation. Disaffection was evident in decline of patriotic fervor, in growing opposition to any peace negotiations and by increased support for Hamas and Islamic Jihad, both organizations seeking to establish Palestine as an Islamic state and both adamantly opposed to recognition of, or peace with, Israel.

Shortly after the uprising began, leaders of the UNC defined their objectives in a document listing 14 conditions for ending the revolt and as the basis for "real peace." The only way to prevent "further violence and blood-shed, and the further deepening of hatred" was to convene an international conference, including the PLO, "the sole legitimate representative of the Palestinian people, as an equal partner." Israel and the international community would have to recognize "Palestinian national rights, including the right of self-determination and the establishment of an independent Palestinian state on Palestinian national soil." The document also demanded an end to emergency regulations, restrictions and prohibitions imposed on the occupied territories. These demands became the charter of the national movement; they were reiterated in one form or another throughout the next few years. The official

Israeli reaction was that "there is nothing to respond to," because the demands were nothing new. After more than a year, and only under international pressure, the Israeli government came up with an indirect response.

One of the first political reactions to the uprising came from Jordan's King Husayn. In July 1988 he abandoned all claims to the West Bank, which had been annexed by his grandfather, King Abdullah, in 1950. For almost 40 years, West Bank Palestinians had been Jordanian subjects, using Jordan's currency, voting in Jordanian elections, serving in Jordan's parliament and in the king's cabinet. The special relationship with Jordan continued even after the occupation in June 1967 and was tacitly accepted by Israel. Some 20,000 West Bank Palestinians who served in the Jordanian civil service continued to receive their salaries from Amman although their offices were under jurisdiction of Israeli military authorities. Jordan continued to subsidize West Bank institutions such as religious foundations, schools, clinics and the like.

Between 1986 and 1988, King Husayn, with U.S. support, floated plans for a $1.3 billion economic rehabilitation scheme to "improve the quality of life" in the territories. The so-called "Jordan option," in which King Husayn would have maintained civil authority under Israeli control of security, had long been favored by Israel's Labor party and was viewed with approval by the United States. When the king proclaimed that "Jordan is not Palestine" and that an "independent Palestinian state will be established on the occupied Palestinian land, after it is liberated . . . ," he ended any Israeli hope of implementing such a settlement.

Although the Intifada initially galvanized Palestinian society, it polarized Israel. The role of policeman in the territories imposed on the IDF had a demoralizing effect on many soldiers required to impose harsh punishments on Palestinian youth and women. Some critics objected to what they perceived as the army's excessive use of force; others demanded that it employ all means possible to quell the uprising. Several new Jewish peace groups emerged opposing the occupation and methods used by the IDF; the number of Israeli objectors to service in the West Bank and Gaza increased substantially. The cost of maintaining many more soldiers in the territories was an added burden. The loss of cheap Arab labor in the construction industry and in agriculture and the decline of Israeli markets due to the Palestine boycott also impacted Israel's economy. By 1990 Israelis were also becoming weary of the war against the Palestinians.

The uprising put great pressure on PLO leaders in Tunis to be more decisive on the political issues involved in the conflict, especially regarding establishment of a Palestinian state and relations with Israel. Until the Intifada, internal disagreements had prevented the Palestine National Council (PNC) from declaring independence and from openly accepting a two-state solution. Reluctance of PLO leaders abroad to take a stand forced the Unified National Command (UNC) of the Intifada to act, as evident in their 14 demands and subsequent proclamations. As political unrest rose within the territories, Arafat authorized his close associates to float a trial balloon proposing accommodation with Israel. His aide, Bassam Abu Sharif, noted in a press statement that despite 70 years of hostility between Jews and Arabs, there were a number of issues on which they had total agreement. Both peoples wanted peace and security; the key lay in direct talks between Israelis and Palestinians without outside intervention. Abu Sharif asked for an internationally supervised referendum in the West Bank and Gaza Strip allowing Palestinian inhabitants to choose between the PLO and any other group of Palestinians advocating self-determination.

Plans were soon underway to convene the PNC, and in November 1988 an emergency session was held in Algiers. The session, called the "Intifada meeting," had two major accomplishments: (1) a declaration of a Palestinian state with its capital in Jerusalem and (2) a political program calling for solution of the conflict based on Security Council Resolutions 242 and 338. The PNC renounced the use of violence outside the territories and declared willingness to negotiate with Israel in the context of an international peace conference. The declaration emphasized the importance of the Intifada, implying that it had led to the new PLO and PNC peace program. In April 1989, the PLO executive committee reinforced the declaration of independence by unanimously electing Arafat as the first president of the state of Palestine.

After the Algiers meeting, several nations recognized the new Palestinian state, although it still had no territory of its own. Israel immediately dismissed the declaration of independence and its accompanying documents as irrelevant and unimportant, and the IDF clamped a curfew on Gaza and the West Bank to prevent unruly celebrations. By 1989 more than 100 nations recognized the declaration of independence; the degree of recognition varied from establishment of full diplomatic ties to mere acknowledgment. The United States still kept its distance, asserting that the Algiers documents were not adequate proof of Arafat's renunciation of violence and terrorism or convincing evidence of PLO willingness to recognize and coexist peacefully with Israel. After several weeks of secret negotiations and further "clarification" by Arafat, acceptable wording was devised and a PLO statement issued making it possible for the United States to declare that it too was ready for "a substantive dialogue with PLO representatives." The first official public meetings between the United States and the PLO began in mid-December 1988.

Were it not for the Intifada, neither the PLO nor the United States would have altered their policies. The insurrection convinced Washington that negotiations with the PLO were inevitable if there were to be any new credible peace initiatives. The PLO was finally forced to abandon its policy of "constructive ambiguity" on key issues such as recognition of Israel, accepting U.N. Resolutions 242 and 338 and renunciation of terrorism. The Intifada thrust the Palestine problem and the Arab-Israel conflict back to the forefront of world attention and started a new round of negotiations for a Middle East peace settlement.

PEACE NEGOTIATIONS

The PNC November 1988 proclamations, Arafat's U.N. declaration of the PLO's acceptance of Resolutions 242 and 338 and of Israel's legitimacy and the new relationship between the PLO and the United States, again raised hopes that the conflict could be peacefully resolved. The new situation also put pressure on Israel to come forward with fresh proposals. In May 1989, the Shamir government issued a detailed plan proposing Palestinian elections in the West Bank and Gaza for representatives to negotiate with Israel. The scheme, originally developed by Defense Minister Rabin, was later adapted in a four-point plan issued by Prime Minister Shamir as the "Peace Initiative of the Israel Government."

The peace initiative reaffirmed the 1978 Camp David accord providing for Palestinian autonomy in the occupied territories (see above). It called on the United States and Egypt to persuade other Arab states to "replace belligerency and boycott with negotiation and cooperation" and to "join direct bilateral negotiations aimed at normalization and peace." The plan emphasized the need for a solution for the Arab refugee problem with special attention to the approximately 300,000 refugee camp residents in the West Bank and Gaza. "Free elections" would be conducted among Arab residents of the territories for a delegation to negotiate an interim settlement in which a self-governing administration would be set up. This "interim period" would serve as a "test of cooperation and coexistence," to be followed by further negotiations on a final settlement.

West Bank and Gaza inhabitants and leaders of the Intifada raised several questions about the election plan: Would they be able to select PLO officials as their representatives? Would Arab residents of East Jerusalem annexed by Israel be permitted to vote or stand for election? Would international supervision of elections be permitted? Would Israeli occupation authorities be authorized to place restrictions on election campaigning? Would Jewish settlement in the territories be suspended during implementation of the peace process? Would Israel eventually agree to withdraw from the territories as part of final peace settlement?

Answers to these questions became the subject of bitter dispute between the Labor and Likud members of the National Unity government (NUG). Labor favored a broader interpretation, whereas Prime Minister Shamir was a strict constructionist who answered all the Palestinian queries negatively. Several Likud militants opposed to any Arab elections in the territories threatened to topple the government.

Egyptian President Hosni Mubarak offered a 10-point elaboration intended to win Palestinian acceptance. Labor members of the government welcomed Mubarak's suggestions, but Shamir, backed by Likud, totally discounted them. U.S. Secretary of State James Baker also attempted to break the impasse, but to no avail. The main problem was the composition of Palestinian representation in negotiations with Israel. Both Labor and Likud adamantly opposed any contact with the PLO, while the Palestinians insisted that only the PLO could represent them.

Disagreements over the peace process caused collapse of the NUG when Labor demanded that Prime Minister Shamir accept a compromise offered by Baker. The demand led to Shamir's dismissal of Deputy Prime Minister Shimon Peres, leader of the Knesset Labor bloc and to withdrawal of all Labor members from the NUG. This left Likud in control of the government and resulted in formation of a new hard line, greater unrest among Palestinians in the territories, and deterioration of relations between Israel and the United States. Symptomatic of the worsening relations was American support in the Security Council for a resolution condemning Israel for the way it handled a riot in Jerusalem when at least 18 Arabs were killed and over 100 wounded, only the third time in U.N. history that the United States had voted to condemn Israel.

Events in the Arab-Israel conflict were overshadowed by the second Gulf War that began with Iraq's invasion of Kuwait on August 2, 1990. The war divided the Arab world between supporters of Iraqi President Saddam Husayn and those who opposed his invasion and occupation of a fellow Arab League member. Egypt, Saudi Arabia, Syria, Kuwait, Bahrain, Qatar, Morocco, Oman and the United Arab Emirates supported the American-led U.N. coalition effort against the invasion with troops or financial contributions. Other Arab states, including Libya, Sudan, Yemen and Jordan, were either ambivalent or supported Saddam Husayn.

There was a large measure of sympathy toward Saddam among Palestinians and PLO leaders. They admired his daring, Nasser-like challenge to the United Nations and to world powers, especially the United States, Israel's chief ally and major source of sustenance. Quite a few Palestinians believed that he would score an easy victory against the West and back their claims to Palestine. Their support for Saddam was also reinforced by the humiliating treatment they had suffered in Kuwait and the surrounding countries during and after the Gulf War. Although some Palestinians assisted the invading Iraqis many observers believed that they were only a small minority. There were also Palestinians who actively participated in the Kuwaiti resistance against Iraq.

Arafat's support for Saddam caused a financial and diplomatic disaster for the PLO. It lost several of its largest contributors, including Saudi Arabia and Kuwait, which had funded many Palestinian institutions and activities with hundreds of millions of dollars. For several years after the war, Arafat was ostracized by former Arab supporters angered by his choice of the wrong side.

The most immediate impact of the Gulf War on Israel was caused by Iraqi Scud missile attacks on Tel Aviv and Haifa. Although casualties were few, hundreds of dwellings were destroyed, adding to an already critical housing shortage. One of the first emergency measures taken by the government was to keep Arab labor in the occupied territories from entering Israel. Loss of these approximately 100,000 workers undermined plans to construct new housing, worsening the problems of absorbing several hundred thousand new Jewish immigrants from the Soviet Union.

The impact on the occupied territories was far more severe. In addition to closing the bridges to Jordan, the longest curfew during the 24 years of occupation was imposed on Gaza and the West Bank. The economy of the territories was brought almost to a total halt. Farmers were unable to water, harvest or market their crops, and most business ceased. By the time the curfew was lifted in March 1991, economists estimated that the territories were working at only 25% of capacity. The situation was so bad that the United Nations appealed for funds to feed Palestinians, and the European Community prepared an $8 million food-aid package for them. The West Bank and Gaza have never fully recovered from the war crisis. Israel has continued to limit the number of workers permitted to enter from the territories; between the Intifada and the Gulf War, the Palestinian economy still suffers high unemployment as well as low economic growth and productivity.

Following Iraq's defeat and conclusion of the Gulf War on March 6, 1991, President George Bush addressed a joint session of the U.S. Congress to announce his goals for the Middle East. They included restructuring security in the Persian Gulf, a regional arms reduction program and fostering economic development to achieve fresh opportunities for peace and stability.

The foundation of the new program was the Madrid Middle East Peace Conference, opened on October 20, 1991. The conference was facilitated by the altered international environment in the region and the changing relationship between the United States and the Soviet Union, characterized by cooperation rather than competition. The end of the Cold War led formerly rejectionist Arab states to participate more willingly in the peace process now that they could no longer receive economic, military and diplomatic support from the Soviet Union. Neither Syria nor the PLO could depend any longer on Moscow's financial aid or support for hard-line positions at the United Nations and were now therefore more amenable to negotiations based on compromise.

Both Israel and the United States insisted that there was no linkage between the Gulf War and the Arab-Israel conflict. However, the conflict was a catalyst for convening the Madrid conference. Preparations required eight trips to the Middle East by U.S. Secretary of State Baker to reconcile conflicting preconditions. The Shamir government stood by its opposition to participation of Palestinian inhabitants of Jerusalem or members of the PLO; only residents of the West Bank and Gaza were acceptable to Shamir, and they had to attend as part of the Jordanian delegation, not as a separate delegation. Shamir also opposed U.N. sponsorship or participation in the conference, but he agreed to Soviet cosponsorship on condition that Moscow reestablish diplomatic relations with Israel, broken during the 1967 war. Palestinian insistance on PLO representation was met by permitting PLO "observers" and "advisors" to assist Palestinians attached to the Jordan delegation.

At the opening session in October, many acrimonious statements were exchanged, yet it was the first conference in which Israel and Syria, Lebanon, Jordan and the Palestinians engaged in open, public and direct peace negotiations. The Madrid phase of the negotiations dealt with ceremonial and procedural rather than substantive matters. It would take at least another two years before the first practical results could be seen.

After Madrid, bilateral talks began between Israel and the Arabs. The Israelis met separately with Syrian, Lebanese, Jordanian and Palestinian delegations. The key issues in each case were largely territorial—Israel's occupation of the Golan Heights and the security zone in south Lebanon, continued occupation of the West Bank and Gaza and minor border disagreements with Jordan.

During January 1992, the participants agreed in Moscow to initiate a series of multilateral miniconferences parallel to the bilateral meetings. Five committees or working groups were organized, each made up of a score or more nations. They were to deal with functional matters related to peace and stability in the Middle East: environment, water, economic development, refugees, disarmament and security. During the next few years, these functional meetings continued to discuss theoretical and practical matters such as improving living conditions for refugees, reunion of Palestinian families separated by the previous wars, arms control measures and water distribution. So far no official agreements have been reached, other than on doing research.

The stalemate in bilateral negotiations between the Shamir government and the Arab negotiators was overcome by Labor's victory in the 1992 Knesset elections and the formation of a new government more committed to serious peace talks. Labor Prime Minister Yitzhak Rabin appointed a new team much more willing to consider territorial concessions in the Golan in exchange for a comprehensive peace, to permit Jerusalem Arabs and those affiliated with the PLO to participate in the talks and to authorize elections for a 15-member administrative council to carry out day-to-day functions in the West Bank and Gaza. Rabin also agreed to join the multilateral working groups on refugees and economic development previously boycotted by Shamir, who disapproved of Palestinian participation.

Among the Palestinians and in Israel, militantly nationalist factions opposed the peace negotiations and were determined to sabotage them. The most militant Israeli opposition came from orthodox Jewish settlers who vowed never to abandon their homes in the West Bank and to fight both Arab and Israeli authorities if confronted with orders to leave. The opposition Likud and nationalist parties in the Knesset were also highly critical of Rabin's willingness to concede territory for peace.

Palestinians opposed to peace with Israel included the left-wing PLO factions, PFLP and DFLP, and the Islamic fundamentalist groups Hamas and Islamic Jihad. The fundamentalists attempted to sabotage the negotiations by creating an atmosphere of terror among both Palestinians and Israelis. After attacks on Jews in the territories and inside the Green Line, Rabin decided to deport some 400 Palestinians affiliated with Hamas for a one-year period. The 400 were exiled to the no-man's-land just north of Israel's Lebanese "security zone," where they lived for the next several months in makeshift tent encampments. Their expulsion led to international condemnation and another Security Council resolution censuring Israel. The deportations also interrupted the peace talks when Arab participants suspended their meetings with Israel to protest the move. Under U.S. pressure, Israel modified the expulsion orders, permitting a few deportees to return and scheduling a phased repatriation of the others.

The peace negotiations were stalled by the summer of 1993. Progress was stymied between Israel and Lebanon and Syria because of an impasse over the Golan Heights. Syria demanded total withdrawal from Golan and complete restoration of Syrian sovereignty there. Without approval from Damascus, whose troops occupied much of Lebanon and whose President Hafiz al-As'ad dictated the course of politics in Beirut, there was little likelihood of progress in the Israel-Lebanon talks. Furthermore, continued attacks on Israel and its South Lebanese Army allies by the Iranian-backed Hizbullah diminished the chances that Israel would leave its "security zone" in Lebanon. Although Rabin indicated willingness to withdraw from part or even most of Golan in return for a full peace with Syria, including exchange of ambassadors, open borders and normalization of relations, the critical question was who would move first: Would Israel withdraw before a total and comprehensive peace agreement, would such an agreement precede withdrawal or could a compromise be devised for phased withdrawal and a gradual move toward peace?

Talks with the Palestinians faltered over several issues: the fate of Jewish settlements and settlers in the West Bank and Gaza, the future status of Arab Jerusalem, the composition and authority of a Palestinian self-governing body, and the release of several thousand Palestinian prisoners in Israeli jails and detention camps. The Palestinians insisted that Jerusalem and the Jewish settlements be given immediate attention; Israel maintained that discussion on these matters be deferred until the end of a five-year transition period.

Negotiations between Israel and Jordan were the least troublesome. There was general agreement between the two countries on most issues such as border rectification, division of water resources and the like. However Jordan was initially reluctant to consummate a peace settlement unless there was progress in the other negotiations between Israel and its neighbors.

There were signs of changing Israeli attitudes toward the Palestinians. In January 1993 the Knesset repealed a 1986 law barring contacts with the PLO, until then labeled a "terrorist" organization. Statements by Labor party leaders calling for direct negotiations with the PLO and for Israeli withdrawal from the Gaza Strip followed.

By summer 1993, reports were circulating about "back-channel diplomacy" between Israel and the PLO in Oslo, Norway. The secret talks had begun in January 1993 between two Israeli academics and a PLO representative, sponsored by Norwegian Foreign Minister Johan Jörgen Holst. At first the discussions dealt with possibilities of economic cooperation; later they discussed a joint declaration of principles. While the secret parleys took place in Oslo, official peace negotiations, part of the Madrid process, continued in Washington with not much success. Early in 1993, the 10th round of official talks ended.

Rabin, who assumed office with a promise to conclude peace, was becoming increasingly frustrated by the lack of progress. It was evident that little could be accomplished without direct PLO involvement; therefore it would be necessary for Israel to change its policy regarding the Palestinians. Negotiations would be greatly facilitated by direct contact with the leaders instead of dealing with second- or third-level representatives who ultimately received their instructions from PLO headquarters. The secret meetings in Oslo opened the way to direct talks and broke the taboo on contacts or relations with the PLO.

Conditions were also pushing Arafat toward ending the conflict. The PLO had lost its financial backing from Saudi Arabia and other Arab Persian Gulf states because of Arafat's support for Saddam Husayn in the Gulf War. Financial and diplomatic support from Moscow also ended with the disintegration of the Soviet Union. Enthusiasm for the Intifada was waning in the West Bank and Gaza due to increasing economic hardship and war-weariness. This combination of circumstances gradually eroded Arafat's popularity and control. He decided that a dramatic move was required to rescue his reputation and save the PLO from collapsing.

Early in September, Arafat convened a meeting of Fatah's executive committee to secure approval of a draft accord with Israel. He was supported by a vote of nine to three, plus his own vote, with only 13 of the committee's 18 members present. When he failed to convene the PNC to obtain its backing, there was a storm of protest, and several PLO officials resigned. The Israeli cabinet backed Rabin, approving the draft accord and arrangements for Palestinian self-government.

In letters exchanged on September 10, Arafat stated: "The signing of the Declaration of Principles marks a new era in the history of the Middle East . . . The PLO recognizes the right of the State of Israel to exist in peace and security . . . The PLO commits itself to the Middle East peace process and to a peaceful resolution of the conflict between the two sides . . . The PLO renounces the use of terrorism and other acts of violence . . . [and] affirms that those articles of the Palestinian Covenant which deny Israel's right to exist . . . are now inoperative and no longer valid." Rabin's letter to Arafat confirmed that "the government of Israel has decided to recognize the PLO as the representative of the Palestinian people and commence negotiations with the PLO within the Middle East peace process."

The Oslo meetings and exchange of letters between Arafat and Rabin set the stage for an agreement signed on September 13 at a public White House ceremony in Washington, D.C. presided over by President Bill Clinton. The pact was sealed with a historic handshake between Arafat and Rabin symbolizing a major breakthrough after a century of conflict.

The September 13 Declaration of Principles on Interim Self-Governing Arrangements for Palestinians in the Gaza Strip and Jericho (DOP) was really an agenda of items that Israel and the PLO agreed to discuss within the context of a peace settlement. The Israeli government had already decided to proceed with self-governing arrangements and withdrawal from Gaza, but Arafat also wanted to establish at least a symbolic Palestinian presence in the West Bank. Israel, however, was not yet prepared to deal with the future of the whole West Bank. The small town of Jericho was added to the agreement in token cognizance of Palestinian interests in West Bank; thus the pact was also called the Gaza-Jericho First agreement.

The DOP established a five-year transition period in which a final settlement would be negotiated. Transfer of authority from Israel to the Palestinians was originally scheduled to begin in late 1993 followed by elections in July 1994 for a Palestine Interim Self-Government Authority

(PISGA), with executive and legislative powers; PISGA would establish a Palestinian police force to replace the Israeli army. The DOP and its associated annexes and protocols also called for creation of a joint Israeli-Palestinian Committee for Economic Cooperation and technical committees to deal with electricity, water, transport and communications, trade, labor relations, social welfare and environment. Talks on the permanent status of the West Bank and Gaza were to begin by December 1995.

Many Palestinians who approved of the peace process objected to PISGA's limited powers and to the small area placed under its jurisdiction. Arafat wanted the Jericho self-governing region to cover an area of more than 100 square miles, that is, the total Jericho District as defined by the British mandate. Israel wanted to concede only the town itself, less than 10 square miles. They compromised on a 24-square-mile Jericho self-governing region. PISGA's authority was restricted to management of taxation, health, education, social welfare, culture, tourism and local police. Israel retained control over foreign affairs, defense, overall security and the border crossings between Egypt and Gaza and Jordan and Jericho.

Despite initial optimism generated by the DOP, it would take many months before it could be implemented. The establishment of PISGA, redeployment and withdrawal of Israeli troops and elections for the Palestinian Governing Authority were delayed because of disagreements between Israel and Arafat. The Palestinians insisted on the DOP as the first step toward an independent state whereas Israel treated the agreement as a guarantee of autonomy, *not* of independence.

Several committees were set up to work out details such as the deployment and functions of the Palestine police force, economic relations between the occupied territories and Israel and the status of Jewish settlers. The economy of Gaza and the West Bank was close to collapse, and there was a serious question about the ability of PISGA to function without financial assistance. A survey by the World Bank published on the eve of the DOP reported that the economy of the occupied territories was "currently in turmoil. Income levels have stagnated . . . unemployment and underemployment are rising rapidly; public infrastructure and social services are grossly overstretched; and the fragile natural resource base is threatened with irreversible damage . . . The resulting sense of despair and dependency, juxtaposed against the high expectations derived from exposure to Israeli living standards within the OT [occupied territories] and in Israel, is clearly a major impediment to achieving peace and stability in the region . . . [there is an] urgent need for stimulating economic development in the OT." The bank believed initial public investment was required to upgrade water supplies, sewage plants, solid waste disposal, the road system, electricity grids and education and health facilities.

Soon after the DOP was signed, an international donors' conference of 43 countries pledged $2.3 billion in assistance to the Palestinian authority over the next five years, including $600 million from the European Community and $500 million from the United States. By the end of 1995, little of this amount was available because of disagreements between the donors and the PLO over methods of distributing the funds and accountability for their use.

After several months of long and protracted discussions on implementing the DOP, Israel and the PLO reached an agreement in Cairo on May 4, 1994, to begin withdrawal of the IDF from the West Bank and Jericho. The agreement spelled out the first details of Palestinian self-government, but a full program remained to be worked out over the next five years.

The major points in the Cairo agreement called for complete Israeli withdrawal from the Gaza Strip and Jericho within three weeks (except from areas required for security of Jewish settlements). Israel would retain authority over Jewish settlements in these areas, keep a military base on the Egyptian border and control certain roads linking Jewish settlements with Israel. According to some estimates, the area to be retained by Israel for security constituted about 20% of the Gaza Strip. The amount of water to be allocated to Palestinians, Jewish settlements and the Gaza military base was to be determined by Israel; Jewish settlements would continue to receive quantities obtained before the agreement, that is, several times the per capita amount available to the indigenous Palestinian population.

A Palestinian authority of 24 members with legislative and executive powers was to be established, and a Palestinian police force of up to 9,000 was authorized, including 7,000 from outside the territories; the force would be equipped with light weapons and wheeled armored vehicles. About 5,000 of the 13,000 to 14,000 Palestinian prisoners would be released within five weeks, and negotiations would continue for release of the others. A joint committee would be formed to consider repatriation to the West Bank of the 800,000 Palestinians displaced during the 1967 war. Arrangements would be made for safe passage of Palestinians with special permits between Gaza and Jericho along specific routes. Four hundred international observers, instructors and experts from five or six countries would be deployed for six months, with the option to continue their presence longer. The five-year interim period for negotiating a permanent solution was to begin with signing of the agreement.

Israel withdrew its forces from the areas specified in the Cairo agreement within the next few weeks, but establishment of the 24-member Palestine authority took much longer. Their appointment, as did most important administrative decisions in Gaza and Jericho, depended on Arafat. He delayed his first visit to Gaza and Jericho until July 1994, when he was sworn in as head of the authority and appointed several of the 24 council members. As the IDF withdrew, it was replaced by contingents of Palestinian police and security officials from Egypt, Jordan, Tunisia and other Arab countries. In the absence of a civil administration, these imported police took charge of daily affairs in the evacuated areas. When they arrived, the new Palestinian officers were received enthusiastically by the local Palestinian inhabitants. Hamas and Islamic Jihad at first refrained from carrying out their threats to sabotage the new Palestinian regime. In Israel, however, right-wing militants staged large protest demonstrations against the IDF evacuation and Arafat's arrival in the territories.

An additional agreement between Israel and the Palestinians was signed in September 1995 after months of arduous negotiations. Details were confirmed at Taba, Egypt, on September 18 and the agreement signed in Washington on September 28 by PLO chairman Arafat and prime minister Rabin in the presence of presidents Clinton and Mubarak and King Husayn. The Taba agreement, also known as "Oslo II," expanded Palestinian self-rule in the West Bank and Gaza, provided for elections to a Palestinian council, and called for Israel to release an additional 5,000 Palestinian prisoners.

According to the agreement Israeli forces were to be withdrawn from three regions in the West Bank. In Area A, with about a third of the Palestinian population in the six largest towns, constituting between 3 and 5 percent of the area of the West Bank, full administrative authority was turned over to the Palestinian Authority. In Area B, including over 400 Palestinian villages and rural areas, about 25 percent of the West Bank's area, the Palestinians assumed administrative and police authority, but Israel retains control of security. Movement of Palestinian police from Area A to Area B requires Israeli approval. Redeployment of Israeli forces from Area B occurred prior to the Palestinian Council elections in January 1996. Sparsely settled or uninhabited Area C, constituting over two thirds of the West Bank, includes Israeli settlements and military areas; these were to remain under Israeli control until establishment of the council when Israel was to begin a phased further redeployment in six-month stages to be completed by the end of 1997. This process was suspended after the Hamas terror bombings of February and March 1996.

The general election for the 88-member Palestine Council and its president was held on January 20, 1996 with some 500 observers from Australia, Cyprus, the European Union, Canada, Egypt, Korea, Japan, Jordan, Morocco, Norway, Russia, South Africa, Switzerland and the United States (former president Jimmy Carter was one of the American observers). There were few irregularities and the election was rated by many of the observers as one of the most credible ever held in the Arab world. The overall rate of participation in the West Bank was 68.46 percent and in Gaza over 80 percent.

Arafat received more than 90 percent of the votes for president; he had only token opposition, from a relatively unknown woman. Fifty members elected to the council represented official Fatah lists and were approved by Arafat. Others elected included seven Islamic candidates perceived as pro-Hamas, two independents affiliated with the PFLP, and one associated with the DFLP. Most of the rest were "independents," many associated with Fatah but not approved by Arafat. Four women were elected, including Hanan Ashrawi, a human rights advocate who had resigned as PLO spokesperson in 1993 in protest of Arafat's leadership. Six members were Christian.

Negotiations to conclude a full peace agreement between Israel and the Palestinians were to have begun in May 1996 and be completed by 1999. However, this phase of negotiations was to include the most difficult issues, such as the borders between Israel and the Palestinians, the political status of Palestine, the fate of Jewish settlers in the territories and Palestinian refugees who left in 1948–49, and the future of Jerusalem. These talks also were put into some doubt by the events of early 1996.

All major Israeli political parties were determined to maintain Jerusalem united as their national capital, under Israel's exclusive jurisdiction. Jerusalem was important to religious and secular Jews as the historic capital of ancient Jewish kingdoms and the focus of Jewish prayer. The Old City, in East Jerusalem, was of special historic significance.

The Palestinians and most Arab and Islamic countries regarded Jerusalem as an integral part of the Arab/Islamic world. Arafat consistently referred to Jerusalem as the capital of Palestine. The city was important, not only for its religious and historical significance, but as a major center of Palestinian cultural, social and economic life. Jerusalem was the main intersection between the northern and southern parts of the West Bank and it was a potent symbol of Palestinian nationalism.

Compromise proposals to resolve the Jerusalem problem included plans to make the city the capital of both Israel and Palestine; division of the city into separate Arab and Jewish boroughs under a central authority; and extending the borders to include larger Jewish and Arab sectors, each responsible for its own local affairs under a joint central administration. By 1996 none of these compromises was yet acceptable to either Israel or the PLO.

Most Israelis also opposed return of the 1948 refugees (see above). They feared that a large Arab influx would undermine the Jewish character of Israel and that returning refugees would be a security risk. Neither Israel nor Palestine could within the forseeable future absorb the nearly two million refugees from Lebanon, Syria and Jordan. Yet these refugees had to be considered in a peace settlement. Attempts to bypass them would likely cause political unrest in the host countries and undermine the peace process and the PLO's credibility. Consideration was given to compensation payments (see above), but the problem was complicated by counterclaims of Jews from Arab countries and technical difficulties such as property identification and evaluation.

Israelis were deeply divided on questions including the legal status of the Palestinian entity (as either a state or a lesser autonomous unit), its borders with Israel and the status of the more than 100 Jewish settlements in the West Bank, Gaza and the Golan Heights. Even within the Labor party, leaders disagreed over these issues. The Labor mainstream and parties to its left gradually moved toward accepting a Palestinian state. Most were willing to concede all of Gaza, but there were wide differences over the area to be evacuated in the West Bank and the Golan. Differing conceptions of national security created a wide gap in the amount of land various politicians were willing to give up.

By 1996 the future of Jewish settlements in the occupied territories was still in doubt. Rabin and his successor Shimon Peres refrained from discussing plans to remove the settlers. Indeed, they continued projects started by the previous Likud government to enlarge and develop settlements in the greater Jerusalem region, extending well into the West Bank. The settlers formed a powerful political bloc with support from Likud and parties to its right and large Jewish constituencies in the diaspora.

The PLO was determined to remove the settlers, although some considered permitting those who would accept obligations of Palestinian citizenship to stay. By the middle of 1993, many settlers who had moved to the West Bank for economic rather than nationalist or religious reasons indicated that they would accept compensation to relocate within the Green Line. But a hard core of zealous nationalists has vowed never to leave the occupied territories.

Although progress was slow toward a settlement between Israel and the Palestinians, the most important component in the Arab-Israel conflict, differences had to be settled with the other Arab "front-line" states bordering Israel—Jordan, Syria and Lebanon. Egypt and Israel had developed a relatively friendly working relationship. President Hosni Mubarak frequently acted as an intermediary between Israel and the rest of the Arab world, and Cairo became one of the meeting places where Israeli and Arab officials frequently conducted their negotiations.

After the DOP was signed in September 1993, Jordan's King Husayn became less cautious about public negotiations with Israel. The day after signing the DOP in Washington, Israel and Jordan agreed on a formal agenda for negotiations. Many of the items in their agreement had been settled in parleys during the previous year, including plans to facilitate travel between the two countries, setting up telephone and other communication links, resolving water allocation disputes and proposals for joint industrial and maritime projects.

It took almost a year before further talks between Israel and Jordan expanded the areas of cooperation leading to a peace treaty on October 26, 1994. In June 1994, the two countries agreed to build a road linking Egypt to their Red Sea ports, the towns of Eilat in Israel and Aqaba in Jordan. They also decided to set up a commission on boundaries, water, economy and environment. Israel and Jordan authorized the United States to consolidate into one master plan their respective blueprints for development of the Jordan Valley. They agreed to end a dispute over two small areas totaling 129 square miles along their mutual border. These "agreements to agree" did not constitute a full peace, but rather a list of items to be included in the 1994 final settlement.

The Jordan-Israel treaty was the second full peace agreement signed between Israel and an Arab state (the first was the 1979 Egypt-Israel treaty signed in Washington [see above]). The treaty was signed on the Israel-Jordan border by King Husayn and Prime Minister Rabin in the presence of President Clinton. It called for full diplomatic relations and exchange of ambassadors and broad cooperation in tourism, water, energy, transportation, environmental protection, agriculture and economic development. Within six months, the two countries were to negotiate trade, banking and other financial arrangements. Israel agreed to recognize Jordan's claims to Islamic shrines in Jerusalem and to give "high priority" to the king's interest in resolution of the Jerusalem question. Jordan promised not to join any anti-Israel alliance or to allow its territory to be used as a base for attacks on Israel. Border disputes were settled by return to Jordan of 300 square kilometers with provision for a 25-year lease of several hundred acres to Israeli farmers who had been cultivating the region. The water question was settled by Israeli agreement to yield several million cubic meters of Yarmuk River waters annually and to cooperate in construction of two dams to provide Jordan with water.

Husayn was also concerned that Arafat's pact with Israel might undermine Jordan's relations with the Palestinians who constituted about 60% of Jordan's four million people. Would Jordan be locked out of the Palestinian market as a result of tariff arrangements between Israel and the PLO? How would Palestinian autonomy affect the hundreds of millions of dollars per year in trade with Jordan? Would the Palestine entity continue to use Jordanian currency or issue its own? What would be the status of the five Jordanian banks operating in the West Bank? Finally, what citizenship would the two million Palestinians in Jordan have; would they remain Jordanians, become Palestinians or hold dual citizenship? These questions remain open.

The negotiations between Israel and Syria remained the most difficult. The impasse was over which was to come first: Israeli withdrawal from the Golan or a full peace settlement. U.S. Secretary of State Warren Christopher shuttled 17 times on diplomatic missions between the two countries but was unable to change the position of either. Various proposals were floated for a phased withdrawal and demilitarization with areas of limited troop deployment on each side of the border. Some called for a gradual Israeli withdrawal of up to eight years. Neither Israel nor Syria was able to make generous concessions because of militant domestic opposition. By 1996, a comprehensive settlement between Israel and Syria still appeared remote. A hopeful sign was the participation of both governments in American-sponsored talks with no preconditions beginning in 1995, but these too were suspended after the Hamas actions of February and March 1996. Then on May 29 came the election as Israel's prime minister of Binyamin Netanyahu of the Likud, who explicitly opposed the idea of returning the Golan to Syria at all.

Despite the difficulties in resolving the Arab-Israel conflict, progress was made in the four years following the Madrid Middle East Conference that started the peace process in October 1991. Israel and all the bordering Arab states participated. Mutual recognition of Jewish and Palestinian Arab national movements and their agreement on the principle of territorial compromise was significant, though the election of Netanyahu has thrown some doubt on Israel's continuing commitment to it. Several other Arab states also agreed to deal with Israel, and Israeli diplomats participated in meetings in Morocco, Tunisia, Jordan and Oman. It was now acceptable in most of the Arab world to deal with Israel directly on issues of importance in the Middle East and beyond, although it is fair to say that as of the election of Netanyahu to head Israel's government, the continuation of this state of affairs is far from certain.

PART II

GUIDE TO FURTHER RESEARCH

GLOSSARY OF NAMES, ACRONYMS AND TERMS USED IN TEXT

Abdul Hamid II Ottoman Sultan at time of Young Turk coup in 1908.
Abdullah Ibn Husayn Emir of Transjordan, later king of Jordan.
Abu Nidal (Sabri al-Banna) Leader of Palestinian splinter terrorist faction opposed to PLO.
Abu Sharif, Bassam One of PLO leader Arafat's principal aides.
Absentee Property Law Israel legislation applied to Palestine Arab refugee property after 1948 war.
Agranat Commission Israeli commission established to investigate setback in 1973 war.
Ahad Ha'am (Asher Ginsberg) Early Russian Zionist writer who emphasized cultural nationalism; warned of conflict with Arabs.
Aliya "Ascent"; Zionist term for Jewish immigration to Israel.
Aliya Bet Illegal Jewish immigration to Palestine during mandate.
Allenby, General Sir Edmund Commander of British forces that conquered Palestine from Turkey in World War I.
Anglo-American Committee of Inquiry Joint government committee appointed to investigate Palestine problem in 1945–46.
Aqaba, Gulf of Body of water between the Sinai and the Arabian peninsula, bordered by Egypt, Israel, Jordan and Saudi Arabia; opens to the Red Sea through the Straits of Tiran at its southern end.
Arab Higher Committee Palestine Arab nationalist leadership body established in 1936; first led by Haj Amin al-Husayni.
Arab League Organization of Arab states established in 1945.

Arab Legion Transjordanian army established by Emir Abdullah with British support.

Arab Liberation Army Arab force during first Arab-Israel war, 1947–48.

Arab Literary Club Palestine Arab nationalist group formed in early years of British mandate.

Arab National Fund Body formed by Palestine Arab nationalists to collect funds for purchase of Arab lands to prevent their acquisition by Jews.

Arafat, Yasir A founder of Fatah, PLO leader since 1967 and first president of Palestine entity.

Ashkenazi Term applied to Jews of eastern European origin.

al-As'ad (Assad), Hafez President of Syria from 1971 to the present.

Aswan High Dam Major Nile River project of Egyptian revolution in the 1950s and 1960s.

Attrition, War of Conflict over Suez Canal between Israel and Egypt in 1970–71; continuation of 1967 Six-Day War.

Ba'ath Arab Socialist Resurrection party, the ruling party of Syria and Iraq. Founded in Syria.

Baghdad Pact Defunct treaty for regional security signed by Turkey, Iran, Iraq, Pakistan and Great Britain in 1955.

Baker, James U.S. secretary of state during Bush administration who fostered peace arrangements leading to Madrid Conference.

Balfour, Arthur James British foreign secretary responsible for Balfour Declaration.

Balfour Declaration Statement during World War I by Great Britain supporting Jewish "national home" in Palestine.

Bandung Conference 1955 meeting of nonaligned (Third World) nations where Nasser played important role.

Bar-Lev Line Israeli fortifications along Suez Canal prior to 1973 war.

Basel Program Program of World Zionist Organization, established in Basel, Switzerland in 1897.

Begin, Menachem Leader of IZL, founder of Herut and Israeli prime minister in Likud government from 1977 to 1983.

Ben-Gurion, David Leader of Labor (Mapai) party in Yishuv; first prime minister and defense minister of Israel.

Bernadotte, Count Folke Swedish diplomat, first U.N. mediator in 1948 Palestine war; assassinated in Jerusalem by Lehi.

Biltmore Program 1942 Zionist program calling for establishment of Jewish "commonwealth" in Palestine.

Bilu Movement of Jewish settlers in Palestine from Russia in 1880s.

Black September Dissident Palestinian terrorist group.

Bunche, Ralph U.S. and U.N. diplomat, successor to Bernadotte as U.N. mediator in 1948; negotiated 1949 armistices.

Cairo Agreement, May 1994 Agreement between Israel and PLO to implement 1993 Declaration of Principles (DOP) on self-rule in Gaza and Jericho.

Camp David Agreements, September 1978 Frameworks for peace agreement between Israel and Egypt and for West Bank and Gaza autonomy arrangement, sponsored by U.S. President Jimmy Carter.

CCP See UNCCP.

Churchill White Paper, 1922 Defined favorable British policy toward Zionist objectives in Palestine.

Christopher, Warren U.S. secretary of state during Clinton administration; attempted to mediate Middle East peace.

Clapp, Gordon Former head of Tennessee Valley Authority; headed 1949 Middle East economic survey mission.

Constantinople Agreement, 1915 World War I agreement dividing Ottoman Empire among Russia, France and Great Britain.

Custodian of Absentee Property Israeli authority responsible for property left by Arab refugees from 1948 war.

Damascus congresses, 1919–20 Arab nationalist congresses in Syria prior to French takeover of country under a League of Nations mandate.

Dayan, Moshe Israeli general and politician. He was chief of staff in the 1950s, defense minister in Labor cabinets of the 1960s and 1970s, responsible for occupied territories, and foreign minister in Likud cabinets of the late 1970s.

demilitarized zones (DMZs) Demilitarized areas established in 1949 armistices on borders between Israel and Egypt, Syria and Jordan.

DFLP Democratic Front for the Liberation of Palestine; left-wing political paramilitary group affiliated with PLO.

disengagement agreements Agreements negotiated between Israel and Egypt and Syria by U.S. secretary of state Kissinger after 1973 war.

Dome of the Rock Mosque on site from which Prophet Muhammad is said to have ascended to heaven and returned. Third holiest Islamic site; in "Noble Sanctuary" (Haram al-Sharif), Jerusalem.

DOP September 13, 1993, Declaration of Principles on Interim Self-Governing Arrangements for Palestinians in the Gaza Strip and Jericho; signed between Israel and PLO.

DPF Democratic Popular Front, a left-wing group belonging to the PLO.

Dreyfus, Captain Alfred French Jewish army officer falsely accused of treason in the 1890s. One of the most scandalous incidents of European anti-Semitism prior to World War I; it became an international cause célèbre and a factor in the growth of the Zionist movement.

Druze Arabic-speaking ethnic group in Syria, Lebanon and Israel; offshoot of Shi'ite Islam.

dunum Traditional Middle East unit of land; about a quarter of an acre.
Dayr Yasin Arab village near Jerusalem; inhabitants slaughtered by Jewish terrorist groups IZL and Lehi in 1948.
elected assembly (Assifat ha-Nivharim) Representative body of Yishuv during mandate.
Evans, Harold Designated U.N. commissioner for Jerusalem in 1948; never assumed post because of 1948 war.
Exodus 1947 Illegal immigrant ship carrying European Jewish refugees to Palestine after World War II. Passengers were sent back to Europe by British, and the ship became a symbol for Zionist nationalists.
Faysal Ibn Husayn Son of Sharif Husayn; king of Syria, later Iraq.
Fatah Arabic acronym for Palestinian National Liberation Movement led by Yasir Arafat.
Fatah Revolutionary Command Dissident Palestinian terrorist faction led by Abu Nidal; also called Black September.
Federation of Arab Republics 1972–73 Libyan plan for federation to include Egypt, Syria, Libya and Sudan.
Fighters for the Freedom of Israel See LEHI below.
al-Futuwwah (Chivalry) Palestinian Arab paramilitary youth group formed by mufti of Jerusalem, Haj Amin al-Husayni, in 1930s.
Gahal Right-wing nationalist party formed from Herut and General Zionists in 1960s.
Gaza Strip Southwestern coastal area of Palestine occupied by Egypt from 1948 to 1967 and by Israel from 1967 to 1994.
General Authority for Palestine Refugees Syrian agency established to deal with Palestinian refugees from the 1948 war.
General Zionists Centrist Zionist party.
Geneva Middle East Peace Conference, 1973 Unsuccessful two-day conference after 1973 war.
Golan Heights Part of Syria occupied by Israel in 1967 war.
Grady, Henry American diplomat; coauthor of 1946 Morrison-Grady plan for Palestine solution.
Green Line 1949 armistice frontiers of Israel with Egypt, Jordan, Syria and Lebanon.
Gulf War, 1991 Conflict fought to reverse Iraq's invasion and occupation of Kuwait in 1990; Iraq was defeated by U.S.-led U.N. coalition force.
Haganah Mandate-era Jewish paramilitary defense organization.
Hamas Fundamentalist Islamic resistance movement formed in Gaza in 1987; rejects peace with Israel.
Haram al-Sharif "Noble Sanctuary," site of Dome of the Rock and al-Aksa mosques; supposed site of Jewish temple in Jerusalem (Western, or Wailing, Wall is thought to be the last temple remnant).

Hassan II King of Morocco since 1961; intermediary between Israel and Arabs on many occasions.

Haycraft, Sir Thomas Chief justice of Palestine during early 1920s; headed commission to investigate 1921 riots.

Herut Nationalist party formed from IZL by Menachem Begin in 1948.

Herzl, Theodor Author of *The Jewish State* and founder of modern Zionist movement in 1890s.

Histdadrut Israel General Federation of Labor; founded during mandate.

Hizbullah "Party of God"; Lebanese Shi'ite fundamentalist faction.

Holocaust Destruction of European Jewry by Nazis in World War II.

Holst, Johan Jörgen Foreign minister of Norway during early 1990s; hosted secret Oslo peace talks between Israel and PLO in 1993.

Hoveve Zion (Lovers of Zion) East European Zionist group in late 19th century.

al-Husayni, Haj Amin Mufti of Jerusalem and Arab nationalist leader during mandate; member of influential Palestinian family.

al-Husayni, Musa Kazem Palestine Arab nationalist leader in early years of mandate.

Husayn (Hussein), King King of Jordan since 1952; negotiated 1994 peace with Israel.

Husayn (Hussein), Saddam President of Iraq; invaded Kuwait in 1990, but was defeated in the Gulf War, 1991.

IDF Israel Defense Forces; replaced Haganah when Israel was established in 1948.

Independence, War of Israeli name for first Arab-Israel war in 1948.

Intifada Palestine Arab uprising against Israeli occupation of West Bank and Gaza begun in December 1987; from Arabic, "shaking off."

Islamic Jihad Palestinian Arab Fundamentalist group opposed to Israeli occupation and to peace settlement.

Istiqlal (Independence) party Palestinian nationalist party, formed 1932.

IZL (Irgun Zvai Leumi—"National Military Organization") Militant Jewish paramilitary offshoot of Haganah formed in 1930s.

Jabotinsky, Vladimir (Zvi) Founder of nationalist Revisionist Zionist Organization in 1925; spiritual father of IZL, Herut, Likud.

Jarring, Gunnar Swedish diplomat assigned as special representative by United Nations as intermediary in Arab-Israel conflict after 1967 war.

Jemayel (Gemayel), Bashir Leader of right-wing Lebanese Phalange party and paramilitary forces allied with Israel; assassinated 1982.

Jewish Agency for Palestine Established during mandate to obtain support of diaspora Jews for Jewish "homeland" in Palestine. Responsible for immigration and other Zionist functions.

Jewish Brigade Largely Palestinian Jewish unit that fought in World War II with the British army.

Jewish National Fund Organization affiliated with world Zionist movement to raise funds for development in Palestine.

Jewish rural special police Formed by British during World War II in Palestine as a kind of home guard.

Johnston, Eric President, Motion Picture Industry Association of America; special Middle East representative appointed by President Eisenhower.

Johnston Plan Plan for joint Arab-Israel development of Jordan River and other water development schemes.

Khartoum Conference, 1967 Arab summit meeting after 1967 war.

kibbutz (pl. kibbutzim) Jewish collective agricultural settlements in Palestine and Israel.

Kissinger, Henry U.S. secretary of state in Nixon and Ford administrations who negotiated post-1973 war disengagement agreements.

Kuneitra Largest Syrian town in Golan Heights; returned by Israel as part of 1973 disengagement agreement.

Kurds Mostly Islamic ethnic group in Turkey, Iraq, Iran, and Syria.

Lausanne Conference, 1949 Unsuccessful first attempt to settle Arab-Israel conflict after the 1948 war.

Lebanese Forces Paramilitary force led by Phalange in civil war; largely Maronite Christian.

Lehi (Lohemi Herut Israel—"Fighters for the Freedom of Israel") Paramilitary offshoot of IZL.

Likud (Unity) Right-wing bloc formed in 1973 opposed to return of territory captured in 1967 war; led until 1983 by Menachem Begin.

London, Treaty of, 1915 Allied treaty dividing Ottoman Empire.

ma'abarot Immigrant transition camps in Israel during 1950s.

MacDonald White Paper British policy statement in 1931 on Jewish settlement in Palestine (after Prime Minister Ramsay MacDonald). Called "Black Paper" by Arabs.

Madrid Middle East Peace Conference, 1991 First public peace negotiations between Israel and Syria, Lebanon, Jordan and the Palestinians.

mandate system League of Nations' system of governing territories of defeated Central Powers Turkey and Germany after World War I.

Maronites Largely Lebanese Christian community affiliated with Catholic Church.

McMahon, Sir Henry British high commissioner in Egypt; conducted Husayn-McMahon correspondence in 1915.

Medina Second holiest site in Islam; in Saudi Arabia.

Mecca Holiest site in Islam; in Saudi Arabia.

Meir, Golda Israel's first woman cabinet minister; prime minister 1969-1974.

millet system Ottoman system of governing through religious communities.

Mitla and Gidi passes Strategic areas in Sinai peninsula.

mixed armistice commissions (MACs) Commissions of Israeli and Arab representatives established by 1949 armistice agreements.

Morrison-Grady Plan 1946 British-American plan for Palestine.

moshav (pl. moshavim) Jewish agricultural settlements in Palestine and Israel.

Moyne, Lord Walter G. British official assassinated by Lehi in 1944.

Mubarak, Hosni President of Egypt since 1981; intermediary between Israel and PLO.

Mufti of Jerusalem Islamic religious leader and ex-officio head of Islamic religious and charitable institutions in all of Palestine. The British-appointed mufti during the mandate period was Haj Amin al-Husayni.

Muslim Brotherhood Muslim fundamentalist organization founded in Egypt during 1920s.

Nashashibi Notable Palestinian Arab family opposed to mufti in the mandate period.

Nasser, Gamal Egyptian president, 1952–1970; leader of 1952 revolution.

National Defense party Mandate-era political party established by Nashashibis and their supporters.

national water carrier Israeli system diverting water from Jordan River.

Negev Semidesert in southern Israel; approximately half the area of mandate Palestine.

Netanyahu, Binyamin Successor to Yitzhak Shamir as leader of Likud; narrowly elected Israel prime minister in May 1996 on a platform of opposition to Rabin-Peres peace policies.

Ottoman Decentralization party Political party established in 1912 by Syrian Arabs living in Cairo.

Ottoman Empire The Turkish empire that governed Palestine, Lebanon, Syria, Jordan and Iraq from the 16th century to the end of World War I.

OPEC Organization of Petroleum Exporting Countries.

Pale of Settlement Area of pre-World War I Russian Empire to which Jews were confined.

Palestine Arab party Mandate-era political party established by followers of mufti of Jerusalem, Haj Amin al-Husayni.

Palestine Liberation Army Military arm of PLO.

Palestine Liberation Organization (PLO) Organization representing Palestinians established in 1964; headed by Yasir Arafat.

Palestine National Council (PNC) Palestinian parliament in exile; elected body of PLO.

Palestine National Fund Fundraising and financial institution of PNC/PLO.

Palestine National Guidance Council West Bank political group established in 1978 to coordinate opposition to Israel occupation.

Palmach Strike force of Haganah.

Passfield White Paper 1930 British policy statement limiting British obligations to Jewish community in Palestine.

Peace for Galilee Israel's name for its 1982 invasion of Lebanon.

Peel Commission 1937 royal commission recommending partition of Palestine.

Peta Tikva Oldest Zionist colony in Palestine.

Peres, Shimon Israeli Labor party politician and cabinet minister; became prime minister after the 1995 assasination of Yitzhak Rabin.

PFLP (Popular Front for the Liberation of Palestine) Left-wing political and paramilitary group affiliated with PLO.

Phalange Right-wing, largely Maronite Lebanese political party.

PISGA Palestine Interim Self-Governing Authority under DOP.

pogroms Organized attacks on Jews, often government-instigated, in pre–World War I Russian Empire.

al-Qasim, Shayk Iss al-Din Palestine Arab guerrilla leader killed in 1935; became hero of Palestine Arab nationalists.

Qibya Jordanian village attacked by Israel in 1953.

Rabin, Yitzhak Israeli Labor party politician and former IDF general; prime minister who signed peace agreement with PLO and Jordan. Assassinated by a right-wing Israeli in 1995.

Ramadan War Arab name for 1973 October War; called the Yom Kippur War by Israelis.

Reagan plan President Ronald Reagan's 1982 Middle East peace plan.

Rejectionist Front Arab countries refusing to participate in peace negotiations with Israel.

Revisionists (1) Zionist political group founded by Vladimir Jabotinsky in 1925; opposed to any plan that would give a Zionist state less than all of mandate Palestine and the East Bank of the Jordan.

Revisionists (2) A group of historians—mainly Israeli, Palestinian, American and British—who emerged in the late 1970s and 1980s to challenge accepted Israeli and Western views of Zionist history. Their work is based partly on research in newly available archives and private papers.

Rishon le-Zion Early Zionist colony in Palestine.

Rogers, William U.S. secretary of state during early Nixon administration; proposed Rogers plans I and II for Middle East peace settlement.

Rothschild, Baron Lionel Walter Early British Zionist leader; recipient of letter containing Balfour Declaration.

Sabra and Shatilla Palestine refugee camps in Beirut; sites of Phalange massacre of Palestinians during Israeli invasion, 1982.

Sadat, Anwar Successor to Nasser as president of Egypt; signed Camp David Accords, first Arab peace agreement with Israel, 1978.

Said, Edward Leading independent Palestinian-American intellectual; professor of English at Columbia University, former member of PNC, leading critic of Arafat and PLO, articulate defender of Palestinian rights and interests.

Sa'iqa Palestinian military unit organized by Syria.

Samuel, Sir Herbert First British high commissioner for Palestine.

Sarkis, Elias President of Lebanon during early years of civil war.

Sephardi Term applied to Jews of Spanish, later Afro-Asian, origin; also called Oriental or Eastern Jews.

Shamir, Yitzhak Successor to Menachem Begin as Likud prime minister of Israel; former leader of Lehi.

Sharia Islamic system of law, codified in the Middle Ages.

Sharm al-Sheikh Southernmost point in Sinai, at Straits of Tiran; marks entrance from Red Sea to Gulf of Aqaba; point of Egyptian-Israeli conflict.

Sharon, Ariel Former IDF general and Likud politician; defense minister responsible for 1982 invasion of Lebanon.

Sheikh al-Islam Head of Islamic community in Ottoman Empire.

Shi'ite The smaller of the two major branches of Islam; its largest following is in Iran, where it constitutes a majority; large numbers also present in Iraq and Lebanon.

Shukairi, Ahmed Palestinian nationalist leader; first head of PLO.

Sinai War, 1956 See *Suez War*.

Six-Day War Conflict of June 5–10, 1967 between Israel and Egypt, Syria, Iraq and Jordan. A major watershed in modern Middle East history, it left Israel in possession of the Sinai, Gaza, Golan, East Jerusalem and the West Bank and established Israeli military superiority in the region.

South Lebanese Army Largely Christian force allied with Israel in Israel's south Lebanon "security zone."

Suez War War fought over control of the Suez Canal and Sinai; between Egypt and Britain, France and Israel.

Sunni Largest branch of Islam with about 90 percent of all Muslims.

Supreme Muslim Council Principal Islamic body in mandatory Palestine, headed by Haj Amin al-Husayni.

Sykes-Picot Agreement World War I secret agreement between Britain and France dividing Arab provinces of Ottoman Empire.

Syrian Social National Movement "Greater Syria" (including Palestine and Lebanon) nationalist movement established in 1930s.

Taba Disputed area on Israel-Egyptian Sinai border; last place evacuated by Israel as part of 1979 peace treaty. In September 1995 it was the site of an agreement between Israel and the PLO.

Tanzimat Ottoman reform period from 1839 to 1876.

Tehiya Militant nationalist Israeli party; broke from Likud in opposition to 1978 peace agreement with Egypt.

Tiran, Straits of Straits between Red Sea and Gulf of Aqaba; point of conflict between Israel and Egypt.

Unified National Command (UNC) Leadership of the Intifada.

UNCCP U.N. Conciliation Commission for Palestine; established 1949.

UNDOF U.N. Disengagement Observer Force; established after 1973 October War.

U.N. Economic Survey Mission Established by UNCCP, 1949.

UNEF U.N. Emergency Force; established after 1956 Suez/Sinai War.

UNIFIL U.N. Interim Force in Lebanon, established 1978.

U.N. mediator in Palestine Position created in 1948 by secretary-general; first mediator, Count Bernadotte, assassinated by Jewish terrorists.

UNRWA U.N. Relief and Works Agency for Palestine Refugees in the Near East; established in 1949.

UNSCOP U.N. Special Committee on Palestine; established 1947.

UNTSO U.N. Truce Supervision Organization; established 1949.

U.N. Resolution 181(II) General Assembly partition resolution, November 1947.

U.N. Resolution 242 Security Council resolution passed November 1967 after Six-Day War, outlining grounds for settlement.

U.N. Resolution 338 Security Council resolution passed after October 1973 War to reinforce Resolution 242.

Va'ad Leumi "National council"; governing body of the Yishuv during mandate.

village leagues Arab civic groups established by Likud government in an unsuccessful attempt to counter PLO in occupied territories.

Waqf Private property endowed to an Islamic institution.

War of Attrition 1968–1970 fighting between Egypt and Israel along Suez Canal, following the 1967 Six-Day War.

Weizmann, Chaim World Zionist leader; first president of Israel.

West Bank Area of Palestine between Jordan River and 1949 armistice border of Israel; captured by Israel from Jordan in 1967.

White Paper, 1939 British policy statement on Palestine limiting Jewish immigration, land purchases and other privileges or rights under mandate.

Woodhead (Partition) Commission Established in 1938 to investigate ways to implement Peel Commission partition recommendations.

World Organization of Jews from Arab Countries (WOJAC) Organization established to represent Jews who left Arab countries after establishment of Israel in 1948.

World Zionist Congress Periodic meetings of World Zionist Organization.

Yishuv Jewish community in Palestine prior to establishment of Israel.

Yom Kippur War Israeli name for 1973 October War; called Ramadan War by Arabs.

Young Turks Group of Turkish nationalist politicians, intellectuals and army officers who called for reform of Ottoman Empire early in the 20th century. Seized Ottoman government in coup in 1908.

Zion Mule Corps Jewish unit attached to British army in World War I.

Zionism International movement for establishment of Jewish national "home" or state in Palestine.

CHRONOLOGY

70 A.D.: Rome captures Jerusalem, destroys Jewish temple and exiles most Jewish inhabitants.

622: Prophet Muhammad's flight (Hijra) from Mecca to Medina; year one in Islamic calendar.

644: Islamic/Arab state is established in Palestine and surrounding countries.

1516–17: Ottoman conquest and rule of Palestine and Arab Middle East.

1839–76: Period of Tanzimat (Ottoman reform).

1853–56: Crimean War.

1858 Ottoman Land Law.

1860 Theodor Herzl, founder of modern Zionist movement, is born (died 1904).

1864: Ottoman Wilayat (Provincial) Law.

1876–1909: Reign of Ottoman sultan Abdul Hamid II.

1878: Peta Tikva, oldest Zionist colony, in Palestine, is established.

1880s: Beginning of Arab nationalist movement; Russian pogroms against Jews.

1882–1903: First wave of immigration (aliya) of Jews from eastern Europe to Palestine. Hoveve Zion (Lovers of Zion) establishes early Jewish colony, Rishon le-Zion, in 1882.

1894: Trial of Captain Alfred Dreyfus in France.

1896: Herzl publishes *Der Judenstaat* (*The Jewish State*).

The Arab-Israel Dispute

1897: First World Zionist Congress in Basel, Switzerland.

1904–1914: Second Aliya of Jews from eastern Europe.

1905: Najib 'Azuri publishes in Paris *Le Reveil de la Nation Arabe* (*The Awakening of the Arab Nation*), early Arab nationalist statement; it warns against Zionism.

1908: Young Turk Revolution.

1909: Abdul Hamid II, sultan of the Ottoman Empire, is deposed; Tel Aviv, first all-Jewish city in Palestine, is established.

1912: Ottoman Decentralization party calling for multinational Ottoman Empire is established in Cairo.

1913: Al-Fatat convenes first congress of Arab nationalist groups in Paris.

1914–18: World War I; Ottoman Empire (Turkey) joins Central Powers (Germany, Austria-Hungary, Bulgaria) against Allies (Great Britain, France, Russia and others).

1915–16: Constantinople Agreement among Great Britain, France and Russia; Treaty of London—Italy joins Allies; Husayn-McMahon Correspondence; Sykes-Picot Agreement (Anglo-French plan to divide Ottoman Empire).

1916: Arab revolt against Turks begins.

1917: Balfour Declaration; British capture Jerusalem.

1918: Beginning of Muslim-Christian associations.

1919–23: Third Aliya from eastern Europe.

1920–1948: Period of British mandate in Palestine.

1920: Arab National Congress in Damascus proclaims Faysal king of Syria in March—he is expelled by French in July and given throne of Iraq by British; San Remo Conference assigns mandate for Palestine to Great Britain; British end military rule in Palestine and appoint Herbert Samuel first high commissioner; Samuel appoints civilian advisory council of Palestine Jews, Christians and Muslims; outbreak of Arab riots against mandate; Histadrut (Jewish labor federation) is founded.

1921: Second outbreak of Arab riots against mandate; Haganah is formed; Haj Amin al-Husayni is appointed mufti of Jerusalem and president of Supreme Muslim Council by Herbert Samuel; Haycraft investigates Arab unrest.

1922: Palestine mandate is ratified by League of Nations; Churchill White Paper; British Colonial Office excludes Transjordan from provisions of Balfour Declaration; Palestine Order in Council is passed by British Parliament; plan for 23-member Palestine legislative council is proposed, and rejected by Jews and Arabs.

1924–28: Fourth Aliya.

1925: Jabotinsky launches Zionist Revisionist Movement.

1929: Riots in Jerusalem over Jewish rights at Western (Wailing) Wall; massacre and exodus of Jews from Hebron; attacks on Jews in Safed; Mapai (Workers' party of Israel) is founded.
1930: Shaw Commission report.
1931: MacDonald statement, called "Black Paper" by Arabs, modifies restrictions on Jewish settlement.
1932: Istiqlal (Independence) party (Palestinian) is formed.
1933–39: Hitler assumes control in Germany; Fifth Aliya from Germany and Central Europe.
1934: Nashashibis form National Defense party.
1935: Palestine Arab party is formed by Husaynis; Shaykh Izz al-Din al-Qasim's revolt is crushed, and he is killed by British.
1936–39: Arab Revolt against Great Britain and Zionists; many Palestinian Arab leaders are expelled.
1936: Arab Higher Committee is formed; Arab general strike is proclaimed.
1937: Peel Royal Commission report recommends partition of Palestine.
1938: Woodhead Palestine Partition Commission is sent to investigate implementation of Peel plan.
1939–1945: World War II.
1939: London Round Table Conference; 1939 White Paper restricting Jewish immigration, settlement and land purchases in Palestine.
1941–45: The Holocaust; destruction of European Jewry by Nazis.
1942: Biltmore Program calls for Jewish commonwealth in Palestine.
1945: Arab League is founded in Cairo; Anglo-American Committee of Inquiry on refugees recommends trusteeship in Palestine; Jewish illegal immigration; beginning of Jewish revolt against British in Palestine.
1946: Morrison-Grady Plan; President Truman supports partition.
1947: British refer Palestine problem to United Nations; special session of General Assembly on Palestine; UNSCOP is established and recommends partition; General Assembly passes Resolution 181(II) on November 29 recommending partition of Palestine into Jewish and Arab states and an international zone in greater Jerusalem area; beginning of civil war between Palestine Jews and Arabs; Arab Liberation Army is formed.
1948: *January*—Arab Liberation Army enters Palestine; civil war begins to be internationalized; *March*—United States proposes U.N. trusteeship in Palestine; *April*—Haganah seizes Tiberias, Haifa, Safed, Jaffa, Acre and West Jerusalem; Dayr Yassin massacre, beginning of Arab flight from Palestine; Arabs blow up *Palestine Post*, attack Hadassah Hospital convoy; United Nations establishes special Jerusalem Truce Commission; *May 14*—Provisional government issues Israel Declaration of Independence; U.S. de facto recognition of Israel; *May 15*—Mandate ends and British depart from Haifa; armed forces of Egypt, Transjordan, Syria, Lebanon

and Iraq are sent to fight Israel; *May 17*—Soviet Union grants Israel de jure recognition; *May 20*—Count Bernadotte is appointed U.N. mediator; *June 11*—first truce; *July 8*—fighting resumes in Palestine; *July 19*—U.N. orders second truce after Israel captures most of Galilee; *September 17*—Bernadotte is assassinated in Jerusalem by Lehi and replaced by acting mediator Ralph Bunche; *December*—Abdullah takes over East Jerusalem and West Bank; U.N. General Assembly passes Resolution 194(III) dealing with Palestine refugees and establishing CCP; beginning of large-scale Jewish immigration from Europe.

1949: *January 6*—Israel and Egypt announce cease-fire; *January 12*—Egypt-Israel armistice talks begin in Rhodes; *January 25*—Israel holds first Knesset election, Ben-Gurion becomes prime minister; *February 24*—Israel and Egypt sign armistice agreement; *March 11*—Israel and Transjordan sign armistice; *March 23*—Israel-Lebanese armistice signed; *April 26*—Transjordan becomes Hashemite Kingdom of Jordan; *April*—Lausanne peace talks begin; *July 20*—Israel-Syria armistice is signed; *July 27*—Bunche announces end of military phase of conflict; *August 12*—U.N. Security Council terminates office of acting mediator; *December*—UNRWA established by United Nations.

1950: *January*—Most of Israeli government is moved from Tel Aviv to Jerusalem; Knesset proclaims that Holy City has "always" been capital of Jewish nation; *April*—Jordan parliament ratifies annexation of West Bank and East Jerusalem (recognized only by Great Britain and Pakistan); Tripartite Agreement among United States, Great Britain and France regulating arms flow to Middle East.

1951: *July 20*—King Abdullah is assassinated in East Jerusalem.

1952: *July 23*—King Farouk is overthrown in Egyptian revolution.

1953: *May 2*—Husayn becomes king of Jordan; *October*—Israel conducts raid on Jordanian village of Qibya.

1953–55: Eric Johnston develops plan for Jordan River development.

1955: *February*—massive Israeli attack on Gaza; *April*—Nasser attends Bandung Conference in Indonesia; Baghdad Pact is signed; Nasser turns to Soviet Bloc for arms after rejection by West.

1956: *July*—United States withdraws offer to assist Egypt with Aswan High Dam (Egypt later turns to Soviet Union for help); *July 26*—Nasser nationalizes Suez Canal; *August–September*—Great Britain, France and Israel plan joint invasion of Egypt to overthrow Nasser; *October 29*—Israel invades Sinai and Gaza; *October 31*—Great Britain and France attack Egypt; *November*—Great Britain, France and Israel accept cease-fire; UNEF is established and sent to Egypt.

1957: *March*—United States pressures Israel to withdraw from Sinai and Gaza; Eisenhower Middle East Doctrine.

1958: *July*—Civil war in Lebanon; monarchy is overthrown in Iraq.

1962: First direct sale of U.S. weapons to Israel.

1964: *January*—First Arab summit; *May*—Founding conference of PLO.

1965: First Fatah guerrilla attack on Israel.

1966: *November*—Egypt and Syria sign defense treaty.

1967: *April*—Border clashes between Israel and Syria; mounting border tensions between Israel and Egypt; *June 1*—Levi Eshkol turns Israel defense ministry over to Dayan; National Unity Government with Begin is formed; *June 5*—Israel initiates preemptive attack on Egypt, Syria and Iraq; Jordan joins Arab forces; *June 10*—Cease-fire on all fronts, and Israel occupies Sinai, Gaza, Golan, East Jerusalem and West Bank; *August–September*—Khartoum Conference; *November 22*—U.N. Security Council passes Resolution 242; *December*—Jarring begins peace mission.

1968: Battle of Karameh between Israel and Palestinian guerrillas.

1969–70: War of Attrition along Suez Canal.

1969: Israel constructs Bar-Lev Line along Suez Canal; PNC elects Arafat as PLO Chairman; Secretary of State William Rogers proclaims "even-handed" U.S. Middle East policy and presents new peace proposals.

1970: Rogers Middle East Plan II is offered; Begin leaves Israel cabinet because of opposition to Rogers plan; *August*—Cease-fire takes effect in War of Attrition; *September*—Palestinian uprising against Jordan government; *September 28*—Nasser dies and is succeeded by Anwar Sadat; *November*—Hafez al-Assad assumes power in Syria.

1971: Soviet-Egyptian Treaty of Friendship.

1972: Egyptian-Syrian plan for war with Israel; Sadat expels Soviet advisors from Egypt, and Moscow increases arms aid to Egypt.

1973: *October 6*—Egypt and Syria attack Israel, beginning October War, also known as Yom Kippur or Ramadan War; *October 22*—U.N. orders cease-fire, Security Council passes Resolution 338; Arab oil embargo on United States; *November*—Agranat Commission is established in Israel to investigate setback in October War; *December*—Likud Party gains strength in Israel election; *December 21*—Geneva Middle East Peace Conference.

1974: U.N. General Assembly recognizes PLO and invites Arafat to address it; Egypt and Syria resume relations with United States; Arab Summit at Rabat recognizes PLO as sole legitimate representative of the Palestinians.

1974–75: Secretary of State Henry Kissinger negotiates Disengagement agreements between Israel and Egypt and Syria.

1975: Sadat permits Suez Canal to reopen after eight years; U.N. General Assembly passes resolution equating Zionism and racism; second civil war begins in Lebanon.

1976: Pro-PLO candidates sweep West Bank municipal elections.

1977: *May*—Begin's Likud wins Knesset election, Begin begins expansion of Jewish settlements in West Bank; *November 19*—Sadat flies to Jerusalem to discuss peace and address Knesset, followed by difficult stalemated negotiations.

1978: *March–June*—Israel occupies and withdraws from south Lebanon, and UNIFIL is established; *September*—Camp David peace negotiations, and accords between Israel, Egypt and United States are signed; *December*—Sadat and Begin jointly receive Nobel Peace Prize.

1979: *March 26*—Egyptian-Israeli peace treaty is signed in Washington, D.C.; *March 31*—Egypt is expelled from Arab League and league headquarters are moved from Cairo to Tunis; *April 30*—First Israeli ship is permitted through Suez Canal; *May 9*—Egypt is expelled from Islamic Conference; *May 25*—Israel begins withdrawal from Sinai.

1980: Israel and Egypt exchange ambassadors; Egyptian National Assembly repeals boycott of Israel; regular passenger flights begin between Israel and Egypt; Egypt sells Israel Sinai oil; Israel officially annexes all of Jerusalem.

1981–82: Sharon attempts to impose civil administration and village leagues on West Bank; violent demonstrations occur against occupation.

1981: *June 7*—Israel bombs Iraqi nuclear reactor at Osirak; *October 6*—Sadat is assassinated by Islamic militants and succeeded by Hosni Mubarak; *December 14*—Israel annexes Golan Heights.

1982: *April*—Israel returns last of Sinai except Taba to Egypt; *June 6*—Israel invades Lebanon in operation Peace for Galilee; *August 21*—PLO and Syrians withdraw from Beirut; IDF is replaced by multinational force; *September*—Reagan peace plan; Arab League Fez peace plan; *September 14*—Bashir Jemayel, leader of Lebanese Forces, is assassinated; Israel reoccupies West Beirut; *September 16*—Sabra and Shatilla massacre; *September 23*—Amin Jemayel (Bashir's brother) is elected president of Lebanon; *September 28–29*—Israel leaves West Beirut, first step in withdrawal from Lebanon.

1983–85: Israel is attacked by guerrilla forces in Lebanon and undertakes phased withdrawal.

1983: *May*—Israel and Lebanon sign peace accord, but it is annulled by Lebanese government in March 1984; *August*—Begin resigns as prime minister of Israel and is succeeded by Yitzhak Shamir; *October*—U.S. Marine barracks in Beirut is blown up by Lebanese guerrillas.

1984: *January*—Islamic Conference readmits Egypt; *February*—U.S. peacekeeping force leaves Lebanon; as result of Knesset election, Labor-Likud unity government formed.

1985: *June*—Israel completes withdrawal from Lebanon except for "security zone" in south; *October*—Israel attacks PLO headquarters in Tunis.

1987: *November*—Arab summit in Amman; *December 9*—Intifada breaks out.

1988: *July*—King Husayn renounces Jordan claims to West Bank and states PLO is responsible for Palestine; *September*—international arbitration panel gives Taba to Egypt; *November*—PNC meeting in Algiers issues Palestine Declaration of Independence; *December*—Arafat addresses U.N. General Assembly in Geneva, accepts Resolutions 242 and 338 and Israel.

1989–91: Secretary of State James Baker negotiates terms for convening Middle East peace conference.

1989: *April*—Shamir's Middle East peace plan; *May*—Egypt is readmitted to Arab League.

1990: *March*—Shamir's government falls in disagreement with Labor over U.S. peace initiative; *August*—Iraq invades Kuwait.

1991: *January–February*—Gulf War, defeat of Iraq by U.N. coalition force, Iraqi missile attack on Israel; *October 30*—Middle East Peace Conference opens in Madrid.

1992: *January*—Moscow meeting initiates five functional multilateral meetings as part of peace process; *June*—Likud is defeated in Knesset election, Labor returns to power and modifies terms for negotiations and peace accord; *December*—Rabin deports over 400 Palestinians affiliated with Hamas.

1993: *January*—beginning of secret Israel-PLO talks in Oslo; *September 13*—Arafat and Rabin sign Declaration of Principles accord in Washington; *September 11*—Israel and Jordan agree on peace agenda in Washington.

1994: *May 4*—Israel and PLO sign Cairo accord on withdrawal of IDF from Gaza and Jericho in West Bank; *July*—Arafat returns to Gaza and Jericho to establish PISGA; Palestine police assume authority in Gaza and Jericho; *June–July*—Further Israel-Jordan negotiations on peace agenda; *July*—King Hussayn and Rabin meet in Washington; *October 26*—Israel-Jordan peace treaty is signed on border.

1995: Israel and Jordan sign agreements to construct railway lines linking Jordan with Haifa port, Dead Sea and Elat, open direct postal service, and cooperate in agricultural marketing, hygiene, research, technology and tourism; Israel turns over to Jordan 132 square miles of territory in the Negev; Jordan's Council of Ministers approves bill to end laws boycotting Israel; *January*—Palestine National Authority (PNA) announces it has received only $250 million of $787 million pledged by donor nations, U.N. agencies and World Bank in 1994; PLO and Jordan sign accord turning over control of Muslim holy sites in Jerusalem to PLO provided PLO acquires authority over East Jerusalem; accord stipulates that Jordan dinar will become official currency in PNA-administered territory; *Febru-*

ary—PLO chairman Arafat, Israeli prime minister Rabin, Jordan's King Husayn and Egyptian president Mubarak attend summit meeting in Cairo to discuss Middle East peace process; Foreign Minister Peres and Omani foreign minister agree in Aqaba, Jordan to open mutual interest sections; *March*—Israel participates in Cairo International Trade Fair for first time since 1987; *April*—Israel and Jordan exchange ambassadors; PNA and Israel agree to plan to accept $60 million from international donors toward meeting PNA's $136 million budget gap; *May*—PNA acquires jurisdiction over banking, energy, industry, labor and securities in West Bank; at meeting in Morocco Peres informs King Hassan II that Israel views Golan Heights as Syrian land; *June*—Israel agrees to transfer all civilian powers to elected Palestinian authorities in Palestinian-controlled areas of West Bank and Gaza after 1996 elections; *September 24*—Israeli and Palestinian authorities initial agreement in Taba on elections for Palestinian council, withdrawal of Israeli troops and extending Palestinian self-rule; *September 27*—Knesset approves September 24 Taba agreement; *September 28*—PLO chairman Arafat and prime minister Rabin sign Taba interim agreement known as "Oslo II" in Washington, D.C. in presence of presidents Clinton and Mubarak and King Husayn; *October 6*—Knesset approves Oslo II accord by vote of 61 to 59; *November 4*—Prime Minister Rabin assassinated in Tel Aviv by Israeli orthodox Jewish student and is replaced as prime minister by foreign minister Shimon Peres.

1996: Israel withdraws from some areas specified in Oslo II interim agreement with Palestinians; *January 20*—first Palestinian elections for 88-member assembly and its president; Arafat wins presidency in election with wide participation; Arafat's Fatah wins most seats; *May 29*—Peres loses extremely close election for prime ministership to Likud leader Binyamin Netanyahu, who ran against the Rabin-Peres program for achieving peace.

ANNOTATED BIBLIOGRAPHY

BOOKS AND PAMPHLETS

Abbas, Mahmoud (Abu Mazen). *Through Secret Channels*. Reading, England: Garnet Publishing, 1995. Account of secret negotiations leading to Declaration of Principles by Palestinian leader who participated.

Abboushi, W. F. *The Angry Arabs*. Philadelphia: Westminster Press, 1974. A Palestinian-American's discussion of Arab grievances against the West with emphasis on the Palestine problem.

———. *The Unmaking of Palestine*. Boulder, Colo.: Rienner, 1985. Palestine during the mandate to 1948. Use of British documentation.

Abcarius, Michael F. *Palestine Through the Fog of Propaganda*. London: Hutchinson, 1946. An early account of conflict between Palestine Arabs and Jews.

Abdel Hamid, [Princess] Dina. *Duet for Freedom*. London: Quartet Books, 1988. Account of Israeli 1982 invasion of Lebanon by former wife of King Hussayn, later married to imprisoned PLO official.

Abed, George T. *The Economic Viability of a Palestinian State*. Washington, D.C.: Institute of Palestine Studies (IPS), 1990. Discussion of economic plans for Palestinian state.

———. *The Palestinian Economy: Studies in Development Under Prolonged Occupation*. London: Routledge, 1988. Collection of papers on Palestinian economy with emphasis on West Bank and Gaza.

Abed, Shukri. *Israeli Arabism: The Latest Incarnation of Orientalism*. Kingston, Ontario, Canada: 1986. An Arab critique of Israeli scholarship on Arab affairs.

Abed-Rabbo, Samir, and Doris Safie, eds. *The Palestinian Uprising*. Belmont, Mass.: Association of Arab-American University Graduates, 1990. Collection of articles on the Intifada.

al-Abid, Ibrahim. *Human Rights in the Occupied Territories, 1971*. Beirut Palestine Research Center, 1973. Study of Israeli abuses in territories by PLO Research Office.

Abu 'Amr, Ziad. *The Intifada: Causes and Factors of Continuity*. Jerusalem: Palestinian Academic Society for the Study of International Affairs (Passia), 1989. A Palestinian social scientist's account of the Intifada.

———. *Islamic Fundamentalism in the West Bank and Gaza*. Bloomington: Indiana University Press, 1994. An insider's view of fundamentalist influence on and competition with the PLO in occupied territories.

Abu-Ghazaleh, Adnan M. *Arab Cultural Nationalism in Palestine During the British Mandate*. Beirut: Institute of Palestine Studies, 1973. Study of Palestinian Arab nationalist writing and writers to 1948.

Abu Iyad (Salah Khalaf), with Eric Rouleau. *My Home, My Land: A Narrative of the Palestinian Struggle*. New York: Times Books, 1981. Account of Arab-Israel conflict by a former PLO leader.

Abu-Lughod, Ibrahim, ed. *The Arab-Israeli Confrontation of June 1967: An Arab Perspective*. 2d ed. Evanston, Ill.: Northwest University Press, 1987. Collection of papers on the June 1967 war.

———. *Palestinian Rights: Affirmation and Denial*. Wilmette, Ill: Medina Press, 1982. Collection of papers focusing on Israeli denial of Palestinian rights.

———. *The Transformation of Palestine: Essays on the Origin and Development of the Arab-Israeli Conflict*. 2d ed. Evanston, Ill.: Northwest University Press, 1987. Collection of articles by diverse scholars from an Arab perspective.

Aburish, Said. *Children of Bethany: The Story of a Palestinian Family*. Bloomington: Indiana University Press, 1989. History of the author's family during the 20th century in a West Bank town.

———. *Cry Palestine: Inside the West Bank*. Boulder, Colo.: Westview Press, 1993. Palestinians under the Israeli occupation.

———. *The Forgotten Faithful: The Christians in the Holy Land*. London: Quartet, 1993. Discusses decline of Palestine Christian community.

el-Ad, Avri. *Decline of Honor*. Chicago: Regnery, 1976. Memoirs of an Israeli secret agent involved in 1954 Cairo scheme.

Adams, Michael. *Chaos or Rebirth: The Arab Outlook*. London: BBC Books, 1968. How Arabs perceive the Arab-Israel conflict.

Adams, William C., ed. *Television Coverage of the Middle East*. Norwood, N.J.: ABLEX, 1981. American TV coverage of the Middle East with emphasis on Palestine problem.

Adan, Avraham. *On the Banks of the Suez: An Israel General's Personal Account of the Yom Kippur War*. San Rafael, Calif.: Presidio Press, 1980. Personal account of the 1973 war.

Adnan, Etel. *Sitt Marie Rose*. Sausalito, Calif.: Post-Apollo Press, 1982. Novel about a Lebanese Christian woman who supported Palestinians.

Adonis [Ali Ahmad Said], Mahmoud Darwish and Samih al-Qasim. *Victims of a Map: A Bilingual Anthology of Arabic Poetry*. London: Al-Saqi Books, 1984. English translation of Arabic poetry collection about Palestine.

Adoofi, Ibrahim S. *Struggle for Freedom: United Nations Palestine Question and Super Powers*. New Delhi, India. H. K. Publishers & Distributors, 1990. An Indian perspective on the Arab-Israel conflict and role of the United Nations.

Aharoni, Dov. *General Sharon's War Against Time Magazine: His Trial and Vindication*. New York: Steimatzky/Shapolsky, 1985. Account of a libel trial involving Sharon; deals with his role in 1982 war.

Aker, Frank. *October 1973: The Arab-Israeli War*. Hamden, Conn.: Archon Books, 1985. Account of Yom Kippur War with introduction by General George Patton, Jr.

Alamuddin, Najib. *Turmoil: The Druzes, Lebanon and the Arab-Israeli Conflict*. London: Quartet Books, 1993. Reactions of Lebanese Druze to Arab-Israel conflict.

Alexander, Yonah, ed. *Crescent and Star: Arab and Israeli Perspectives on the Middle East Conflict*. New York: AMS Press, 1973. Collection of articles, essays and addresses.

Allen, David, and Alfred Pijpers, eds. *European Foreign Policy-Making and the Arab-Israeli Conflict.* The Hague, Netherlands: Martinus Nijhoff, 1984. Policies of European Community members.

Allen, Peter. *The Yom Kippur War.* New York: Scribner, 1982. Study of the 1973 war.

Allen, Richard. *Imperialism and Nationalism in the Fertile Crescent: Sources and Prospects of the Arab-Israeli Conflict.* 2d ed. Boulder, Colo.: Westview Press, 1985.

Alpher, Joseph, and Shai Feldman, eds. *The West Bank and Gaza: Israel's Options for Peace.* Tel Aviv: Jaffee Center, Tel Aviv University, 1989. Six options for West and Gaza offered by an Israeli study group.

Alroy, Gil Carl. *The Kissinger Experience: American Policy in the Middle East.* New York: Horizon Press, 1975. Highly critical account of Kissinger's Middle East activities.

Alteras, Issac. *Eisenhower and Israel: U.S.-Israel Relations, 1953–1960.* Gainesville: University of Florida Press, 1993. Examines how U.S. commitment to Israel was sustained through Israel's 1956 attack on Egypt.

Altoma, Salih Jawasi. *Palestinian Themes in Modern Arabic Literature, 1917–1970.* Cairo: Anglo-Egyptian Bookshop, 1972. The Palestinian cause in Arabic literature.

Amad, Adnan, comp. and ed. *Israeli League for Human and Civil Rights (The Shahak Papers).* Beirut: Palestine Research Center, 1973. Describes work of Israeli League vis-à-vis Palestine Arabs.

American Friends of the Middle East. *The Jordan Water Problem.* Washington, D.C.: 1964. Analysis and summary of documents on Jordan water problem.

American Friends Service Committee. *A Compassionate Peace: A Future for the Middle East.* New York: Hill & Wang, 1982. Quaker study of Middle East problems with emphasis on Arab-Israel conflict.

Amos, John W. *Arab Israeli Military/Political Relations: Arab Perceptions and the Politics of Escalation.* New York: Pergamon Press, 1979. Emphasis on "escalatory patterns" in Arab-Israel conflict during 1960s and 1970s.

———. *Palestinian Resistance: Organization of a Nationalist Movement.* New York: Pergamon Press, 1980. Detailed study of Palestinian resistance movements.

Amun, Hasan, et al. *Palestinian Arabs in Israel: Two Case Studies.* London: Ithaca Press, 1977. Study of an Arab village and of Arab university students.

Anabtawi, Samir N. *Palestinian Higher Education in the West Bank and Gaza.* London: KPI, 1986. Critique of Palestinian higher education in West Bank and Gaza.

Ang, Swee Chai. *From Beirut to Jerusalem.* London: Grafton Books, 1989. Experiences of woman physician working with Palestinians in 1982 war.

Angeloglou, Christopher, and Brian Haynes, eds. *The Holy War*. London: Cornmarket, 1967. The Six-Day War, as covered by *London Sunday Times* and photographers.

Antonius, George. *The Arab Awakening: The Story of the Arab National Movement*. New York: Capricorn Books, 1965. Classic study of rise of Arab nationalism in 19th and 20th centuries.

Antonius, Soraya. *The Lord*. London: Hamish Hamilton, 1986. Novel about Palestine during British mandate.

———. *Where the Jinn Consult*. London: Hamish Hamilton, 1987. Novel based on Palestinian Arab author's 1948 and subsequent experiences.

Arab Republic of Egypt, Ministry of Foreign Affairs. *White Paper on Peace Initiatives Undertaken by President Anwar al-Sadat, 1971–1977*. Cairo: Ministry of Foreign Affairs, 1978. Extensive documentation and source material.

———. *Egypt and the Palestinian Question, 1945–1980: Performance Report*. Cairo: Ministry of Foreign Affairs, 1980. Egyptian government position on relations with Israel.

Arad, Yitzhak. *The Partisan: From the Valley of Death to Mt. Zion*. New York: Holocaust Library, Schocken Books, 1979. Personal narrative of Jewish partisan in Europe from 1939 to Israel-Arab war of 1948.

Arakie, Margaret. *The Broken Sword of Justice: America, Israel and the Palestine Tragedy*. London: Quartet Books, 1973. Critique of U.S. involvement in the Arab-Israel conflict sympathetic to Palestinians.

Arnon, Itzhak. *From Fellah to Farmer: A Study of Change in Arab Villages*. Rehovot, Israel: Settlement Study Center, 1980. Changes in economy of Israeli-Arab farmers.

Arnoni, M. S. *Rights and Wrongs in the Arab-Israeli Conflict*. Passaic, N.J.: Minority of One Press, 1968. An Israeli critique of Israel government policy towards Arabs.

Aron, Raymond. *De Gaulle, Israel and the Jews*. New York: Praeger, 1969. French intellectual's critique of De Gaulle's policy on Israel.

Aronson, Geoffrey. *Israel, Palestinians, and the Intifada: Creating Facts on the West Bank*. Washington, D.C.: Institute of Palestine Studies, 1990. Critical examination of Israeli policy in West Bank.

Aronson, Shlomo. *Conflict and Bargaining in the Middle East: An Israeli Perspective*. Baltimore: Johns Hopkins University Press, 1978. An Israeli strategist's study of Israel's foreign policy 1949–77.

Arora, J. S. *West Asia War, 1973, that Shook the World and Brought Us to the Brink of the Third World War*. New Delhi: New Light, 1973. An Indian perspective; states 1973 war led to brink of World War III.

Guide to Further Research

Aruri, Nasser H., ed. *Middle East Crucible: Studies on the Arab-Israeli War of October 1973*. Wilmette, Ill.: Medina University Press, 1975. Collection of papers on 1973 war and its impact on Arabs and Israelis.

———. *Occupation: Israel Over Palestine*. 2d ed. Belmont, Mass.: Association of Arab-American University Graduates, 1989. Collection of papers on Israeli occupation policies and Intifada.

———. *The Palestinian Resistance to Israeli Occupation*. Wilmette, Ill.: Medina University Press, 1970. Collection of papers on Palestinian resistance movement to Israeli occupation and in diaspora.

Aruri, Nasser H., and Edmond Ghareeb. *Enemy of the Sun: Poetry of Palestinian Resistance*. Washington, D.C.: Drum & Spear Press, 1970. Anthology of English translations.

Asher, Jerry. *Duel for the Golan: The 100-Hour Battle that Saved Israel*. New York: Morrow, 1987. Battle over Golan Heights in 1973 war.

Ashkenasi, Abraham. *Palestinian Identities and Preferences: Israel's and Jerusalem's Arabs*. New York: Praeger, 1992. Discussion of ethnic relations between Israeli Jews and Arabs.

Ashrawi, Hanan. *This Side of Peace: A Personal Account*. New York: Simon & Schuster, 1995. An account of peace negotiations in the early 1990s by spokeswoman of the Palestinian delegation.

al-Asmar, Fouzi. *Through the Hebrew Looking Glass—Arab Stereotypes in Children's Literature*. London: Zed Books, 1986. Study of Israel childrens' literature.

———. *To Be an Arab in Israel*. London: Frances Pinter, 1978. Autobiography illustrating discrimination against Israeli Arabs.

———. *The Wind Driven Reed and Other Poems*. Washington, D.C.: Three Continents Press, 1979. English translations of al-Asmar's poems with Arabic originals.

al-Asmar, Fouzi, Uri Davis and Naim Khadr. *Towards a Socialist Republic of Palestine*. London: Ithaca Press, 1981. Text of discussion among authors calling for democratic, secular, socialist Palestine state to replace Israel and occupied territory.

Assaf, Michael. *The Arab Movement in Palestine*. New York: 1937. A Palestinian Jewish scholar's appraisal.

Associated Press. *Lightning Out of Israel: The Six-Day War in the Middle East*. New York: Associated Press, 1967. Compilation of Associated Press accounts of 1967 war.

Astor, David, and Valerie Yorke. *Peace in the Middle East*. London: Corgi Press, 1978. Covers Jewish-Arab relations and Middle East politics from 1945 to late 1970s.

Ata, Ibrahim Wade. *The West Bank Palestinian Family*. London: KPI, 1986. Sociological study of West Bank Arab family structure.

Ateek, Naim S., Marc C. Ellis and Rosemary R. Ruether, eds. *Faith and the Intifada*. Maryknoll, N.Y.: Orbis Books, 1992. Collection of articles dealing with plight of Palestinian Christian Arabs in Intifada.

Augustin, Ebba, ed. *Palestinian Women: Identity and Experience*. London: Zed Books, 1993. Fifteen essays and two poems dealing with Palestinian women under occupation.

Australia, Parliament of. Joint Committee on Foreign Affairs and Defense. *The Middle East: Focal Point of Conflict, the Interests of the Powers*. Canberra: Australian Government Publishing Service, 1977. An Australian perspective.

Aved, Joe. *Ami: A Novel*. New York: Shengold, 1981. Novel covering period of 1948 and 1956 wars.

Avineri, Shlomo, ed. *Israel and the Palestinians*. New York: St. Martin's Press, 1971. Collection of perspectives by Israeli doves.

Avinoam, Reuben. *Such Were Our Fighters*. New York: Herzl Press, 1965. Anthology of writings by Israeli soldiers who died in combat.

Avneri, Arieh L. *The Claim of Dispossession: Jewish Land Settlement and the Arabs*. New Brunswick, N.J.: Transaction Books, 1984. An Israeli argument against Arab claims of Zionist dispossession.

Avnery, Uri. *Israel Without Zionists: A Plea for Peace in the Middle East*. New York: Collier Books, 1971. An Israeli critique of Zionism and Israeli policies.

———. *My Friend, The Enemy*. Westport, Conn.: Lawrence Hill, 1986. An account of the author's meetings with Arafat and other Palestinians.

Azcarte, Pablo de. *Mission in Palestine, 1948–1952*. Washington, D.C.: Middle East Institute, 1966. Account of 1948 war and UNCCP by an early U.N. representative.

Badr, Ahmed M. *Education of the Palestinians: An Annotated Bibliography*. Detroit, Mich.: Association of Arab American University Graduates, 1977. Annotated bibliography of articles and books in Arabic and English.

el-Badri, Maj. Gen. Hazzan, Maj. Gen. Taha el Magdoub and Maj. Gen. Mohammed Dia el Din Zohdy. *The Ramadan War*. Fairfax, Va.: Hero Books, 1978. Three Egyptian generals describe the 1967 Six-Day War.

Bahbah, Bishara, with Linda Butler. *Israel and Latin America: The Military Connection*. New York: St. Martin's Press, 1986. Study of Israeli arms sales to rightist Latin American countries and importance to Israeli arms industry.

Bahiri, Simcha. *Industrialization in the West Bank and Gaza*. Boulder, Colo.: Westview Press, 1987. Problems of economic development in the occupied territories.

Guide to Further Research

Bailey, Clinton. *Bedouin Poetry from Sinai and the Negev: Mirror of Culture*. Oxford: Clarendon Press, 1991. Extensive study of Bedouin oral poetry in context of daily life.

———. *Jordan's Palestinian Challenge, 1948–1983: A Political History*. Boulder, Colo.: Westview Press, 1984. Study of the Palestinian challenge to Jordan's regime since 1948.

Bailey, Sydney D. *Four Arab-Israeli Wars and the Peace Process*. New York: St. Martin's Press, 1990. Discussion of mediation and peacemaking since 1948.

———. *The Making of Resolution 242*. The Hague: Nijhoff Press, 1985. Study of 1967 war and attempts to attain a cease-fire.

Bain, Kenneth R. *The March to Zion: United States Policy and the Founding of Israel*. College Station: Texas A&M University Press, 1979. Critique of American involvement in Palestine problem and of U.S. recognition of Israel.

Ball, George. *Error and Betrayal in Lebanon: An Analysis of Israel's Invasion of Lebanon and the Implications for U.S.-Israeli Relations*. Washington, D.C.: Foundation for Middle East Peace, 1984. A highly critical account of U.S. policy by a former undersecretary of state.

Ball, George W., and Douglas B. Ball. *The Passionate Attachment: America's Involvement with Israel, 1947 to the Present*. New York: Norton, 1992. Authors maintain U.S. Middle East policy is a captive of Israel lobby.

Banks, Lynne Reid, ed. *Torn Country: An Oral History of the Israeli War of Independence*. New York: Watts, 1982. Personal narratives of 1948–49 war.

Barakat, Halim. *Days of Dust*. Wilmette, Ill.: Medina University Press, 1974. A Palestinian novel about the 1967 Six-Day War.

Barbour, Nevill. *Nisi Dominus: A Survey of the Palestine Controversy*. London: Harrap, 1946. A British critique of Zionism and British Palestine policy.

Bar-Gal, Yoram, and A. Soffer. *Geographical Changes in the Traditional Arab Villages in Northern Israel*. Durham, England: University of Durham, 1981. An Israeli account of urbanization and other changes in Arab villages.

Bar-Joseph, Uri. *The Best of Enemies: Israel and Transjordan in the War of 1948*. London: Cass, 1987. Examines the secret relationship between the Yishuv, later Israel, and King Abdullah.

Bar-On, Mordechai. *The Gates of Gaza: Israel's Road to Suez and Back, 1955–1957*. New York: St. Martin's Press, 1994. Account by Israeli participant in 1956 war and its diplomacy.

Bar-Siman Tov, Yaacov. *Israel and the Peace Process 1977–1982: In Search of Legitimacy for Peace*. Albany, N.Y.: State University of New York Press, 1994. An Israeli scholar's account, emphasis on Israel-Egypt relations and peace process.

———. *The Israeli-Egyptian War of Attrition, 1969–1970.* New York: Columbia University Press, 1980. An Israeli scholar's study of the accelerating conflict.

Bar-Yaacov, Nissim. *The Israel-Syrian Armistice: Problems of Implementation, 1949–1966.* London: Oxford University Press, 1967. An Israeli account of the border conflict with Syria.

Bar-Zohar, Michael. *Ben-Gurion: A Biography.* New York: Delacorte Press, 1978. An authorized biography of Israel's first prime and defense minister.

———. *Embassies in Crisis: Diplomats and Demagogues Behind the Six-Day War.* Englewood Cliffs, N.J.: Prentice-Hall, 1970. An Israeli's critical account of Western polices.

———. *Facing a Cruel Mirror: Israel's Moment of Truth.* New York: Scribner, 1990. A critical account of Israel-Arab relations from 1949 to 1967.

Bar-Zohar, Michael, and Eitan Haber. *The Quest for the Red Prince.* New York: Morrow, 1983. Deals with Palestinian terrorism; focus on Ali Hassan Salameh.

Bard, Mitchell G. *The Water's Edge and Beyond: Defining the Limits to Domestic Influence on United States Middle East Policy.* New Brunswick, N.J.: Transaction, 1991. Discusses role of American Jews in Middle East policy-making.

Bard, Mitchell G., and Joel Himelfarb. *Myths and Facts: A Concise Record of the Arab-Israel Conflict.* Washington, D.C.: Near East Report. Propaganda pamphlet reflecting perspective of AIPAC (Israel lobby).

Barghuthi, Iyad. *Palestinian Americans: Socio-Political Attitudes of Palestinian Americans Towards the Arab-Israeli Conflict.* Durham, England: Durham University Middle East & Islamic Centre, 1989. Survey of Palestinian-American attitudes; Occasional Paper series.

Barker, A. J. *Arab-Israeli Wars.* London: Allan, 1980. A military history/survey.

———. *Yom Kippur War.* New York: Ballantine Books, 1974. Illustrated history of the 1973 war.

Barnett, Michael N. *Confronting the Costs of War: Military Power, State and Society in Egypt and Israel.* Princeton: Princeton University Press, 1992. Uses Egypt and Israel as model for comparative study of state power and international security considerations.

Bashan, Refa'el. *The Victory: The Six-Day War of 1967.* Chicago: Quadrangle Books, 1968. A laudatory Israeli account translated from Hebrew.

Basisu, Mu'in. *Descent into the Water: Palestinian Notes From Arab Exile.* Wilmette, Ill.: Medina Press, 1980. Memoirs of Palestinian life in Gaza from 1952 to 1963.

Bassiouni, M. Cherif, and Louise Cainker, eds. *The Palestinian Intifada–December 9, 1987–December 8, 1988: A Record of Israeli Repression.* Chicago:

DataBase Project on Palestinian Human Rights, 1989. Documentation of Israeli human rights violations in first year of Intifada.

Bazzaz, Sa'd. *Gulf War: The Israeli Connection*. Baghdad, Iraq: Dar Al-Ma'mun, 1989. Iraqi account, translated from Arabic, of Israel's role in Iraq-Iran War.

Becker, Abraham Samuel. *Israel and the Palestinian Occupied Territories: Military-Political Issues in the Debate*. Santa Monica, Calif.: Rand Corporation, 1971. Report prepared for Defense Department by Rand Corporation.

Becker, Jillian. *The PLO: The Rise and Fall of the Palestine Liberation Organization*. New York: St. Martin's Press, 1984. Critique of the PLO.

Beg, Aziz, and Nasim Ahmad. *Pakistan and the Arab-Israel War*. Lahore, Pakistan: Babur & Amer, 1973. Pakistani account highly critical of Zionism and Israel.

Begin, Menachem. *The Revolt*. Los Angeles: Nash, 1972. Memoirs of IZL, Herut and Likud leader and former Israel prime minister.

Behbehani, Hashim S. H. *China's Foreign Policy in the Arab World, 1955–1975: Three Case Studies*. London: Kegan Paul, 1981. Includes China's policy toward Palestine issue, 1955–73.

Beinin, Joel. *Was the Red Flag Flying There? Marxist Policies and the Arab-Israeli Conflict in Egypt and Israel, 1948–1965*. Berkeley, Calif.: University of California Press, 1990. Study of left-wing and labor political attitudes to conflict.

Beirut Massacre: The Complete Kahan Commission Report. Princeton, N.J.: Karz-Cohl, 1983. Report of Israeli investigation commission on the Sabra and Shatilla massacre.

Beit-Hallahmi, Benjamin. *Original Sins: Reflections on the History of Zionism and Israel*. Boulder, Colo.: Westview Press, 1991. An Israeli Jewish critique of Zionist mythology.

———. *The Israeli Connection: Who Israel Arms and Why*. New York: Pantheon, 1987. Survey of Israeli ties with right-wing regimes in South Africa and Latin America.

Beling, Willard A., ed. *Middle East Peace Plans*. New York: St. Martin's Press, 1986. Compilation of various peace plans for Middle East conflicts.

Bell, J. Bowyer. *Terror Out of Zion: Irgun Zvai Leumi, LEHI, and the Palestine Underground, 1929–1949*. New York: St. Martin's Press, 1977. Account of pre-Israel and early Israeli underground groups.

———. *The Long War: Israel and the Arabs Since 1946*. Englewood Cliffs, N.J.: Prentice-Hall, 1969. Study of Arab-Israeli conflicts from 1946 to 1967.

Bellow, Saul. *To Jerusalem and Back: A Personal Account*. New York: Viking Press, 1976. American Jewish author's description of Israel and its conflict with Arabs.

Ben-Ami, Yitshaq. *Years of Wrath, Days of Glory: Memoirs From the Irgun*. 2d ed. New York: Shengold, 1983. Personal account by IZL participant covering late 1930s to 1948.

Ben-Dak, Joseph, and George E. Assousa. *Peace in the Near East, the Palestinian Imperative*. Muscatine, Iowa: Stanley Foundation, 1974. Occasional paper emphasizing importance of Palestinians to any prospective peace settlement.

Ben-Dor, Gabriel, and David B. Dewitt, eds. *Confidence Building Measures in the Middle East*. Boulder, Colo.: Westview Press, 1994. Collection of papers by an Israeli and an American scholar.

Bendt, Ingela, and James Downing. *We Shall Return: Women of Palestine*. Westport, Conn.: Lawrence Hill, 1982. Portrayal of Palestinian women, mostly in 1970s south Lebanon.

Ben Gad, Yitschak. *Politics, Lies, and Videotape: 3,000 Questions and Answers on the Mideast Crisis*. New York: Shapolsky, 1991. Jewish-Arab relations and Arab politics from an Israeli perspective.

Ben-Meir, Alon. *Israel: The Challenge of the Fourth Decade*. New York: Cyrco Press, 1978. Discussion of Israeli politics, including Arab-Israeli relations.

Ben-Meir, Yehuda. *National Security Decision-Making: The Israeli Case*. Boulder, Colo.: Westview Press, 1986. Study of Israel's security policy.

Ben-Porath, Yoram. *The Arab Labor Force in Israel*. Jerusalem: Falk Institute for Economic Research in Israel, 1966. Israeli economist's survey of Israeli Arab workers.

Benson, Alex. *The 48 Hour War*. New York: IN, 1967. Covers 1967 war.

Bentwich, Norman D. *Israel: Two Fateful Years, 1967–69*. New York: Drake Publishers, 1972. Influence of the 1967 war on Israel.

Bentwich, Norman, and Helen Bentwich. *Mandate Memoirs, 1918–1948*. New York: Schocken Books, 1965. Memoirs of Jewish former high-ranking Palestine British official.

Benvenisti, Eyal. *Legal Dualism: The Absorption of the Occupied Territories into Israel*. Boulder, Colo.: Westview Press, 1990. Examines differences between legal system for Jews and Arab in occupied territories.

Benvenisti, Meron. *Conflicts and Contradictions*. New York: Villard Books, 1986. Personal account of Zionism and Palestinians by former deputy mayor of Jerusalem.

———. *Intimate Enemies: Jews and Arabs in a Shared Land*. Berkeley: University of California Press, 1995. Former Jerusalem deputy mayor discusses Arab-Jewish relations with controversial proposal for a shared Israel/Palestine homeland.

———. *Jerusalem: The Torn City*. Minneapolis: University of Minnesota Press, 1976. Account of ethnic relations in city by Israeli former deputy mayor.

———. *The West Bank Data Project: A Study of Israel's Policies.* Washington, D.C.: American Enterprise Institute, 1984. Extensive data collection on Israel-occupied West Bank.

———. *West Bank Data Project 1986 Report: Demographic, Economic, Legal, Social and Political Developments in the West Bank.* Boulder, Colo.: Westview Press, 1986. Survey of West Bank developments 1884–1985.

———. *The West Bank Data Project 1987 Report: Demographic, Economic, Legal, Social and Political Developments in the West Bank.* Boulder, Colo.: Westview Press, 1987. Survey of West Bank and Gaza development in 1986 and early 1987.

Benvenisti, Meron, with Ziad Abu-Zayed and Danny Rubinstein. *The West Bank Handbook: A Political Lexicon.* Boulder, Colo.: Westview Press, 1986. Extensive collection of data on all aspects of the West Bank.

Benvenisti, Meron, and Shlomo Khayat. *The West Bank and Gaza Atlas.* Jerusalem: West Bank Data Base Project, distributed by the *Jerusalem Post,* 1988. Detailed maps and analysis on demography, water, education, health, etc.

Ben-Zvi, Abraham. *Between Lausanne and Geneva: International Conferences and the Arab-Israel Conflict.* Boulder, Colo.: Westview Press, 1990. Covers peace conferences from 1949 to 1970s; published for Jaffee Center for Strategic Studies, Tel Aviv University.

———. *The United States and Israel: The Limits of the Special Relationship.* New York: Columbia University Press, 1993. Several case studies of "coercive measures" by United States between 1953 and 1991 in relationship with Israel.

Bercuson, David J. *Canada and the Birth of Israel: A Study of Canadian Foreign Policy.* Toronto, Canada: University of Toronto Press, 1985. Detailed study of Canada's policy on Palestine issues to 1949.

———. *The Secret Army.* New York: Stein & Day, 1984. Examines foreign participation in the 1948–49 war.

Beres, Louis Rene, ed. *Security or Armageddon: Israel's Nuclear Strategy.* Lexington, Mass.: Lexington Books, 1986. Papers discussing whether Israel should have nuclear weapons.

Bergen, Kathy, ed. *Justice and the Intifada: Palestinians and Israelis Speak Out.* New York: Friendship Press, 1991. Collection of interviews with Israeli Jews and Palestinian Arabs.

Berger, Earl. *The Covenant and the Sword: Arab-Israeli Relations, 1948–1956.* London: Kegan Paul, 1965. Examines background of the 1948 and 1956 wars.

Berger, Elmer. *Judaism or Jewish Nationalism: The Alternative to Zionism.* New York: Bookman Associate, 1957. Views of a leading American anti-Zionist rabbi.

———. *Peace for Palestine: First Lost Opportunity.* Gainesville: University of Florida Press, 1993. Examines 1949 armistices and early possibilities for peace.

———. *Who Knows Better Must Say So!* New York: American Council for Judaism, 1958. Collection of letters by Berger critical of Zionism and Israel.

Berindranath, Dewan. *War and Peace in West Asia.* New Delhi, India: Topical Publications, 1969. An Indian perspective on Arab-Israeli wars.

Berkman, Ted. *Sabra.* New York: Harper & Row, 1969. Account of 1967 Six-Day War sympathetic to Israel.

Bernadotte, Folke. *To Jerusalem.* Westport, Conn.: Hyperion Press, 1976. Personal account of 1948 conflict by U.N. Palestine mediator.

Bernards, Neal. *The Palestinian Conflict: Identifying Propaganda Techniques.* San Diego, Calif.: Greenhaven Press, 1990. Short monograph discussing perceptions in juvenile literature of Arab-Israel conflict.

Beshir, Mohamed Omer. *Terramedia: Themes in Afro-Arab Relations.* London: Ithaca Press, 1982. Arab-African relations in context of Israel-South Africa ties.

Bethell, Nicholas. *The Palestine Triangle: The Struggle for the Holy Land, 1935–48.* New York: Putnam, 1979. Struggle between British, Arabs and Jews from Arab Revolt to 1948.

Bhargava, G. S. *India and West Asia: A Survey of Public Opinion.* New Delhi: Popular Book Services, 1967. Survey of Indian public opinion on Arab-Israel tensions.

Bhutani, Surendra. *Arab East Today.* New Delhi: Academic Press, 1981. An Indian overview of Arab-Israel conflict, Soviet-Egyptian relations and Arab attitudes to Iraq-Iran war.

———. *The United Nations and the Arab-Israeli Conflict.* Gurgaon, India: Academic Press, 1977. An Indian perspective of the United Nations and the Arab-Israel conflict.

Bialer, Uri. *Armed Forces in Foreign Territories Under the Terms of Peace Agreements: Historical Implications.* Tel Aviv: Tel Aviv University, 1979. Center for Strategic Studies; discusses Israeli bases in West Bank.

———. *Between East and West: Israel's Foreign Policy Orientation 1948–1956.* Cambridge: Cambridge University Press, 1990. An Israeli scholar's study of early Israeli foreign policy.

Bickerton, Ian J., and Carla L. Klausner. *A Concise History of the Arab-Israeli Conflict.* 2d ed. Englewood Cliffs, N.J.: Prentice Hall, 1995. Basic text containing maps, chronology, bibliography, documents.

Bilby, Kenneth. *New Star in the New East.* New York: Doubleday, 1950. Report on Israel's first days by an American reporter.

Guide to Further Research

Bindra, Atam Parkash Singh. *Suez Thrombosis: Causes and Prospects*. Delhi, India: Vikas Publications, 1969. An Indian account of the 1956 Sinai/Suez War and events leading to it.

Binur, Yoram. *My Enemy, My Self*. New York: Penguin, 1990. An Israeli Jewish journalist account of his experiences when disguised as an Arab worker during the late 1980s.

Birkland, Carol. *Unified in Hope: Arabs and Jews Talk About Peace*. New York: Friendship Press, 1988. Interviews with Israeli Jews and Palestinian Arabs on the conflict.

Bisharat, George E. *Palestinian Lawyers and Israeli Rule: Law and Disorder in the West Bank*. Austin: University of Texas Press, 1989. Legal status of Palestine Arabs and rule of law in West Bank.

Black, Ian, and Benny Morris. *Israel's Secret Wars: A History of Israel's Intelligence Services*. New York: Viking Penguin, 1991. Activities of Israel's Mossad against Palestinians and Arab states.

Blake, Gerald H., and Richard N. Schofield, eds. *Boundaries and State Territory in the Middle East and North Africa*. The Cottons, Cambridgeshire, England: Middle East & North African Studies Press, 1987. Collection of articles on Egypt-Israel borders, water, and Middle East maritime boundaries.

Blatt, Martin, Uri Davis and Paul Kleinbaum. *Dissent and Ideology in Israel: Resistance to the Draft, 1948–73*. London: Ithaca Press, 1980. Biographical sketches of Israeli Jewish conscientious objectors.

Blitzer, Wolf. *Between Washington and Jerusalem: A Reporter's Notebook*. Oxford, England: Oxford University Press, 1986. Examines Israel-U.S. relations, Israel and Congress, U.S. Jews.

Blow, Desmond. *"Take Now Thy Son": The Yom Kippur War*. Cape Town, South Africa: Timmins, 1974. Looks at South Africa's involvement with Israel and 1973 October War.

Blum, Yehuda Z. *The Juridical Status of Jerusalem*. Jerusalem: Hebrew University, Papers on Peace Problems, 1974. Presents Israel's legal case for keeping Jerusalem.

———. *Secure Boundaries and Middle East Peace in the Light of International Law and Practice*. Jerusalem: Institute for Legislative Research and Comparative Law, 1971. Legal study of boundaries by Israeli diplomat and law professor.

Bober, Arie, ed. *The Other Israel: The Radical Case Against Zionism*. Garden City, N.Y.: Anchor Books, 1972. Statements issued by radical Matzpen party on Palestine problem, Oriental Jews and Arab citizens and other contemporary issues.

Bonds, Joy, Jimmy Emerman, Linda John, Penny Johnson and Paul Rupert. *Our Roots Are Still Alive: The Story of the Palestinian People*. New York:

Institute for Independent Social Journalism, 1981. A leftist perspective, sympathetic to Palestinians, covering period from the late 19th century to conflict in south Lebanon in late 1970s.

Bondy, Ruth, ed. *Mission Survival: The People of Israel's Story in Their Own Words, From the Threat of Annihilation to Miraculous Victory*. London: Allen, 1968. Based on interviews and personal narratives with Israelis concerning the 1967 Six-Day War.

Bookbinder, Hyman, and James G. Abourezk. *Through Different Eyes: Two Leading Americans, A Jew and an Arab, Debate U.S. Policy in the Middle East*. Bethesda, Md.: Adler & Adler, 1987. Two leading lobbyists debate their respective positions.

Boudreault, Jody, Emma Naughton, and Yasser Salaam, eds. *U.S. Official Statements—Israeli Settlements/the Fourth Geneva Convention*. Washington, D.C.: Institute of Palestine Studies, 1992. Collection of documents on U.S. policy toward Jewish settlements in occupied territories.

Boulding, Elise, ed. *Building Peace in the Middle East: Challenges for States and Civil Society*. Bolder, Colo.: Rienner, 1994. Emphasis on civil society, nongovernmental and intergovernmental roles in Middle East peacemaking.

Boullata, Kamal. *Faithful Witnesses: Palestinian Children Recreate Their World*. New York: Olive Branch Press, 1989. West Bank and Gaza children illustrations of Arab-Israel relations.

Boullata, Kamal, and Mir'enne Ghossein, eds. *The World of Rashid Hussein: A Palestinian Poet in Exile*. Detroit: Association of Arab-American University Graduates, 1979. Essays on life and work of deceased Israeli/Palestinian Arab poet.

Bovis, H. Eugene. *The Jerusalem Question, 1917–1968*. Stanford, Calif.: Hoover Institution Press, 1971. Study of international attempts to deal with the Jerusalem question.

Bowie, Robert R. *Suez 1956: International Crises and the Role of Law*. New York: Oxford University Press, 1974. Examines international legal aspects of 1956 war.

Bowker, Robert. *Beyond Peace: The Search for Security in the Middle East*. Boulder, Colo.: Lynne Riener Publishers, 1996. Examination of security dimensions in the Arab-Israel peace process, including problems of water, defense, regional security.

Bradley, C. Paul. *The Camp David Peace Process: A Study of Carter Administration Policies, 1977–1980*. Hamden, Conn.: Shoe String Press, 1981. Study of U.S. foreign relations with emphasis on Israel-Egypt peace.

Brand, Laurie A. *Palestinians in the Arab World: Institution Building and the Search for State*. New York: Columbia University Press, 1988. Study of Palestinians and their organizations in Egypt, Kuwait and Jordan.

Guide to Further Research

Braverman, Libbie (Levin), and Samuel M. Silver. *The Six-Day Warriors: An Introduction to Those Who Gave Israel Its Vigor and Its Victories*. New York: Bloch, 1969. Brief biographies of Israelis who participated in the Six-Day War.

Brecher, Michael. *The Foreign Policy System of Israel: Setting, Images, Process*. New Haven, Conn.: Yale University Press, 1972. Extensive study of how Israel foreign policy is made and what influences it.

Brecher, Michael, and Benjamin Geist. *Decisions in Crisis: Israel, 1967 and 1973*. Berkeley: University of California Press, 1980. Decision-making in 1967 and 1973 wars; part of the International Crisis Behavior Project.

Brenner, Lenni. *The Iron Wall: Zionist Revisionism From Jabotinsky to Shamir*. London: Zed Books, 1984. Critical study of revisionism and its offshoots—IZL, Lehi, Herut, Likud.

Briefing Papers on Twenty Years of Israeli Occupation of the West Bank and Gaza. Ramallah, West Bank: Al-Haq/Law in the Service of Man, 1987. Examination of Israeli military government and situation of human rights by affiliate of International Commission of Jurists.

Briemberg, Mordecai. *Sand in the Snow: Images of the Middle East in Canadian English-Language Literature and Commentary*. Washington, D.C.: International Center for Research & Public Policy, 1986. Study of pro-Israel and anti-Arab bias, in series of occasional papers dealing with American public opinion and Arab-Israel relations.

Brinner, William, and Moses Rischin, eds. *Like All the Nations? The Life and Legacy of Judah L. Magnes*. Albany, N.Y.: State University of New York: SUNY Press, 1987. Edited papers of Zionist American-Jewish ex-Hebrew University president who favored binational state.

Brook, David. *Preface to Peace: The United Nations and the Arab-Israel Armistice System*. Washington, D.C.: Public Affairs Press, 1964. Study of the 1948 war and 1949 Arab-Israel armistice agreements.

Brookings Middle East Study Group. *Toward Peace in the Middle East: Report of a Study Group*. Washington, D.C.: Brookings Institution, 1975. Report by group of prominent Americans; calls for comprehensive settlement including Palestinian self-determination.

Brookings Study Group on Arab-Israeli Peace. *Toward Arab-Israeli Peace: Report of a Study Group*. Washington, D.C.: Brookings Institution, 1988. Report by group of prominent Americans; calls for study of convening an international conference with Palestinian participation.

Brooman, Josh. *The Arab-Israeli Conflict: Arabs, Jews, and the Middle East Since 1900*. New York: Longman, 1989. Part of Longman's Twentieth-Century History Series.

Brown, L. Dean. *The Land of Palestine: West Bank Not East Bank.* Washington, D.C.: Middle East Institute, 1982. The institute's "Problem Paper 23"; gives an answer to "Jordan is Palestine" argument.

Brown, William R. *The Last Crusade: A Negotiator's Handbook.* Chicago: Nelson-Hall, 1980. Critique of U.S., especially Kissinger's, Middle East negotiations.

Brynen, Rex. *Sanctuary and Survival: The PLO in Lebanon.* Boulder, Colo.: Westview Press, 1990. Study of the PLO's use of Lebanon as a base for armed activities.

Brynen, Rex, ed. *Echoes of the Intifada: Regional Repercussions of the Palestinian-Israeli Conflict.* Boulder, Colo.: Westview Press, 1991. Collection of papers on wider impact of the Intifada.

Budeiri, Musa. *The Palestine Communist Party, 1919–48: Arab and Jew in the Struggle for Internationalism.* London: Ithaca Press, 1979. Arab-Jewish relations in the Palestine Communist movement before 1948.

Buehrig, Edward. *The U.N. and the Palestine Refugees: A Study in Nonterritorial Administration.* Bloomington: Indiana University Press, 1971. Study of the work and administration of UNRWA.

Bull, Odd. *War and Peace in the Middle East: The Experiences and Views of a U.N. Observer.* London: Cooper, 1976. Memoirs of former head of UNTSO during the period of Six-Day War.

Bull, Vivian A. *The West Bank—Is It Viable?* Lexington, Mass.: Lexington Books, 1975. Study of the economy of the West Bank.

Bulloch, John. *Death of a Country: The Civil War in Lebanon.* London: Weidenfeld & Nicolson, 1977. Discusses the role of the Palestinians in early days of civil war.

———. *The Making of a War: The Middle East from 1967 to 1973.* London: Longman, 1974. Discusses background and causes of 1973 war.

Burdett, Winston. *Encounter With the Middle East: An Intimate Report on What Lies Behind the Arab-Israeli Conflict.* New York: Atheneum, 1969. Account of the Six-Day War by an American journalist.

Burns, Gen. E. L. M. *Between Arab and Israeli.* New York: Obolensky, 1963. Experiences of Canadian head of UNTSO and UNEF in 1950s.

Busailah, Reja-e. *We Are Human Too: Poems on the Palestinian Condition.* Wilmette, Ill.: Medina Press, 1970. Poems by a Palestinian-American English professor at Indiana University.

Byford-Jones, W. *The Lightning War.* Indianapolis: Bobbs-Merrill, 1968. Account of the 1967 Six-Day War.

Calvocoressi, Peter. *Suez: Ten Years After.* New York: Pantheon, 1967. British journalist's appraisal of 1956 war and its impact.

Cameron, James. *The Making of Israel.* New York: Taplinger, 1977. Discusses 1947 partition and 1948 Arab-Israel War.

Campbell, R. K. *Sea Power and South Africa: Lessons of the Falklands and Arab-Israel Conflicts*. Pretoria, South Africa: University of Pretoria, Institute for Strategic Studies, 1984. Discusses South Africa and the Arab-Israel conflict.

Caplan, Neil. *Futile Diplomacy, Vol. 1: Early Arab-Zionist Negotiation Attempts, 1913–131* and *Vol. 2: Arab-Zionist Negotiations and the End of the Mandate*. London: Cass, 1983. Documented study of Zionist-Arab contacts, including relevant documents in last half of Volume 2.

———. *The Lausanne Conference, 1949: A Case Study in Middle East Peacemaking*. Tel Aviv: Tel Aviv University, Moshe Dayan Center, 1993. Detailed study of the reasons for failure of 1949 Lausanne Conference.

———. *Palestine Jewry and the Arab Question, 1917–1925*. London: Cass, 1978. The conflict during early British administration of Palestine.

Carter, Jimmy. *The Blood of Abraham*. Boston: Houghton Mifflin, 1985. Former president's observations based on 1983 Middle East visit.

Caspi, Mishael, and Julia Ann Blessing. *Weavers of the Songs: The Oral Poetry of Arab Women in Israel and the West Bank*. Washington, D.C.: Three Continents Press, 1991. Palestinian history and folklore in poetry.

Cattan, Henry. *Palestine and International Law: The Legal Aspects of the Arab-Israel Conflict*. 2d ed. London: Longman, 1976. A Palestinian lawyer's rejection of Zionist claims and Israel's legality; illegality of the Palestine mandate.

———. *The Palestine Question*. London: Croom Helm, 1988. A juridical analysis of Palestine question to 1982.

———. *Palestine, the Arabs and Israel: The Search for Justice*. London: Longman, 1969. Strong presentation by Palestinian international lawyer with proposals for settlement based on "law and justice."

———. *The Question of Jerusalem*. New York: St. Martin's Press, 1981. History of Jerusalem with emphasis on illegal Israeli actions.

———. *To Whom Does Palestine Belong?* Beirut: Institute of Palestine Studies, 1969. Monograph (Series 8) asserting Palestinians' right to all Palestine.

Catudal, Honore M. *Israel's Nuclear Weaponry: A New Arms Race in the Middle East*. London: Grey Seal, 1991. Political history of Israel's nuclear weapons program.

Chace, James, ed. *Conflict in the Middle East*. New York: Wilson, 1969. Influence of the 1967 war.

Chacour, Elias, with David Hazard. *Blood Brothers*. Grand Rapids, Mich.: Chosen Books, 1984. Personal account of a Palestinian Christian priest from his 1948 expulsion from Galilee village to early 1980s.

Chacour, Elias, with Mary E. Jensen. *We Belong to the Land: The Story of a Palestinian Israeli Who Lives for Peace and Reconciliation*. San Francisco:

Harper San Francisco, 1990. Account of Palestinian Christian Melchites (Byzantine rite).
Chafets, Ze'ev. *Double Vision: How the Press Distorts America's Vision of the Middle East*. New York: Morrow, 1984. An Israeli journalist's critique of "anti-Israel bias" of U.S. Press.
Chaliand, Gerard. *The Palestinian Resistance*. Baltimore: Penguin Books, 1972. French journalist's sympathetic account of Palestinian resistance based on his experiences.
Charney, Leon H. *Special Counsel*. New York: Philosophical Library, 1984. Personal account of international lawyer involved in U.S. Middle East policy and Arab-Israel conflict.
Charters, David A. *The British Army and Jewish Insurgency in Palestine, 1945–47*. New York: St. Martin's Press, 1989. Account of the Yishuv's revolt against Great Britain after World War II.
Chesler, Muriel, ed. *A Shield About Me*. Cape Town: Nasionale Boekhandel, 1968. Personal narratives of Six-Day War in letters from Israel.
Chesnoff, Richard Z. *If Israel Lost the War*. New York: Coward-McCann, 1969. Fictional account of disaster to Israel if it lost the Six-Day War.
Childers, Erskine B. *The Road to Suez: A Study of Western-Arab Relations*. London: MacGibbon & Kee, 1962. Western misconceptions of Arabs and 1956 tripartite aggression.
Chill, Dan S. *The Arab Boycott of Israel: Economic Aggression and World Reaction*. New York: Praeger, 1976. Volume in Praeger Special Studies in International Economics and Development; Arab-Jewish relations from 1917.
Chomsky, Noam. *The Fateful Triangle: The U.S., Israel and the Palestinians*. Boston: South End Press, 1984. Strong critique of U.S. pro-Israel policy.
———. *Peace in the Middle East? Reflections on Justice and Nationhood*. New York: Vintage Books, 1974. Essays and reflections by a leading American Jewish scholar supporting Palestinian rights; critical of Israel and United States.
———. *Pirates and Emperors: International Terrorism and the Real World*. Montreal: Black Rose Books, 1987. Critique of conventional wisdom and disinformation in U.S. press about terrorism and neglect of Israel's "state terrorism."
Chouraqui, Andre. *Between East and West: The Jews of North Africa*. Philadelphia: Jewish Publication Society, 1968. Account of Oriental (Sephardi) Jews.
Churchill, Randolph S. *The Six Day War*. Boston: Houghton Mifflin, 1967. Winston Churchill's son's journalistic account.
Clawson, Patrick. *The Economic Consequences of Peace for Israel, the Palestinians, and Jordan*. Washington, D.C.: Washington Institute for Near East Policy, 1991. Monograph in policy papers series.

Cleeve, Roger. *Daughters of Jerusalem*. Bethesda, Md.: Adler & Adler, 1986. Fictional account of the Six-Day War.

Clifton, Tony, and Catherine Leory. *God Cried*. London: Quartet Books, 1983. Pictorial account with narrative of atrocities against Palestinians in 1976 and in 1982 war.

Cobban, Helena. *The Palestinian Liberation Organization: People, Power and Policies*. New York: Cambridge University Press, 1984. Sympathetic, scholarly study of Palestine resistance movement from 1948 to 1980s conflicts in Lebanon.

Cohen, Abner. *Arab Border Villages in Israel: A Study of Continuity and Change in Social Organization*. Manchester, England: Manchester University Press, 1972. An anthropological study of Israeli Arab social change.

Cohen, Aharon. *Israel and the Arab World*. Boston: Beacon Press, 1976. Study of Arab Zionist/Israel relations by Israeli leftist scholar.

Cohen, Akiba, and Gadi Wolfsfeld. *Framing the Intifada: People and Media*. Norwood, N.J.: Ablex, 1993. Jewish-Arab relations and the Intifada as seen in the media.

Cohen, Amnon. *Jewish Life Under Islam: Jerusalem in the Sixteenth Century*. Cambridge, Mass.: Harvard University Press, 1984. Israeli scholar's account of Jewish minority in 16th-century Jerusalem.

———. *Palestine in the 18th Century: Patterns of Government and Administration*. Jerusalem: Magnes Press, 1973. Scholarly account of 18th century Ottoman administration.

———. *Political Parties in the West Bank Under the Jordanian Regime, 1949–1967*. Ithaca, N.Y.: Cornell University Press, 1982. Study of Arab Nationalist Movement, Muslim Brothers, Communist and Liberation parties.

Cohen, Esther R. *Human Rights in the Israeli-Occupied Territories 1967–82*. Manchester, England: Manchester University Press, 1986. An Israeli international lawyer's justification of Israeli policy.

Cohen, Kitty O., and Jane S. Gerber, eds. *Perspectives on Israeli Pluralism*. New York: Israel Colloquium, 1991. Proceedings of conference on pluralism in Israel.

Cohen, Michael J. *Churchill and the Jews*. London: Cass, 1985. Study of Winston Churchill's outlook on Jews and Zionists, 1919–48.

———. *The Origins and Evolution of the Arab-Zionist Conflict*. Berkeley: University of California Press, 1987. Interpretive examination of Arab-Zionist conflict to 1948.

———. *Palestine and the Great Powers, 1945–1948*. Princeton, N.J.: Princeton University Press, 1982. British and American policies on Palestine—mandate's end to 1948.

———. *Palestine: Retreat From the Mandate: The Making of British Policy, 1936–1945*. New York: Holmes & Meier, 1978. Decline of British support for Zionism after Palestine Arab revolt.

———. *Palestine to Israel: From Mandate to Independence*. Savage, Md.: Rowman & Littlefield, 1989. History of the mandate era.

Cohen, Michael J., ed. *The Rise of Israel: Palestine and Arab Federation, 1938–1945*. New York: Garland, 1987. Volume in collection of history sources.

Cohen, Mitchell. *Zion and State: Nation, Class and the Shaping of Modern Israel*. Oxford: Basil Blackwell, 1987. Critical study of Zionism with emphasis on Labor movement.

Cohen, Ramond. *Culture and Conflict in Egyptian-Israeli Relations: A Dialogue of the Deaf*. Bloomington: Indiana University Press, 1990. Examines how Egyptian and Israeli policymakers are beset by difficulties of intercultural communication.

Cohen, Shaul Ephraim. *The Politics of Planting: Israeli-Palestinian Competition for Control of Land in the Jerusalem Periphery*. Chicago: University of Chicago Press, 1993. Examines contentious battle between Israelis and Palestinians over land use in Jerusalem area.

Cohen, Stanley, with Mohammed Haj. *Crime, Justice and Social Control in the Israeli Arab Population*. Tel Aviv: International Center for Peace in the Middle East, 1989. Study of criminal justice system as applied to Israeli Arabs.

Cohen, Yinon. *War and Social Integration: The Effects of the Israeli-Arab Conflict on Jewish Emigration from Israel*. Tel Aviv: Golda Meir Institute for Social & Labour Research, 1987. Monograph on impact of Jewish-Arab relations on emigration.

Collins, Larry, and Dominique Lapierre. *O Jerusalem!*. New York: Simon & Schuster, 1988. French journalist's account of Battle for Jerusalem in 1948 war.

Comay, Michael. *U.N. Peace-Keeping in the Arab-Israel Conflict, 1948–1975: An Israeli Critique*. Jerusalem: Hebrew University, Leonard Davis Institute for International Relations, 1976. Critique of the United Nations by a former high-ranking Israeli diplomat.

Commanders of the Six Day War and Their Battle Reports. Tel Aviv: Ramdor, 1967. Photographs and biographies of 1967 Israeli IDF commanders.

Cooley, John K. *Green March, Black September: The Story of the Palestinian Arabs*. London: Cass, 1973. Discussion of mostly diaspora Palestinians, their organizations, literature and supporters and Israeli perceptions of them.

Congressional Quarterly. The Middle East. 7th ed. Washington, D.C.: 1990. Useful compendium of articles on Middle East oil, Arab-Israel conflict, arms sales, Islam, country profiles, chronology, etc.

Coordinator of Government Operations in Judea & Samaria, Gaza District, Sinai, Golan Heights: A Thirteen Year Survey (1967–1980). Tel Aviv: Ministry of Defense, 1981. Presents Israeli government account of accomplishments.

Corbin, Jane. *The Norway Channel: The Secret Talks That Led to the Middle East Peace Accord.* New York: Atlantic Monthly Press, 1994. Story behind secret negotiations leading to 1993 Oslo accords.

Cordesman, Anthony H. *After the Storm: The Changing Military Balance in the Middle East.* Boulder, Colo.: Westview Press, 1993. Comprehensive survey of military capabilities of Middle Eastern and North African states with historical overview.

———. *The Arab-Israel Military Balance and the Art of Operations: An Analysis of Military Lessons and Trends and Implications for Future Conflicts.* Washington, D.C.: American Enterprise Institute, 1987.

———. *Arms and the Middle East Balance.* Washington, D.C.: Middle East Institute 1983. Study of Jordanian military capability.

———. *The Gulf and the Search for Strategic Stability: Saudi Arabia, The Military Balance in the Gulf, and Trends in the Arab-Israeli Military Balance.* Boulder, Colo.: Westview Press, 1984.

Corm, Georges G. *Fragmentation in the Middle East: The Last Thirty Years.* London: Hutchinson, 1988. Translation of a Lebanese interpretation of how the Middle East has slid "into chaos and anarchy" since 1956.

Cossali, Paul, and Clive Robson. *Stateless in Gaza.* London: Zed Books, 1986. Life in the Gaza Strip under Israeli occupation; position of women.

Crossman, Richard. *Palestine Mission: A Personal Record.* New York: Harper, 1947. Experiences of British MP on Anglo-American Palestine Commission.

Crow, Ralph E., Philip Grant and Saad E. Ibrahim, *Arab Nonviolent Political Struggle in the Middle East.* Boulder, Colo.: Rienner, 1990. Discussion of nonviolent political action in Arab world, including arguments for and against nonviolent tactics in West Bank and Gaza.

Cozic, Charles P., ed. *Israel: Opposing Viewpoints.* San Diego, Calif.: Greenhaven Press, 1994. Covers diverse views on Arab-Israel conflict, Palestinians, etc.

Curtis, Michael, *et al.*, eds. *The Palestinians: People, History, Politics.* New Brunswick, N.J.: Transaction Books, 1975. Collection of articles by diverse specialists.

Curtiss, Richard H. *A Changing Image: American Perceptions of the Arab-Israeli Dispute.* Washington, D.C.: American Educational Trust, 1986. Critique of U.S. policy and influence of Israel lobby.

Cutting, Pauline. *Children of the Siege*. London: Heinemann, 1988. Account of British surgeon in Beirut Palestine refugee camp, 1980s.

Dajani, Souad R. *Eyes Without Country: Searching for a Palestinian Strategy of Liberation*. Philadelphia: Temple University Press, 1994. An attempt to develop theoretical insights from the Intifada.

Damas, Michael J. *The Day Israel Died . . . and Lived*. Philadelphia: Dorrance, 1974. Fiction about early Israel-Arab border conflicts.

Dan, Uri. *To the Promised Land*. New York: Doubleday, 1988. History of Arab-Israel conflicts from late 1920s to late 1940s.

Dann, Uriel. *King Hussein and the Challenge of Arab Radicalism: Jordan, 1955–1967*. Oxford, England: Oxford University Press, 1989. Covers King Hussein's conflicts with Palestinian nationalists.

Darwish, Mahmoud. *The Music of Human Flesh*. Washington, D.C.: Three Continents Press, 1980. Translations of Palestinian poetry.

———. *Sand and Other Poems*. London: KPI, 1986. Translations of leading Palestinian nationalist poet.

———. *Selected Poems*. Chatham, England: W & J Mackey, 1983.

———. *Splinters of Bone: Poems by Mahmoud Darwish*. Greenfield Center, N.Y.: Greenfield Review Press, 1974.

Davis, John H. *The Evasive Peace: A Study of the Zionist-Arab Problem*. Cleveland, Ohio: Dillow Liederbach, 1976. Account of conflict, highly critical of U.S. policy, Israel and Zionists, by former commissioner-general of UNRWA.

Davis, Moshe, ed. *Seminar on World Jewry and the Yom Kippur War*. New York: Arno Press, 1974. Proceedings of seminar in Jerusalem, 1973.

Davis, Uri. *The Golan Under Israeli Occupation, 1967–1981*. Durham, England: Durham University Centre for Middle Eastern & Islamic Studies, 1983. Monograph highly critical of Israeli occupation policies.

———. *Israel: An Apartheid State*. London: Zed Books, 1987. Author charges political Zionism is racist; calls for democratic, unified Palestine state.

———. *Israel: Utopia Incorporated: A Study of Class, State and Corporate Kin Control*. London: Zed Books, 1977. Author charges Zionism/Israel is colonial, controlled by small circle of Israeli Jewish families.

———. *The State of Palestine*. Reading, England: Ithaca Press, 1991. Monograph with author's solution (Palestine state) to conflict.

Davis, Uri, Andrew Mack and Nira Yuval-Davis, eds. *Israel and the Palestinians*. London: Ithaca Press, 1975. Collection of papers, highly critical of Israel, supportive of Palestinian rights, critical of West.

Davis, Uri, and Norton Mezvinsky, eds. *Documents from Israel 1967–1973: Readings for a Critique of Zionism*. London: Ithaca Press, 1975. Translated from Israel press critical of Zionism and Israel policies.

Day, Arthur R. *East Bank/West Bank: Jordan and the Prospects for Peace*. New York: Council of Foreign Relations, 1986. Analysis of Jordan society and policies and relations with Palestinians.

Dayan, David. *Strike First! A Battle History of Israel's Six-Day War*. New York: Pitman, 1968. Account of Six-Day War translated from Hebrew.

Dayan, Moshe. *Breakthrough: A Personal Account of the Egypt-Israel Peace Negotiations*. New York: Knopf, 1981. Memoirs of Dayan and his role in Israel-Egypt peace agreement.

Dayan, Yael. *Israel Journal, June 1967*. New York: McGraw Hill, 1967. Personal narrative by Moshe Dayan's daughter.

———. *A Soldier's Diary: Sinai 1967*. London: Weidenfeld & Nicolson, 1967. Personal narratives.

Death of a Mediator. London: Newman Neame for Institute of Palestine Studies, 1968. Documents related to Bernadotte's work, including 1948 progress report.

Declaration of Principles on Interim Self-Government Arrangements. Jerusalem: Ministry of Foreign Affairs, 1993. Official Israel-PLO agreement on Gaza, Jericho and West Bank.

Dehter, Aaron. *How Expensive Are the West Bank Settlements? A Comparative Analysis of the Financing of Social Services*. Boulder, Colo.: Westview Press, 1987. Detailed study on the cost of West Bank Jewish settlements.

Deonna, Lawrence. *The War with Two Voices: Testimonies by Women From Egypt and Israel*. Washington, D.C.: Three Continents Press, 1989. Portraits of women, in their own words, about suffering from war losses.

De Vore, Ronald M. *The Arab-Israeli Conflict: A Historical, Political & Military Bibliography*. Santa Barbara, Calif.: Clio Books, 1976. Extensive bibliography of books, articles, documents, etc.

Diamond, James S. *Homeland or Holy Land? A Canaanite Critique of Israel*. Bloomington: Indiana University Press, 1986. Views of an Israeli "nativist" faction rejecting Zionism.

Dib, Georges Moussa. *Israel's Violation of Human Rights in the Occupied Territories: A Documented Report*. Beirut: Institute of Palestine Studies, 1970. Critical account of Israel's human rights violations.

Di Giovanni, Janine. *Against the Stranger: Lives in Occupied Territory*. London: Viking Press, 1993. Account of a traveler covering Intifada and territories since 1973.

Dimbleby, Jonathan. *The Palestinians*. New York: Quartet, 1980. Sympathetic account of Palestinian resistance with photos.

Dobson, Christopher. *Black September, Its Short, Violent History*. New York: Macmillan, 1974. Critical account of Palestinian terrorist organization.

Divine, Donna Robinson. *Politics and Society in Ottoman Palestine: The Arab Struggle for Survival and Power*. Boulder, Colo.: Rienner, 1994. Survey of

political, economic and social developments among Palestine Arabs in Ottoman era.
Dodd, C. H., and M. E. Sales. *Israel and the Arab World.* New York: Barnes & Noble, 1970. Collection of documents and readings up to 1968; diverse views.
Dodd, Peter, and Halim Barakat. *River Without Bridges: A Study of the Exodus of the 1967 Palestinian Arab Refugees.* Beirut: Institute of Palestine Studies, 1969. A sociological study based on interviews with 1967–68 refugees.
Donovan, Robert J. *Six Days in June; Israel's Fight for Survival.* New York: New American Library, 1967. Six-Day War compiled from coverage by *Los Angeles Times* staff.
Douglas-Home, Charles. *The Arabs and Israel.* London: Bodley Head, 1970. History of Arab-Jewish/Israel relations sympathetic to Israel.
Downing, David, and Gary Herman. *War Without End, Peace Without Hope: Thirty Years of the Arab-Israeli Conflict.* London: New English Library, 1978. Survey of Arab-Israel conflicts from 1948 to 1978.
Dowty, Alan. *Middle East Crisis: U.S. Decision-Making in 1958, 1970, and 1973.* Berkeley: University of California Press, 1984. Study of U.S. policy-making in Lebanon crisis, 1958; Jordan and PLO, 1970; and 1973 October War.
Draper, Theodore. *Israel and World Politics: Roots of the Third Arab-Israeli War.* New York: Viking Press, 1968. Background and causes of the Six-Day War, sympathetic to Israel.
Draper, Thomas. *Israel and the Middle East.* New York: Wilson, 1983. Covers Israel-Arab relations from late 1940s to 1973.
Drysdale, Alasdair, and Raymond A. Hinnebusch. *Syria and the Middle East Peace Process.* New York: Council on Foreign Relations Press, 1991. Emphasizes importance of Syria in comprehensive peace settlement.
Dumper, Michael. *Islam and Israel: Muslim Religious Endowments and the Jewish State.* Washington, D.C.: Institute of Palestine Studies, 1994. Discusses waqf administration from Ottoman to Israeli times with focus on land question.
Dunkelman, Ben. *Dual Allegiance: An Autobiography.* New York: Crown, 1976. Personal account of Canadian who served in Israel army in the 1948 war.
Dupuy, Trevor N. *Elusive Victory: The Arab-Israeli Wars, 1947–1974.* 3d ed. Dubuque, Iowa: Kendall/Hunt, 1992. Massive study of Arab-Israel wars by American military analyst.
Dupuy, Trevor N. and Paul Nartell. *Flawed Victory—The 1982 War in Lebanon.* Fairfax, Va.: Hero Books, 1985. Extensive military history of Israel's Lebanon war.
EAFORD [International Organization for the Elimination of All Forms of Racism] and AJAZ [American Jewish Alternatives to Zionism]. *Judaism or*

Zionism: What Difference for the Middle East. London: Zed Books, 1985. Compilation of 1983 conference papers critical of Zionism and its impact on the Middle East.

Eban, Abba. *An Autobiography*. New York: Random House, 1977. Autobiography of former Israeli foreign minister and U.N. and U.S. ambassador.

Eden, Anthony. *The Suez Crisis of 1956*. Boston: Beacon Press, 1968. Memoir by Britain's prime minister during 1956 Suez War.

Efrat, Elisha. *Geography and Politics in Israel Since 1967*. London: Cass, 1988. Israeli land settlement, ethnic relations, historical geography.

The Egyptian-Israeli Treaty: Text and Selected Documents. Beirut: Institute of Palestine Studies, 1979.

Eisenberg, Laura Z. *My Enemy's Enemy: Lebanon in the Early Zionist Imagination 1900–1948*. Detroit: Wayne State University Press, 1994. Examination of Zionist-Lebanese relationship based on study of Hebrew and Arabic press, interviews and documents.

Eisenstadt, Michael. *Arming for Peace? Syria's Elusive Quest for "Strategic Parity."* Washington, D.C.: 1990, Washington Institute for Near East Policy. Claims Syria's motivation for joining peace talks is to buy time while acquiring arms to destroy Israel.

———. *The Sword of the Arabs: Iraq's Strategic Weapons*. Washington, D.C.: Washington Institute for Near East Policy, 1990. Discussion of Iraq's strategic forces vis-à-vis Israel.

Eitan, Raphael. *A Soldier's Story: The Life and Times of an Israeli War Hero*. New York: Shapolsky, 1991. Autobiography of Israeli former chief of staff who planned the 1982 war.

Elazar, Daniel J., ed. *Governing Peoples and Territories*. Philadelphia: Institute for the Study of Human Issues, 1982. Papers discussing autonomy with focus on Palestine.

———. *Judea, Samaria, and Gaza: Views of the Present and the Future*. Washington, D.C.: American Enterprise Institute, 1982. Collection of papers on plans for the occupied territory.

———. *Self Rule/Shared Rule*. Ramat Gan, Israel: Turtledove, 1979. Discussion of future of occupied territories.

———. *Self Rule/Shared Rule: Federal Solutions to the Middle East Conflict*. Lanham, Md.: University Press of America, 1984. Reprint of earlier edition; Palestine solutions.

Eliav, Arie L. *Land of the Hart: Israelis, Arabs, the Territories, and a Vision of the Future*. Philadelphia: Jewish Publication Society, 1974. Visionary account of the future by Israeli dove, former Labor party leader.

Elkordy, Abdul-Hafez M. *Crisis of Diplomacy: The Three Wars and After*. San Antonio, Tex.: Naylor, 1971. An Arab account of Arab-Israel conflicts and the role of the United Nations.

Ellisen, Stanley A. *Who Owns the Land?: The Arab Israeli Conflict*. Portland, Oreg.: Multnomah, 1991. Bible prophecies and Jewish-Arab relations.

Elon, Amos. *The Israelis: Founders and Sons*. New York: Holt, Rinehart & Winston, 1971. An Israeli journalist discusses origins of Israel and Zionism.

———. *Jerusalem: City of Mirrors*. Boston: Little, Brown, 1989. Israel's leading journalist's impressions and history of Jerusalem.

Elon, Amos, and Sana Hassan. *Between Enemies: A Compassionate Dialogue Between an Israeli and an Arab*. New York: Random House, 1974. Text of discussion between Israeli journalist and Egyptian woman.

Eppel, Michael. *The Palestine Conflict in the History of Modern Iraq. The Dynamics of Involvement 1928–1948*. Essex, England: Frank Cass, 1994. Discusses the influence of the Palestine conflict on modern Iraq.

Elliot, Elisabeth. *Furnace of the Lord: Reflections on the Redemption of the Holy City*. Garden City, New York: Doubleday, 1969. American missionary's account of trip to Israel after 1967 war, her disillusionment with Israel and sympathy for Palestinians.

Elmessiri, A. W. M. *A Lover From Palestine and Other Poems*. Syracuse, N.Y.: Syracuse University Press, 1970. Collection of Palestinian poetry emphasizing loss of homeland.

Ennis, James, Jr. *Assault on the Liberty: The True Story of the Israeli Attack on the American Intelligence Ship*. New York: Random House, 1980. Account of Israeli attack on U.S. ship in 1967 war and cover-up.

Epp, Frank H. *The Israelis: Portrait of a People in Conflict*. Scottdale, Pa.: Herald Press, 1980. Discusses Jewish-Arab relations, Israeli politics, conflict.

———. *The Palestinians: Portrait of a People in Conflict*. Scottdale, Pa.: Herald Press, 1976. Companion work to portrait of Israelis.

———. *Whose Land Is Palestine? The Middle East Problem in Historical Perspective*. Grand Rapids, Mich.: Eerdmans, 1970. A Mennonite minister's examination of the problem from a religious-historical perspective, sympathetic to Palestinians.

ESCO Foundation for Palestine. *Palestine: A Study of Jewish, Arab and British Policies*. 2 vols. New Haven, Conn.: Yale University Press, 1947. Massive study of problem; vol. 1 covers emergence of Zionism, World War I, to 1929; vol. 2 covers up to 1946 Anglo-American committee.

Eshkol, Joseph. *The Six Days' War*. Tel Aviv: Ministry of Defense, 1967. Official account of Six-Day War with maps and photos.

Evans, Mike. *Israel—America's Key to Survival*. Plainfield, N.J.: 1981. Examines Israel-Arab conflicts with theme of Israel's value to United States.

Evensen, Bruce J. *Truman, Palestine and the Press: Shaping Conventional Wisdom at the Beginning of the Cold War*. Westport, Conn.: Greenwood Press, 1992. Examines role of U.S. media during 1947–48 Palestine crisis.

Evron, Yair. *Israel's Nuclear Dilemma*. Ithaca, N.Y.: Cornell University Press, 1994. Critique of Israel's nuclear policy by leading Israeli strategist.

———. *The Middle East: Nations, Superpowers and Wars*. New York: Praeger, 1973. An Israeli scholar's analysis of strategic implications of conflict for the powers from 1948 to early 1970s.

Fahmy, Ismail. *Negotiating for Peace in the Middle East*. Baltimore, Md.: Johns Hopkins Press, 1983. Critical account of Sadat's peace initiative by Egyptian foreign minister who resigned in protest against it.

Farah, Tawfic E., and Yasumasa Kuroda. *Political Socialization in the Arab States*. Boulder, Colo.: Rienner, 1987. Collection of papers, several on Palestinians, on political attitudes.

Farahat, Albir. *The Sun Rises from the South: The Israeli Aggression Against South Lebanon: Facts and Testimony*. Beirut: Dar Al-Farabi, 1978. Discusses border conflict with Israel after 1948.

Farid, Abdel Majid, and Hussein Sirriyeh, eds. *Israel and Arab Water: An International Symposium*. London: Ithaca Press, 1985. Collection of papers accusing Israel of aspirations to obtain Arab water from Litani in Lebanon, Hasbani in Syria and Nile in Egypt.

el-Farra, Muhammed. *Years of Decision*. London: KPI, 1987. Autobiography of former Jordanian U.N. ambassador during late 1960s.

Farsoun, Samih K. and Christina Zacharia. *Palestine and the Palestinians*. Boulder, Colo.: Westview Press, 1996. Examination of social, economic and political development of the Palestinians from antiquity to the present.

Feinberg, Nathan. *The Arab-Israel Conflict in International Law: A Critical Analysis of the Colloquium of Arab Jurists in Algiers*. Jerusalem: Magnes Press, Hebrew University, 1970. Noted Israeli international law scholar's answer to Arabs.

———. *On an Arab Jurist's Approach to Zionism and the State of Israel*. Jerusalem: Magnes Press, 1971. Feinberg's counter-arguments to Henry Cattan's arguments against Zionism and Israel (see above).

———. *Studies in International Law: With Special Reference to the Arab-Israel Conflict*. Jerusalem: Magnes Press, 1979. Feinberg's addresses, essays, lectures on mandate and Jewish Arab relations.

Feintuch, Yossi. *U.S. Policy on Jerusalem*. Westport, Conn.: Greenwood Press, 1987. Covers U.S. Policy from 1919 to 1980s, based on U.S. and U.N. archives.

Feis, Herbert. *The Birth of Israel: The Tousled Diplomatic Bed*. New York: Norton, 1969. Critique of American and other policy leading to establishment of Israel.

Feldman, Emanuel. *The 28th of Iyar*. New York: Bloch, 1968. Personal narratives of Israelis in 1967 war.

Feldman, Shai. *The Raid on Osiraq: A Preliminary Assessment.* Tel Aviv: Tel Aviv University Center for Strategic Studies, 1981. Analysis of Israel's 1981 air attack on Iraq's nuclear reactor.

Feldman, Shai, and Ariel Levite, eds. *Arms Control and the New Middle East Security Environment.* Boulder, Colo.: Westview Press, 1994. Discusses lessons in other areas for Middle East arms control.

Fernea, Elizabeth Warnock, and Mary E. Hocking, eds. *The Struggle for Peace: Israelis & Palestinians.* Austin: University of Texas Press, 1992. Part of "Perspectives on Peace: The Middle East," a larger project including documentary film with emphasis on peacemaking and coexistence among Israelis and Palestinians.

Feste, Karen A. *Plans for Peace: Negotiation and the Arab-Israeli Conflict.* New York: Greenwood Press, 1991. A study about "negotiation potential."

Feuerlicht, Roberta S. *The Fate of the Jews: A People Torn Between Israeli Power and Jewish Ethics.* New York: Times Books, 1983. Condemnation of Zionism and Israel as incompatible with Jewish ethics.

Feuerwerger, Marvin C. *Congress and Israel: Foreign Aid Decision-Making in the House of Representatives: 1969–1976.* Westport, Conn.: Greenwood Press, 1979. Study of congressional attitudes on aid to Israel.

Findley, Paul. *Facing the Facts about the U.S.-Israeli Relationship.* Brooklyn: Lawrence Hill Books, 1993. Sharp critique of Israel policies and relations with United States.

———. *They Dare to Speak Out: People and Institutions Confront Israel's Lobby.* Westport, Conn.: Lawrence Hill, 1985. Former U.S. congressman's account of media suppression by Israel lobby.

Fischer, Stanley, *et al. The Economics of Middle East Peace: Views from the Region.* Cambridge, Mass.: MIT Press, 1993. Based on 12 papers at Harvard Institute for Social and Economic Policy in the Middle East.

Fischer, Stanley, *et al. Securing Peace in the Middle East: The Project on Economic Transition.* Cambridge, Mass.: MIT Press, 1994. Conclusions of study group on economic transition to peace between Israel and Palestinians.

Fisher, Eugene M., and Cherif Bassiouni. *Storm Over the Arab World: A People in Revolution.* Chicago: Follett, 1972. Sympathetic account of Arab aspirations with focus on Arab-Israel conflict.

Fisher, Roger. *Dear Israelis, Dear Arabs: A Working Approach to Peace.* New York: Harper & Row, 1972. Harvard law professor offers draft exchange of letters.

FitzGerald, Garret. *The Israeli-Palestinian Issue: A Report to the Trilateral Commission.* New York: Trilateral Commission, 1990. The Trilateral Commission's proposals for solving conflict.

Fitzsimons, M. A. *Empire by Treaty: Britain and the Middle East in the Twentieth Century*. Notre Dame, Ind.: University of Notre Dame Press, 1964. Britain's role in the Middle East with some focus on Palestine.

Flamhaft, Ziva. *Israel on the Road to Peace: Accepting the Unacceptable*. Boulder, Colo.: Westview Press, 1996. Reaction of diverse segments of Israeli society to the peace process.

Flapan, Simha. *The Birth of Israel: Myths and Realities*. New York: Pantheon, 1988. Israeli revisionist account of 1948–51 period; presents series of conventional "myths" about Arab-Israel conflict.

———. *Zionism and the Palestinians*. New York: Barnes & Noble Books, 1979. Israeli revisionist history of Zionist-Arab relations in Palestine up to 1948; maintains peaceful solution was possible.

Flapan, Simha, ed. *When Enemies Dare to Talk: An Israeli-Palestinian Debate*. London: Croom Helm, 1979. Text of 1978 debating sessions between Israeli and Palestinian moderates.

Flint, Roy K. *The Arab-Israeli Wars, The Chinese Civil War, and the Korean War*. Wayne, N.J.: Avery, 1987. History Department, West Point Military History Series. Comparative study.

Fofanah, Ibrahim Mohammed. *The Middle East Conflict: An In-Depth Study of the 1973 War as a Catalyst for a Peaceful Settlement*. Lawrenceville, Va.: Brunswick Press, 1991. Discusses U.S. role in conflict and peace possibilities.

For the Record, Intransigence Leads to Escalation: Who Is Responsible. London: The Arab League Office, 1972. Arab League account of the Six-Day War.

Forman, James D. *My Enemy, My Brother*. New York: Meredith, 1969. Fictional account of boy who is released from concentration camp, moves to kibbutz and finds life threatened by Arab-Israel conflict.

Forrest, A. C. *The Unholy Land*. Toronto, Canada: McClelland & Stewart, 1971. Account by Canadian minister of his visit to Middle East, sympathetic to Palestinians.

Frangi, Abdullah. *The PLO and Palestine*. London: Zed Books, 1983. Account of Palestine problem by former PLO/Arab League representative.

Frank, Gerald. *The Deed: The Assassination of Lord Moyne*. New York: Simon & Schuster, 1963. Account of Lehi (Stern Gang) assassination of British minister of state in Cairo in 1944.

Frankel, Glenn. *Beyond the Promised Land: Jews and Arabs on the Hard Road to a New Israel*. New York: Simon & Schuster, 1994. Jewish (Israel)—Arab relations since the 1970s.

Frankel, William. *Israel Observed: An Anatomy of the State*. New York: Thames & Hudson, 1980. Examination of Israeli politics.

Fraser, T. G. *The Arab-Israel Conflict*. New York: St. Martin's Press, 1995. Reevaluation of Arab-Israel conflict in light of recent agreements between Israel and the PLO.

———. *The USA and the Middle East Since World War 2*. New York: St. Martin's Press, 1989. U.S. policy and the Arab-Israel conflicts.

Freedman, Robert O., ed. *The Intifada: Its Impact on Israel, the Arab World, and the Superpowers*. Miami: Florida International University Press, 1991. Edited papers by diverse scholars.

———. *The Middle East Since Camp David*. Boulder, Colo.: Westview Press, 1984. Collection of papers on policies of superpowers, Israel, PLO, etc.

———. *Soviet Policy Toward the Middle East Since 1970*. 3d ed. New York: Praeger, 1982. Detailed study of Soviet Middle East policy with Palestine emphasis.

———. *World Politics and the Arab-Israeli Conflict*. New York: Pergamon Press, 1979. Collection of papers by diverse authors on Middle East and international politics.

Friedlander, Dov, and Calvin Goldscheider. *The Population of Israel*. New York: Columbia University Press, 1979. Demographic trends in Israel and in pre-1948 Palestine.

Friedlander, Melvin A. *Sadat and Begin: The Domestic Politics of Peacekeeping*. Boulder, Colo.: Westview Press, 1983. Study of talks leading to 1979 peace treaty and domestic influences.

Friedlander, Saul, and Mahmoud Hussein. *Arabs and Israelis: A Dialogue*. New York: Holmes & Meier, 1975. Text of three-day dialogue between an Israeli and three Egyptians.

Friedman, Georges. *The End of the Jewish People*. Garden City, N.Y.: 1967. French Jew's argument that Zionism/Israel will cause end of Jewish people.

Friedman, Isaiah. *Germany, Turkey, and Zionism, 1897–1918*. Oxford: Clarendon Press, 1977. Thorough study of German relations with Zionist movement and Ottomans.

———. *The Question of Palestine, 1914–1918: British-Jewish-Arab Relations*. New York: Schocken Books, 1973. Detailed study of diplomacy, Balfour Declaration and Husayn-McMahon correspondence.

Friedman, Isaiah, ed. *The Rise of Israel: Opposition to Zionism, 1919*. New York: Garland, 1987. Collection of sources in series on Israel.

Friedman, Thomas L. *From Beirut to Jerusalem*. New York: Farrar, Straus & Giroux, 1991. Experiences and observations of *New York Times* correspondent covering Middle East & Arab-Israel conflict.

Friesel, Evyatar. *The British, Zionism and Palestine: Perceptions and Policies During the Mandate Period*. Totowa, N.J.: Cass, 1989.

Fromkin, David, *A Peace to End All Peace: Creating the Modern Middle East, 1914–1922*. New York: Holt, 1989. Study of diplomacy leading to post-World War I Arab states and Palestine.

Fuldheim, Dorothy. *Where Were the Arabs?* Cleveland, Ohio: World, 1967. Covers Six-Day War.

Fuller, Graham E. *The West Bank of Israel: Point of No Return?* Santa Monica, Calif.: Rand, 1989. Discussion of West Bank, Intifada and U.S. and Israel policy.

Furlonge, Sir Geoffrey. *Palestine Is My County: The Story of Musa Alami*. New York: Praeger, 1969. Biography of leading Palestinian educator and political figure.

Gabbay, Rony E. *A Political Study of the Arab-Jewish Conflict*. New York: Lounz, 1959. One of the earliest studies, focuses on refugees, compensation, etc.

Gabriel, Richard A. *Operation Peace for Galilee: The Israeli-PLO War in Lebanon*. New York: Hill & Wang, 1984. Apologetic account of Israel's 1982 invasion of Lebanon.

Gainsborough, J. R. *The Arab-Israeli Conflict: A Politico-Legal Analysis*. London: Gower Press, 1986. Analysis of legal and political issues in five major Arab-Israel wars.

Galnoor, Itzhak. *The Partition of Palestine: Decision Crossroads in the Zionist Movement*. Albany: State University of New York Press, 1995. An Israeli scholar's examination of Zionist reactions to 1937 Peel Commission partition proposal.

el-Gamasy, Mohamed Abdel Ghani. *The October War: Memoirs of Field Marshal El-Gamasy of Egypt*. Cairo: American University in Cairo Press, 1993. Memoirs of Egyptian chief of staff and war minister in 1967 and 1973 wars.

Ganin, Avi. *Truman, American Jewry, and Israel, 1945–1948*. New York: Holmes & Meier, 1979. Analysis of Truman's perceptions, attitudes and policies toward Israel.

Garaudy, R. *The Case of Israel: A Study of Political Zionism*. London: Shorouk, 1983. Critique of "myth" upon which Israel was founded.

Garfinkle, Adam M. *Israel and Jordan in the Shadow of War: Functional Ties and Futile Diplomacy in a Small Place*. New York: St. Martin's Press, 1992. Discusses how "functional" ties between Israel and Jordan were more successful than diplomatic negotiations.

Gavron, Daniel. *Israel After Begin: Israel's Options in the Aftermath of the Lebanon War*. Boston: Houghton Mifflin, 1984. Discusses domestic and foreign policy developments after 1982 war.

Gawrych, George W. *Key to the Sinai: The Battles for Abu Ageila in the 1956 and 1967 Arab-Israeli Wars*. Fort Leavenworth, Kan.: U.S. Army Command and General Staff College; dist. Superintendent of Documents,

Washington, D.C., 1990. U.S. Army General Staff College study of Israel-Egypt battles in 1956 and 1967 wars.

Gazit, Mordechai. *The Peace Process, 1969–1973: Efforts and Contacts.* Jerusalem: Magnes Press, Hebrew University, 1983. Critical study by former high-ranking Israeli diplomat.

———. *President Kennedy's Policy Toward the Arab States and Israel: Analysis and Documents.* Tel Aviv: Shiloah Center, Tel Aviv University, 1983. Critical account by Israeli diplomat who participated in events.

Geddes, Charles L. *An Analytical Guide to the Bibliographies on the Arab Fertile Crescent.* Denver: American Institute of Islamic Studies, 1975. Contains a section on the Arab-Israeli conflict.

Geddes, Charles L., ed. *A Documentary History of the Arab-Israeli Conflict.* New York: Praeger, 1991. Annotated documentation collection with bibliography and sources.

George, Donald E. *Israeli Occupation: International Law and Political Realities.* Hicksville, New York: Exposition Press, 1980. Discusses West Bank and Gaza occupation in light of politics.

Gerber, Haim. *Ottoman Rule in Jerusalem 1890–1914.* Berlin: Klaus Schwarz Verlag, 1985. Study of government modernization in Jerusalem province.

Gerner, Deborah J. *One Land, Two Peoples: The Conflict Over Palestine.* 2d ed. Boulder, Colo.: Westview Press, 1994. Good introductory text to Arab-Israel conflict.

Gershoni, Haim. *Israel: The Way It Was.* New York: Cornwall Books, 1989. Biographical account of American Jewish participant in 1948 War.

Gerson, Allan. *Israel, the West Bank and International Law.* London: Cass, 1978. An international lawyer's perspective, supporting that of Israel's government.

Gervasi, Frank. *The Case for Israel.* New York: Viking, 1967. American journalist's fervent presentation of Israeli case from biblical times to post-1967 war.

Ghabra, Shafeeq N. *Palestinians in Kuwait: The Family and the Politics of Survival.* Boulder, Colo.: Westview Press, 1987. Study of Palestinian community and family networks in Kuwait.

Ghanayem, Ishaq I., and Alden H. Voth. *The Kissinger Legacy: American Middle East Policy.* New York: Praeger, 1984. Critical examination of Kissinger's Middle East policies.

Gharaibeh, Fawzi A. *The Economies of the West Bank and Gaza Strip.* Boulder, Colo.: Westview Press, 1985. Examines various sectors of economy and impact on Israeli policies.

Ghareeb, Edmund, ed. *Split Vision: The Portrayal of Arabs in the American Media.* Washington, D.C.: American-Arab Affairs Council, 1983. Collection of studies covering editorials, cartoons, fiction, TV and textbooks illustrating anti-Arab bias in American media.

Giacaman, Rita. *Life and Health in Three Palestinian Villages*. London: Ithaca Press, 1987. Examines health conditions with focus on women and children.

Giannou, Chris. *Beseiged: A Doctor's Story of Life and Death in Beirut*. New York: Olive Branch Press, 1992. Experiences of Canadian surgeon in Palestine Red Crescent hospital in Shatilla refugee camp from 1985 to 1988.

Gilbert, Martin. *Atlas of the Arab-Israeli Conflict*. 6th ed. New York: Oxford University Press, 1993. Covers conflict from biblical era to present with pro-Israel view; 146 maps with some commentary.

———. *Jerusalem: Rebirth of a City*. New York: Viking, 1985. Illustrated account of Jerusalem "Reawakening," 1838–1898.

Gilboa, Eytan. *American Public Opinion Toward Israel and the Arab-Israeli Conflict*. Lexington, Mass.: Lexington Books, 1987. Jewish and American attitudes to Israel and Arab-Israel conflict.

———. *Simulation of Conflict and Conflict Resolution in the Middle East*. Jerusalem: Magnes Press, 1980. Simulation methods in Middle East conflict.

Gilmour, David. *Dispossessed: The Ordeal of the Palestinians, 1917–1980*. London: Sphere Books, 1980. Sympathetic account of Palestinians in Palestine, Israel, occupied territories, diaspora and refugee camps since 1917.

Ginat, J. *Analysis of the Arab Vote in the 1984 Elections*. Tel Aviv: Dayan Center, Tel Aviv University, 1987. Dayan Center for Middle Eastern and African Studies Occasional Paper.

———. *Blood Disputes Among Bedouin and Rural Arabs in Israel*. Pittsburgh, Pa.: University of Pittsburgh Press, 1987. Study by an Israeli scholar on Arab affairs.

———. *Women in Muslim Rural Society: Status and Role in Family and Community*. New Brunswick, N.J.: Transaction Books, 1982. Study of Israel/Palestinian Arab women.

Glassman, Jon D. *Arms for the Arabs: The Soviet Union and War in the Middle East*. Baltimore, Md.: Johns Hopkins University Press, 1975. Soviet policy in the Middle East, Egypt and Arab-Israel conflict.

Glubb, Sir John Bagot. *Peace in the Holy Land: An Historical Analysis of the Palestine Problem*. London: Hodder & Stoughton, 1971. Former British commander of Arab Legion's account of Arab-Israel conflict from ancient era to present; sympathetic to Palestinians.

———. *A Soldier With the Arabs*. New York: Harper, 1967. Autobiography of former British commander of Jordan's Arab Legion.

Goitein, S. D. *Jews and Arabs: Their Contacts Through the Ages*. New York: Schocken Books, 1964. Classic account by Israeli scholar of Jewish/Arab common origins and mutual religious and cultural interactions through the ages.

Golan, Galia. *Moscow and the Middle East: New Thinking on Regional Conflict.* New York: Council on Foreign Relations Press, 1992. Study by Israeli scholar of Cold War's end in the Middle East.

———. *Yom Kippur and After: The Soviet Union and the Middle East Crisis.* London: Cambridge University Press, 1977. Detailed account of Soviet Union's role in 1973 and aftermath.

Golan, Matti. *The Secret Conversations of Henry Kissinger: Step-by-Step Diplomacy in the Middle East.* New York: Quadrangle, 1976. An Israeli journalist's revelations about Kissinger's "shuttle-diplomacy" during 1973–1975.

———. *Shimon Peres: A Biography.* London: Weidenfeld & Nicolson, 1982. Biography of Israeli foreign and prime minister who negotiated peace agreements with PLO and Jordan.

Goldberg, Giora, Gad Barzali and Efraim Inbar. *The Impact of Intercommunal Conflict: The Intifada and Israeli Public Opinion.* Jerusalem: Leonard Davis Institute, Hebrew University, 1991. Policy Studies of Davis Institute, no. 43.

Goldring, Benjamin. *Analytic Study in Treatment of Palestinians in Israel-Occupied West Bank and Gaza, Report of the National Lawyers Guild 1977 Middle East Delegation.* New York: National Lawyers Guild, 1979.

Goodman, Hirsh. *The Future Battlefield and the Arab-Israeli Conflict.* New Brunswick: Transaction Books, 1990. Military analysis by Israel's leading military correspondent.

Goren, Arthur A., ed. *Dissenter in Zion: From the Writings of Judah L. Magnes.* Cambridge, Mass.: Harvard University Press, 1982. Collection of writings from 1900 to 1948 by former president of Hebrew University, critic of Zionism who favored binational state.

Gordon, Haim, and Rivca Gordon, eds. *Israel/Palestine: The Quest for Dialogue.* Maryknoll, N.Y.: Orbis Books, 1991. Dialogue between Jewish Israelis and Palestinian Arabs.

Gordon, Hayim. *Dance, Dialogue, and Despair: Existentialist Philosophy and Education for Peace in Israel.* University, Ala.: University of Alabama Press, 1986. Deals with study and teaching for peace in higher education.

Gorkin, Michael. *Days of Honey, Days of Onion: The Story of a Palestinian Family in Israel.* Berkeley: University of California Press, 1993. Case studies of social conditions and relations of Israeli Arabs.

Gorny, Yosef. *The British Labour Movement and Zionism, 1917–1948.* London: Frank Cass, 1983. Study of British Labor party's stand on Zionism and a Jewish state.

———. *Zionism and the Arabs 1882–1948: A Study in Ideology*. New York: Oxford University Press, 1987. Study of early Zionist ideology toward the "Arab question."

Gothelf, Yehuda. *Israel and the New Left; A Collection of Articles and Essays*. Tel Aviv: World Labour Zionist Movement, 1969. Exchanges between Israeli Laborites and New Left (Socialists and Labor movement).

Gowers, Andrew, and Tony Walker. *Behind the Myth: Yasser Arafat and the Palestinian Revolution*. New York: Olive Branch Press, 1992. Biography of PLO leader Arafat.

Graham-Brown, Sarah. *Education, Repression & Liberation: Palestinians*. London: World University Service, 1984. Study of Palestinian education in relation to national liberation.

———. *Palestinians and Their Society, 1880–1946: A Photographic Essay*. London: Quartet Books, 1980. Collection of photographs with narrative covering rural and urban Palestinians.

———. *The Palestinian Situation*. Geneva: World Alliance of Young Men's Christian Associations, 1989. Palestinian-Israeli relations and conflicts since 1948.

Great Britain, Central Office of Information Reference Services. *Britain and the Arab-Israel Conflict*. London: HMSO, 1993. Survey of official British policy.

Granott, A. *The Land System in Palestine: History and Structure*. London: Eyre & Spottiswoode, 1952. Detailed study of the land system during the mandate.

Green, D. F., ed. *Arab Theologians on Jews and Israel: Extracts From the Proceedings of the Fourth Conference of the Academy of Islamic Research*. 3d ed. Geneva: Editions de l'Avenir, 1976.

Green, Stephen. *Living by the Sword: America and Israel in the Middle East 1968–87*. Brattleboro, Vt.: Amana Books, 1988. Highly critical account of America's "unreserved support" for Israel.

———. *Taking Sides: America's Secret Relations With a Militant Israel*. New York: Morrow, 1984. Highly critical of American support for Israel.

Greenberg, Stanley B. *Race and State in Capitalist Development: Comparative Perspectives*. New Haven: Yale University Press, 1980. Comparative study of ethnic domination of blacks in South Africa and Alabama, Catholics in Northern Ireland and Palestinians in Israel.

Greenwald, Norman D. *Portraits of Power*. Freeport, N.Y.: Books for Libraries Press, 1969. Series of radio and TV lectures (WGBH Boston) dealing with prominent leaders, including one on David Ben-Gurion.

Greffenius, Steven. *The Logic of Conflict: Making War and Peace in the Middle East*. Armonk, N.Y.: Sharpe, 1993. Case studies of decision-making in Middle East wars.

Gresh, Alain. *The PLO: The Struggle Within: Towards an Independent Palestinian State*. 2nd ed. Totowa, N.J.: Zed Books, 1988. Account by French scholar of Palestinian national movement.

Gresh, Alain, and Dominique Vidal. *The Middle East: War Without End?* London: Lawrence & Wishart, 1988. General analysis of Palestinian-Israel struggle and historical roots.

Grose, Peter A. *A Changing Israel*. New York: Vintage Books, for Council on Foreign Relations, 1985. Analysis of changes in Israeli society with trend to binationalism.

———. *Israel in the Mind of America*. New York: Knopf, 1983. History of American attitudes toward and perceptions of Israel.

Grossman, David. *Sleeping on a Wire: Conversations with Palestinians in Israel*. New York: Farrar, Straus & Giroux, 1993. Israeli writer's meetings with country's Arabs who describe their plight as second-class citizens.

———. *The Yellow Wind*. New York: Farrar, Straus & Giroux, 1988. Grossman's meetings and conversations with Arabs in West Bank.

Gruber, Ruth. *Israel on the Seventh Day*. New York: Hill & Wang, 1968. Enthusiastic account of Israel in 1967 Six-Day War.

Guillaume, Alfred. *Zionists and the Bible: A Criticism*. N.p., n.d., no publisher. Brief refutation of Zionist claims to biblical promises.

Gunn, Janet Varner. *Second Life: A West Bank Memoir*. Minneapolis: University of Minnesota Press, 1995. Memoirs of a human rights worker with Palestinians.

Haber, Eitan, Zeev Schiff and Ehud Yarri. *The Year of the Dove*. New York: Bantam Books, 1979. Account of the 1973 war followed by peace negotiations and treaty with Egypt.

Habiby, Emile. *The Secret Life of Saeed: The Pessoptimist*. Columbia, La.: Readers International, 1989. Satirical novel about Arab minority in Israel by noted Israeli Arab writer, a former leader of Communist party.

Hadawi, Sami. *Bitter Harvest: A Modern History of Palestine*, 4th ed. Brooklyn, N.Y.: Interlink Publishing Group, 1991. General history of Palestine conflict by Palestinian scholar.

———. *Palestine: Loss of a Heritage*. San Antonio, Tex.: Naylor, 1963. Evaluation of Palestinian property confiscated by Israel.

———. *The Palestine Problem Before the United Nations, 1966*. Beirut: Institute of Palestine Studies, 1967. Collection of official U.N. documents and proceedings on Palestine.

———. *Palestine Rights and Losses in 1948: A Comprehensive Study*. Atlantic Highlands, N.J.: Saqi Books, 1988. Extensive study and evaluation of Palestinian Arab property left in Israel and work of UNCCP in evaluation; maps, documents, tables.

Haddad, Mohanna Yousuf Salim. *Arab Perspectives of Judaism: A Study of Image Formation in the Writings of Muslim Arab Authors, 1948–1978.* Utrecht: Rijksuniversiteit te Utrecht, 1984. Ph.D. thesis at Utrecht University in Netherlands.

Haim, Yehoyada. *Abandonment of Illusions: Zionist Political Attitudes Toward Palestinian Arab Nationalism.* Boulder, Colo.: Westview Press, 1983. Study of diverse Zionist attitudes toward Palestinians and changes.

Haidar, Aziz. *The Palestinians in Israeli Social Science Writings.* Washington, D.C.: International Center for Research & Public Policy, 1987. Study of what Israeli social scientists write about Arabs.

———. *Social Welfare Services for Israel's Arab Population.* Boulder, Colo.: Westview Press, 1991. Study undertaken with International Center for Peace in the Middle East.

al Haj, Majid. *Arab Local Government in Israel.* Boulder, Colo.: Westview Press, 1990. Part of study of status and condition of Israeli Arabs.

———. *Education, Empowerment and Control: The Case of the Arabs in Israel.* Albany, N.Y.: State University of New York Press, 1994. Part of study of status and condition of Israeli Arabs.

———. *Social Change and Family Processes: Arab Communities in Shefar-A'm.* Boulder, Colo.: Westview Press, 1987. Study of Israeli Arab family structure.

Halabi, Rafik. *The West Bank Story.* Rev. ed. San Diego: Harcourt Brace Jovanovich, 1985. An account by Israeli Druze journalist of West Bank occupation.

Halderman, John W., ed. *The Middle East Crisis: Test of International Law.* Dobbs Ferry, N.Y.: Oceana Publications, 1969. Symposium on legal aspects of Arab-Israel conflict; diverse views.

Halevi, Ilan. *A History of the Jews: Ancient and Modern.* London: Zed Books, 1987. History of Jews with critical emphasis on Zionism as colonialist.

Hallaba, Saadallah A. *Euro-Arab Dialogue.* Brattleboro, Vt.: Amana Books, 1984. Examination of post-1983 Arab-European relations and Palestine.

Halloum, Ribhi. *Palestine Through Documents.* Istanbul, Turkey: Belge Uluslararasi Yayincilik, 1988. Documentary study of Arab-Jewish relations since 1917.

Halperin, Samuel. *The Political World of American Zionism.* Detroit, Mich.: Wayne State University Press, 1961. Study of political influence of American Zionism, 1918–1945.

Halper, Jeffrey. *Between Redemption and Revival: The Jewish Yishuv of Jerusalem in the Nineteenth Century.* Boulder, Colo.: Westview Press, 1991. Sympathetic examination of Jewish community in 19th-century Jerusalem.

Halpern, Ben. *The Idea of the Jewish State*. 2d ed. Cambridge, Mass.: Harvard University Press, 1969. History of political Zionism to 1948; relations with world Jewry.

Halsell, Grace. *Journey to Jerusalem: A Journalist's Account of Christian, Jewish, and Muslim Families in the Strife-Torn Holy Land*. New York: Macmillan, 1981. Halsell's portrayal of Jewish and Arab families with whom she lived; sympathetic account of Palestinian suffering.

———. *Prophecy and Politics: Militant Evangelists on a Path to Nuclear War*. Westport, Conn.: Lawrence Hill, 1986. A critique of American militant evangelists who support Israel.

Halter, Marek. *The Jester and the Kings: A Political Autobiography*. New York: Arcade, 1989. Halter's account of his efforts to bring Jews and Arabs together.

Hammel, Eric M. *Six Days in June: How Israel Won the 1967 Arab-Israeli War*. New York: Scribner's, 1992. Account of the war, its causes, military history; sympathetic to Israel.

Hanna, Paul L. *British Policy in Palestine*. Washington, D.C.: American Council on Public Affairs, 1942. Critical account of British policy during the mandate.

Handel, Michael I. *Perception, Deception, and Surprise: The Case of the Yom Kippur War*. Jerusalem: Leonard Davis Institute, Hebrew University, 1976. Davis Institute for International Relations paper on peace problems.

Har-Shefi, Yoella. *Beyond the Gunsights: One Arab Family in the Promised Land*. Boston: Houghton Mifflin, 1980. Social conditions; Israeli Arab family's relations with Jews.

Harari, Yehi'el, ed. *The Arabs in Israel: Statistics and Facts*. Givat Haviva, Israel: Center for Arab & Afro-Asian Studies, 1972. Factual monograph with statistics on Israeli Arabs.

Hareven, Alouph, ed. *A Chance for Peace: Risks and Hopes*. Jerusalem: Van Leer Jerusalem Foundation, 1980. Jewish-Arab relations, Van Leer Foundation conference papers.

Hareven, Alouph, ed. *Every Sixth Israeli: Relations Between the Jewish Majority and the Arab Minority in Israel*. Jerusalem: Van Leer Jerusalem Foundation, 1983. Collection of scholarly papers and personal accounts by Israeli Jews and Arabs.

Harkabi, Yehoshafat. *Arab Attitudes to Israel*. 2d ed. Jerusalem: Israel Universities Press, 1974. Social psychology analysis based on Arab writings.

———. *Arab Strategies and Israel's Response*. New York: Free Press, 1977. Deals with pre- and post-1967 Arab objectives and Israel's responses.

———. *The Bar Kokhba Syndrome: Risk and Realism in International Politics*. Chappaqua, N.Y.: Rossel Books, 1983. Dangers posed to Israel by its intransigent policies.

———. *Fedayeen Action and Strategy*. London: Institute for Strategic Studies, 1968. Adelphi Paper 53 by former chief of Israeli army intelligence.

———. *Israel's Fateful Hour*. New York: Harper & Row, 1988. Warning about Israel's dangerous policies vis-à-vis Palestinians.

———. *The Palestinian Covenant and Its Meaning*. 2d ed. Totowa, N.J.: Vallentine Mitchell, 1979. Detailed, article-by-article analysis of PLO covenant.

Harkavy, Robert T. *Spectre of a Middle East Holocaust: The Strategic and Diplomatic Implications of the Israeli Nuclear Weapons Program*. Denver, Colo.: University of Denver Graduate School of International Affairs, 1977. Published in Monograph Series in World Affairs.

Harlow, Barbara. *Resistance Literature*. London: Methuen, 1987. Comparative study of resistance literature, including Palestinians; covers poetry, narratives, prison memoirs, etc.

Haron, Miriam Joyce. *Palestine and the Anglo-American Connection 1945–1950*. New York: Peter Lang, 1986. Documented study of U.S.-British policies on Palestine.

Harris, William Wilson. *Taking Root: Israeli Settlement in the West Bank, the Golan and Gaza Sinai, 1967–1980*. Chichester, England: Research Studies Press, 1980. Detailed study of Israeli settlements; maps, statistics, photos.

Hart, Aaron. *A Mortal Danger*. New York: Vantage Press, 1987. Examines Israel's relations with Arab countries.

Hart, Alan. *Arafat, a Political Biography*. Bloomington: Indiana University Press, 1989. Sympathetic account of Arafat and of Palestinian resistance.

Hart, Harold H. *Yom Kippur Plus 100 Days: The Human Side of the War and Its Aftermath*. New York: Hart, 1974. 1973 war as shown through columns of *Jerusalem Post*.

Hart, Vada Nakby. *Burning Hope*. Cairo: Arab Writer, 1967. Novel about 1948–49 Arab-Israel War.

Hashavi, Arye. *A History of the Six-Day War*. Tel Aviv: Ledory, 1969. Translation from Hebrew; Israeli writer's account of 1967 war.

Hassan bin Talal, Crown Prince of Jordan. *Palestinian Self-Determination: A Study of the West Bank and Gaza Strip*. New York: Quartet Books, 1981. Covers West Bank and Gaza 20th-century history and international status.

———. *Search for Peace: The Politics of the Middle Ground in the Arab East*. New York: St. Martin's Press, 1984. Covers Jewish-Arab relations from 1949.

Hattis, Susan Lee. *The Bi-National Idea in Palestine During Mandatory Times*. Haifa, Israel: Shikmona Press, 1970. Study of the bi-national movement in the Yishuv.

Hays, Peter. *Thirteen Days*. London: Cape, 1959. Fictional account of 1948–49 war.

Hazan, Barukh. *Soviet Propaganda: A Case Study of the Middle East Conflict.* New York: Wiley, 1976. Examines Soviet propaganda (1945–79) and Arab-Israel conflict.

Hazelton, Lesley. *Jerusalem, Jerusalem: A Memoir of War and Peace, Passion and Politics.* New York: Penguin Books, 1987. Passionate portrayal by ex-Israeli disillusioned by experiences.

Heiberg, Marianne, and Geir Ovensen. *Palestinian Society in Gaza, West Bank and Arab Jerusalem: A Survey of Living Conditions.* Oslo, Norway: FAFO (Institute for Applied Social Science), 1993. Extensive survey of 2,500 Palestinian households covering health, education, status of women, employment and political views.

Heikal, Mohammed Hasanayn. *Autumn of Fury: The Assassination of Sadat.* New York: Random House, 1983. Unflattering account of Sadat by former associate and editor of Egypt's leading daily and former diplomat.

Heikal, Mohammed H. *The Cairo Documents: The Inside Story of Nasser and His Relationships with World Leaders.* New York: Doubleday, 1973. First-hand account of Nasser's relations with Dulles, Eden, Khruschev, Hammarskjöld, Kennedy, Johnson, Tito, Nehru and others.

———. *The Road to Ramadan.* New York: Balantine, 1977. Heikal's account of 1973 war and events from 1967 leading to war.

———. *The Sphinx and the Commissar: The Rise and Fall of Soviet Influence in the Middle East.* New York: Harper & Row, 1978. Author's account of his experiences as personal advisor to Nasser.

Heckelman, A. Joseph. *American Volunteers and Israel's War of Independence.* New York: KTAV, 1974. American volunteers' participation in 1948–49 war.

Heller, Mark. *A Palestinian State: The Implications for Israel.* Cambridge, Mass.: Harvard University Press, 1983. An Israeli proposal for Palestinian self-determination and its political, economic and security implications for Israel.

Heller, Mark, and Sari Nusseibeh. *No Trumpets, No Drums: A Two-State Settlement of the Israeli-Palestinian Conflict.* New York: Hill & Wang, 1991. Compromise peace proposals of Israeli Jew and Palestinian Arab.

Hempstone, Smith. *In the Midst of Lions.* New York: Harper & Row, 1968. Novel about the 1967 war.

Hen-Tov, Jacob. *Communism and Zionism in Palestine: The Comintern and the Political Unrest in the 1920's.* Cambridge, Mass.: Schenkman, 1974. Study of Comintern's relations with Palestine Communist Party, emphasis on 1929 Wailing Wall riots.

Hershlag, Z. Y., ed. *The Economic Implications of Peace in the Middle East.* Tel Aviv: Tel Aviv University, David Horowitz Institute, 1973. Research report of David Horowitz Institute for the Research of Developing Countries.

Hertzberg, Arthur, ed. *The Zionist Idea: A Historical Analysis and Reader*. New York: Atheneum, 1972. Collection of Zionist writings from 1847 to 1944.

Herzl, Theodor. *The Complete Diaries of Theodor Herzl*. Edited by Raphael Patai. New York: Herzl Press, 1960. Covers period from 1895 to 1904.

———. *Diaries of Theodor Herzl*. Edited by Marvin Lowenthal. New York: Grosset & Dunlap, 1982. Selections from Herzl's diaries.

———. *The Jewish State: An Attempt at a Modern Solution of the Jewish Question*. London: Central Office of Zionist Organization, 1934. Herzl's pamphlet leading to first World Zionist Congress in 1897.

Herzog, Chaim. *The Arab-Israeli Wars: War and Peace in the Middle East*. Rev. ed. New York: Vintage Books, 1984. History of Israel's wars by former Israeli general, diplomat and president.

———. *The War of Atonement, October, 1973*. Boston: Little Brown, 1975. Account of the 1973 war by former Israeli general.

Hewat, Tim, ed. *War File*. London: Panther, 1967. Items about 1967 war.

Hiltermann, Joost R. *Behind the Intifada: Labor and Women's Movements in the Occupied Territories*. Princeton, N.J.: Princeton University Press, 1991. Detailed discussion of diverse Palestinian women's organizations.

———. *Israel's Deportation Policy in the Occupied West Bank and Gaza*. Ramallah, West Bank: Al-Haq/Law in the Service of Man, affiliate of International Commission of Jurists, 1988. Documented study of Israel's 1985 deportation of Palestinians.

Hirst, David. *The Gun and the Olive Branch: The Roots of Violence in the Middle East*. New York: Harcourt Brace Jovanovich, 1977. British journalist's account of Palestine conflict, sympathetic to Palestinians, critical of Zionists and Israel.

Hirst, David, and Irene Beeson. *Sadat*. London: Faber & Faber, 1982. Critical account of Sadat's peace arrangements with Israel.

Hof, Frederic C. *Galilee Divided: The Israeli-Lebanon Frontier, 1916–1984*. Boulder, Colo.: Westview Press, 1985. Study of border issues between Israel and Lebanon, tracing roots to post-World War I agreements; deals with issues such as water, etc.

Hofman, John E., *et al*. *Arab-Jewish Relations in Israel: A Quest in Human Understanding*. Bristol, Ind.: Wyndham Hall Press, 1988. Collection of scholarly papers written by both Israeli Jews and Arabs.

Horowitz, Dan, and Moshe Lissak. *Origins of the Israeli Polity: Palestine Under the Mandate*. Chicago: University of Chicago Press, 1978. Impact of the Yishuv before 1948 on state of Israel after 1948.

Houston, S. J. *Conflict in Palestine*. New York: Longman, 1989. Study of Arab Israeli conflicts from 1917 to 1949.

Howard, Harry N. *The King-Crane Commission: An American Inquiry in the Middle East*. Beirut: Khayats, 1963. Scholarly study of commission sent by President Woodrow Wilson to Middle East after World War I to determine wishes of inhabitants.

Howe, Irving, and Carl Gershman, eds. *Israel, the Arabs, and the Middle East*. New York: Quadrangle Books, 1972. Collection of addresses, essays and lectures on Arab-Jewish relations.

Hudson, Michael, ed. *Alternative Approaches to the Arab-Israeli Conflict: A Comparative Analysis of the Principal Actors*. Washington, D.C.: Georgetown University Center for Contemporary Arab Studies, 1980. Papers on Israeli, Arab, Soviet and U.S. approaches to the conflict.

Hudson, Michael, and Ronald G. Wolfe, eds. *The American Media and the Arabs*. Washington, D.C.: Georgetown University Center for Contemporary Arab Studies, 1980. Symposium papers from conference on treatment of Arabs in media.

Hudson, Michael C. *Arab Politics: The Search for Legitimacy*. New Haven, Conn.: Yale University Press, 1977. Analysis of Arab politics with emphasis concerning Palestine.

Hunt, Paul. *Justice? The Military Court System in the Israeli-Occupied Territories: Including an Introduction to Relevant International Human Rights and Humanitarian Law*. Ramallah, West Bank: Al-Haq, 1987. Sharp critique of Israeli courts' human rights violations.

Hunter, F. Robert. *The Palestinian Uprising: A War by Other Means*. Berkeley: University of California Press, 1991. Study of the first two and one-half years of the Intifada.

Hurewitz, J. C. *The Struggle for Palestine*. New York: Schocken Books, 1976. Detailed study of Palestine under the mandate, including 1948 war and establishment of Israel.

Hurewitz, J. C., ed. *Oil, The Arab-Israeli Dispute, and the Industrial World: Horizons of Crisis*. Boulder, Colo.: Westview Press, 1976. Collection of essays from Middle East Institute Conference.

Hurwitz, Deena, ed. *Walking the Red Line: Israelis in Search of Justice for Palestine*. Philadelphia: New Society Publishers, 1992. Discussion of Israelis, Palestinians and human rights.

Hussaini, Hatem I. *The Arab Israeli Conflict: An Annotated Bibliography*. Washington, D.C.: Palestine Information Office, 1980. Bibliography presenting Arab viewpoint with lengthy annotations.

Hussein, King, of Jordan. *My 'War' With Israel*. New York: Morrow, 1969. King's account of 1967 conflict as told to two journalists.

Hussein, Mahmoud, and Saul Friedlander. *Arabs & Israelis: A Dialogue*. New York: Holmes & Meier, 1975. Dialogue between Israeli and Arab moderated by Jean Lacouture.

Hutchinson, Elmo H. *Violent Truce: A Military Observer Looks at the Arab-Israeli Conflict, 1951–1955*. New York: Devin-Adair, 1956. Memoir of U.S. naval commander who served with UNTSO; highly critical of Israel.

Hyamson, Albert M. *Palestine Under the Mandate*. London: Methuen, 1950. Account by Jewish former high-ranking British mandatory official.

Ilan, Amitzur. *Bernadotte in Palestine, 1948: A Study in Contemporary Humanitarian Knight-Errantry*. New York: St. Martin's Press, 1989. Covers U.N. mediator's role in Palestine conflict, 1948–49.

Indian Society of International Law. *The Arab-Israel Conflict: Documents & Comments*. New Delhi: 1967. An Indian perspective.

Indinopulos, Thomas A. *Jerusalem Blessed, Jerusalem Cursed: Jews, Christians, and Muslims in the Holy City from David's Time to Our Own*. Chicago: Ivan R. Dee, 1991. Discusses the three religion's claims, with emphasis on Jewish.

Ingrims, Doreen, ed. *Palestine Papers, 1917–1922: Seeds of Conflict*. New York: Braziller, 1973. Excerpts from important documents with explanations.

Insight Team of the *London Sunday Times*. *Insight on the Middle East War*. Garden City, New York: Doubleday, 1974. Expanded articles on 1973 war from *London Sunday Times*.

Institute for Palestine Studies (IPS). *The Arab-Israeli Armistice Agreements, February–July 1949: U.N. Texts and Annexes*. Beirut: IPS, 1967. Collection of armistice documents.

———. *Documents on Palestine*. Kuwait: Kuwait University, annual from 1967 to 1977. Documents from United Nations, Israel and Arab and other countries.

———. *The Palestinian-Israeli Peace Agreement: A Documentary Record*. Washington, D.C.: IPS, 1994. Extensive collection of major documents from Camp David Accords to 1993 Declaration of Principles.

———. *A Survey of Palestine*. Washington, D.C.: IPS, 1991. Reprint of two volumes and supplement prepared by Palestine mandatory government, 1945–1947, for international investigation commissions.

———. *United Nations Resolutions on Palestine and the Arab-Israeli Conflict, 1947–1991*. 4 vols. Washington, D.C.: IPS, 1988–93. Four volumes that include U.N. resolutions from 1947 to 1991.

———. *U.S. Official Statements*. 5 vols. (*The Palestinian Refugees*; *Golan Heights*; *Status of Jereusalem*; *Israeli Settlements /Fourth Geneva Convention*; *UN Resolution 242*). Washington, D.C.: IPS, 1992–94. Official statements by U.S. government on conflict issues.

International Conference on the Question of Palestine. *Report of the International Conference on the Question of Palestine: Geneva, Aug. 29–Sept. 7, 1983*. New York: United Nations, 1983. First international meeting of nongovernmental organizations (NGOs) on the question of Palestine.

International NGO Meeting on the Question of Palestine (Geneva-1984). New York: United Nations, Division for Palestine Rights, 1985.

International Symposium on Israeli Settlements in the Occupied Arab Territories (Washington, 1985). New York: League of Arab States, 1979. Covers period of Israeli settlement from 1967.

International Symposium on the Military Aspects of the Arab-Israeli Conflict, Jerusalem, Israel, 1975. Tel Aviv: University Publications Projects, 1975. Report on symposium conducted under patronage of Defense Minister Shimon Peres.

The Investigation Commission to Investigate the Events in the Refugee Camps in Beirut. *The Beirut Massacre: The Complete Kahan Commission Report*. Princeton, N.J.: Karz-Cohl, 1983. Official Israeli government report on Sabra and Shatilla massacres.

Irani, George E. *The Papacy and the Middle East: The Role of the Holy See in the Arab-Israeli Conflict, 1962–1984*. Notre Dame, Ind.: University of Notre Dame Press, 1986. Scholarly study of Vatican's role in Arab-Israel conflict, including Jerusalem, from Second Vatican Council in 1984.

The Iraqi Nuclear Threat—Why Israel Had to Act. Jerusalem: Ministry of Foreign Affairs, Atomic Energy Commission, 1981. Israel's account and explanation of bombing Iraq's nuclear plant at Osirak in 1981.

Isaac, Rael Jean. *Israel Divided: Ideological Politics in the Jewish State*. Baltimore, Md.: Johns Hopkins University Press, 1976. Examination of nationalist Land of Israel Movement and Israeli peace movements.

———. *Party and Politics in Israel: Three Visions of a Jewish State*. New York: Longman, 1981. Compares three principal trends in Israeli politics and their views and perceptions of Arab-Israel relations.

Islamic Summit. *Report on Second Islamic Summit, 1974, Lahore, Pakistan, February 22–24, 1974*. Islamabad: Pakistan Ministry of Information & Broadcasting, 1974. Official discussions of Israel-Arab conflict.

Israel Ministry of Foreign Affairs. *Israel's Peace Offers to the Arab States, 1948–1963*. Jerusalem: Ministry of Foreign Affairs, 1963. Israeli government presentation of peace offers.

Israeli, Raphael. *Muslim Fundamentalism in Israel*. London: Brassey's, 1993. Case study based on three Israeli Arab villages.

———. *Palestinians Between Israel and Jordan: Squaring the Triangle*. New York: Praeger, 1991. Discusses relations between Israelis and Palestinians.

———. *Peace in the Eye of the Beholder*. New York: Mouton, 1985. Discusses Arab perceptions of Israel, anti-semitism, peace.

The Israeli Army and the Intifada: Policies that Contribute to the Killings. New York: Middle East Watch, 1990. Middle East Watch (affiliated with Amnesty International) report.

Israeli Obstacles to Economic Development in the Occupied Territories. Jerusalem: Jerusalem Media & Communications Centre, 1992. Study of West Bank economic conditions; Israel government policies.

Jabara, Abdeen, and Janice Terry, eds. *The Arab World From Nationalism to Revolution.* Wilmette, Ill.: Medina University Press, 1971. Collection of papers on world's media and Arabs, Zionism and Palestine.

Jabbour, Hala Deeb. *A Woman of Nazareth.* New York: Olive Branch Press, 1989. Fictional account of uprooted Palestinian woman.

Jabra, Jabra I. *Hunters in a Narrow Street.* Washington, D.C.: Three Continents Press, n. d. Novel about diaspora Palestinians in Baghdad during 1940s.

———. *The Ship.* Washington, D.C.: Three Continents Press, 1985. Novel of post-1948 Palestinian exile in symbolic terms.

Jackson, Elmore. *Middle East Mission: The Story of a Major Bid for Peace in the Time of Nasser and Ben-Gurion.* New York: Norton, 1983. Memoir of American Quaker on Middle East peace mission.

Jacobs, Paul. *Between the Rock and the Hard Place.* New York: Random House, 1970. Journalist's account of efforts to bring Jews and Arabs together.

Jammal, Laila. *Contributions of Palestinian Women to the National Struggle for Liberation.* Washington, D.C.: Middle East Public Relations, 1985. Women in Palestinian nation movement; women political prisoners.

Jansen, G. H. *Zionism, Israel and Asian Nationalism.* Institute for Palestine Studies, Beirut: 1971. Indian journalist presents Zionism as European colonial movement.

Jansen, Michael E. *The Battle of Beirut: Why Israel Invaded Lebanon.* London: Zed Books, 1982. Strong condemnation of Israel's actions in 1982 invasion.

———. *Dissonance in Zion.* London: Zed Books, 1987. Examines conflict between Israeli peace movement and right wing.

Japheth, Maurice David, and P. K. Rajiv. *The Arab Israel Conflict: An Indian Viewpoint.* Bombay, India: Pearl Publications, 1967. Covers Arab-Israel conflict from 1949 to 1967.

Jayyusi, Selma Khadra, ed. *Anthology of Modern Palestinian Literature.* New York: Columbia University Press, 1992. Largest and most comprehensive anthology of Palestinian literary writing in Western language with selections from some 100 20th-century Palestinian authors.

Jeffries, J. M. N. *Palestine: The Reality.* Westport, Conn.: Hyperion Press, 1976. Extensive presentation of Arab case; strongly condemns Britain.

Jeryis, Naseem. *Small-Scale Enterprises in Arab Villages: A Case Study from the Galilee Region in Israel.* Uppsala, Sweden: Uppsala University, 1990. Analysis of characteristics and development of small-scale Arab enterprises in northern Israel.

Jiryis, Sabri. *The Arabs in Israel, 1948–1966*. 2d ed. New York: Monthly Review Press, 1976. Former Israeli Arab's examination of Israeli discrimination.

John, Robert, and Sami Hadawi. *The Palestine Diary*. 2d ed. 2 vols. New York: New World Press, 1971. Extensive documentation of Palestine question; vol. 1 covers British involvement from World War I to 1945, vol. 2 from end of World War II to 1948.

Johnson, Nels. *Islam and the Politics of Meaning in Palestinian Nationalism*. London: Kegan Paul, 1982.

Jones, Christina. *The Untempered Wind: Forty Years in Palestine*. London: Longman, 1975. Autobiography of Christian missionary in Palestine from 1922 to 1956; sympathetic to Palestinian Arabs.

Jones, Martin. *Failure in Palestine: British and United States Policy After the Second World War*. London: Mansell, 1986. Critical account of British policy for failure to adopt divide-and-rule Arab policy; extensive use of British archives.

Jubran, Glenn M. *Our Struggle: The Palestine Revolution, 1968–70*. New York: Vantage Books, 1972. Examines role of Palestinian guerrillas (fedayeen) in conflict.

Judea-Samaria and the Gaza District Since 1967. Jerusalem: Israel Information Center, 1986. Israeli government's account of accomplishments in first two decades of occupation.

Jureidini, Paul, and William E. Huzen. *The Palestinian Movement in Politics*. Lexington, Mass.: Lexington Books, 1976. Examines Palestinian movement from 1920s to 1975 with attention to guerrilla organizations and relations with Arab states.

Kadi, Leila S. *Arab Summit Conferences and the Palestine Problem 1934–1950*. Beirut: Palestine Research Center, 1966. Examines how Arab summit conferences dealt with Palestine issue.

———. *The Arab-Israeli Conflict: The Peaceful Proposals, 1948–1972*. Beirut: Palestine Research Center, 1973. Examines Arab peace proposals from 1948 to 1972.

Kahalani, Avigdor. *The Heights of Courage: A Tank Leader's War on the Golan*. New York: Praeger, 1992. An Israeli officer's account of June 1973 war on Golan Heights.

Kahan, David. *Agriculture and Water Resources in the West Bank and Gaza (1967–1987)*. Boulder, Colo.: Westview Press, 1987. Discusses Palestinian and Jewish agriculture in occupied territories and possibilities of development.

Kahane, Rabbi Meir. *Israel: Revolution or Referendum*. Secaucus, N.J.: Barricade Books, 1990. Hard-line position by assassinated American-Israeli political activist; attacks Israeli government for "soft" position toward Arabs.

———. *They Must Go*. New York: Grosset & Dunlap, 1981. Presents position that Israel must get rid of Arab population.

Kaleh, Hala, and Simonetta Calderini. *The Intifada—The Palestinian Uprising in the West Bank and Gaza Strip: A Bibliography of Books and Articles 1987–1992*. Oxford: Middle East Libraries Committee, Oxford Middle East Centre, 1993. Index of major monographs and journal and magazine articles on first five years of Intifada.

Kally, Elisha, and Gideon Fishelson. *Water and Peace: Water Resources and the Arab-Israeli Peace Process*. Westport, Conn.: Praeger, 1993. Covers water rights, conflict and development; published in cooperation with Armand Hammer Fund for Economic Development in Middle East.

Kamel, Mohammed Ibrahim. *The Camp David Accords: A Testimony*. Boston: Routledge & Kegan Paul, 1986. Account by Sadat's foreign minister who resigned in protest against Camp David accords.

Kanafani, Ghassan. *Men in the Sun and Other Palestinian Stories*. Washington, D.C.: Three Continents Press, 1983. Fictional accounts of Palestinian condition by Palestinian author and political figure (assassinated by Israeli intelligence).

———. *Palestine's Children*. Washington, D.C.: Three Continents Press, 1984. Stories of Palestinian life through child's eyes.

Kana'nah, Sharif. *Socio-Cultural and Psychological Adjustment of the Arab Minority in Israel*. San Francisco: R & E Research, 1976. Social conditions and their impact on Israeli Arabs.

Kanofsky, Eliahu. *The Economic Impact of the Six-Day War; Israel, the Occupied Territories, Egypt, Jordan*. New York: Praeger, 1970. Economic analysis by an Israeli/American economist.

Karetzky, Stephen, and Norman Frankel, eds. *The Media's Coverage of the Arab-Israeli Conflict*. New York: Shapolsky, 1989. How the *New York Times* covers and influences public opinion on the Arab-Israel conflict and the Intifada.

Kark, Ruth. *Jaffa: A City in Evolution, 1799–1917*. Jerusalem: Yad Izhak Ben-Zvi Press, 1990. Analysis of political, demographic, social, economic and regional factors shaping Jaffa's development in 19th century.

———. *Jerusalem Neighborhoods: Planning and By-Laws (1855–1930)*. Jerusalem: Magnes Press, 1991. Some 80 by-laws dealing with Jerusalem neighborhoods.

The Karp Report: An Israeli Government Inquiry into Settler Violence Against Palestinians on the West Bank. Washington, D.C.: Institute for Palestine Studies, 1984. English translation from Hebrew of report by Israel's deputy attorney general.

Karsh, Efraim. *The Cautious Bear: Soviet Military Engagement in Middle East Wars in the Post-1967 Era*. Boulder, Colo.: Westview Press, 1986. Military analysis for Jaffee Center Strategic Studies, Tel Aviv.

Karsh, Efraim, ed. *Peace in the Middle East: The Challenge for Israel.* Essex, England: 1994. Various authors discuss the implications of peace for Israel.

Kasher, Aryeh. *Jews, Idumaeans, and Ancient Arabs: Relations of the Jews in Eretz-Israel With the Nations of the Frontier and the Desert in the Hellenistic and Roman Era (332 B.C.E.–70 C.E.)*. Tubingen: Mohr, 1988. Covers Maccabees, Edomites and early Jewish-Arab relations.

Kass, Ilana. *Soviet Involvement in the Middle East: Policy Formulation, 1966–1973*. Boulder, Colo.: Westview Press, 1978. Covers Soviet involvement in Arab-Israel conflict.

Kassim, Anis F., ed. *The Palestine Yearbook of International Law*. Nicosia, Cyprus: Al-Shaybani Society of International Law, 1984–85. Articles, texts and documents on legal aspects of Palestine problem.

Katz, Shmuel. *Battleground: Fact and Fantasy in Palestine*. New York: Bantam Books, 1973. Katz's "exposé" of media bias against Israel.

———. *Follow Me! A History of Israel's Military Elite*. London: Arms and Armour, 1989. Study of Israel's military leaders.

———. *Guards Without Frontiers: Israel's War Against Terrorism*. London: Arms & Armour, 1990. Examination of Israel's anti-terrorism policies.

———. *Israel's Tank Battles: Yom Kippur to Lebanon*. London: Arms & Armour, 1988. Covers Israeli tank activities in 1973 and 1982 (Lebanon) wars.

Kaufman, Edy, Shukri Abed and Robert L. Rothstein, eds. *Democracy, Peace, and the Israeli-Palestinian Conflict*. Boulder, Colo.: Rienner, 1993. Papers discussing possibilities of sustaining democracy in Israel and among Palestinians in context of the conflict.

Kayyali, Abdul Wahhab. *Palestine: A Modern History*. London: Croom Helm, 1979. Chronological history of Palestine from 1881 to 1939.

Kayyali, Abdul Wahhab, ed. *Zionism, Imperialism and Racism*. London: Croom Helm, 1978. Essays on imperialist and racist nature of Zionism.

Kazziha, Walid W. *Palestine in the Arab Dilemma*. New York: Barnes & Noble, 1979. Essays on the Palestinians and the Arab world; Lebanese Civil War; Sadat's peace initiative; critical of Arab regimes.

———. *Revolutionary Transformation in the Arab World: Habash and His Comrades from Nihilism to Marxism*. New York: St. Martin's Press, 1975. Study of how the Arab nationalist movement spawned the Popular Front for the Liberation of Palestine and other leftist Arab movements.

Kedourie, Elie. *Arabic Political Memoirs and Other Studies*. London: Cass, 1974. Essays on Arab nationalism in the 19th and 20th centuries.

Kedourie, Elie, and Sylvia Haim, eds. *Palestine and Israel in the 19th and 20th Centuries*. London: Cass, 1982. Collection of articles from *Middle Eastern Studies* published in London.

———. *Zionism and Arabism in Palestine and Israel*. London: Cass, 1982. Collection of papers on various aspects of Palestine problem.

Keesing's Research Report. *The Arab-Israeli Conflict: The 1967 Campaign*. New York: Scribner's, 1968. Extracts from *Keesing's Contemporary Archives*.

Keller, Adam. *Terrible Days: Social Divisions and Political Paradoxes in Israel*. Amstelveen, The Netherlands: Cypres, 1987. Discussion of Israelis opposed to government's Arab policies.

Kelman, Herbert C. *Understanding Arafat*. Tel Aviv: International Center for Peace in the Middle East, 1983. Short monograph sympathetic to Arafat.

Kemp, Geoffrey. *The Control of the Middle East Arms Race*. Washington, D.C.: Carnegie Endowment for International Peace, 1991. Strategic outlook on Middle East arms race by former National Security Council and Defense Department staff member.

Kenan, Amos. *Israel: A Wasted Victory*. Tel Aviv: Amikan, 1970. Selected articles by dissident Kenan on Arab-Israel relations.

———. *The Road to Ein Harod*. London: Saqi Books, 1986. Fictional account of Israeli and Palestinian in flight from Israel.

Kerr, Malcolm H. *The Arab Cold War: Gamal 'Abd al-Nasir and His Rivals, 1958–1970*. 3d ed. New York: Oxford University Press, 1971.

Kerr, Malcolm H., ed. *The Elusive Peace in the Middle East*. Albany: State University of New York Press, 1975. Articles, diverse authors on official & non-official peace efforts.

Khadduri, Majdia D., ed. *The Arab-Israeli Impasse*. Washington, D.C.: Luce, 1968. Collection of diverse articles on causes of 1967 war, refugees, etc.

Khaled, Leila. *My People Shall Live: Autobiography of a Revolutionary*. London: Hodder & Stoughton, 1973. Autobiography of woman guerrilla noted for 1970 hijacking.

Khalidi, Raja. *The Arab Economy in Israel: Dynamics of a Region's Development*. London: Croom Helm, 1988. Study of Israeli Arab economy; integration into Israeli economy.

Khalidi, Rashid. *British Policy Towards Syria and Palestine, 1906–1914: A Study of the Antecedents of the Hussein-McMahon Correspondence, the Sykes-Picot Agreement, and the Balfour Declaration*. London: Ithaca Press, 1980. Study of Britain's conflicting commitments based on archives.

———. *Conflict and Violence in Lebanon*. Cambridge, Mass.: Harvard University Center for International Affairs, 1979. History of Lebanese Civil War and aftermath of Israeli 1978 invasion.

———. *Palestine Reborn*. New York: St. Martin's Press, 1992. Covers Israel-Arab relations, conflict and U.S. policy.

———. *Under Siege: P.L.O. Decisionmaking During the 1982 War*. New York: Columbia University Press, 1986. PLO decisions during Beirut siege based on PLO & other documents.

Khalidi, Walid. *Before Their Diaspora: A Photographic History of the Palestinians, 1876–1948*. Washington, D.C.: Institute for Palestine Studies, 1984. Photo collection with text illustrating pre-1948 Palestinian life.

Khalidi, Walid, ed. *All That Remains: The Palestinian Villages Occupied and Depopulated by Israel in 1948*. Washington, D.C.: Institute for Palestine Studies, 1992. Detailed listing and description of several hundred Palestinian villages.

———. *From Haven to Conquest: Readings in Zionism and the Palestine Problem Until 1948*. Beirut, Lebanon: IPS, 1971. Collection of diverse documents, letters and accounts from pre-Israel era.

Khalidi, Walid, and Jill Khadduri, eds. *Palestine and the Arab-Israeli Conflict: An Annotated Bibliography*. Beirut, Lebanon: IPS, 1974. Extensive bibliography of books and articles in several languages.

Khalifa, Sahar. *Wild Thorns*. London: Saqi Books, 1985. Novel about West Bank life under occupation.

el-Khawas, Mohamed, and Samir Abed Rabbo. *American Aid to Israel: Nature and Impact*. Brattleboro, Vt.: Amana Books, 1984. Critique of U.S. aid to Israel with General Accounting Office report.

Khouri, Fred J. *The Arab-Israeli Dilemma*. 3d ed. Syracuse, N.Y.: Syracuse University Press, 1985. Detailed analysis of conflict with extensive coverage on United Nations.

Khurshid, Ghazi, and Ibrahim al-Abid, eds. *Human Rights in the Occupied Territories*. Beirut: Near East Ecumenical Bureau for Information & Interpretation, 1973. Critique of Israel's human rights violations in Gaza and West Bank.

Kieval, Gershon R. *Party Politics in Israel and the Occupied Territories*. Westport, Conn.: Greenwood Press, 1983. Discussion of positions of Israeli parties toward West Bank.

Kimche, David. *The Last Option: After Nasser, Arafat & Saddam Hussein: The Quest for Peace in the Middle East*. New York: Scribner's, 1991. Account of Israel-Arab relations 1967–73 by former high-ranking Israeli diplomat and intelligence officer.

Kimche, David, and Dan Bawley. *The Sandstorm: The Arab-Israeli War of June 1967: Prelude and Aftermath*. New York: Stein & Day, 1968. Account of 1967 war by former Israeli diplomat and intelligence officer.

Kimche, Jon. *The Seven Fallen Pillars*. New York: Praeger, 1953. Account of Jewish-Arab relations and 1948 war.

———. *There Could Have Been Peace*. New York: Dial Press, 1973. Author's analysis of lost peace opportunities in Arab-Israel conflict from 1917 to 1973; blames big powers, not Jews or Arabs.

Kimche, Jon, and David Kimche. *Both Sides of the Hill*. London: Secker & Warburg, 1960. Account of the 1948 war (see below).

———. *A Clash of Destinies: The Arab-Jewish War and the Founding of the State of Israel*. New York: Praeger, 1960. Chronological account of the 1948 war (see above) from early 1948.

Kimmerling, Baruch. *Zionism and Economy*. Cambridge, Mass.: Schenkman, 1983. Critical analysis of Zionist state-building in Israel with reference to economic relations with Palestinians.

———. *Zionism and Territory: The Socio-Territorial Dimensions of Zionist Politics*. Berkeley: University of California Institute of International Studies, 1983. Critical analysis of Zionist land policies.

Kimmerling, Baruch, ed. *The Israeli State and Society: Boundaries and Frontiers*. Albany, N.Y.: State University of New York Press, 1989. Collection of essays, some refer to Israeli relations with Arabs.

Kimmerling, Baruch, and Joel S. Migdal. *Palestinians: The Making of a People*. New York: Free Press, 1993. History of the Palestinians from 1834 revolt to 1987 Intifada.

King, John. *Handshake in Washington: The Beginning of Middle East Peace?* London: Ithaca Press, 1994. An optomistic assessment of the 1993 Oslo accords.

King, Michael C. *The Palestinians and the Churches: vol. 1 1948–1956*. Geneva: Commission on Inter-Church Aid, World Council of Churches, 1981. Covers church work with Palestine refugees, 1948–1956.

Kirisci, Kemal. *The PLO and World Politics: A Study of Mobilization of Support for the Palestinian Cause*. New York: St. Martin's Press, 1986. Discussion of how the PLO rallied support among Palestinians, Arab states and Third World and East and West European countries.

Kirkbride, Sir Alec Seath. *From the Wings: Amman Memoirs, 1947–1951*. London: Cass, 1976. Account by former British diplomat of Jordan and 1948 war.

Kissinger, Henry. *The White House Years*. Boston: Little Brown, 1979. Includes ex-Secretary of State's account of his Middle East diplomacy.

Klieman, Aaron. *Statecraft in the Dark: Israel's Practice of Quiet Diplomacy*. Boulder, Colo.: Westview Press, 1988. Examines cases such as Israel's relations with Morocco and Jordan.

———. *Israel, Jordan, Palestine, the Search for a Durable Peace*. Beverly Hills, Calif.: Sage, 1981. Sage Policy Paper for Strategic & International Studies Center.

Klieman, Aaron, ed. *Israel in American Middle East Policy*. New York: Garland, 1991. Collection of articles on Israel and United States since 1945.

———. *The Rise of Israel: Arab-Jewish Relations, 1921–1937*. New York: Garland, 1987. Collection of sources with bibliographical references.

Knohl, Dov, ed. *Siege in the Hills of Hebron: The Battle of the Etzion Bloc*. New York: Yoseloff, 1958. Personal narratives dealing with battle in 1948 war.

Kochler, Hans, ed. *The Legal Aspects of the Palestine Problem, With Special Regard to the Question of Jerusalem*. Vienna: Wilhelm Braumuller, 1981. Papers presented at a conference in Vienna in 1980.

el-Kodsy, Ahmed, and Eli Lobel. *The Arab World and Israel*. New York: Monthly Review Press, 1970. Two critical leftist essays on Arab nationalism and class struggle.

Koestler, Arthur. *Promise and Fulfillment: Palestine, 1917–1949*. London: Macmillan, 1979. British author's account of events leading to Israel's creation.

Kohler, Foy D., and Mose L. Harvey. *The Soviet Union and the October 1973 Middle East War; the Implications for Detente*. Coral Gables, Fla.: University of Miami Center for Advanced International Studies, 1974. Soviet and American relations and the Middle East conflict.

Kokole, Omari H. *Dimensions of Africa's International Relations*. Delmar, N.Y.: Caravan Books, 1993. African political scientist looks at Africa and Arab-Israel conflicts.

Korany, Bahgat, and Ali E. Hillal Dessouki. eds. *The Foreign Policies of Arab States*. Boulder, Colo.: Westview Press, 1984. Collection of articles by diverse authors on Arab state foreign policies with attention to Arab-Israel conflict, PLO, Palestine.

Korn, David A. *Assassination in Khartoum*. Bloomington: Indiana University Press, 1993. Covers Palestinian terrorism and kidnapping of U.S. diplomat in Sudan.

———. *Stalemate: The War of Attrition and Great Power Diplomacy in the Middle East, 1967–1970*. Boulder, Colo.: Westview Press, 1992. Covers Israel-Egypt border conflicts from 1949 to post-1967 war.

Kosman, William Youssef. *Sadat's Realistic Peace Initiative*. New York: Vantage Press, 1981. Sadat and Israel-Egyptian relations.

Kosut, Hal. *Israel & the Arabs: The June 1967 War*. New York: Facts On File, 1968. Compiled from *Facts On File World News Digest*.

Kotler, Yair. *Heil Kahane*. New York: Adama Books, 1986. Study of Meir Kahane and his Kach Movement, which calls for expulsion of Arabs from Israel and occupied territories.

Kramer, Gudran. *The Jew in Modern Egypt, 1914–1952*. Seattle: University of Washington Press, 1989. Study of Egyptian Jews and conditions leading to their exodus.

Kretzmer, David. *The Legal Status of the Arabs in Israel.* Boulder, Colo.: Westview Press, 1990. Published in cooperation with International Center for Peace in the Middle East.

Kreutz, Andrej. *Vatican Policy on the Palestinian-Israeli Conflict: The Struggle for the Holy Land.* New York: Greenwood Press, 1990. The Catholic church and Zionism; Israel-Vatican relations.

Kriesberg, Louis. *International Conflict Resolution: The U.S.-USSR and Middle East Cases.* New Haven, Conn.: Yale University Press, 1992. Case studies of diplomacy in international relations.

Kuniholm, Bruce Robellet. *The Palestinian Problem and United States Policy: A Quick Guide to Issues and References.* Claremont, Calif.: Regina Books, 1986. Reference guide with extensive bibliography.

Kunstel, Marcia, and Joseph Albright. *Their Promised Land: Arab Versus Jew in History's Cauldron: One Valley in the Jerusalem Hills.* New York: Crown, 1990. Jewish-Arab relations in Sorek Valley 1917–1949.

Kunz, Diane B. *The Economic Diplomacy of the Suez Crisis.* Chapel Hill: University of North Carolina Press, 1991. Examines U.S. use of economic clout in 1956–57 Suez crisis.

Kupferschmidt, Uri M. *The Supreme Muslim Council: Islam Under the British Mandate for Palestine.* Leiden, The Netherlands: Brill, 1987. Account of Palestine's Supreme Muslim Council; role of Haj Amin.

Kuroda, Alice K., and Yasumasa Kuroda. *Palestinians Without Palestine: A Study of Political Socialization Among Palestinian Youths.* Washington, D.C.: University Press of America, 1978. Attitude formation among Palestinian youth; uses survey research.

Kurzman, Dan. *Ben-Gurion: Prophet of Fire.* New York: Simon & Schuster, 1983. Highly laudatory biography of Ben-Gurion's role in the creation of Israel.

———. *The First Arab-Israeli War.* New York: New American Library, 1970. Enthusiastic account of Israel's birth, based on interviews.

Kushner, David, ed. *Palestine in the Late Ottoman Period: Political, Social and Economic Transformation.* Leiden, The Netherlands: Brill, 1986. Scholarly study of pre–World War I Palestine.

Kuttab, Jonathan, and Raja Shehadeh. *Civilian Administration in the Occupied West Bank: Analysis of Israeli Military Order No. 947.* Ramallah, West Bank: Law in the Service of Man, 1982. Legal analysis by two Palestinian lawyers of Israel's 1981 introduction of "civil administration."

Kyle, Keith. *Suez.* New York: St. Martin's Press, 1991. In-depth history of 1956 Suez crisis by former *Economist* Washington correspondent.

Laffin, John. *Fedayeen: The Arab-Israeli Dilemma.* New York: Free Press, 1973. British journalist's account of Palestinian guerrillas.

Lakhanpal, P.L. *Documents and Notes on the Arab-Israeli Question*. Delhi: International Books, 1968. Document collection.

Lakin, Martin. *Arab and Jew in Israel: Case Study in Human Relations Training Approach to Conflict*. New York: American Academic Association for Peace in the Middle East, 1969. Social psychologist's study of intergroup relations.

Lall, Arthur. *The UN and the Middle East Crisis, 1967*. New York: Columbia University Press, 1968. Detailed account by ex-Indian ambassador of U.N. role in conflict from eve of 1967 war to adoption of Resolution 242 in November.

Landau, Jacob M. *The Arab Minority in Israel, 1967–1991: Political Aspects*. New York: Oxford University Press, 1993. Israeli scholar's study of Israeli Arabs. Critical of Palestinian nationalists but calls for Arab integration into Israel state.

———. *The Arabs in Israel: A Political Study*. Oxford, England: Oxford University Press, 1969. An earlier study of Israeli Arabs by Landau.

Landau, Michael. *Israel and the Arabs: A Handbook of Basic Information*. Jerusalem: Israel Communications, 1971. A quasi-official account of Jewish-Arab relations.

Landow, Eli. *Jerusalem the Eternal: The Paratroopers' Battle for the City of David*. Tel Aviv: Otpaz, 1968. Laudatory account of Israel's 1967 capture of Jerusalem.

Langer, Felicia. *These Are My Brothers: Israel and the Occupied Territories, Part II*. London: Ithaca Press, 1979. Israel leftist lawyer's account; her defense of Palestinian Arab political prisoners.

———. *With My Own Eyes: Israel and the Occupied Territories, 1967–1973*. London: Ithaca Press, 1975. Earlier account of Israeli lawyer's defense of Arab political prisoners.

Langfur, Stephen. *Confession from a Jericho Jail: "What Happened When I Refused to Fight the Palestinians."* New York: Grove Weidenfeld, 1992. Personal account of an Israeli Jewish conscientious objector.

Lapidoth, Ruth, and Moshe Hirsch, eds. *The Arab-Israel Conflict and Its Resolution: Selected Documents*. Boston: Nijhoff, 1992. Includes U.N. and other documents.

Lapp, John Allen. *The View From East Jerusalem*. Scottdale, Pa.: Herald Press, 1980. Critical account of Israel's rule in Arab Jerusalem.

Laqueur, Walter. *Confrontation; The Middle East and World Politics*. New York: Quadrangle/*New York Times* Books, 1974. Role of the superpowers in the 1973 war.

———. *The Road to Jerusalem: Origin and Aftermath of the Arab-Israel Conflict, 1967/8*. Baltimore: Penguin Books, 1969. Account of 1967 war sympathetic to Israel.

Laqueur, Walter, and Barry Rubin. *The Israel-Arab Reader: A Documentary History of the Middle East Conflict*. 4th ed. New York: Facts On File, 1985. Extensive collection of documents, speeches, etc. since 1880s.

Larkin, Margaret. *The Hand of Mordechai*. London: Gollancz, 1968. Account of battle in 1948 war over Kibbutz Yad Mordechai.

Laskier, Michael M. *The Jews of Egypt 1920–1970 in the Midst of Zionism, Anti-Semitism, and the Middle East Conflict*. New York: New York University Press, 1992. Comprehensive history of recent Egyptian Jewish history.

Laufer, Leopold Yehuda. *U.S. Aid to the West Bank and Gaza: Policy Dilemmas*. Jerusalem: Leonard Davis Institute, Hebrew University, 1985. Monograph in Policy Studies from Institute for International Relations.

Lavie, Smadar. *The Poetics of Military Occupation: Mzeina Allegories of Bedouin Identity Under Israeli and Egyptian Rule*. Berkeley: University of California Press, 1990. Anthropological study of how bedouin coexist with Israel.

The Lebanese Border. Tel Aviv: Israel Defense Forces, 1981. IDF's account of tension on Lebanese-Israel border 1949–75.

Lebow, Richard Ned, and Janice Gross Stein. *We All Lost the Cold War*. Princeton, N.J.: Princeton University Press, 1994. Includes sections on Soviet Union, U.S. and Arab-Israel conflicts.

Lederman, Jim. *Battle Lines: The American Media and the Intifada*. Boulder, Colo.: Westview Press, 1993. American journalist's survey of U.S. media and the Intifada.

Legal Aspects of the Arab Boycott. New York: Practicing Law Institute, 1977. Corporate law and practice course handbook series.

Legum, Colin, and Haim Shaked, eds. *Arab Relations in the Middle East: The Road to Realignment*. New York: Holmes & Meier, 1979. Collection of essays from *The Middle East Contemporary Survey*, annual published by Shiloah Center, Tel Aviv University.

Lehn, Walter, and Uri Davis. *The Jewish National Fund*. London: Kegan Paul, 1988. Critical study of Jewish National Fund land policies emphasizing discriminatory practices vis-à-vis Arabs.

Lerner, Abba, and Haim Ben Shahar. *The Economics of Efficiency and Growth: Lessons from Israel and the West Bank*. Cambridge, Mass.: Ballinger, 1975. Critique of Israeli policies by an American and an Israeli economist.

Lesch, Ann Mosely. *Arab Politics in Palestine, 1917–1939: The Frustration of a Nationalist Movement*. Ithaca, N.Y.: Cornell University Press, 1979. Scholarly account of Palestinian Arab nationalist development.

———. *Israel's Occupation of the West Bank: The First Two Years*. Santa Monica, Calif.: Rand, 1970. Description of Israeli occupation—1967–1969.

———. *Political Perceptions of Palestinians on the West Bank and the Gaza Strip*. Washington, D.C.: Middle East Institute, 1980. Study of Palestinian attitudes after Camp David agreements.

———. *Transition to Palestinian Self-Government: Practical Steps Toward Israeli-Palestinian Peace*. Bloomington: Indiana University Press, 1992. Report of a study group convened by American Academcy of Arts & Sciences in Cambridge, Mass.

Lesch, Ann M. and Mark Tessler. *Israel, Egypt, and the Palestinians: From Camp David to Intifada*. Bloomington: Indiana University Press, 1989. Collection of essays by Lesch and Tessler on Israel, Egypt and Palestinian relations—1980–1988.

Levins, Hoag. *Arab Reach: The Secret War Against Israel*. Garden City, N.Y.: Doubleday, 1983. Account of Israel-Arab conflicts sympathetic to Israel.

Levitt, Zola. *Israel in Agony: The Beginning of the End?* Irvine, Calif.: Harvest House Publishers, 1975. Bible prophecies and the 1973 war.

Lewin-Epstein, Noah, and Moshe Semyonov. *The Arab Minority in Israel's Economy: Patterns of Ethnic Inequality*. Boulder, Colo.: Westview Press, 1993. Discusses differential nature of economic inequality and its negative impact on Israeli Arab minority.

Lewis, Bernard. *Semites and Anti-Semites: An Inquiry into Conflict and Prejudice*. New York: Norton, 1986. Argument by noted historian that struggle against Israel caused new form of Arab anti-Semitism.

Lewis, William, and Robert W. Stookey, eds. *The End of the Palestine Mandate*. Austin: University of Texas Press, 1986. Essays on U.S., British, Arab and Zionist attitudes on mandate's end.

A License to Kill: Israeli Operations Against "Wanted" and Masked Palestinians. New York: Human Rights Watch, 1993. Israeli undercover operations against Palestinians in Gaza and the West Bank.

Liden, Anders. *Security and Recognition: A Study in Change in Israel's Official Doctrine 1967–1974*. Lund, Sweden: Studentlitt., 1980. Thesis from Lund University.

Lieber, Robert J. *Oil and the Middle East War—Europe in the Energy Crisis*. Cambridge, Mass.: Harvard International Affairs Center, 1976. Impact of the 1973 war on Europe's energy supply and economy.

Lieblich, Amia. *Seasons of Captivity: The Inner World of POWs*. New York: New York University Press, 1994. Personal narratives of and psychological effects on Israeli POWs.

Lilienthal, Alfred M. *What Price Israel?* Chicago: Regnery, 1953. An early critical account of Zionism, Israel, Zionist lobby and its influence on U.S. policy by American Jewish anti-Zionist.

———. *The Zionist Connection II: What Price Peace?* New Brunswick, N.J.: North American, 1983. Extensive critique of U.S. policy and media manipulation by Zionists.

———. *The Other Side of the Coin: An American Perspective.* New York: Devin-Adair, 1965. Critical account by American Jew of Israel, Zionism and U.S. policy.

Lipman, Beata. *Israel: The Embattled Land: Jewish and Palestinian Women Talk About Their Lives.* London: Pandora Press, 1988. Jewish woman Holocaust survivor's interviews showing oppression of Palestinian and Israeli women.

Living Conditions of the Palestinian People in the Occupied Territories. New York: United Nations, 1985. Prepared for the U.N. Committee on the Exercise of the Inalienable Rights of the Palestinian People.

Livingston, Harold. *No Sword: An American Volunteer in the Israeli Air Force During the 1948 War of Independence.* Chicago: Edition Q, 1994. Biography of American flight radio operator in 1948 war.

Locke, Richard, and Anthony Stewart. *Bantustan Gaza.* London: Zed Books, 1985. Gaza's history and conditions under occupation and as a source of cheap labor.

Lockman, Zachary, and Joel Beinin, eds. *Intifada: The Palestinian Uprising Against Israeli Occupation.* Boston: South End Press, 1989. Collection of articles, impressions, documents, poetry of Intifada.

Lorch, Netanel. *Israel's War of Independence, 1947–1949.* 2d ed. Hartford, Conn.: Hartmore House, 1968. Account of 1948 war campaigns by Israeli military historian.

Love, Kenneth. *Suez: The Twice-Fought War, A History.* New York: McGraw Hill, 1969. Background of events leading to 1956 war; postscript on 1967 war.

Lowi, Miriam R. *Water and Politics: The Politics of a Scarce Resource in the Jordan River Basin.* New York: Cambridge University Press, 1993. Analysis of history and current status of dispute between Israel and Arabs over Jordan River waters; various plans for development of Jordan River system.

Luciani, Giacomo, and Ghassan Salame, eds. *The Politics of Arab Integration.* London: Croom Helm, 1988. Collection of diverse articles with several on Arab-Israel conflict.

Lukacs, Yehuda, ed. *The Israeli-Palestinian Conflict: A Documentary Record 1967–1990.* Cambridge, England: Cambridge University Press, 1992. Extensive documentation, including U.S., Israel, Arab and international documents, speeches, letters, pronoucements.

Lukacs, Yehuda, and Abdalla Battah, eds. *The Arab-Israeli Conflict: Two Decades of Change.* Boulder, Colo.: Westview Press, 1988. Collection of diverse views on conflict since 1967 war, emphasizing policies of regional actors and superpowers; includes the peace process.

Lustick, Ian S. *Arabs in the Jewish State: Israel's Control of a National Minority.* Austin: University of Texas Press, 1980. Study of Israeli methods to control its Arab citizens.

———. *For the Land and the Lord: Jewish Fundamentalism in Israel.* New York: Council on Foreign Relations, 1988. Study of Jewish fundamentalists and West Bank settlers, including their attitudes to Arabs.

———. *Israel and Jordan: The Implications of an Adversarial Relationship.* Berkeley: University of California Institute of International Studies, 1978. Monograph on Israel-Jordan "adversarial partnership" after 1967.

———. *Unsettled States, Disputed Lands: Britain and Ireland, France and Algeria, Israel and the West Bank.* Ithaca, N.Y.: Cornell University Press, 1994. Comparative study; attempts theoretical scheme on disputed lands.

Lustick, Ian S., ed. *Arab-Israeli Relations: A Collection of Contending Perspectives and Recent Research.* 10 vols. (1. *Arab-Israel Relations: Historical Background and Origins of the Conflict*; 2. *Triumph and Catastrophe: The War of 1948, Israeli Independence, and the Refugee Problem*; 3. *From War to War: Israel vs. the Arabs 1948–1967*; 4. *From Wars Toward Peace in the Arab-Israeli Conflict 1969–1992*; 5. *Religion, Culture, and Psychology in Arab-Israeli Relations*; 6. *Economic, Legal, and Demographic Dimensions of Arab-Israeli Relations*; 7. *The Conflict With the Arabs in Israeli Politics and Society*; 8. *The Conflict With Israel in Arab Politics and Society*; 9. *Palestinians Under Israeli Rule*; 10. *Arab-Israeli Relations in World Politics*). Hamden, Conn.: Garland, 1994. Collection of over 170 articles by diverse authors covering Arab-Israel conflict from 19th century to 1991.

Luttwak, Edward. *Sea Power in the Mediterranean: Political Utility and Military Constraints.* Beverly Hills, Calif.: Sage Publications, 1979. Case study of superpower diplomacy in the 1973 war.

Lynd, Staughton, Sam Bahour and Alice Lynd. *Homeland: Oral Histories of Palestine and Palestinians.* New York: Olive Branch Press, 1994. Interviews with diverse Palestinians in 1991–92.

MacBride, Sean, and Richard Falk, eds. *Israel in Lebanon: Report of the International Commission to Enquire into Reported Violations of International Law by Israel During Its Invasion of Lebanon.* London: Ithaca Press, 1983. Commission chaired by McBride; strongly condemned Israel for crimes against humanity and occupation of Lebanon.

Mackinlay, John. *The Peacekeepers: An Assessment of Peacekeeping Operations at the Arab-Israeli Interface.* London: Unwin Hyman, 1989. Study of U.N. forces in Lebanon, Golan Heights, Sinai—1970s–80s—and of Beirut Second Multinational Force—1982–84.

MacLeish, Roderick. *The Sun Stood Still.* New York: Atheneum, 1967. Account of the 1967 war.

al Madfai, Madiha Rashid. *Jordan, the United States and the Middle East Peace Process, 1974–1991.* New York: Cambridge University Press, 1993. Jordan's role in peacemaking during Carter, Reagan and Bush administrations culminating in Hussein's separation from West Bank.

Madrid, Robin, ed. *Statements and Position Papers of Major American Organizations on Middle East Peace*. Rev. ed. Washington, D.C.: Washington Middle East Associates, 1987. Collection of diverse statements.

Maghroori, Ray, and Stephen M. Gorman. *The Yom Kippur War: A Case Study in Crisis Decision-Making in American Foreign Policy*. Washington, D.C.: University Press of America, 1981. Covers U.S. Middle East policy in 1969–74 period.

Magnes, Judah L., *et al. Palestine: Divided or United? The Case for a Bi-national Palestine Before the United Nations*. Westport, Conn.: Greenwood Press, 1983. Reissue of 1947 testimony by Zionists (Ihud) before UNSCOP favoring binational state.

Magnus, Ralph H., ed. *Documents on the Middle East*. Washington, D.C.: American Enterprise Institute, 1969. Several documents cover Arab-Israel conflict.

Mahmood, M. *Soviet Policy Towards the Arab-Israeli Conflict, 1948–1988*. New Delhi, India: Gian, 1989. An Indian perspective on Soviet Middle East policy.

Makofvsky, David. *Making Peace with the PLO*. Boulder, Colo.: Westview Press, 1996. Detailed account of secret negotiations leading to Declaration of Principles.

Mallison, W. Thomas, and Sally Mallison. *An International Law Analysis of the Major United Nations Resolutions Concerning the Palestine Question*. New York: United Nations, 1979. Legal analysis of partition, refugees, Jerusalem, Palestinian status.

———. *The Palestine Problem in International Law and World Order*. New York: Longman, 1983. Treatment of legal aspects of Balfour Declaration, U.N. Partition Resolution, Jerusalem, Israeli settlements, Palestinian rights.

Mandell, Brian S. *The Sinai Experience: Lessons in Multimethod Arms Control Verification and Risk Management*. Ottawa: Arms Control & Disarmament Division, Department of External Affairs, 1987. Part of Canadian government's Arms Control Verification Studies.

Mandel, Neville J. *The Arabs and Zionism Before World War I*. Berkeley: University of California Press, 1976. Covers Arab reaction to Zionism from 1880s to 1914.

al-Mani, Saleh. *The Euro-Arab Dialogue*. New York: St. Martin's Press, 1983. Arab-West European relatons and the Palestine problem.

Manna, 'Adil. *Jerusalem and the Administered Territories, 1967–1976: A Select Bibliography*. Jerusalem: Hebrew University, Harry S. Truman Research Institute, 1977. Prepared for June 1977 seminar on Jerusalem and administered territories.

Mannin, Ethel. *The Road to Beersheba*. Chicago: Regnery, 1964. Fictional account of Palestinian refugees in 1948 war.

Mansour, Attalah. *Waiting for the Dawn*. London: Secker & Warburg, 1975. Personal account of Israeli Arab journalist, critical of Jews and Arabs.

Mansour, Camile. *Beyond Alliance: Israel in U.S. Foreign Policy*. Washington, D.C.: Institute for Palestine Studies, 1994. Examines U.S. policy toward Arab-Israel conflict from 1948 to 1992.

Ma'oz, Moshe. *Ottoman Reform in Syria and Palestine, 1840–1861: The Impact of the Tanzimat on Politics and Society*. Oxford, England: Clarendon Press, 1968. Covers Ottoman rule, including military, taxes, minorities, etc.

———. *Palestinian Arab Politics*. Jerusalem: Jerusalem Academic Press, 1975. Papers on Palestinian politics, parties and literature under British and Jordanians.

———. *Palestinian Leadership on the West Bank: The Changing Role of the Mayors Under Jordan and Israel*. Totowa, N.J.: Cass, 1984. An Israeli scholar's examination of Palestinian politics during occupation.

Ma'oz, Moshe, ed. *Studies on Palestine During the Ottoman Period*. Jerusalem: Magnes Press, 1975. Documented study of Ottoman era from 1516 to 1917.

Marantz, Paul, and Janice G. Stein, eds. *Peace-Making in the Middle East: Problems and Prospects*. Totowa, N.J.: Barnes & Noble, 1985. Papers on role of outside powers in Middle East conflict.

al-Marayati, Abid. A., ed. *International Relations of the Middle East and North Africa*. Cambridge, Mass.: Schenkman, 1984. Survey of Middle East international relations with much focus on Palestine issue.

Mar'i, Sami K. *Arab Education in Israel*. Syracuse, N.Y.: Syracuse University Press, 1978. Critical account of Israeli Arab education in context of problems.

Marks, Shannee. *Where Is Palestine? The Arabs of Israel*. London: Pluto Press, 1986. Description of Israeli oppression of Arab citizens and occupied territory.

Marlowe, John. *The Seat of Pilate: An Account of the Palestine Mandate*. London: Cresset Press, 1959. Critical account of Britain in Palestine, 1917–48.

Marshall, S. L. A. *Swift Sword; The Historical Record of Israel's Victory, June, 1967*. New York: American Heritage, 1967. Account of 1967 war based on UPI reports; includes combat photos.

Marton, Kati. *A Death in Jerusalem*. New York: Pantheon Books, 1994. Account of assassination of U.N. mediator Count Bernadotte in 1948.

Marx, Emanuel, ed. *The Changing Bedouin*. New Brunswick, N.J.: Transaction Books, 1984. Anthropological studies of Israeli bedouin; economic and social changes.

Masalah, Nur. *Expulsion of the Palestinians: The Concept of "Transfer" in Zionist Political Thought, 1882–1948*. Washington, D.C.: Institute for Palestine

Studies, 1992. Analysis of Zionist ideas about and plans for Arab expulsion, which author maintains were implemented in 1948 war.

Masalah, Nur, ed. *The Palestinians in Israel: Is Israel the State of All Its Citizens and "Absentees"?* Haifa: Galilee Centre for Social Research, 1993. Collection of articles highly critical of Israel's treatment of its Arab citizens.

Mattar, Philip. *The Mufti of Jerusalem: Al-Hajj Amin al-Husayni and the Palestinian Movement*. New York: Columbia University Press, 1988. Objective account of Mufti's life based on archival research.

Mayer, Thomas. *Egypt and the Palestine Question, 1936–1945*. Berlin: Klaus Schwarz Verlag, 1982. Detailed study of Egypt's involvement in Palestine from Arab Revolt to establishment of Arab League.

Mayhew, Christopher, and Michael Adams. *Publish It Not: The Middle East Cover-Up*. London: Longman, 1973. Critical account of press coverage of Palestine by two Britons.

McDowall, David. *Palestine and Israel: The Uprising and Beyond*. Berkeley: University of California Press, 1989. Examines Israel-Palestinian relations and background of Intifada.

———. *The Palestinians: The Road to Nationhood*. Concord, Mass.: Minority Rights Publications, 1995. Describes the weak status of the Palestinians despite the recent peace accords.

McForan, Desmond. *The World Held Hostage: The War Waged by International Terrorism*. New York: St. Martin's Press, 1987. The role of terrorism in the Arab-Israel conflict.

McKinnon, Clinton Dan. *Bullseye One Reactor*. San Diego: House of Hits, 1987. Account of Israel's 1981 attack on Iraq's nuclear reactor.

McTague, John J. *British Policy in Palestine, 1917–1922*. Lanham, Md.: University Press of America, 1983. Covers period from Balfour Declaration to League of Nations mandate.

Meinhertzhagen, Col. Richard. *Middle East Diary, 1917–1956*. London: Cresset Press, 1959. Diaries of British colonial official who became ardent Zionist.

Meir, Shmuel. *Strategic Implications of the New Oil Reality*. Boulder, Colo.: Westview Press, 1986. The influence of oil on Israel's security and on Middle East conflict.

Melman, Yossi, and Dan Raviv. *Beyond the Uprising: Israelis, Jordanians, and Palestinians*. Westport, Conn.: Greenwood Press, 1989. Covers Israel's relations with Jordan and Palestinians and U.S. involvement.

Mendelsohn, Everett, ed. *A Compassionate Peace: A Future for the Middle East*. New York: Hill & Wang, 1982. Report prepared for the American Friends Service Committee (Quakers).

Mendes-Flohr, Paul R., ed. *A Land of Two Peoples: Martin Buber on Jews and Arabs.* New York: Oxford University Press, 1983. Collection of Buber's writings on Jewish-Arab relations, 1918–45.

Mergui, Raphael, and Philippe Simonnot. *Israel's Ayatollahs: Meir Kahane and the Far Right in Israel.* Atlantic Highlands, N.J: Saqi Books, 1988. Interview with Kahane and descriptions of right-wing Israeli organizations.

Merlin, Samuel. *The Search for Peace in the Middle East: The Story of President Bourguiba's Campaign for a Negotiated Peace Between Israel and the Arab States.* South Brunswick, N.J.: Yoseloff, 1969. Covers efforts by Tunisia's former president to resolve conflict.

Metzger, Jan, Martin Orth and Christian Sterling. *This Land Is Our Land: The West Bank Under Israeli Occupation.* London: Zed Books, 1983. Broad study of Israeli occupation, Jewish settlements, Palestinians.

The Middle East. 6th ed. Washington, D.C.: Congressional Quarterly, 1986. Extensive coverage of Middle East with sections on Arab-Israel conflict.

Migdal, Joel S., *et al. Palestinian Politics and Society.* Princeton, N.J.: Princeton University Press, 1979. Collection by various authors on Palestinian society from Ottoman era to present.

Mihanna, Muhammad Nasr. *The Role of Egypt in the Middle Eastern Peace Process Since 1967.* Cairo: Anglo-Egyptian Bookshop, 1984. Egypt and the Arab-Israel conflict.

Miller, Aaron David. *The PLO and the Politics of Survival.* New York: Praeger, 1983. Study of internal, inter-Arab and Israeli constraints on PLO.

Miller, Ylana N. *Government and Society in Rural Palestine, 1920–1948.* Austin: University of Texas Press, 1984. Study of mandatory government impact on Arab village life.

Mishal, Shaul. *The PLO under 'Arafat: Between Gun and Olive Branch.* New Haven, Conn.: Yale University Press, 1986. Internal problems of PLO and relations with West Bank.

———. *West Bank, East Bank: The Palestinians in Jordan, 1949–1967.* New Haven, Conn.: Yale University Press, 1976. Palestinians under Jordanian rule between 1948 and 1967 wars.

Mishal, Shaul, and Reuben Aharoni. *Speaking Stones: Communiques From the Intifada Underground.* Syracuse, N.Y.: Syracuse University Press, 1994. Collection of Intifada leaflets (Fatah, Hamas, documentation and commentary).

Mogannam, Matiel. *The Arab Woman and the Palestine Problem.* London: Herbert Joseph, 1937. Early feminist account of Palestinian women.

Moore, John Norton, ed. *The Arab-Israeli Conflict.* 3 vols. Princeton, N.J.: Princeton University Press, 1974. Extensive collection of primary documents, readings, articles; volumes 1 and 2—readings; volume 3—documents.

———. *The Arab-Israeli Conflict.* Vol. 4, *The Difficult Search for Peace*, in two parts. Princeton, N.J.: Princeton University Press, 1991. This volume covers 1975–88.

Mor, Ben D. *Decision and Interaction in Crisis: A Model of International Crisis Behavior.* London: Praeger, 1993. Psychological aspects of conflict; emphasis on 1967 Six-Day War.

Morris, Benny. *The Birth of the Palestinian Refugee Problem.* Cambridge, England: Cambridge University Press, 1987. Israeli revisionist account of causes and impact of refugee problem.

———. *Israel's Border Wars, 1949–1956: Arab Infiltration, Israeli Retaliation and the Countdown to the Suez War.* New York: Oxford University Press, 1993. Account of Israel-Arab border tensions leading to 1956 war.

———. *1948 and After: Israel and the Palestinians.* New York: Oxford University Press, 1990. An Israeli revisionist account of 1948 Arab-Israel War and its historiography.

Moskin, J. Robert. *Among Lions: The Battle for Jerusalem, June 5–7, 1967.* New York: Arbor House, 1982. Laudatory account of Israel's capture of East Jerusalem.

Mroz, John Edwin. *Beyond Security: Private Perspectives Among Arabs and Israelis.* New York: International Peace Academy, 1980. Arab and Israeli perceptions of threats based on author's interviews.

Muhawi, Ibrahim, and Sharif Kanaana. *Speak, Bird, Speak Again: Palestinian Arab Folktales.* Berkeley: University of California Press, 1989. Translation of 45 popular Palestinian folk tales with analysis.

Mullen, George. *The Jew and the Arab: A Puzzle Solved; A Realistic Proposal for Peace in the Mideast.* San Diego: San Diego, 1994. Unique proposal for resolving the conflict.

The Multinational Force and Observers. Rome: Office of Public Affairs, Multinational Force & Observers, 1987. Official account of work of Sinai force.

Murphy, Jay, ed. *For Palestine.* New York: Writers & Readers, 1993. Collection of articles covering history of Palestine from 16th century to Oslo accords; highly sympathetic to Palestinian cause.

Musallem, Sami. *The Palestine Liberation Organization: Its Structure and Function.* Brattleboro, Vt.: Amana Books, 1988. Account of PLO by director of PLO chairman Arafat's office.

Musallem, Sami, ed. *United Nations Resolutions on Palestine, 1947–1972.* Beirut: Institute for Palestine Studies, 1973. Collection of U.N. resolutions on Palestine through 1972; voting tables.

Mushtak, Hazim T. *The Arab Rejection of Israel: A Philosophical Approach and Analysis.* Baghdad: Al-Ani Press, 1976. Lectures delivered by author, 1964–71.

Muslih, Muhammad Y. *The Origins of Palestinian Nationalism*. New York: Columbia University Press, 1988. Scholarly study of 1850s to 1920s based on archival research.

Mutawi, Samir A. *Jordan in the 1967 War*. Cambridge: Cambridge University Press, 1987. Background of Jordan's entry into 1967 war; impact, consequences.

Nachmani, Amikam. *Great Power Discord in Palestine: The Anglo-American Committee of Inquiry into the Problems of European Jewry and Palestine, 1945*. London: Cass, 1987. Detailed study of Anglo-American Committee based on British and U.S. documents.

Nachmias, Nitza. *Transfer of Arms, Leverage, and Peace in the Middle East*. New York: Greenwood Press, 1988. Examines U.S.-Israel military relations.

Nahas, Dunia Habib. *The Israeli Communist Party*. New York: St. Martin's Press, 1976. Covers Communist movement from 1948 prestate era, 1965 split of party into Jewish and Arab factions, role of Rakkah in 1970s.

Naidu, A. G. *U.S. Policy Towards the Arab-Israeli Conflict*. New Delhi: Tulsi, 1981. An Indian perspective on Zionist and Israel relations with United States.

Najjar, Orayb Aref, and Kitty Warnock. *Portraits of Palestinian Women*. Salt Lake City: Utah University Press, 1992. Intimate interviews with women activists, intellectuals, homemakers and professionals.

Nakleh, Emile. *The West Bank and Gaza: Toward the Making of a Palestinian State*. Washington, D.C.: American Enterprise Institute, 1979. Examination of West Bank and Gaza local government institutions.

Nakleh, Emile, ed. *A Palestinian Agenda for the West Bank and Gaza*. Washington, D.C.: American Enterprise Institute, 1980. Collection of papers about future education, agriculture, social work, local government, etc., by West Bank and Gaza Palestinians.

Nakleh, Issa. *Encyclopedia of the Palestine Problem*. 2 vols. New York: Intercontinental Books, 1991. Covers Palestine problem from 1917 from an ardent Palestinian perspective.

Nakleh, Khalil. *Indigenous Organizations in Palestine: Towards a Purposeful Societal Development*. Jerusalem: Arab Thought Forum, 1991. Emphasis on local and community development societies.

Nakleh, Khalil, and Elia Zureik, eds. *The Sociology of the Palestinians*. New York: St. Martin's Press, 1980. Collection of papers dealing with class, demography, women, etc.

Narkiss, Uzi. *The Liberation of Jerusalem: The Battle of 1967*. London: Vallentine, Mitchell, 1983. Account of 1967 Battle for Jerusalem by Israeli commander.

Nashif, Taysir N. *The Palestinian Arab and Jewish Political Leaderships: A Comparative Study*. New York: Asia, 1979. Based on quantitative comparisons of class, social background, education, occupation, etc. Covers 1920 to 1948.

Nasru, Fathiya Said. *Education in the West Bank Government Schools, 1968/69–1976/77.* Birzeit, West Bank: Birzeit University Research Office, 1977. Covers impact of 1967 war and occupation on West Bank education.

Nassar, Jamal, and Roger Heacock, eds. *Intifada: Palestine at the Crossroads.* New York: Praeger, 1990. Collection of articles on the Palestinian uprising.

Nassib, Selim, and Caroline Tisdall. *Beirut: Frontline Story.* London: Pluto Press, 1983. Account of 1982 Israeli invasion of Lebanon.

A Nation Under Siege: al-Haq Annual Report on Human Rights in the Occupied Palestinian Territories. Ramallah, West Bank: al-Haq, 1990. Annual report of Palestinian human rights organization.

National Lawyers Guild, 1977 Middle East Delegation. *Treatment of Palestinians in Israeli-Occupied West Bank and Gaza.* New York: National Lawyers Guild, 1978. Report of the American National Lawyers Guild 1977 delegation.

Nazzal, Nafez. *The Palestinian Exodus From Galilee, 1948.* Beirut: Institute for Palestine Studies, 1978. Detailed study of Palestinian 1948 exodus during 1947–48 war.

Neff, Donald. *Fallen Pillars: U.S. Policy Towards Palestine and Israel, 1947–1994.* Washington, D.C.: Institute for Palestine Studies, 1995. Critique of American policy toward Israel-Palestinian conflict.

———. *Warriors Against Israel.* Brattleboro, Vt.: Amana Books, 1988. Account of Arab-Israel conflict after Nasser's death in 1970 with attention to 1973 war, Israel-Egypt peace agreement and Palestinians.

———. *Warriors at Suez: Eisenhower Takes America into the Middle East.* Brattleboro, Vt.: Amana Press, 1988. Account of 1956 Suez crisis and tripartite aggression.

Neff, Donald, ed. *Warriors for Jerusalem: The Six Days that Changed the Middle East.* New York: Simon & Schuster, 1984. Account of 1967 war, its background and aftermath.

Netanyahu, Benjamin. *A Place Among the Nations: Israel and the World.* New York: Bantam Books, 1993. A Likud leader's account of Israel's foreign relations.

Newman, David. Population, Settlement, and Conflict: Israel and the West Bank. Cambridge: Cambridge University Press, 1991. Importance of demography and population in solution of Arab-Israel conflict.

Newman, David, ed. *The Impact of Gush Emunim: Politics and Settlement in the West Bank.* New York: St. Martin's Press, 1985. Essays about militant Jewish West Bank settlers' movement.

Nicosia, Francis R. *The Third Reich and the Palestine Question.* Austin: University of Texas Press, 1985. Study of Nazi 1930s policies favoring Jewish Palestine settlement.

Nijim, Basheer, and Muammar Bishara, eds. *Toward the De-Arabization of Palestine/Israel, 1945–1977.* Dubuque, Iowa: Kendall Hunt, 1984. Documented, village-by-village examination of uprooted Palestinian villages taken over by Israel; maps and tables.

Nimrod, Dan. *Peace Now: Blueprint for National Suicide.* Dollard Des Ormeaux, Quebec: Dawn, 1984. Critical account of Israel's doves after 1973.

Nir, Yeshayahu. *The Israeli-Arab Conflict in Soviet Caricatures, 1967–1973.* Tel Aviv: Tcherikover, 1976. A research monograph in visual communications.

Nisan, Mordechai. *Toward a New Israel: The Jewish State and the Arab Question.* New York: AMS Press, 1992. Covers Muslim and Arab relations with Jews, Zionism, Israel.

Nissenson, Hugh. *Notes From the Frontier.* New York: Dial Press, 1968. Personal narratives about kibbutzim and 1967 war.

Nurenberg, Thelma. *The Time of Anger.* New York: Abelard-Schuman, 1975. Friendship between kibbutz/Arab neighbors threatened by 1967 war.

Nuseibeh, Hazem Z. *Palestine and the United Nations.* New York: Quartet Books, 1981. Collection of speeches on Palestine by former Jordanian U.N. representative.

Nutting, Anthony. *Nasser.* London: Constable, 1972. Former British foreign minister's attack on Nasser.

———. *No End of a Lesson: The Story of Suez.* New York: Clarkson & Potter, 1967. Account of Suez by British foreign minister who resigned during crisis.

O'Ballance, Edgar. *The Arab-Israeli War, 1948.* 1956. Reprint. Westport, Conn.: Hyperion Press, 1981. Account of 1948 war by British military analyst.

———. *The Electronic War in the Middle East, 1968–70.* London: Faber & Faber, 1974. Account of the 1970–71 War of Attrition.

———. *No Victor, No Vanquished: The Yom Kippur War.* San Rafael, Calif.: Presidio Press, 1978. Account of the 1973 war.

———. *The Third Arab-Israeli War.* Hamden, Conn.: Archon, 1972. Account of the 1967 war.

O'Brien, Conor Cruise. *The Siege: The Saga of Israel and Zionism.* New York: Simon & Schuster, 1986. Massive pro-Zionist history of Palestine struggle from 19th century to 1985 by prominent international political figure; sympathetic to Israel.

O'Brien, William V. *Law and Morality in Israel's War with the PLO.* New York: Routledge, 1991. Argues that Israel is engaged in a "just war," therefore its behavior toward the Palestinians is justified.

Oded, Arye. *Africa and the Middle East*. Boulder, Colo.: Rienner, 1987. Account of African ties with Israel and Arab states after 1973.

Ofek, Uriel. *Smoke Over Golan*. New York: Harper & Row, 1979. Account of 10-year-old Israeli boy near front in 1973 war.

'Omer, Devorah. *Path Beneath the Sea*. New York: Funk & Wagnalls, 1969. Novel about Israeli frogman and his important 1967 war mission.

O'Neil, Bard E. *Armed Struggle in Palestine: A Political-Military Analysis*. Boulder, Colo.: Westview Press, 1978. Detailed examination of Palestine resistance movement and origins.

———. *Revolutionary Warfare in the Middle East: The Israelis Vs. the Fedayeen*. Boulder, Colo.: Paladin Press, 1974. Account of Israeli war with Palestinian guerrillas.

The Ordeal of South Lebanon: A Documented Study. Beirut: 1980. Israel-Lebanon border conflict, 1949–1980.

Oren, Michael. *Origins of the Second Arab-Israel War: Egypt, Israel, and the Great Powers, 1952–56*. Portland, Ore.: Cass, 1992. Account of the 1956 Suez/Sinai War, its causes and impact.

Oren, Nissan, ed. *Termination of Wars: Processes, Procedures, and Aftermaths*. Jerusalem: Magnes Press, Hebrew University, 1982. Case studies using Arab-Israel wars.

Osman, Hassan. *The October War: An Authentic Illustrated Record*. Cairo: General Egyptian Book Organization, 1977. Official Egyptian account of 1973 war using mostly illustrations.

Osia, Kumirum. *Israel, South Africa and Black Africa: A Study of the Primacy of the Politics of Expedience*. Washington, D.C.: University Press of America, 1981. Critical account of Israel-South Africa relations and Arab ties to South Africa.

Ott, David H. *Palestine in Perspective: Politics, Human Rights & the West Bank*. London: Quartet Books, 1980. Critique of Israeli autonomy proposals in light of international law.

Ovendale, Ritchie. *Britain, The United States, and the End of the Palestine Mandate, 1942–1948*. London: Boydell Press, 1989. Discussion of Anglo-American tensions caused by Palestine question.

———. *The Origins of the Arab-Israeli Wars*. New York: Longman, 1984. Covers conflict since rise of Zionism; includes 1948, 1956, 1967, 1973 wars.

Ovensen, Geir. *Responding to Change: Trends in Palestinian Household Economy*. Washington, D.C.: Institute for Palestine Studies, 1994. Extensive survey including tables, charts and graphs of dynamics of change in West Bank and Gaza Palestinian households.

Owen, Roger, ed. *Studies in the Economic and Social History of Palestine in the Nineteenth and Twentieth Centuries*. Carbondale: Southern Illinois University Press, 1982. Collection of studies by diverse authors covering economy, society and government.

Oz, Amos. *Black Box*. New York: Vintage Books, 1989. Novel by leading Israeli author covering Jewish-Arab relations.

———. *In the Land of Israel*. New York: Harcourt Brace Jovanovich, 1983. Account of Oz's conversations with Israelis on diverse matters, including relations with Arabs.

Palestine: Profile of an Occupation. Atlantic Highlands, N.J.: Zed Books, 1989. Collection by diverse authors covering Israel-Arab relations.

Palestine Royal Commission. *Report: Presented by the Secretary of State for the Colonies to Parliament by Command of His Majesty July, 1937*. London: HM Stationery Office, 1937. Detailed report on Palestine; also known as Peel Commission Report.

Palestinian Arabs in Israel: Two Case Studies. London: Ithaca Press, for the Middle East Research & Action Group, 1977. Collection of articles critical of treatment of Israeli Arabs in institutions of higher education in Israel.

Palestinian Education: A Threat to Israel's Security: The Israeli Policy of School Closures in the Occupied West Bank and Gaza Strip. Jerusalem: Jerusalem Media & Communication Centre, 1989. Critical account of school closure by Israeli military authorities.

Palestinian External Trade Under Israeli Occupation. New York: UNCTAD, 1989. Examines economic conditions in occupied territories and Israeli government trade restrictions.

The Palestinian-Israeli Peace Agreement: A Documentary Record. Washington, D.C.: Institute for Palestine Studies, 1993. Documents on September 1993 accord between Israel and the PLO.

Palestinians in Profile: A Guide to Leading Palestinians in the Occupied Territories. East Jerusalem: Panorama-Center for the Dissemination of Alternative Information, 1993. Biographical data and interviews with 251 leading Palestinians.

Palit, D. K. *Return to Sinai: The Arab-Israeli War, 1973*. Salisbury, England: Compton Russell, 1974. An Indian account of the 1973 war.

Palumbo, Michael. *Imperial Israel: The History of the Occupation of the West Bank and Gaza*. London: Bloomsbury Press, 1992. Highly critical account of Israeli occupation; compares to South Africa.

———. *The Palestinian Catastrophe: The 1948 Expulsion of a People From Their Homeland*. New York: Olive Branch Press, 1989. Highly critical account of Israeli 1948 policy toward Arabs.

Pappe, Ilan. *Britain and the Arab-Israeli Conflict, 1948–51*. New York: St. Martin's Press, 1988. Detailed study based on archival materials of British policy.

———. *The Making of the Arab-Israeli Conflict, 1947–51.* New York: Tauris, 1992. Diplomatic history of the 1948 war, background and aftermath.

Parker, Richard B. *The Politics of Miscalculation in the Middle East.* Bloomington: Indiana University Press, 1993. Critical examination of U.S. policy in three Middle East crises—1967 war, 1970–71 War of Attrition, 1982 Israeli invasion of Lebanon.

Parker, Thomas. *The Road to Camp David: U.S. Negotiating Strategy Towards the Arab-Israeli Conflict.* New York: Lang, 1989. Examines U.S. Middle East policy from 1973 to 1981.

Parkes, James. *Whose Lands? A History of the Peoples of Palestine.* New York: Taplinger, 1970. History by ardent Christian Zionist of Jews, Arabs (Christians and Muslims) and others in Palestine from ancient times.

Parmenter, Barbara McKean. *Giving Voice to Stones: Place and Identity in Palestinian Literature.* Austin: University of Texas Press, 1994. Discusses how Palestinian writers represent their national experiences since World War I.

Patai, Raphael. *Journeyman in Jerusalem: Memories and Letters, 1933–1947.* Salt Lake City: University of Utah Press, 1992. Autobiography of Hungarian Jewish immigrant and Middle East scholar in mandatory Jerusalem; covers 1936–39 Arab Revolt.

———. *The Seed of Abraham: Jews and Arabs in Contact and Conflict.* Salt Lake City: University of Utah Press, 1986. Israeli anthropologist's comparison of relations between Jews and Arabs from ancient times.

Patai, Raphael, ed. *Encyclopedia of Zionism and Israel.* 2 vols. New York: McGraw Hill, 1971. Reference work on all aspects of Zionism from the 1880s.

Paz, Ury. *The Shortest War. Israeli Fights for Survival.* Tel Aviv: Ramdor Press, 1967. Israeli account of the 1967 Six-Day War.

Peace and the Palestinians: Record of Proceedings: London Seminar. London: British Section of Parliamentary Association for Euro-Arab Co-operation, 1977. Papers and proceedings of September–October 1977 seminar.

Peacewatch Anthology: Analysis of the Arab-Israeli Peace Process From the Madrid Peace Conference to the Eve of President Clinton's Inauguration. Washington, D.C.: Washington Institute for Near East Policy, 1993. Collections of papers from policy forum on peace process.

Pearson, Anthony. *Conspiracy of Silence.* London: Quartet Books, 1978. Investigation into Israeli attack on U.S. ship (*Liberty*) during 1967 war.

Peck, Juliana S. *The Reagan Administration and the Palestinian Question: The First Thousand Days.* Washington, D.C.: Institute for Palestine Studies, 1984. Examines early Reagan policy, including 1982 Lebanon war and Reagan peace plan.

Peleg, Ilan, and Ofira Seliktar, eds. *The Emergence of a Binational Israel: The Second Republic in the Making*. Boulder, Colo.: Westview Press, 1989. Collection of essays on Israel-Arab relations in post-1967 era.

Pelcovits, Nathan A. *The Long Armistice: U.N. Peacekeeping and the Arab-Israeli Conflict, 1948–1960*. Boulder, Colo.: Westview Press, 1993. Role of U.N. forces in 1948 and 1956 wars.

———. *Peacekeeping on Arab-Israeli Fronts: Lessons from the Sinai and Lebanon*. Boulder, Colo.: Westview Press, 1984. Examines role of international forces in Sinai and Lebanon peacekeeping.

———. *Security Guarantees in a Middle East Settlement*. Beverly Hills, Calif.: Sage Publications, 1976. General discussion of international role in security guarantees.

Peres, Shimon. *Battling for Peace: A Memoir*. New York: Random House, 1995. Memoir by Israel's prime minister.

———. *David's Sling*. London: Weidenfeld & Nicolson, 1970. Israeli foreign and prime minister's account of search for security.

———. *The New Middle East*. New York: Holt, 1993. Peres' vision for Middle East future, economic integration, etc.

Peretz, Don. *Intifada: The Palestinian Uprising*. Boulder, Colo.: Westview Press, 1990. Account of Intifada—background, causes, impact on Israel and Arabs.

———. *Israel and the Palestine Arabs*. Washington, D.C.: Middle East Institute, 1958. Israel's policy toward Arab minority and Palestine refugees.

———. *The West Bank: History, Politics, Society, and Economy*. Boulder, Colo.: Westview Press, 1986. Examination of West Bank from Ottoman era through Israeli occupation.

Peretz, Don, Evan Wilson and Richard J. Ward. *A Palestine Entity*. Washington, D.C.: Middle East Institute, 1970. Background and problems in establishing Palestinian West Bank Gaza entity.

Peri, Yoram. *Between Battles and Ballots: Israeli Military in Politics*. Cambridge: Cambridge University Press, 1983. Study of military role in Israeli politics.

Perlmutter, Amos. *Politics and the Military in Israel 1967–1977*. London: Cass, 1978. Covers role of IDF in politics and its influence in 1973 war; sequel to *Military and Politics in Israel 1948–1967*.

Perlmutter, Amos, Michael Handel and Uri Bar-Joseph. *Two Minutes Over Baghdad*. London: Vallentine, Mitchell, 1982. Israeli 1981 attack on and destruction of Iraq's nuclear plant.

Perry, Mark. *A Fire in Zion: The Israeli-Palestinian Search for Peace*. New York: Morrow, 1994. Israeli-Arab relations from 1973 to September 1993 PLO accord.

Persson, Sune O. *Mediation or Assassination: Count Bernadotte's Mission to Palestine 1948*. London: Ithaca Press, 1979. Bernadotte's mission as U.N. Palestine mediator and his 1948 assassination.

Peteet, Julie M. *Gender in Crisis: Women and the Palestinian Resistance Movement*. New York: Columbia University Press, 1991. Discusses Palestinian women's movements and women's plight from 1920s to 1982.

Peters, F. E. *Jerusalem and Mecca: The Typology of the Holy City in the Near East*. New York: New York University Press, 1987. Comparison and role of the two cities in Islamic history.

———. *Jerusalem: The Holy City in the Eyes of Chroniclers, Visitors, Pilgrims, and Prophets From the Days of Abraham to the Beginnings of Modern Times*. Princeton, N.J.: Princeton University Press, 1985. Selections from eyewitness accounts.

Peters, Joan. *From Time Immemorial: The Origins of the Arab-Israeli Conflict Over Palestine*. New York: Harper & Row, 1984. Highly controversial attempt to discredit Arab claims to Palestine.

Pfaff, Richard H. *Jerusalem: Keystone of an Arab-Israeli Settlement*. Washington, D.C.: American Enterprise Institute, 1969. Study of and proposals for resolution of Jerusalem issue.

Pinner, Walter. *How Many Arab Refugees*. London: Macgibbon & Kee, 1959. An early attempt to estimate number of refugees; on the low side.

Plascov, Avi. *A Palestinian State? Examining the Alternatives*. London: International Institute for Strategic Studies, 1981. Adelphi Paper examines diverse solutions; favors Palestine state.

Platt, Alan, ed. *Arms Control and Confidence Building in the Middle East*. Washington, D.C.: U.S. Institute of Peace Press, 1992. Four authors discuss how to control Middle East arms race.

Playfair, Emma, ed. *International Law and Administration of Occupied Territories: Two Decades of Israeli Occupation of the West Bank and Gaza Strip*. New York: Oxford University Press, 1992. Collection of essays from 1988 conference in East Jerusalem.

Pogany, Istvan S. *The Security Council and the Arab-Israeli Conflict*. New York: St. Martin's Press, 1984. Account of U.N. Security Council and Arab-Israel conflict.

Polk, William R. *The Elusive Peace: The Middle East in the Twentieth Century*. New York: St. Martin's Press, 1979. Short history of Arab-Israel conflict; U.S. role; impact on Lebanon.

Polk, William, David Stamler and Edmund Asfour. *Backdrop to Tragedy: The Struggle for Palestine*. Boston: Beacon Press, 1957. History of conflict—three perspectives from 19th century to creation of Israel; refugee problem, economic impact.

Pollock, David. *The Politics of Pressure: American Arms and Israeli Policy Since the Six Day War*. Westport, Conn.: Greenwood Press, 1982. U.S. use of arms supplies to influence Israeli policies.

Porath, Yehoshua. *The Emergence of the Palestinian National Movement, 1918–1929*. London: Cass, 1973. Scholarly study of the rise of the Palestinian national movement.

———. *The Palestinian Arab National Movement, From Riots to Rebellion*. Vol. 2. *1929–1939*. London: Cass, 1978. Continuation of Porath's study to end of Arab Rebellion.

Portugali, Juval. *Implicate Relations: Society and Space in the Israeli-Palestinian Conflict*. Boston: Kluwer, 1993. Geographic study of Jewish-Arab relations since 1973.

Posner, Steve. *Israel Undercover: Secret Warfare and Hidden Diplomacy in the Middle East*. Syracuse, N.Y.: Syracuse University Press, 1987. Account of Israel undercover operations in Lebanon, Egypt, etc.

Postal, Bernard, and Henry W. Levy. *And the Hills Shouted for Joy: The Day Israel Was Born*. New York: McKay, 1973. Laudatory account of Israel's birth, background, history from 1917.

Prison Conditions in Israel and the Occupied Territories. New York: Human Rights Watch, 1991. Palestinian prison conditions, political prisoners and civil rights.

Pry, Peter. *Israel's Nuclear Arsenal*. Boulder, Colo.: Westview Press, 1984. Examines Israel's military nuclear capability.

Pryce-Jones, David. *The Face of Defeat: Palestinian Refugees and Guerrillas*. New York: Holt, Rinehart & Winston, 1972. Journalistic account based on interviews with guerrillas.

Punamaki-Gital, Raija-Leena. *Childhood Under Conflict: The Attitudes and Emotional Life of Israeli and Palestinian Children*. Tampere, Finland: Tampere Peace Research Institute, 1987. Psychological impact of conflict on Arab and Jewish children.

Punishing a Nation: Human Rights Violations During the Palestinian Uprising, December 1987–December 1988. Ramallah, West Bank: al-Haq/Law in the Service of Man, 1988. Documented study of human rights violations; by affiliate of the International Commission of Jurists.

Puschel, Karen L. *U.S.-Israeli Strategic Cooperation in the Post-Cold War Era: An American Perspective*. Boulder, Colo.: Westview Press, 1992. Monograph on U.S.-Israel strategic relations after Cold War.

Qleibo, Ali H. *Before the Mountains Disappear: An Ethnographic Chronicle of the Modern Palestinians*. Cairo: Kloreus, 1992. Collection of essays, anecdotes and personal observations of Palestinian anthropologist returning to homeland during Intifada.

Quandt, William B. *Camp David: Peacemaking and Politics.* Washington, D.C.: Brookings Institution, 1986. Detailed study of U.S. Middle East diplomacy leading to Israel-Egypt peace.

———. *Decade of Decisions: American Policy Toward the Arab-Israeli Conflict, 1967–1976.* Berkeley: University of California Press, 1977. History of U.S. involvement in Arab-Israel conflict.

———. *Peace Process: American Diplomacy and the Arab-Israeli Conflict Since 1967.* Berkeley: University of California Press, 1993. Massive account of U.S. Middle East policy since 1967 by former National Security Council Middle East specialist.

Quandt, William B., ed. *The Middle East: Ten Years After Camp David.* Washington, D.C.: Brookings Institution, 1988. Collection of essays and documents covering impact of Camp David.

Quandt, William B., Fuad Jabbar and Ann Mosely Lesch. *The Politics of Palestinian Nationalism.* Berkeley: University of California Press, 1973. Studies of Palestinian national movement from mandate to end of 1960s.

Quarrie, Bruce. *A Wargamers' Guide to the Arab-Israeli Wars Since 1948.* Cambridge, England: Stephens, 1978. Layman's guide to conducting a Middle East war game.

The Quest for Peace: Principal United States Public Statements and Documents Related to the Arab-Israeli Peace Process, 1967–1983. Washington, D.C.: U.S. Department of State, 1984. Extensive collection of documents covering Arab-Israel conflict.

Quigley, John. *Palestine and Israel: A Challenge to Justice.* Durham, N.C.: Duke University Press, 1990. Critical account of Israeli policy by international lawyer.

Rabah, Jamil, and Natasha Fairweather, eds. *Israeli Military Orders in the Occupied Palestinian West Bank: 1967–1992.* Jerusalem: Jerusalem Media & Communication Centre, 1993. Translation and summaries of over 1,300 Israeli military orders.

Rabie, Mohamed. *U.S.-PLO Dialogue: Secret Diplomacy and Conflict Resolution.* Gainesville, Fla.: University of Florida Press, 1995. Discussion of PLO internal debate leading to dialogue with U.S.

Rabin, Yitzhak. *The Rabin Memoirs.* Boston: Little, Brown, 1979. Memoirs of Israeli soldier, diplomat and prime minister including account of his participation in Israel's wars.

Rabinovich, Abraham. *The Battle for Jerusalem, June 5–7, 1967.* Philadelphia: Jewish Publication Society, 1987. Enthusiastic account of Israel's victory.

———. *The Boats of Cherbourg.* New York: Seaver, 1988. Account of Israeli seizure of missile boats in France.

Rabinovich, Itamar. *The Road Not Taken: Early Arab-Israeli Negotiations*. New York: Oxford University Press, 1991. Israeli scholar/diplomat's account of missed opportunities.

———. *The War for Lebanon, 1970–1983*. Ithaca, N.Y.: Cornell University Press, 1984. Account of and background to civil war in Lebanon and Israel's role.

Rabinovich, Itamar, and Jehuda Reinharz, eds. *Israel in the Middle East: Documents and Readings on Society, Politics, and Foreign Relations 1948–Present*. New York: Oxford University Press, 1984. Collection of documents, readings, etc., covering Israel's foreign policy; includes relations with United States, USSR, Arabs.

Rabinovich, Itamar, and Haim Shaked, eds. *From June to October: The Middle East Between 1967 and 1973*. New Brunswick, N.J.: Transaction Books, 1978. Collection of papers by diverse authors on Middle East conflict.

Raeymaeker, Omer de. *Belgium and the Israeli-Arab Conflicts, 1948–1982*. Brussels: Ministry of Foreign Affairs, 1984. Account of Belgium's policy in Arab-Israel conflict.

al-Raheb, Hani. *The Zionist Character in the English Novel*. London: Zed Books, 1985. Study of Zionist characters in English novels offering flattering stereotypes.

Rahman, Mira. *Middle East Impasse: Sadat and Camp David*. Dacca: Asif Rahman, 1982. A perspective from Bangladesh.

Rajab, Jehan S. *Palestinian Folk Costume*. New York: KPI, 1989. Colorful illustrations of mostly woman's garments.

Ramraz-Ra'ukh, Gilah. *The Arab in Israeli Literature*. Bloomington: Indiana University Press, 1989. A study of how Israeli authors treat Arab subjects.

Ramsden, Sally, and Cath Senker, eds. *Learning the Hard Way: Palestinian Education in the West Bank, Gaza Strip and Israel*. London: WUS(UK), 1993. Observations of 1993 study tour investigation of Palestinian education.

Randal, Jonathan C. *Going All the Way: Christian Warlords, Israeli Adventurers, and the War in Lebanon*. New York: Viking, 1983. Account of Lebanon's civil war and Israel-Maronite relations.

Rausch, David A. *The Middle East Maze: Israel and Her Neighbors*. Chicago: Moody Press, 1991. Covers Israel-Jewish and Israel-Arab relations.

Raviv, Yehoshua. *The Arab-Israeli Military Balance (in View of the Israeli-Egyptian Peace Treaty)*. Tel Aviv: Tel Aviv University Center for Strategic Studies, 1980. How the peace treaty affects Israel's security.

Ray, James Lee. *The Future of American-Israeli Relations: A Parting of the Ways?* Lexington: University of Kentucky Press, 1985. Critical account of U.S.-Israel relations and West Bank occupation.

Razien, Esther. *No Rattling of Sabers: An Antohology of Israeli War Poetry.* Austin: University of Texas Press, 1996. Discusses characteristics of Israeli war poetry from 1948 to 1991.

Reich, Bernard. *Quest for Peace: United States-Israel Relations and the Arab-Israeli Conflict.* New Brunswick, N.J.: Transaction Books, 1977. Impact of Arab-Israel conflict on post-1967 U.S.-Israel relations.

———. *The United States and Israel: Influence in the Special Relationship.* New York: Praeger, 1984. Account of Israel-U.S. relations during the Carter and Reagan eras.

Reich, Walter. *A Stranger in My House: Jews and Arabs in the West Bank.* New York: Holt, Rinehart & Winston, 1984. Attitudes of Israeli settlers and Palestinians to each other based on conversations with both.

Reinharz, Jehuda. *Chaim Weizman: The Making of a Zionist Leader.* Oxford, England: Oxford University Press, 1985. Biography to 1913 of the Zionist leader who later became Israel's first president.

Reiser, Stewart. *The Politics of Leverage: The National Religious Party of Israel and Its Influence on Foreign Policy.* Cambridge, Mass.: Harvard University Center for Middle Eastern Studies, 1984. Monograph of the National Religious party's role in coalition government and policy influence.

Reische, Diana L. *Arafat and the Palestine Liberation Organization.* New York: Watts, 1991. Life and career of Yasir Arafat as leader of the PLO.

Reiss, Nira. *The Health of the Arabs in Israel.* Boulder, Colo.: Westview Press, 1991. Examines Arab medical care, social conditions and health services.

el-Rayyes, Riad, and Dunia Nahas. *Guerrillas for Palestine.* New York: St. Martin's Press, 1976. Sympathetic study of Palestine resistance movement, structure, leaders, foreign relations.

Riad, Mahmoud. *The Struggle for Peace in the Middle East.* New York: Quartet Books, 1982. Memoirs of Egyptian general, foreign minister and Arab League secretary-general from the 1967 Six-Day War to the 1978 Camp David meetings.

Rice, Michael. *False Inheritance: Israel in Palestine and the Search for a Solution.* New York: Columbia University Press, 1994. Critique of "exclusionist Jewish State" and Zionist claims based on Old Testament, from non-Palestinian Arab perspective.

Richardson, John P. *The West Bank: A Portrait.* Washington, D.C.: Middle East Institute, 1984. Survey of the West Bank and its history from the Ottomans to occupation by Israel.

Rigby, Andrew. *Living the Intifada.* London: Zed Books, 1991. Detailed history of the Intifada through the Gulf War.

Rikardsson, Gunnel. *The Middle East Conflict in the Swedish Press: A Content Analysis of Editorials in Three Daily Newspapers 1948–1973.* Stockholm:

Esselte Studium, 1978. Covers Swedish public opinion on Arab-Israel conflict.
Rikhye, Indar Jit. *The Sinai Blunder: Withdrawal of the United Nations Emergency Force Leading to the Six-Day War of June 1967*. London: Cass, 1980. Account by commander of UNEF during 1967 crisis.
Rishmawi, Mona. *Planning in Whose Interest? Land Use Planning as a Strategy for Judaization*. Ramallah, West Bank: al-Haq, 1986. Critical examination of Israeli acquisition of West Bank Arab land.
Roberts, Samuel J. *Survival or Hegemony? The Foundations of Israeli Foreign Policy*. Baltimore, Md.: Johns Hopkins University Press, 1973. Critical account of Zionist policy before 1948 and of Israeli policy since 1948 with a section on Israeli imperialism.
Robertson, Terence. *Crisis: The Inside Story of the Suez Conspiracy*. New York: Atheneum, 1965. Account of 1956 war critical of Great Britain, France and Israel.
Robson, Clive, and Paul Cassli. *Stateless in Gaza*. London: Zed Books, 1986. Collection of interviews with Gaza Palestinians.
Rodinson, Maxime. *Cult, Ghetto, and State: The Persistence of the Jewish Question*. London: Saqi Books, 1983. Collection of essays by a French Jewish Middle East scholar.
———. *Israel: A Colonial-Settler State?* New York: Monad Press, 1973. Argues Israel, like South Africa, is a colonial-settler state.
———. *Israel and the Arabs*. New York: Pantheon Books, 1968. Critical account of Israel in its conflict with Arabs to 1967.
Rokach, Livia. *The Catholic Church and the Question of Palestine*. London: Saqi Books, 1987. Critical examination of Catholic church's position on Zionism, Israel and Palestinians.
———. *Israel's Sacred Terrorism: A Study Based on Moshe Sharett's Personal Diary and Other Documents*. 3d ed. Belmont, Mass.: Association of Arab-American University Graduates, 1986. Excerpts from former Israeli foreign and prime minister's account of aggressive policy in 1950s.
Roman, Michael, and Alex Weingrod. *Living Together Separately: Arabs and Jews in Contemporary Jerusalem*. Princeton, N.J.: Princeton University Press, 1991. Arab-Jewish ethnic relations since Israel's occupation of Jerusalem.
Rose, John. *Israel, the Hijack State: America's Watchdog in the Middle East*. London: Bookmarks, 1986. Israel-U.S. relations and the Palestine conflict.
Rose, Norman A. *Chaim Weizmann: A Biography*. New York: Viking Press, 1986. Sympathetic account of Israel's first president.
———. *The Gentile Zionists: A Study in Anglo-Zionist Diplomacy*. London: Cass, 1973. Influence of non-Jewish Zionists on British policy in 1930s.

Rosen, Harry M. *The Arabs and Jews in Israel: The Reality, the Dilemma, the Promise*. Jerusalem: American Jewish Committee Israel Office, Foreign Affairs Department, 1970. Influential American Jewish group's presentation of Arab-Jewish relations.

Rosen, Steven. *Military Geography and the Military Balance in the Arab-Israel Conflict*. Jerusalem: Hebrew University, Leonard Davis Institute for International Relations, 1977. Monograph in Jerusalem Papers on Peace Problems series.

Rosenfeld, Alvin. *The Plot to Destroy Israel: The Road to Armageddon*. New York: Putnam, 1977. Critical account of Arabs and policies of the West.

Rosenne, Shabtai. *Israel's Armistice Agreements With the Arab States: A Juridical Interpretation*. Tel Aviv: Israel Branch, International Law Association, 1951. Israeli legal authority's interpretation of armistices.

Rosensaft, Menachem Z. *Not Backward to Belligerency: A Study of Events Surrounding the "Six-Day War" of June 1967*. New York: Yoseloff, 1969. Diplomatic history of 1967 war with a call for peace.

Rosenwasser, Penny. *Voices From a "Promised Land": Palestinian and Israeli Peace Activists Speak Their Hearts*. Willimantic, Conn.: Curbstone Press, 1992. Interviews with Israeli Jewish and Arab women peace activists.

Rostow, Eugene V., ed. *The Middle East: Critical Choices for the United States*. Boulder, Colo.: Westview Press, 1976. Speeches at convention of National Committee for American Foreign Policy, largely critical of United States and Arabs.

Roth, Stephen, ed. *The Impact of the Six-Day War: A Twenty-Year Assessment*. New York: St. Martin's Press, 1988. Assessments, mostly by Israelis, on the impact of the 1967 war after 20 years.

Rotham, Jay, and Sharon Bray. *A Guide to Arab-Jewish Peacemaking in Israel*. New York: New Israel Fund, 1984. Directory of Israeli peace groups.

Rothschild, Jon, ed. *Forbidden Agendas: Intolerance and Defiance in the Middle East*. London: Saqi Books, 1984. Collection of articles on Israeli society with leftist orientation.

Rowley, Gwyn. *Israel into Palestine*. London: Mansell, 1984. General history of the Palestine question from 19th century to 1982 war.

Roy, Sara. *The Gaza Strip: A Demographic, Economic, Social and Legal Survey*. Boulder, Colo.: Westview Press, 1986. Extensive study of Gaza for West Bank Data Base Project.

———. *The Gaza Strip: The Political Economy of De-Development*. Washington, D.C.: Institute for Palestine Studies, 1995. Detailed study of Gaza's political economy after Israeli occupation, and its deterioration.

Rubenberg, Cheryl A. *Israel and the American National Interest: A Critical Examination*. Urbana: University of Illinois Press, 1986. Sharply critical examination of Israel-U.S. relationship.

———. *The Palestine Liberation Organization: Its Institutional Infrastructure.* Belmont, Mass.: Institute for Arab Studies, 1982. Study of PLO civilian welfare, educational and industrial institutions.

Rubin, Barry. *The Arab States and Palestine.* Syracuse, N.J.: Syracuse University Press, 1981. History of Arab states involvement in Palestine problem.

———. *Revolution Until Victory? The Politics and History of the PLO.* Cambridge, Mass.: Harvard University Press, 1994. Highly critical history and analysis of the PLO.

Rubin, Jeffrey Z., ed. *Dynamics of Third Party Intervention: Kissinger in the Middle East.* New York: Praeger, 1981. Collection of essays on Kissinger's Middle East involvement.

Rubinstein, Amnon. *The Zionist Dream Revisited: From Herzl to Gush Emunim and Back.* New York: Schocken Books, 1984. Critical history of Zionist ideology: "What went wrong?"

Rubinstein, Alvin Z., ed. *The Arab-Israel Conflict: Perspectives.* 2d ed. New York: HarperCollins, 1991. Essays by Israeli and American scholars on Israel, Palestinians and the United States.

Rubinstein, Danny. *The Mystery of Arafat.* South Royalton, Vt.: Steerforth Press, 1995. Sympathetic account of Arafat's problems by Israeli journalist.

———. *The People of Nowhere: The Palestinian Vision of Home.* New York: Times Books, 1991. Sympathetic account by Israeli journalist of Palestinian insistence on "right of return."

Rubinstein, Sondra Miller. *The Communist Movement in Palestine and Israel.* Boulder, Colo.: Westview Press, 1985. Study of Communist movement, mostly during mandatory era.

Ruedy, John, and Janet Abu Lughod. *The Dynamics of Land Alienation and the Demographic Transformation of Palestine.* North Dartmouth, Mass.: American Association of Arab-American University Graduates, 1973. Monograph on Arab land loss to Zionists and displacement from Palestine.

Reuther, Herman, J. *The Wrath of Jonah: The Crisis of Religious Nationalism in the Israeli Palestine Conflict.* San Francisco: Harper & Row, 1989. Liberal Christian critical analysis of Zionism, Israel and U.S. policy.

Saba, Michael. *The Armageddon Network.* Brattleboro, Vt.: Amana Books, 1984. Revelations about Pentagon officials spying for Israel.

Sachar, Howard M. *Egypt and Israel.* New York: Marek, 1981. History of Egyptian-Israeli relations from 1930s to 1979 peace.

———. *A History of Israel From the Rise of Zionism to Our Time.* New York: Knopf, 1976. Detailed history of rise of Israel, including Arab relations.

———. *A History of Israel.* Vol. 2, *From the Aftermath of the Yom Kippur War.* New York: Oxford University Press, 1987. Sequel to Sachar's first volume.

Safran, Nadav. *From War to War: The Arab-Israeli Confrontation, 1948–1967*. Indianapolis, Ind.: Pegasus, 1969. History of Arab-Israel conflict from end of 1948 war to end of 1967 war.

———. *Israel: The Embattled Ally*. Cambridge, Mass.: Harvard University Press, 1978. Extensive survey of Israel foreign policy and U.S. relations.

Safty, Adel. *From Camp David to the Gulf: Negotiations, Language, Propaganda and War*. Montreal: Black Rose Books, 1992. Collection of essays examining statements of personalities, some based on interviews with Sadat, Dayan, Carter, Heikal, etc.

Sahliyeh, Emile. *In Search of Leadership: West Bank Politics Since 1967*. Washington, D.C.: Brookings Institution, 1988. West Bank politics under Israeli occupation; based on interviews.

———. *The PLO After the Lebanon War*. Boulder, Colo.: Westview Press, 1986. Describes impact of 1982 war on PLO.

Said, Edward W. *After the Last Sky: Palestinian Lives*. New York: Pantheon Books, 1986. Portrayal of Palestinian people's lives through photos and text.

———. *The Politics of Dispossession: The Struggle for Palestinian Self-Determination 1969–1994*. London: Chatto & Windus, 1994. Collection of essays by Palestinian-American highly critical of Western, Arab and Palestinian policies.

———. *The Question of Palestine*. New York: Times Books, 1979. Presentation of Palestinian position; Zionist achievement of goals at expense of Palestinian people.

Said, Edward, Christopher Hitchens, eds. *Blaming the Victims: Spurious Scholarship and the Palestinian Question*. New York: Verso, 1987. Collection of essays by diverse authors criticizing Middle East scholarship.

Saliba, Samir N. *The Jordan River Dispute*. The Hague, The Netherlands: Nijhoff, 1968. Discussion of dispute between Israel and Arabs over water.

Salih, Abdul Jawad. *Israel's Policy of De-Institutionalization: A Case Study of Palestinian Local Government*. Amman, Jordan: Jerusalem Center for Development Studies, 1987. Critique of Israeli government's policy toward Arab municipalities.

Salmi, Ralph H. and Issam, Nashashibi, eds. *The Israeli-Palestinian Declaration of Principles: Voices of Dissent in the Palestinian Community*. Boulder, Colo.: Westview Press, 1996. Essays by diverse Palestinian intellectuals critical of DOP.

Samarah, 'Adil. *Industrialization in the West Bank: A Marxist Socio-Economic Analysis, 1967–1991*. Jerusalem: Al-Mashriq, 1992. From Economic & Development Studies; critique of Israeli policy.

Sam'o, Elias, *The June 1967 Arab-Israeli War: Miscalculation or Conspiracy?* Wilmette, Ill.: Medina University Press, 1971. Background and causes of the 1967 war.

Sandler, Shmuel, and Hillel Frisch. *Israel, the Palestinians, and the West Bank: A Study in Intercommunal Conflict*. Lexington, Mass.: Lexington Books, 1984. Examination of Israeli government policies by two Israeli scholars.

Sarna, Aaron J. *Boycott and Blacklist: A History of Arab Economic Warfare Against Israel*. Totowa, N.J.: Rowman & Littlefield, 1986. Examination of Israel-Arab economic relations.

Saunders, Harold H. *The Other Walls: The Arab-Israeli Peace Process in a Global Perspective*. Princeton, N.J.: Princeton University Press, 1991. Revised edition of earlier work on international mediation and conflict resolution in Arab-Israel conflict.

Sayigh, Rosemary. *Palestinians: From Peasants to Revolutionaries*. London: Zed Books, 1979. Sociological study of Palestinian displacement.

———. *Too Many Enemies: The Palestinian Experience in Lebanon*. London: Zed Press, 1994. Case study based on Shatilla refugee camp on outskirts of Beirut.

Sayigh, Yezid. *Arab Military Industry: Capability, Performance, and Impact*. London: Brassey's, for Centre for Arab Unity Studies, 1992. Discusses Arab defense spending, imports, capabilities.

Schack, Howard H. *A Spy in Canaan: My Secret Life as a Jewish American Businessman Spying for Israel*. Thorndike, Maine: Thorndike Press, 1994. Sensational autobiography.

Schenker, Hillel, ed. *After Lebanon-Palestinian Connection*. New York: Pilgrim Press, 1983. Collection of articles on Israeli intervention against Palestinians in Lebanon.

Schiff, Benjamin N. *Refugees unto the Third Generation: U.N. Aid to Palestinians*. Syracuse: Syracuse University Press, 1995. Detailed study of history and operations of UNRWA.

Schiff, Zeev. *Fedayeen: Guerrillas Against Israel*. New York: McKay, 1972. Account by senior Israeli political-military correspondent.

———. *October Earthquake. Yom Kippur, 1973*. Tel Aviv: University Publishing Projects, 1974. Account of 1973 war by Israeli journalist.

———. *Peace with Security: Israel's Minimal Security Requirements in Negotiations with Syria*. Washington, D.C.: Washington Institute for Near East Policy, 1993. Supports land for peace arrangement but emphasizes Israel's security and water requirements for an agreement.

Schiff, Zeev, and Ehud Yaari. *Intifada: The Palestinian Uprising—Israel's Third Front*. New York: Simon & Schuster, 1990. Authors maintain that Intifada is internal war.

———. *Israel's Lebanon War*. New York: Simon & Schuster, 1984. Critical account of Lebanon War by two leading Israeli journalists.

Schleifer, Abdullah. *The Fall of Jerusalem*. New York: Monthly Review Press, 1972. Account of the 1967 Jerusalem battle by Jewish American convert to Islam.

Schnell, Itzhak. *Perceptions of Israeli-Arabs: Territoriality and Identity*. Brookfield, Vt.: Ashgate, 1994. Israeli public opinion vis-à-vis Arab citizens.

Schoenberg, Harris O. *A Mandate for Terror: The United Nations and the PLO*. New York: Shapolsky, 1989. Critique of United Nations' recognition of PLO.

Schoenman, Ralph. *The Hidden History of Zionism*. Santa Barbara, Calif.: Veritas Press, 1988. Attack on pro-Israel myths; sympathetic to Palestinians.

Scholch, Alexander. *Palestine in Transformation, 1856–1882: Studies in Social, Economic and Political Development*. Washington, D.C.: Institute for Palestine Studies, 1993. Studies of 19th-century Palestine; translated from German.

Scholch, Alexander, ed. *Palestinians Over the Green Line: Studies in the Relations Between Palestinians on Both Sides of the Armistice Line Since 1967*. London: Ithaca Press, 1983. Studies relations between Israel Arab citizens and West Bank Arabs.

Scholz, Norbert, ed. *U.S. Official Statements: Palestinian Refugees*. Washington, D.C.: Institute for Palestine Studies, 1994. Fifth book in series of U.S. official policy statements.

Schwartz, Ted. *Walking with the Damned: The Shocking Murder of the Man Who Freed 30,000 Prisoners From the Nazis*. New York: Paragon House, 1992. Biography of Count Folke Bernadotte, U.N. Palestine mediator.

The Search for Peace in the Middle East: Documents and Statements, 1967–79. Washington, D.C.: U.S. Government Printing Office, 1979. Report prepared for the House of Representatives Committee on Foreign Affairs Subcommittee on Europe and the Middle East.

The Search for Peace in the Middle East—Documents and Statements, 1967–88. Buffalo, New York: Hein, 1989. Prepared for the House of Representatives Committee on Foreign Affairs Subcommittee on Europe and the Middle East.

Segal, Jerome M. *Creating the Palestinian State: A Strategy for Peace*. Chicago: Lawrence Hill Books, 1989. Proposal by American Jewish professor to create Palestine state.

Segal, Ronald. *Whose Jerusalem? The Conflicts of Israel*. Baltimore, Md.: Penguin, 1975. Israel-Arab conflict over Jerusalem after 1948.

Seger, Karen, ed. *Portrait of a Palestinian Village: The Photographs of Hilma Granquist*. London: Third World Center for Research and Publishing, 1981. Anthropological study with excellent photos.

Segev, Tom. *1949: The First Israelis*. New York: Free Press, 1986. Israeli journalist's account of Israeli confiscation of Arab property, early Arab policies and initial mishandling of problems.

Seliktar, Ofira. *New Zionism and the Foreign Policy System of Israel*. Carbondale: Southern Illinois University Press, 1986. Describes the growth of more militant Israeli foreign policy.

Sella, Amnon, and Yael Yishai. *Israel: The Peaceful Belligerent, 1967–79*. New York: St. Martin's Press, 1986. Israeli scholar's analysis of events from 1967 war to peace treaty with Egypt.

Selzer, Michael, ed. *Zionism Reconsidered: The Rejection of Jewish Normalcy*. New York: Macmillan, 1970. Collection of essays by Jewish critics of Zionism.

Semyonev, Moshe, and Noah Lewin-Epstein. *Hewers of Wood and Drawers of Water: Noncitizen Arabs in the Israeli Labor Market*. Ithaca, N.Y.: ILR Press, 1987. Examines conditions of Palestinians from occupied territories working in Israel.

Serwer-Bernstein, Blanche. *In the Tradition of Moses and Mohammed: Jewish and Arab Folktales*. Northvale, N.J.: Aronson, 1994.

Shadid, Mohammed Khalil. *The United States and the Palestinians*. New York: St. Martin's Press, 1981. Critical analysis of U.S. policy from pre-1948 to President Carter.

Shafir, Gershon. *Land, Labor and the Origins of the Israeli-Palestinian Conflict, 1882–1914*. Cambridge, England: Cambridge University Press, 1989. Discussion of early causes of Arab-Jewish tension in Palestine.

Shahak, Israel. *Jewish History, Jewish Religion: The Weight of Three Thousand Years*. Boulder, Colo.: Pluto Press, 1994. Highly critical of Orthodox Judaism and Jewish attitudes to Arabs.

Shaham, Nathan, and Mordechai Bar-On. *Israel Defense Forces, The Six Day War*. Philadelphia: Chilton, 1969. Official account of I.D.F. in Six-Day War, published through Israel Ministry of Defense.

Shaheen, Azeez. *Ramallah: Its History and Its Genealogies*. Birzeit, West Bank: Birzeit University Press, 1982. Family genealogies of Ramallah.

Shaheen, Jack G. *The TV Arab*. Bowling Green, Ohio: Bowling Green State University Popular Press, 1984. Documents bias against Arabs on TV.

Shaked, Haim, and Itamar Rabinovich, eds. *The Middle East and the United States: Perceptions and Policies*. New Brunswick, N.J.: Transaction Books, 1990. Collection of articles on Middle East and Israel-U.S. relations.

Shalev, Aryeh. *The Autonomy—Problems and Possible Solutions.* Tel Aviv: Tel Aviv University, 1980. Former Israeli general discusses autonomy arrangements for West Bank and Gaza.

———. *The Intifada: Causes and Effects*. Boulder, Colo.: Westview Press, 1991. Analysis of Intifada by former Israeli West Bank military governor.

———. *Israel and Syria: Peace and Security on the Golan*. Boulder, Colo.: 1994. An Israeli ex-general's discussion of problems of a peace settlement with Syria.

———. *The Israel-Syria Armistice Regime, 1949–1955*. Boulder, Colo.: Westview Press, 1993. Examination of armistice agreement by Israeli participant in Mixed Armistice Commission with Syria.

———. *The West Bank: Line of Defense*. New York: Praeger, 1985. Israeli general argues West Bank is necessary for Israeli defense.

Shalev, Carmel. *Collective Punishment in the West Bank and the Gaza Strip.* Jerusalem: B'tselem, 1990. Critique of Israeli human rights violations; by Israeli human rights group.

Shamgar, Meir, ed. *Military Government in the Territories Administered by Israel, 1967–1980: The Legal Aspects*. Jerusalem: Hebrew University, Harry Sacher Institute for Legislature Research and Comparative Law, 1982. An Israeli official view.

Shammas, Anton. *Arabesques*. New York: Harper & Row, 1988. Autobiographic novel by Israeli Arab; translated from Hebrew.

Shapira, Anita. *Land and Power: The Zionist Resort to Force, 1891–1948*. New York: Oxford University Press, 1992. Examines ideologies, myths and symbols developed by Zionist settlers to justify confrontation with Palestine and other Arabs.

Shapira, Avraham, ed. *The Seventh Day: Soldiers Talk About the Six-Day War*. New York: Scribner, 1971; Baltimore: Penguin, 1971.

Shapiro, Yonathan. *The Road to Power: Herut Party in Israel*. Albany: State University of New York Press, 1991. Analysis of Israel's nationalist/territorialist party.

Sharabi, Hisham. *Palestine and Israel: The Lethal Dilemma*. New York: Pegasus, 1969. Palestinian scholar's discussion of the conflict and its ramifications.

Sharif, Regina. *Non-Jewish Zionism: Its Roots in Western History*. London: Zed Books, 1983. Examines Western Christian beliefs from 16th century to present.

Sharoni, Simona. *Gender and the Israel-Palestinian Conflict: The Politics of Women's Resistance*. Syracuse: Syracuse University Press, 1995. Feminist account of role played by Israeli and Palestinian women in the Arab-Israeli conflict.

Shavit, Yaacov. *Jabotinsky and the Revisionist Movement 1925–1948: The Right in Zionism and in Israel 1925–1985*. Savage, Md.: Rowman & Littlefield, 1989. History of Begin's mentor and roots of Likud bloc in Israel.

———. *The New Hebrew Nation: A Study in Israeli Heresy and Fantasy*. London: Cass, 1987. Examines ideology of new "Hebrew nation" that rejects Zionism but seeks to dominate Middle East.

el-Shazly, Saad. *The Arab Military Option*. San Francisco: American Mideast Research, 1986. Discussion of Israel-Arab conflicts by former Egyptian general.

———. *The Crossing of the Suez*. San Francisco: American Mideast Research, 1980. Egyptian general's account of Egypt's role in 1973 war.

Sheehan, Edward R. F. *The Arabs, Israel and Kissinger: A Secret History of America's Diplomacy in the Middle East*. New York: Reader's Digest Press, 1976. Journalistic account of Kissinger's 1973–74 shuttle diplomacy.

Sheffer, Gabriel, ed. *Dynamics of Dependence: U.S.-Israeli Relations*. Boulder, Colo.: Westview Press, 1987. Collection of essays arguing for special U.S.-Israel relationship.

Shehadeh, Raja. *Occupier's Law: Israel and the West Bank*. Washington, D.C.: Institute for Palestine Studies, 1989. Palestinian lawyer's documented study of human rights violations.

———. *The Sealed Room: Selections from the Diary of a Palestinian Living under Israeli Occupation, September 1990–August 1991*. London: Quartet Books, 1992. Discusses suffering of Palestinians in occupied territories during 1990 Gulf War.

———. *The Third Way: A Journal of Life in the West Bank*. New York: Quartet Books, 1982. First-hand account by Palestinian lawyer of life under occupation.

Shemesh, Moshe. *The Palestinian Entity 1959–1974: Arab Politics and the PLO*. London: Cass, 1988. Detailed study of idea of Palestine state in context of Arab politics.

Sherbiny, Naiem A., and Mark Tessler, eds. *Arab Oil: Impact on the Arab Countries and Global Implications*. New York: Praeger, 1976. Some articles treat relationship of oil to Arab-Israel conflict.

Sherman, John, ed. *The Arab-Israeli Conflict, 1945–1971: A Bibliography*. New York: Garland, 1978. Extensive bibliography on Arab-Jewish relations.

Shiblak, Abbas. *The Lure of Zion: The Case of the Iraqi Jews*. London: Saqi Books, 1986. Study of Iraqi Jewish exodus to Israel in 1950–51.

Shinar, Dov. *Palestinian Voices: Communications and Nation Building in the West Bank*. Boulder, Colo.: Rienner, 1987. Study of West Bank communications: press, radio, TV, family networks, education system, theater, clubs, organizations, etc.

Shinar, Dov, and Danny Rubinstein. *Palestinian Press in the West Bank: The Political Dimension*. Boulder, Colo.: Westview Press, 1987. The treatment of the events of 1985–86 by the Palestinian press under occupation.

Shindler, Colin. *Plowshares into Swords? Israelis and Jews in the Shadow of the Intifada*. New York: Tauris, 1991. Examines reactions of Israeli society—military, religious, press, etc.— and Jewish diaspora communities to Intifada and Palestinians.

Shipler, David K. *Arab and Jew: Wounded Spirits in a Promised Land*. New York: Times Books, 1986; Penguin, 1987. Pulitzer Prize-winning account of Arab and Jewish mutual perceptions by former *New York Times* correspondent.

Shlaim, Avi. *Collusion Across the Jordan: King Abdullah, the Zionist Movement, and the Partition of Palestine*. New York: Columbia University Press, 1988. Study of Jordan-Israel collaboration versus Palestinian nationalists.

———. *Conflicting Approaches to Israel's Relations with the Arabs: Ben Gurion and Sharett, 1953–1956*. Washington, D.C.: Woodrow Wilson International Center for Scholars, Smithsonian Institution, 1981. Clash between two Israeli leaders over foreign policy: Sharett's "dovish" approach versus Ben-Gurion's "hardline."

———. *War and Peace in the Middle East: A Critique of American Policy*. New York: Viking Penguin, 1994. Somewhat polemical critique of Cold War policy and the resultant misreading of Middle East realities; sounds a call for evenhanded approach.

Shokeid, Moshe, and Shlomo Deshen. *Distant Relations: Ethnicity and Politics Among Arabs and North African Jews in Israel*. New York: Praeger, 1982. Anthropological study of Israeli Arabs and Oriental Jews.

Shtainer, Puah. *Forever My Jerusalem: A Personal Account of the Siege and Surrender of Jerusalem's Old City in 1948*. New York: Feldheim, 1987. A personal narrative.

Shukri, Ghali. *Egypt: Portrait of a President 1917–1981: The Counter-Revolution in Egypt, Sadat's Road to Jerusalem*. London: Zed, 1981. Accuses Sadat of betrayal of Palestinians.

Shuqayri, Ahmad. *Liberation, Not Negotiation*. Beirut: PLO Research Center, 1966. Polemic against negotiations with Israel by PLO's first leader.

Sickerman, Harvey. *Broker or Advocate: The U.S. Role in the Arab-Israeli Dispute, 1973–1978*. Philadelphia: Foreign Policy Research Institute, 1978. Monograph critical of U.S. policy as pro-Arab.

———. *Palestinian Autonomy, Self-Government & Peace*. Boulder, Colo.: Westview Press, 1993. Critique of autonomy arrangements for Palestinians.

———. *The Yom Kippur War: End of Illusion?* Beverly Hills, Calif.: Sage, 1976. Sage Foreign Policy Paper (monograph).

Sid-Ahmed, Mohamed. *After the Guns Fall Silent: Peace or Armageddon in the Middle East*. London: Croom Helm, 1976. Egyptian leftist's analysis of Arab-Israel conflict after 1973 war; one of first Arab proposals for peace negotiations with Israel.

Siddiq, Muhammad. *"Man Is a Cause": Political Consciousness and the Fiction of Ghassan Kanafani*. Seattle: University of Washington Press, 1984. Study of leftist Palestinian author who was assassinated by Israel in 1972.

Siilasvuo, Ensio. *In the Service of Peace in the Middle East, 1967–1979*. New York: St. Martin's Press, 1992. Experiences of former U.N. Middle East peacekeeper.

Silver, Eric. *Begin: The Haunted Prophet*. New York: Random House, 1984. Biography of the late prime minister and Likud leader Menachem Begin.

Silverberg, Sanford R. *The Palestinian Arab-Israeli Conflict: An International Legal Bibliography*. Monticello, Ill.: Vance Bibliographies, 1982. Monograph-size reference work.

Simon, Merrill. *God, Allah, and the Great Land Grab: The Middle East in Turmoil*. Middle Village, N.Y.: Jonathan David, 1989. Covers Israel-Arab conflicts and Israel military policy from Israeli perspective.

———. *Oil, Money, Weapons—Middle East at the Brink*. Washington, D.C.: Center for International Security, 1982. Arab-Israel conflicts and U.S.-Israel relations from right-wing perspective.

Simons, Chaim. *International Proposals to Transfer Arabs From Palestine 1895–1947: A Historical Perspective*. Hoboken, N.J.: KTAV, 1988. Study of various, mostly Zionist, proposals to move Arabs.

Sinai, Anne, and I. Robert Sinai. *Israel & the Arabs: Prelude to the Jewish State*. New York: Facts On File, 1972. Covers Jewish-Arab relations and Palestine history, 1929–1948.

Singer, Amy. *Palestinian Peasants and Ottoman Officials*. New York: Cambridge University Press, 1994. Study of rural administration in Ottoman Palestine.

Singer, Howard. *Bring Forth the Mighty Men: On Violence and the Jewish Character*. New York: Funk & Wagnalls, 1969. Israeli and Jewish national characteristics; 1967 war narratives.

Skousen, W. Cleon. *Fantastic Victory: Israel's Rendezvous With Destiny*. Salt Lake City, Utah: Bookcraft, 1967. Laudatory account of Israel's 1967 victory.

Slapikoff, Saul A. *Consider and Hear Me: Voices from Palestine and Israel*. Philadelphia: Temple University Press, 1993. Account of author's travel through Israel and West Bank.

Slater, Robert. *Warrior Statesman: The Life of Moshe Dayan*. New York: St. Martin's Press, 1991. Journalistic account of Dayan's life by *Time* magazine writer.

Slonim, Reuben. *Both Sides Now; A Twenty-Five-Year Encounter with Arabs and Israelis*. Toronto: Clarke, Irwin, 1972. Personal account of experiences with Jews and Arabs.

Smith, Barbara J. *The Roots of Separatism in Palestine: British Economic Policy, 1920–1929*. Syracuse, N.Y.: Syracuse University Press, 1993. British economic policy in mandatory Palestine and its impact on Arabs.

Smith, Charles D. *Palestine and the Arab-Israeli Conflict*. 2d ed. New York: St. Martin's Press, 1992. Good overall introduction covering conflict from Ottomans to 1991.

Smith, David. *Prisoners of God: The Modern-Day Conflict of Arab and Jew*. London: Quartet Books, 1988. Journalistic account of conflict since 1967 based on interviews.

Smith, Gary V., ed. *Zionism: The Dream and the Reality, A Jewish Critique*. New York: Barnes & Noble, 1974. Collection of articles by anti-Zionists and moderate Zionists.

Smith, Pamela Ann. *Palestine and the Palestinians, 1876–1983*. New York: St. Martin's Press, 1984. Social history of the Palestinians, Ottoman era to present.

Smith, Wilbur Moorehead. *Israeli/Arab Conflict and the Bible*. Glendale, Calif.: Regal Books, 1967. Discusses Bible prophecies and present relevance.

Smooha, Sammy. *Arabs and Jews in Israel*. Vol. 1, *Conflicting and Shared Attitudes in a Divided Society*. Boulder, Colo.: Westview Press, 1989. Vol. 2, *Change and Continuity in Mutual Intolerance*. Boulder, Colo.: Westview Press, 1992. Discussion of political and social attitudes based on survey research.

———. *Israel: Pluralism and Conflict*. Berkeley: University of California Press, 1978. Study of intergroup ethnic relations favoring pluralist model.

———. *The Orientation and Politicization of the Arab Minority in Israel*. Haifa: Haifa University Jewish-Arab Center, 1984. Study by Israeli scholar in Middle East Occasional Papers Series.

Smooha, Sammy, ed. *Social Research on Arabs in Israel, 1977–1982: A Bibliography*. Haifa: Haifa University Jewish-Arab Center, 1984.

Smooha, Sammy and Ora Cibulski. *Social Research on Arabs in Israel, 1948–1977: Trends and an Annotated Bibliography*. Ramat Gan, Israel: Turtledove, 1978.

Snetsinger, John. *Truman, The Jewish Vote and the Creation of Israel*. Stanford, Calif.: Hoover Institution Press, 1974. Influence of Zionist lobby and Jewish vote on Truman's Middle East policy.

Snider, Lewis W. *Arabesque: Untangling the Patterns of Supply of Conventional Arms to Israel and the Arab States and the Implications for United States Policy on Supply of "Lethal" Weapons to Egypt*. Denver, Colo.: University of Denver

Graduate School of International Studies, 1977. Monograph series in World Affairs; completed with U.S. military assistance.

Sobel, Lester A., ed. *Israel and the Arabs: The October 1973 War*. New York: Facts On File, 1974. Compiled from *Facts On File World News Digest*.

———. *Palestinian Impasse: Arab Guerrillas & International Terror*. New York: Facts On File, 1977. Compiled from *Facts On File World News Digest*.

———. *Peace-Making in the Middle East*. New York: Facts On File, 1980. Compiled from *Facts On File World News Digest*.

Sous, Ibrahim. *Letter to a Jewish Friend*. London: Quartet, 1989. Letter from a PLO official expressing concern over Israel policy.

Soustelle, Jacques. *The Long March of Israel*. New York: American Heritage Press, 1969. Laudatory account of Israel by admiring French politician.

Spechler, Dina. *Internal Influences on Soviet Foreign Policy: Elite Opinion and the Middle East*. Jerusalem: Hebrew University Soviet & East European Research Centre, 1976. Soviet public opinion and 1973 war and Arab-Israel relations.

Spicehandler, Daniel. *Burnt Offering, a Novel*. New York: Macmillan, 1961. Fictional story about 1948 war from perspective of American Jewish settler in Israel.

Spiegel, Steven L. *The Other Arab-Israeli Conflict: Making America's Middle East Policy From Truman to Reagan*. Chicago: University of Chicago Press, 1985. Detailed account of U.S. policy-making de-emphasizing role of Israel lobby; favorable to Israel.

Spiegel, Steven L., ed. *Conflict Management in the Middle East*. Boulder, Colo.: Westview Press, 1992. Twenty articles by diverse authors on various Middle East conflicts.

———. *The Arab-Israeli Search for Peace*. Boulder, Colo.: Rienner, 1992. Collection on conflict management and arms control in the Middle East.

Spielman, Miriam. *If Peace Comes—: The Future Expectations of Jewish and Arab Children and Youth*. Stockholm: Almqvist & Wiksell, 1984. Survey of children's perceptions and attitudes in the early 1970s in Palestine and Israel.

Sprinzak, Ehud. *The Ascendance of Israel's Radical Right*. New York: Oxford University Press, 1991. Includes radical right perceptions of Arabs & Arab-Israel conflict.

Stebbing, John. *A Structure of Peace: The Arab-Israeli Conflict*. Oxford: New Cherwell Press, 1993. Projection of plans for cooperation between Israel and Arabs.

Stefoff, Rebecca. *Yasir Arafat*. New York: Chelsea House, 1988. Biography of Arafat for juveniles.

Stein, Janice Gross, and Raymond Tanter. *Rational Decision-Making: Israel's Security Choices, 1967*. Columbus: Ohio State University Press, 1980. Background and causes of 1967 war.

Stein, Kenneth W. *The Land Question in Palestine, 1917–1939*. Chapel Hill: University of North Carolina Press, 1984. Discussion of Zionist land acquisition in mandatory Palestine.

Stein, Leonard J. *The Balfour Declaration*. New York: Simon & Schuster, 1961. Historical background of events leading to 1917 Balfour Declaration.

Stendel, Ori. *The Minorities in Israel: Trends in Development of the Arab and Druze Communities 1948–1973*. Jerusalem: Israel Economist, 1973. Discussion of minorities by Israeli scholar.

Stetler, Russell, ed. *Palestine, the Arab-Israeli Conflict*. San Francisco: Ramparts Press, 1972. Collection of articles, lectures, essays, photos on conflict.

Steven, Stewart. *The Spymasters of Israel*. New York: Macmillan, 1980. History of Israel's intelligence (secret) service.

Stevens, Richard P. *American Zionism and U.S. Foreign Policy 1942–1947*. New York: Pageant Press, 1962. Reprint, Washington, D.C.: Institute for Palestine Studies, 1972. Study of Zionist tactics and strategy in pressure politics.

———. *Weizmann & Smuts: A Study of Zionist-South African Cooperation*. Beirut: Institute of Palestine Studies, 1975. Examines close ties between Zionists and apartheid South African leaders.

Stevenson, William. *Strike Zion!* New York: Bantum Books, 1967. Laudatory account of Israel in 1967 war.

Stewart, Desmond. *The Palestinians, Victims of Expediency*. London: Quartet Books, 1982. Journalist's account of his travels to occupied territories in 1980–81; sympathetic to Palestinians.

———. *Theodor Herzl*. Garden City, N.Y.: Doubleday, 1974. Critical biography of founder of Zionist movement.

Stillman, Norman A. *The Jews of Arab Lands: A History and Source Book*. Philadelphia: Jewish Publication Society of America, 1979. History of Jews in Arab countries up to modern era, with documents.

———. *The Jews of Arab Lands in the Modern Period*. Philadelphia: Jewish Publication Society of America, 1991. Covers history of Jews from 19th century to 1990s.

Stock, Ernest. *From Conflict to Understanding: Relations Between Jews and Arabs in Israel Since 1948*. New York: American Jewish Committee Institute of Human Relations Press, 1968. Part of Institute of Human Relations monograph series.

———. *Israel on the Road to Sinai, 1949–1956. With a Sequel on the Six-Day War, 1967*. Ithaca, N.Y.: Cornell University Press, 1967. Account sympathetic to Israel; background to 1956 and 1967 wars.

Stone, Julius. *Israel and Palestine: Assault on the Law of Nations*. Baltimore, Md.: Johns Hopkins University Press, 1981. Analysis of international law favorable to Israel by international lawyer.

Strum, Philippa. *The Women Are Marching: The Second Sex and the Palestinian Revolution*. New York: Lawrence Hill Books, 1992. Journal discussing women's emergence into leadership roles.

Sulaiman, Khalid A. *Modern Arabic Poetry and Palestine*. London: Zed Books, 1984. Poems by Palestinian and other Arab poets with theme of Palestine.

Suleiman, Michael W. *The Arabs in the Mind of America*. Brattleboro, Vt.: Amana Books, 1988. American perceptions of Arabs as influenced by the media.

———. *U.S. Policy on Palestine from Wilson to Clinton*. Normal, Ill.: Association of Arab-American University Graduates, 1995. Diverse Palestinian and American authors examine Palestine policies of U.S. administrations since World War I.

Suleman, Syed Mohamed. *The Zionist Israel*. Rawalpindi, Pakistan: Justice Publications, 1973. A Pakistani view of Israel and the United States as racist, anti-Arab and Nazi-like.

Sullivan, Anthony Thrall. *Palestinian Universities Under Occupation*. Cairo: American University in Cairo Press, 1989. Analysis of Arab higher education in occupied territories.

A Survey of Palestine. Jerusalem: Government of Palestine, 1946. Detailed description of mandatory Palestine as prepared for Anglo-American Commission.

Sussman, Zvi. *Wage Differentials and Equality within the Histadruth: The Impact of Egalitarian Ideology and Arab Labour on Jewish Wages in Palestine*. Ramat Gan, Israel: Massada, 1947. Economic comparison of Israeli Arab and Jewish workers.

Swedenburg, Ted. *Memories of Revolt*. Minneapolis: University of Minnesota Press, 1995. An account of Palestinians in the 1936–39 Arab revolt.

Sykes, Christopher. *Crossroads to Israel*. Cleveland, Ohio: World, 1965; Bloomington, Ind.: Indiana University Press, 1973. Critical account of British policy in Palestine 1917 to 1948.

Tabory, Mala. *The Multinational Force and Observers in the Sinai: Organization, Structure, and Function*. Boulder, Colo.: Westview Press, 1986. Study of Sinai force established by 1979 peace treaty.

Tack, Deane A. *The Palestinian*. Brattleboro, Vt.: Amana Books, 1986. Novel of young Palestinian: fighter, prisoner, student in United States.

Talhami, Ghada Hashem. *Palestine and Egyptian National Identity*. Westport, Conn.: Praeger, 1992. Surveys the range of Egyptian attitudes to Palestine in writings of diverse intellectuals.

Talmon, Jacob L. *The Six Day War in Historical Perspective: Reflections on Jewish Statehood*. Rehovot, Israel: Yad Chaim Weizmann, 1971. Reflections on Israel's condition by noted Israeli historian.

Tannus, 'Izzat. *The Palestinians: A Detailed Documented Eyewitness History of Palestine Under the British Mandate*. New York: I.G.T., 1988. Account of mandate era by militant Palestinian nationalist.

Taras, David, and David H. Goldberg, eds. *The Domestic Battleground: Canada and the Arab-Israeli Conflict*. Kingston, Ontario, Canada: McGill-Queen's University Press, 1989. Canada's Middle East policy and its relations with Israel and the Jewish community.

Tawil, Ramonda. *My Home, My Prison*. New York: Holt, Rinehart & Winston, 1980. Autobiographic account of life under occupation by Palestinian woman.

Taylor, Alan. *Prelude to Israel*. New York: Philosophical Library, 1959. Highly critical account of Zionism and its various forms, to 1948.

———. *The Zionist Mind: The Origins and Development of Zionist Thought*. Beirut: Institute of Palestine Studies, 1974. Critical analysis of Zionism from 19th century to 1970s.

Taylor, Alan, and Richard N. Tetlie. *Palestine: A Search for Truth: Approaches to the Arab-Israel Conflict*. Washington, D.C.: Public Affairs Press, 1970. Collection of readings by Jewish critics of political Zionism.

Taylor, Jim. *Pearl Harbor II: The True Story of the Sneak Attack by Israel Upon the* U.S.S. Liberty, *June 8, 1967*. Washington, D.C.: Mideast Publishing House, 1980. Controversial account of Israeli attack during 1967 war.

Tekiner, Roselle, Samir Abed-Rabbo and Norton Mezvinsky, eds. *Anti-Zionism: Analytical Reflections*. Brattleboro, Vt.: Amana Books, 1988. Collection of articles critical of Zionism by mostly Jewish authors.

Tekoah, Yosef. *In the Face of the Nations: Israel's Struggle for Peace*. New York: Simon & Schuster, 1976. Speeches and reflections of former Israeli diplomat and university president.

Telhami, Shibley. *Power and Leadership in International Bargaining: The Path to the Camp David Accords*. New York: Columbia University Press, 1990. Egypt-Israel relations as a case study in negotiating international disputes.

Terry, Janice J. *Mistaken Identity: Arab Stereotypes in Popular Writing*. Washington, D.C.: American-Arab Affairs Council, 1985. Arab stereotypes in novels, biographies and journalistic accounts.

Teslik, Kennan Lee. *Congress, The Executive Branch, and Special Interests: The American Response to the Arab Boycott of Israel*. Westport, Conn.: Greenwood Press, 1982. U.S. foreign economic relations with Arab countries and Israel.

Tessler, Mark A. *A History of the Israeli-Palestinian Conflict.* Bloomington: Indiana University Press, 1994. Massive history, from Old Testament to Israel-PLO 1993 agreement.

Teveth, Shabtai. *Ben-Gurion and the Palestinian Arabs: From Peace to War.* Oxford, England: Oxford University Press, 1985. Ben-Gurion's perceptions of and views and policy prescriptions vis-à-vis Palestinian Arabs and his changes in attitude from 1906 to 1939.

———. *Ben-Gurion: The Burning Ground 1886–1948.* Boston: Houghton-Mifflin, 1987. Massive documented biography of Israel's first prime minister.

———. *The Cursed Blessing; the Story of Israel's Occupation of the West Bank.* New York: Random House, 1971. Critical account by leading Israeli journalist.

———. *Moshe Dayan: The Soldier, the Man, the Legend.* London: Quartet Books, 1974. Biography by leading Israeli journalist.

———. *The Tanks of Tammus.* New York: Viking Press, 1969. Regimental history of Israeli unit in 1967 war.

Thorpe, Merle, Jr. *Prescription for Conflict: Israel's West Bank Settlement Policy.* Washington, D.C.: Foundation for Middle East Peace, 1984. Highly critical account of Israel's West Bank settlement policy.

Tibawi, A. L. *Arab Education in Mandatory Palestine: A Study in Three Decades of British Administration.* London: Luzac, 1956. Account by former Palestinian Arab educator.

———. *British Interests in Palestine, 1800–1901: A Study of Religious and Educational Enterprise.* London: Oxford University Press, 1961. Survey of British cultural and political interests in 19th-century Palestine.

———. *Jerusalem: Its Place in Islam and Arab History.* Beirut: Institute of Palestine Studies, 1969. Short account of Jerusalem's importance for Arabs and Islam.

———. *Conflict and War in the Middle East, 1967–91: Regional Dynamic and the Superpowers.* New York: St. Martin's Press, 1993. Covers Arab-Israel conflicts and 1991 Persian Gulf War.

Tillman, Seth P. *The United States in the Middle East: Interests and Obstacles.* Bloomington: Indiana University Press, 1982. Analysis of U.S. policy critical of Israel lobby influence.

Timmerman, Jacobo. *The Longest War: Israel in Lebanon.* New York: Vintage Books, 1982. Highly critical account of Israel's 1982 invasion of Lebanon by noted Argentine Jewish editor and writer.

Tivnan, Edward. *The Lobby: Jewish Political Power and American Foreign Policy.* New York: Simon & Schuster, 1987. Thorough investigation of Israel lobby, especially AIPAC (American Israel Public Affairs Committee).

Touval, Saadia. *The Peace Brokers: Mediators in the Arab-Israeli Conflict, 1948–1979*. Princeton, N.J.: Princeton University Press, 1982. History of third-party mediation in Arab-Israel conflict.

Toward Arab-Israeli Peace: Report of a Study Group. Washington, D.C.: Brookings Institution, 1988. Report of high-level Brookings study group.

Toye, Patricia. *Palestine Boundaries, 1833–1947*. Newchatel, Switzerland: Archive Editions, in association with The International Boundaries Research Unit, University of Durham, England, 1989. Four volumes of reprinted original documents, mostly in English, dealing with Palestine border diplomacy.

Treverton, Gregory, ed. *Crisis Management and the Super-Powers in the Middle East*. Montclair, N.J.: Osmun, 1981. Monograph in International Institute for Strategic Studies Adelphi Library.

Trice, Robert H. *Interest Groups and the Foreign Policy Process: U.S. Policy in the Middle East*. Beverly Hills, Calif.: Sage, 1976. Monograph on U.S. policy and pressure groups in Arab-Israel conflict.

Troen, Selwyn Ilan, and Moshe Shemesh, eds. *The Suez-Sinai Crisis, 1956: Retrospective and Reappraisal*. London: Cass, 1990. A new look at the 1956 war.

Tschirig, Dan. *The American Search for Mideast Peace*. New York: Praeger, 1989. Discusses U.S. relations with Israel and Arabs, 1945–1989.

———. *The Politics of Indecision: Origins and Implications of American Involvement with the Palestine Problem*. New York: Praeger, 1983. Discusses factors shaping U.S. Palestine policy from late 1930s.

Tuma, Elias H. *Peacemaking and the Immoral War: Arabs and Jews in the Middle East*. New York: Harper Torchbooks, 1972. Extended essay blaming Arabs and Israel for continued conflict.

Tuma, Elias, and Haim Darin-Drabkin. *The Economic Case for Palestine*. New York: St. Martin's Press, 1978. An Israeli and Palestinian economist discount thesis that Palestinian state is not economically viable.

Turki, Fawaz. *The Disinherited: Journal of a Palestinian Exile*. New York: Monthly Review Press, 1972. Passionate biographical account of author's life as displaced person in a refugee camp and in larger Arab world.

———. *Exile's Return: The Making of a Palestinian-American*. New York: Free Press (Macmillan) 1994. Third book in Turki's odyssey as a displaced Palestinian.

———. *Soul in Exile: Lives of a Palestinian Revolutionary*. New York: Monthly Review, 1988. Further experiences of Palestinian refugee in the United States, France and Australia.

United Nations. *Israeli Settlements in Gaza and the West Bank (Including Jerusalem): Their Nature and Purpose. Parts I and II*. New York: United Nations, 1982, 1984. U.N. reports on Israeli settlements.

United Nations Committee on the Exercise of the Inalienable Rights of the Palestinian People. *Israel's Policy on the West Bank Water Resources.* New York: United Nations, 1980. Account of Israel's use of West Bank water resources.

———. *Social, Economic and Political Institutions in the West Bank and the Gaza Strip.* New York: United Nations, 1982. Describes Palestinian institutions.

———. *The Status of Jerusalem.* New York: United Nations, 1979. Discusses arguments over Jerusalem.

United Nations Security Council Resolution 242: The Building Block of Peacemaking. Washington, D.C.: Washington Institute for Near East Policy, 1993. Discussion by Jordanian U.N. representative and others on 25th anniversary of U.N. Resolution 242.

United Nations Resolutions on Palestine and the Arab-Israeli Conflict. Washington, D.C.: Institute of Palestine Studies, 1993. Compilation of relevant U.N. resolutions.

U.S. Congress. House. Committee on Foreign Affairs. *Resolution of Inquiry Concerning the U.S. Vote in the U.N. Security Council on Israeli Settlements in the Occupied Territories: Hearings before the Committee on Foreign Affairs, House of Representatives*, 96th Cong., 2nd sess., on House Resolution 598, March 12, 21 and 28, 1980. Washington, D.C.: U.S. Government Printing Office, 1980. Extensive hearings on Israeli settlements.

U.S. Congress. House. Committee on Foreign Affairs. Subcommittee on Near East. *Jerusalem: The Future of the Holy City for Three Monotheisms: Hearings before the House Committee on Foreign Affairs, Subcommittee on Near East*, 92nd Cong., 1st sess., July 28, 1971. Washington, D.C.: U.S. Government Printing Office, 1972.

U.S. Congress. House. Committee on Foreign Affairs. Subcommittee on the Near East and South Asia. *The Impact of the October Middle East War. Hearings*, 93rd Cong., 1st sess. Washington, D.C.: U.S. Government Printing Office, 1973.

U.S. Congress. House. Committee on International Relations. Subcommittee on the Middle East and Europe. *Assessment of the 1978 Middle East Camp David Agreements: hearing before the Subcommittee on Europe and the Middle East of the Committee on International Relations.* House of Representatives, 95th Cong., 2nd sess., September 28, 1978. Washington, D.C.: U.S. Government Printing Office, 1978.

U.S. Congress. House. Committee on International Relations. Subcommittee on International Organizations. *Israeli Settlements in the Occupied Territories: hearings before the Subcommittee on Europe and the Middle East of the Committee on International Relations.* House of Representatives, 95th Cong., 2nd sess., September 12, 21 and October 19, 1973. Washington, D.C.: U.S. Government Printing Office, 1978.

U.S. Congress. House. Committee on the Judiciary. *Arab Boycott: hearings before the Subcommittee on Monopolies and Commercial Law of the Committee of the Judiciary*. House of Representatives, 94th Cong., 1st and 2nd sess., July 9, 1975. Includes directory of boycotted companies, Arab sanctions and Israel.

U.S. Congress. House. Committee on Foreign Affairs. Subcommittee on Europe and the Middle East. *Documents and Statements on Middle East Peace, 1979–82*. 97th Cong., 2nd sess., 1982. Washington, D.C.: Library of Congress, 1982. Collection of documents and statements.

U.S. Congress. House. Committee on Foreign Affairs. Subcommittee on Europe and the Middle East. *Documents on Middle East Peace, 1982–88*. 101st Cong., 1st sess., 1989. Washington, D.C.: Library of Congress, 1989. Collection of documents and statements.

U.S. Congress. Senate. Committee on Foreign Relations. Subcommittee on the Near East and South Asia. *The Israeli Air Strike*. Washington, D.C.: U.S. Government Printing Office, 1981. Hearing on Israeli strike at Iraq's nuclear reactor in 1981.

U.S. Congress. Senate. Committee on the Judiciary Immigration and Naturalization. *The Colonization of the West Bank Territories by Israel: hearings before the Subcommittee on Immigration and Naturalization of the Committee of the Judiciary*. United States Senate, 95th Cong., 1st sess., October 17 and 18, 1977. Washington, D.C.: U.S. Government Printing Office, 1978. Discussion of Israeli Settlements in West Bank.

The Uprising. Tunis: *Lotus* Journal of Afro-Asian Writers Association, 1987. Account of the Intifada and Palestinian and Israeli politics and government.

Van Arkadie, Brian. *Benefits and Burdens: A Report on West Bank and Gaza Strip Economies Since 1967*. New York: Carnegie Endowment for International Peace, 1977. Study of occupied territories economic viability.

Van Creveld, Martin L. *Military Lessons of the Yom Kippur War: Historical Perspectives*. Beverly Hills, Calif.: Sage, 1975. A Sage policy paper in Washington Papers series.

Van Leeuwen, Marianne. *Americans and the Palestinian Question: The U.S. Public Debate on Palestinian Nationhood, 1973–1988*. Atlanta, Ga.: Editions Rodophi B.V., 1993. Comprehensive survey of American writing and discussion of Palestine question from 1973 war to Intifada.

Velie, Lester. *Countdown in the Holy Land*. New York: Funk & Wagnalls, 1969. The 1967 war, with emphasis on the Soviet role.

Victor, Barbara. *A Voice of Reason: Hanan Ashrawi and Peace in the Middle East*. New York: Harcourt Brace, 1994. Biography of former spokesperson of Palestine delegation at Middle East peace negotiations.

Vilnay, Zeev. *Jerusalem in the Modern Era: 1860–1967.* New York: John Day, 1974. History of Jerusalem from Ottoman era to Israel's conquest of Arab Old City in 1967 war; by an Israeli authority.
Viorst, Milton. *Reaching for the Olive Branch: UNRWA and Peace in the Middle East.* Washington, D.C.: Middle East Institute, 1989. Monograph with history; work of U.N. Palestine refugee agency.
———. *Sands of Sorrow: Israel's Journey From Independence.* New York: Harper & Row, 1987. Critique of Israeli policy after 1967 war & of U.S. support for Israel by American Jewish former supporter.
Vocke, Harold. *The Lebanese War: Its Origins and Political Dimensions.* London: Hurst, 1978. Includes role of Palestinians and Israel.
Von Horn, Maj. Gen. Carl. *Soldiering for Peace.* New York: McKay, 1967. Memoirs of former Swedish U.N. truce supervision officer in Middle East.
Voth, Alden H. *Moscow Abandons Israel for the Arabs: Ten Crucial Years in the Middle East.* Lanham, Md.: University Press of America, 1980. Discussion of how USSR changed its Middle East policy during the 1950s.
Wagner, Abraham R. *Crisis Decision-Making: Israel's Experience in 1967 and 1973.* New York: Praeger, 1974. Case study of decision-making in crisis situation.
Walinsky, Louis J. *The Implications of Israel-Arab Peace for World Jewry: A Report of the International Economic and Social Commission of the World Jewish Congress.* New York: World Jewish Congress, 1981. Discussion of various proposals and their effects on Jews.
Wallach, Janet, and John Wallach. *Arafat in the Eyes of the Beholder.* Rocklin, Calif.: Prima, 1991. Biography of Arafat by two sympathetic American journalists.
———. *The New Palestinians: The Emerging Generation of Leaders.* Rocklin, Calif.: Prima, 1992. Life histories of 12 mostly West Bank and Gaza Palestinian leaders.
———. *Still Small Voices.* New York: Harcourt Brace Jovanovich, 1989. Portraits of West Bank and Gaza Arabs and Jewish settlers based on interviews.
Waines, David A. *A Sentence of Exile: The Palestinian/Israel Conflict, 1897–1977.* Wilmette, Ill.: Medina University Press, 1977. Canadian historian's account of conflict sympathetic to Palestinians.
Ward, Richard J., Don Peretz and Evan M. Wilson. *The Palestine State: A Rational Approach,* revised ed. Port Washington, New York: Kennikat, 1977. Revision and updating of earlier edition with discussion of options for Palestinians.
Warnock, Kitty. *Land Before Honour: Palestinian Women in the Occupied Territories.* New York: Monthly Review Press, 1990. Discusses Palestinian women in society, work and politics.

Wasserstein, Bernard. *Herbert Samuel: A Political Life*. Oxford, England: Clarendon Press, 1992. Biography of Jewish first British high commissioner of Palestine.

———. *The British in Palestine: The Mandatory Government and the Anglo-Jewish Conflict 1917–1929*. London: Royal Historical Society, 1978. Detailed, documented study of British rule from 1917 to the Wailing Wall incident.

Weiler, Joseph. *Israel and the Creation of a Palestinian State: A European Perspective*. London: Croom Helm, 1985. Examines possibility of Palestinian state integrated with Israel.

Weir, Shelagh. *Palestinian Costume*. Austin: University of Texas Press, 1989. Illustrated with 200 color and 100 black and white photos.

Weisburd, David. *Jewish Settler Violence: Deviance as Social Reaction*. University Park: Pennsylvania State University Press, 1989. Social-psychological study of settlers in occupied territories.

Weissbrod, Lilly. *Arab Relations With Jewish Immigrants and Israel, 1891–1991: The Hundred Years' Conflict*. Lewiston, N.Y.: Mellen Press, 1992. Examines conflict between two national liberation movements.

Weizman, Ezer. *The Battle for Peace*. New York: Bantam Books, 1981. Account of his participation in peace negotiations with Egypt by Israel's president, former air-force commander and defense minister.

Weizmann, Chaim. *Trial and Error: The Autobiography of Chaim Weizmann*. New York: Harper, 1949. Autobiography of interwar Zionist leader and Israel's first president.

Wengler, Wilhelm, and Josef Tittel, eds. *Documents on the Arab Israeli Conflict. The Resolutions of the United Nations Organization*. Berlin: Verlag, 1971. Document collection, including maps.

West, Morris L. *The Tower of Babel: A Novel*. New York: Morrow, 1968. Novel about economic collapse in the Middle East.

The West Bank and Gaza: Israel's Options for Peace: Report of a JCSS Study Group. Tel Aviv: Tel Aviv University, Jaffee Center for Strategic Studies, 1989. Report discusses merits and disadvantages of various peace options.

Whetten, Lawrence L. *The Arab-Israel Dispute: Great Power Behaviour*. London: International Institute for Strategic Studies, 1977. Monograph in ISS Adelphi Papers series.

———. *The Canal War: Four-Power Conflict in the Middle East*. Cambridge, Mass.: MIT Press, 1974. Examines U.S., USSR, Israel and Egypt policies in 1967–70 wars.

Wilson, Evan M. *Decision on Palestine: How the U.S. Came to Recognize Israel*. Stanford, Calif.: Hoover Institution Press, 1979. U.S. policy toward Palestine problem in 1940s and Palestine issue in Anglo-American diplomacy and in U.S. politics.

———. *Jerusalem: Key to Peace*. Washington, D.C.: Middle East Institute, 1970. Account of Jerusalem issue by former U.S. consul-general in Israel, drawing on his own experiences.

Wilson, Mary C. *King Abdullah, Britain and the Making of Jordan*. New York: Cambridge University Press, 1988. Scholarly biography of Abdullah, his dealings with Zionists and his interest in Palestine.

Wiissa, Karim. *The Oil Question in Egyptian-Israeli Relations, 1967–1979: A Study in International Law and Resource Politics*. Cairo: American University in Cairo Press, 1990. The role of oil in Egyptian-Israel relations from 1967 to 1979.

Winternitz, Helen. *A Season of Stones: Living in a Palestinian Village*. New York: Atlantic Monthly Press, 1991. Experiences of American writer in West Bank village near Bethlehem.

Wolinetz, Harvey D. *Arab Philatelic Propaganda Against the State of Israel*. Ann Arbor, Mich.: Wolinetz, 1975. Extended version of 1973 Yeshiva University master's thesis on role of stamps.

Woolfson, Marion. *Prophets in Babylon: Jews in the Arab World.*. London: Faber & Faber, 1980. History of Jews in Arab countries from early times to creation of Israel, emphasizing how Zionists disrupted their lives.

Woolfson, Martin. *Bassam Shaka: Portrait of a Palestinian*. London: Third World Center for Research and Publishing, 1981. Biography of Nablus mayor who was imprisoned, then expelled by Israel.

Wright, Claudia. *Spy, Steal and Smuggle: Israel's Special Relationship With the United States*. Belmont, Mass.: Association of Arab-American University Graduates, 1986. Author believes that Israel's clandestine activities threaten the United States.

Wright, Clifford A. *Facts and Fables: The Arab-Israeli Conflict*. London: Kegan Paul, 1989. Author attempts to discount Zionist "myths."

Wright, Martin, ed. *Israel and the Palestinians*. Chicago: St. James Press, 1989. Collection of articles on Jewish-Arab conflicts and Arab-Israel wars.

Yaari, Ehud. *Strike Terror: The Story of Fatah*. New York: Sabra Books, 1970. An Israeli journalist's account of Fatah.

Yahav, David, ed. *Israel, the "Intifada" and the Rule of Law*. Tel Aviv: Ministry of Defense Publications, 1993. Official Israeli response to human rights organizations' critique of Israel's civil administration rule in occupied territories.

Yaniv, Avner. *Dilemmas of Security: Politics, Strategy, and the Israeli Experience in Lebanon*. New York: Oxford University Press, 1987. Israel scholar's analysis of 1982 invasion, which he believes was dictated by security.

Yaniv, Avner, ed. *National Security and Democracy in Israel*. Boulder, Colo.: Rienner, 1993. Collection of papers by seven Israeli scholars on Israeli security.

Yegar, Moshe. *Neutral Policy-Theory versus Practice: Swedish-Israeli Relations.* Jerusalem: Israeli Council on Foreign Relations, 1993. Sweden's policy under Olaf Palme toward Arab-Israel conflict.

Yehoshua, A. B. *Between Right and Right.* Garden City, N.Y.: Doubleday, 1981. Essays by leading Israeli novelist; argues Arab-Israel dispute is a conflict between two "rights."

Yermina, Dov. *My War Diary: Lebanon June 5–July 1, 1982.* Boston: South End Press, 1984. Israeli kibbutz member and army officer reveals Israeli atrocities.

Yiftachel, Oren. *Planning a Mixed Region in Israel: The Political Geography of Arab-Jewish Relations in Galilee.* Aldershot, England: Avebury, 1992. Author warns of deterioration in Arab-Jewish coexistence if state maintains a policy of spatial control.

Yishai, Yael. *Land or Peace: Whither Israel?* Stanford, Calif.: Hoover Institution Press, 1987. Examines various Israeli perspectives and views—hawks, doves, political parties, etc.—on occupied territories.

Yizhar, S. *Midnight Convoy and Other Stories.* Jerusalem: Institute for the Translation of Hebrew Literature, 1969. Collection of stories, some on war with the Arabs, by leading Israeli novelist.

Yodfat, Aryeh, and Yuval Arnon-Ohana. *PLO Strategy and Tactics.* New York: St. Martin's Press, 1981. Examination of PLO by two Israeli scholars.

The Yom Kippur War. London: Deutch, 1975. The 1973 war as covered by the Sunday *Times* (London) Insight team.

Young, Elsie G. *Keepers of the History: Women and the Israel-Palestinian Conflict.* New York: Teachers College Press, 1992. Covers women and the conflict from 1949 to Intifada.

Young, Peter. *The Israeli Campaign 1967.* London: Kimber, 1967. British brigadier's account of the 1967 war.

Young, Ronald J. *Missed Opportunities for Peace: U.S. Middle East Policy, 1981–1986.* Philadelphia: American Friends Service Committee, 1987. A Quaker (AFSC) critique of U.S. Middle East policy failures.

Zaremba, Alan Jay. *Mass Communication and International Politics: A Case Study of Press Reactions to the 1973 Arab-Israeli War.* Salem, Wis.: Sheffield, 1988. An examination of press and public opinion in Arab-Israel conflict.

Zeadey, Faith, ed. *Camp David: A New Balfour Declaration.* Detroit, Mich.: Association of Arab-American University Graduates, 1979. Collection of articles, some critical, of effect of Camp David on the Palestinians.

Zogby, James J. *Palestinians, the Invisible Victims.* Washington, D.C.: American Arab Anti-Discrimination Committee, 1981. Critique of U.S. policy toward and Israeli treatment of Palestinians.

Zurayq, Constantine K. *The Meaning of the Disaster*. Beirut: Khayyats, 1956. Critique of Arab society's failure to meet Zionist/Israel challenge by leading Arab intellectual.

Zureik, Elia. *The Palestinians in Israel: A Study in Internal Colonialism*. London: Routledge & Kegan Paul, 1979. Sociological study of Israeli Arab minority and its subordinate relationship to the Zionist state.

Zureik, Elia, and Fouad Moughrabi, eds. *Public Opinion and the Palestinian Question*. New York: St. Martin's Press, 1986. Several studies of U.S. and Canadian public opinion on the conflict.

Zweig, Ronald W. *Britain and Palestine During the Second World War*. New York: St. Martin's Press, 1986. Study of British policy from 1939 to 1945, based on documents.

PERIODICALS

Most of the periodicals listed below deal with the Middle East at large but frequently contain articles and material focusing on the Arab-Israel conflict.

Arab Studies Quarterly. Normal, Ill.: Association of Arab-American University Graduates & Institute of Arab Studies.

Challenge: A Magazine of the Israeli Left. Tel Aviv, Israel.

I&P: Israel and Palestine Political Report. Paris, France.

Israel Horizons. New York: Americans for Progressive Israel.

Israeli Foreign Affairs. Sacramento, California.

The Jerusalem Report. Jerusalem, Israel.

Journal of Palestine Studies. Washington: D.C.: Institute for Palestine Studies & Kuwait University. (Quarterly on Palestinian Affairs and the Arab-Israel conflict—perhaps the best single source for information on the Arab-Israel conflict. Includes articles, book reviews, documents and source materials, bibliography of periodical literature and detailed chronology.)

The Link. New York: Americans for Middle East Understanding.

Middle East Insight. Washington, D.C.: International Insight.

Middle East International. London and Washington, D.C.

Middle East Journal. Washington, D.C.: Middle East Institute.

Middle East Policy. Washington, D.C.: Middle East Policy Council.

Middle East Quarterly. Philadelphia, Pa.: Middle East Forum.

Middle East Report. Washington, D.C.: Middle East Research and Information Project (MERIP).

Middle East Watch Report. New York: Middle East Watch.

Middle Eastern Studies. London: Cass.

The Other Israel. Tel Aviv, Israel: Israel Council for Israeli-Palestinian Peace.

Palestine-Israel Journal. Jerusalem, Israel.

Report on Israeli Settlement in the Occupied Territories. Washington, D.C.: Foundation for Middle East Peace.
Tikkun: A Quarterly Jewish Critique of Politics, Culture and Society. Oakland, Calif.: Institute for Labor and Mental Health.
Washington Report on Middle East Affairs. Washington, D.C.: American Educational Trust.

ORGANIZATIONS AND INSTITUTIONS

MIDDLE EAST ORGANIZATIONS

Several of the following organizations deal with the larger context of the Middle East but include in their activities extensive coverage of the Arab-Israel conflict. For a further comprehensive listing of American organizations, see *National Directory of Organizations Concerned with Peaceful Resolution of Arab-Israeli-Palestinian Conflicts*, National Peace Foundation, 1835 K St. NW, Washington DC 20036; (202) 223-1770 (over 90 pages, $10 per yr.).

America-Israel Council for Israel-Palestinian Peace (ICIPP)
4816 Cornell Ave.,
Downers Grove IL 60615
(708) 969-7584

U.S. affiliate of ICIPP, Israeli peace group; publishes *The Other Israel*.

American Alliance for Palestinian Human Rights
2435 Virginia Ave. NW
Washington DC 20037
(202) 342-8347

Organization for defense of Palestinian human rights.

American Coalition for Middle East Dialogue
Stony Point Center
Stony Point NY 10980

Helps organize Arab-Israeli dialogues in the United States.

American Educational Trust (AET)
P.O. Box 53062
Washington DC 20009
(202) 939-6050; (800) 368-5788

Promotes information about Arab-Israel conflict and publishes *Washington Report on Middle East Affairs* monthly.

American Friends Service Committee
1501 Cherry St.
Philadelphia PA 19102
(215) 241-7019

Quaker organization whose activities include work on behalf of Middle East peace and Arab-Jewish reconciliation.

American Israel Public Affairs Committee (AIPAC)
440 First St.
Washington DC 20001
(202) 639-5200

Pro-Israel organization that lobbies Congress concerning legislation affecting

U.S.-Israel relations; publishes weekly *Near East Report* and other publications.

American Jewish Committee
165 East 56 St.
New York NY 10022
(212) 751-4000

Headquarters of Institute of Human Relations, Institute on American Jewish Relations; supports Israel.

American Jewish Congress
15 East 84 St.
New York NY 10028

Publishes various publications; strongly supports Israel.

American-Arab Anti-Discrimination Committee
4201 Connecticut Ave. NW
Washington DC 20008
(202) 244-2990

Organization to protect rights of people of Arab descent; publishes monthly periodical and studies on foreign and domestic issues.

American-Israeli Civil Liberties Coalition
275 Seventh Ave.
New York NY 10001
(212) 696-9603

Publishes newsletter dealing with civil rights in Israel.

Americans for Middle East Understanding
475 Riverside Dr.
New York NY 10115
(212) 870-2053

Organized to promote U.S. understanding of Middle East issues; publishes periodical with frequent focus on Arab-Israel conflict.

Americans for Peace Now
27 W. 20th St.
New York NY 10011
(212) 645-7355

Affiliate of Israeli peace movement Peace Now.

Amnesty International USA
322 8th Ave.
New York NY 10001
(212) 807-8400

Publishes periodic reports on human rights.

Anti-Defamation League of B'nai B'rith
823 U.N. Plaza
New York NY 10017
(212) 490-2525

Organized to counter assaults on rights and image of Jews; various publications with frequent focus on Arab-Israel conflict.

Arab American Institute
918 16 St. NW
Washington DC 20006
(202) 429-9210

Conducts policy research and analysis and publishes on U.S.-Arab issues.

Arab League Information Office
1100 17 St. NW
Washington DC 20036
(202) 265-3210

Distributes information about Arab world and Arab issues.

Association of Arab-American University Graduates
2121 Wisconsin Ave. NW, Suite 310
Washington DC 20007

Publishes *Arab Studies Quarterly* and other publications, with frequent focus on Arab-Israel conflict; organizes conferences.

Campaign for Peace with Justice in the Middle East
c/o AFSC
2161 Massachusetts Ave.
Cambridge MA 02140
(617) 661-6130

Publishes reports on Arab-Israel conflict.

Center for Contemporary Arab Studies
Georgetown University
ICC 485
Washington, DC 20057-1052
(202) 687-5793

Part of Georgetown University School of Foreign Service; publishes material and sponsors conferences with frequent focus on Arab-Israel conflict.

Center for Middle East Peace and Economic Cooperation
444 N. Capitol St. NW
Washington DC 20001
(202) 737-6111

Furthers knowledge of Middle East conflict through seminars, conferences, speakers and internship program.

Center for Policy Analysis on Palestine
2435 Virginia Ave. NW
Washington DC 20037
(202) 336-1290

Presents Palestinian perspective on Arab-Israel conflict with special reports, conferences and meetings.

Center for Strategic & International Studies
1800 K St. NW
Washington DC 20006
(202) 887-0200

Center's Middle East Studies Program includes seminars, research and publications.

Center for the Study of Israel & the Contemporary Middle East
Baltimore Hebrew University
5800 Park Heights Ave.
Baltimore MD 21215
(410) 578-6921

Affiliate of Baltimore Hebrew University offering courses, lectures, conferences and Middle East library.

Churches for Middle East Peace
110 Maryland Ave. NE
Washington DC 20008
(202) 546-8425

Represents 16 Protestant and Catholic groups in lobbying on Middle East issues; offers congressional briefings.

Committee on Israeli Censorship
1903 W. Newport
Chicago, IL 60654
(312) 549-6421

Committee of librarians that exposes and protests against censorship of Middle East materials; publishes occasional newsletter.

Council for the National Interest
1511 K St. NW
Washington DC 20009
(202) 628-6962

Presents information on Middle East with focus on Arab-Israel conflict through grass-roots lobbying, speakers and publications.

The Dialogue Project
1601 Connecticut Ave. NW
Washington DC 20009
(202) 797-8961

Organizes dialogues and conferences.

Foundation for Global Community
222 High St.
Palo Alto CA 94301-1097

Educational movement, formerly Beyond War, with Middle East Task Force;

booklets, audio and video programs and newsletter.

Foundation for Middle East Peace
555 13 St. NW
Washington DC 20004
(202) 637-6558

Furthers understanding of Arab-Israel conflict through books, articles and *Report on Israeli Settlements in the Occupied Territories.*

Friends of Yesh Gvul (There's a Limit/Border)
1678 Shattuck Ave.
Berkeley CA 94709
(510) 848-9391

U.S. affiliate of Israeli organization of conscientious objectors.

Givat Haviva Educational Foundation
27 W. 20th St.
New York NY 10011
(212) 255-1991

U.S. representative of Israeli institute for Arab-Jewish relations.

Initiative for Peace and Cooperation in the Middle East
(*see* **Search for Common Ground**)

Institute for Middle East Peace & Development
33 W. 42d St.
New York NY 10036

Sponsors meetings on Middle East peace.

Institute for Palestine Studies
3501 M St. NW
Washington DC 20007
(202) 342-3990

Publishes books, reprints, monographs and *Journal of Palestine Studies*; has archives, organizes research on Arab-Israel conflict.

International Center for Peace in the Middle East
P.O. Box 20511
Dag Hammarskjöld Center
New York NY 10017
(212) 288-2350

Offers information on Arab-Israel conflict.

International Jewish Peace Union
P.O. Box 20854
Tompkins Sq. Station
New York NY 10009
(212) 979-8754

Jewish peace organization with occasional publications.

International Security Council
2401 Pennsylvania Ave. NW
Washington DC 20037
(202) 828-0802

Concerned with U.S. security and defense policies with periodic focus on Middle East.

Jewish Committee on the Middle East
P.O. Box 18367
Washington DC 20036
(202) 234-5397

Association of American Jewish supporters of Palestinian statehood and reduction of aid to Israel; occasional publications and videos.

Jewish Institute for National Security Affairs
1717 K St. NW
Washington DC 20006
(202) 833-0020

Concerned with U.S. and Israel security affairs.

Jewish Peace Fellowship
P.O. Box 271

Nyack NY 10960
(914) 358-4601

American Jewish pacifist organization; periodic publications.

Jewish Peace Lobby
8401 Colesville Rd.
Silver Spring MD 20910
(301) 589-8764

Focuses on Israel-Palestine conflict; lobbies on behalf of peace projects.

Middle East Institute
1761 N St. NW
Washington DC 20036
(202) 785-1141

Principal Middle East research and information organization in United States; publishes *Middle East Journal*, newsletter, books; offers outreach grants; holds annual conference; extensive library.

Middle East Policy Council
1730 M St. NW
Washington DC 20036
(202) 296-6767

Publishes *Middle East Policy*; conducts teachers' workshops, conferences.

Middle East Research and Information Project (MERIP)
1400 Massachusetts Ave. NW
Washington DC 20005
(202) 223-3677

Publishes *Middle East Report*, special publications.

Middle East Watch
485 5th Ave.
New York NY 10017
(212) 972-8400

Affiliate of Amnesty International; publishes *Middle East Watch Report*.

National Association of Arab Americans
1212 New York Ave. NW
Washington DC 20005
(202) 842-1840

Lobbies on behalf of Arab Americans; distributes information about Arab world; publishes reports on U.S. Middle East policy.

National Council on U.S.-Arab Relations
1735 I St. NW
Washington DC 20006
(202) 293-0801

Organizes educational and cross-cultural exchanges, school and university outreach programs and fellowship for travel/study in the Middle East.

New Israel Fund
1101 15th St. NW
Washington DC 20005
(202) 223-3333

Raises funds for projects in Israel; sponsors lectures and seminars; publications, resource materials and speakers.

Palestine Affairs Center
1730 K St. NW
Washington DC 20006
(202) 785-8394

Registered foreign agent for Arab League representing Palestinian affairs; lectures, publications.

Palestine Aid Society
2025 I St. NW
Washington DC 20006
(202) 728-9425

Raises funds for Palestinians; seminars, newsletter.

Palestine Solidarity Committee
P.O. Box 372, Peck Slip Station
New York NY 10272
(212) 227-1435

Activities in support of Palestinians; publishes *Palestine Focus*.

Project Nishma
1225 15 St. NW
Washington DC 20005
(202) 462-4268

Distributes information about Israeli security in context of peace process; briefings, speakers, information packets.

Resource Center for Nonviolence
Middle East Program
515 Broadway
Santa Cruz CA 95060
(408) 423-1626

Provides information about peaceful approaches to conflict.

Search for Common Ground—Initiative for Peace and Cooperation in the Middle East
1601 Connecticut Ave. NW
Washington DC 20009
(202) 265-4300

Seeks to develop working groups and projects for Jewish-Arab cooperation in Middle East.

Search for Justice and Equality in Palestine/Israel
P.O. Box 3452
Framingham, MA 01701

Distributes information about Israel-Palestinian relations.

United States Institute of Peace
1550 M St. NW
Washington DC 20005
(202) 457-1700

Quasi-governmental institute fostering research, lectures, conferences, publications with frequent focus on Arab-Israel conflict.

UNITED NATIONS ORGANIZATIONS

U.N. Committee on the Exercise of the Inalienable Rights of the Palestinian People
U.N. Division for Palestinian Rights
U.N. Plaza
New York NY 10017
(212) 754-8231

U.N. Division for Palestinian Rights
U.N. Plaza
New York NY 10017

U.N. Relief & Works Agency for Palestine Refugees in the Near East (UNRWA)
United Nations
New York, NY 10017

U.N. Special Committee to Investigate Israel Practices Affecting the Human Rights of Population
U.N. Plaza
New York NY 10017

AMERICAN EDUCATIONAL INSTITUTIONS—MIDDLE EAST OUTREACH PROGRAMS

University of Arizona
Center for Middle Eastern Studies
Tucson AZ 85721
(602) 621-5450.

State University of New York (SUNY), Binghamton
Middle East Program (SWANA)
Binghamton NY 13902-6000
(607) 777-4738

University of California at Berkeley
Center for Middle East Studies

Stephens Hall
Berkeley CA 94720-22314
(510) 642-8208

University of California at Los Angeles
Near East Studies Center
Bunche Hall
Los Angeles CA 90024
(310) 206-2406

University of Chicago
Middle East Studies Center
5848 South University Ave.
Chicago IL 60637
(312) 702-8297

Columbia University
Middle East Institute
International Affairs Bldg.
New York NY 10027
(212) 854-1741

Georgetown University
Center for Contemporary Arab Studies
Washington DC 20057
(202) 687-5793

Harvard University
Middle Eastern Studies Center
1737 Cambridge St.
Cambridge MA 02138
(617) 495-4055

The Johns Hopkins University
Middle East Studies Program
School for Advanced International Studies
1740 Massachusetts Ave. NW
Washington DC 20036
(202) 663-5676

University of Michigan
Middle East Outreach Program
Lane Hall
Ann Arbor MI 48109-1290
(313) 764-0350

New York/Princeton Universities Joint Center for Near East Studies
Hagop Kevorkian Center
50 Washington Sq. S
New York NY 10003
(212) 598-2697 (NYU);
(609) 452-4272 (Princeton)

Ohio State University
Middle East Program
Oxley Hall
1712 Neil Ave.
Columbus OH 43210
(614) 292-9660

University of Pennsylvania
Middle East Center
Williams Hall
Philadelphia PA 19104
(215) 898-6335

University of Texas at Austin
Middle East Resource Center
Austin TX 78712-1193
(512) 471-3881

University of Utah
Middle East Outreach Council
Salt Lake City UT 84112
(801) 581-6181 or -7143

University of Washington
Near East Resource Center
Thompson Hall
Seattle WA 98195
(206) 543-7236

PART III

DOCUMENTS

1. THE BASEL PROGRAM 1897

The aim of Zionism is to create for the Jewish people a home in Palestine secured by public law.

The Congress contemplates the following means to the attainment of this end:

1. The promotion, on suitable lines, of the colonization of Palestine by Jewish agricultural and industrial workers.

2. The organization and binding together of the whole of Jewry by means of appropriate institutions, local and international, in accordance with the laws of each country.

3. The strengthening and fostering of Jewish national sentiment and consciousness.

4. Preparatory steps towards obtaining government consent, where necessary, to the attainment of the aim of Zionism.

2. From the HUSAYN-McMAHON CORRESPONDENCE 1915

Sharif Husayn to Sir Henry McMahon Mecca, Ramadan 2, 1333 [July 14, 1915]

Whereas the entire Arab nation without exception is determined to assert its right to live, gain its freedom and administer its own affairs in name and in fact;

And whereas the Arabs believe it to be in Great Britain's interest to lend them assistance . . .

And whereas it is similarly to the advantage of the Arabs . . . to prefer British assistance . . .

For these reasons, the Arab nation has decided to approach the Government of Great Britain with a request for the approval . . . of the following basic provisions . . .

1. Great Britain recognises the independence of the Arab countries . . .
2. Great Britain will agree to the proclamation of an Arab Caliphate for Islam.
3. The Sharifian Arab Government undertakes, other things being equal, to grant Great Britain preference in all economic enterprises in the Arab countries . . .
5. Great Britain agrees to the abolition of the Capitulations in the Arab countries . . .

In his response, dated August 30, Sir Henry stated that the question regarding the frontiers of the proposed Arab state was premature and "a waste of time." Husayn was adamant on this point.

Sir Henry McMahon to Sherif Husayn
Cairo, October 24, 1915

. . . I regret to find that you inferred from my last note that my attitude towards the question of frontiers and boundaries was one of hesitancy and lukewarmth . . . All I meant was that I considered that the time had not yet come in which that question could be discussed in a conclusive manner.

But, having realized from your last note that you considered the question important, vital and urgent, I hastened to communicate to the Government of Great Britain the purport of your note . . .

As for the regions lying within the proposed frontiers, in which Great Britain is free to act without detriment to the interests of her ally France, I am authorised to give you the following pledges on behalf of the Government of Great Britain, and to reply as follows to your note:

(1) That, subject to the modifications stated above, Great Britain is prepared to recognise and uphold the independence of the Arabs in all the regions lying within the frontiers proposed by the Sharif of Mecca;

(2) That Great Britain will guarantee the Holy Places against all external aggression, and will recognise the obligation of preserving them from aggression . . .

3. From the SYKES-PICOT AGREEMENT 1915–16

Sir Edward Grey to Paul Cambon, May 16, 1916

It is accordingly understood between the French and British Governments—

1. That France and Great Britain are prepared to recognize and protect an independent Arab State or a Confederation of Arab States in the areas (A) and (B) marked on the annexed map [not reproduced], under the suzerainty of an Arab chief. That in area (A) France, and in area (B) Great Britain, shall have priority of right of enterprise and local loans. That in area (A) France, and in area (B) Great Britain, shall alone supply advisers or foreign functionaries at the request of the Arab State or Confederation of Arab States.

2. That in the blue area France, and in the red area Great Britain, shall be allowed to establish such direct or indirect administration or control as they desire and as they may think fit to arrange with the Arab State or Confederation of Arab States.

3. That in the brown area there shall be established an international administration, the form of which is to be decided upon after consultation with Russia, and subsequently in consultation with the other Allies, and the representatives of the Shereef of Mecca.

4. That Great Britain be accorded (1) the ports of Haifa and Acre . . .

5. That Alexandretta shall be a free port as regards the trade of the British Empire . . .

That Haifa shall be a free port as regards the trade of France, her dominions and protectorates . . .

6. That in area (A) the Bagdad Railway shall not be extended southwards beyond Mosul, and in area (B) northwards beyond Samarra, until a railway connecting Baghdad with Aleppo via the Euphrates Valley has been completed, and then only with the concurrence of the two Governments.

7. That Great Britain has the right to build, administer, and be sole owner of a railway connecting Haifa with area (B), and shall have a perpetual right to transport troops along such a line at all times.

It is to be understood by both Governments that this railway is to facilitate the connexion of Baghdad with Haifa by rail . . .

8. . . . There shall be no interior customs barriers between any of the above-mentioned areas. The customs duties leviable on goods destined for the interior shall be collected at the port of entry and handed over to the administration of the area of destination.

9. It shall be agreed that the French Government will at no time enter into any negotiations for the cession of their rights and will not cede such rights

in the blue area to any third Power, except the Arab State or Confederation of Arab States without the previous agreement of His Majesty's Government, who, on their part, will give a similar undertaking to the French Government regarding the red area . . .

11. The negotiations with the Arabs as to the boundaries of the Arab State or Confederation of Arab States shall be continued through the same channel as heretofore on behalf of the two Powers.

12. It is agreed that measures to control the importation of arms into the Arab territories will be considered by the two Governments . . .

4. The BALFOUR DECLARATION 1917

Foreign Office,
November 2nd, 1917

Dear Lord Rothschild,

I have much pleasure in conveying to you, on behalf of His Majesty's Government, the following declaration of sympathy with Jewish Zionist aspirations which has been submitted to, and approved by, the Cabinet.

"His Majesty's Government view with favour the establishment in Palestine of a national home for the Jewish people, and will use their best endeavours to facilitate the achievement of this object, it being clearly understood that nothing shall be done which may prejudice the civil and religious rights of existing non-Jewish communities in Palestine, or the rights and political status enjoyed by Jews in any other country."

I should be grateful if you would bring this declaration to the knowledge of the Zionist Federation.

[Signed]
Arthur James Balfour

5. From the CHURCHILL WHITE PAPER 1922

Statement of British Policy in Palestine Issued by Mr. Churchill in June, 1922.

. . . The tension which has prevailed from time to time in Palestine is mainly due to apprehensions, which are entertained both by sections of the Arab and by sections of the Jewish population. These apprehensions, so far as the Arabs are concerned, are partly based upon exaggerated interpretations of the meaning of the Declaration favouring the establishment of a Jewish National Home in Palestine, made on behalf of His Majesty's Government on 2nd November, 1917. Unauthorized statements have been made to the effect that the purpose in view is to create a wholly Jewish Palestine. Phrases have been used such as that Palestine is to become "as Jewish as England is English." His Majesty's Government regard any such expectation as impracticable and have no such aim in view. Nor have they at any time contemplated, as appears to be feared by the Arab Delegation, the disappearance or the subordination of the Arabic population, language, or culture in Palestine. They would draw attention to the fact that the terms of the Declaration referred to do not contemplate that Palestine as a whole should be converted into a Jewish National Home, but that such a Home should be founded *in Palestine*. In this connection it has been observed with satisfaction that at the meeting of the Zionist Congress, the supreme governing body of the Zionist Organization, held at Carlsbad in September, 1921, a resolution was passed expressing as the official statement of Zionist aims "the determination of the Jewish people to live with the Arab people on terms of unity and mutual respect, and together with them to make the common home into a flourishing community, the upbuilding of which may assure to each of its peoples an undisturbed national development."

It is also necessary to point out that the Zionist Commission in Palestine, now termed the Palestine Zionist Executive, has not desired to possess, and does not possess, any share in the general administration of the country. Nor does the special position assigned to the Zionist Organization in Article IV of the Draft Mandate for Palestine imply any such functions. That special position relates to the measures to be taken in Palestine affecting the Jewish population, and contemplates that the Organization may assist in the general development of the country, but does not entitle it to share in any degree in its Government.

Further, it is contemplated that the status of all citizens of Palestine in the eyes of the law shall be Palestinian, and it has never been intended that they, or any section of them, should possess any other juridical status.

So far as the Jewish population of Palestine are concerned it appears that some among them are apprehensive that His Majesty's Government may depart from the policy embodied in the Declaration of 1917. It is necessary, therefore, once more to affirm that these fears are unfounded, and that that Declaration, re-affirmed by the Conference of the Principal Allied Powers at San Remo and again in the Treaty of Sèvres, is not susceptible of change.

During the last two or three generations the Jews have recreated in Palestine a community, now numbering 80,000, of whom about one-fourth are farmers or workers upon the land. This community has its own political organs; an elected assembly for the direction of its domestic concerns; elected councils in the towns; and an organization for the control of its schools. It has its elected Chief Rabbinate and Rabbinical Council for the direction of its religious affairs. Its business is conducted in Hebrew as a vernacular language, and a Hebrew Press serves its needs. It has its distinctive intellectual life and displays considerable economic activity. This community, then, with its town and country population, its political, religious, and social organizations, its own language, its own customs, its own life, has in fact "national" characteristics. When it is asked what is meant by the development of the Jewish National Home in Palestine, it may be answered that it is not the imposition of a Jewish nationality upon the inhabitants of Palestine as a whole, but the further development of the existing Jewish community, with the assistance of Jews in other parts of the world, in order that it may become a centre in which the Jewish people as a whole may take, on grounds of religion and race, an interest and a pride. But in order that this community should have the best prospect of free development and provide a full opportunity for the Jewish people to display its capacities, it is essential that it should know that it is in Palestine as of right and not on sufferance. That is the reason why it is necessary that the existence of a Jewish National Home in Palestine should be internationally guaranteed, and that it should be formally recognized to rest upon ancient historic connection.

This, then, is the interpretation which His Majesty's Government place upon the Declaration of 1917, and, so understood, the Secretary of State is of opinion that it does not contain or imply anything which need cause either alarm to the Arab population of Palestine or disappointment to the Jews.

For the fulfilment of this policy it is necessary that the Jewish community in Palestine should be able to increase its numbers by immigration. This immigration cannot be so great in volume as to exceed whatever may be the economic capacity of the country at the time to absorb new arrivals. It is essential to ensure that the immigrants should not be a burden upon the people of Palestine as a whole, and that they should not deprive any section of the present population of their employment. Hitherto the immigration has fulfilled these conditions. The number of immigrants since the British occupation has been about 25,000 . . .

. . . it is not the case, as has been represented by the Arab Delegation, that during the war His Majesty's Government gave an understanding that an independent national government should be at once established in Palestine. This representation mainly rests upon a letter dated the 24th October, 1915, from Sir Henry McMahon, then His Majesty's High Commissioner in Egypt, to the Sherif of Mecca, now King Hussein of the Kingdom of the Hejaz. That letter is quoted as conveying the promise to the Sherif of Mecca to recognise and support the independence of the Arabs within the territories proposed by him. But this promise was given subject to a reservation made in the same letter, which excluded from its scope, among other territories, the portions of Syria lying to the west of the district of Damascus. This reservation has always been regarded by His Majesty's Government as covering the vilayet of Beirut and the independent Sanjak of Jerusalem. The whole of Palestine west of the Jordan was thus excluded from Sir H. McMahon's pledge.

Nevertheless, it is the intention of His Majesty's Government to foster the establishment of a full measure of self-government in Palestine. But they are of opinion that, in the special circumstances of that country, this should be accomplished by gradual stages and not suddenly. The first step was taken when, on the institution of a Civil Administration, the nominated Advisory Council, which now exists, was established. It was stated at the time by the High Commissioner that this was the first step in the development of self-governing institutions, and it is now proposed to take a second step by the establishment of a Legislative Council containing a large proportion of members elected on a wide franchise. It was proposed in the published draft that three of the members of this Council should be non-official persons nominated by the High Commissioner, but representations having been made in opposition to this provision, based on cogent considerations, the Secretary of State is prepared to omit it. The Legislative Council would then consist of the High Commissioner as President and twelve elected and ten official members. The Secretary of State is of opinion that before a further measure of self-government is extended to Palestine and the Assembly placed in control over the Executive, it would be wise to allow some time to elapse. During this period the institutions of the country will have become well established; its financial credit will be based on firm foundations, and the Palestinian officials will have been enabled to gain experience of sound methods of government. After a few years the situation will be again reviewed, and if the experience of the working of the constitution now to be established so warranted, a larger share of authority would then be extended to the elected representatives of the people . . .

6. From the BRITISH MANDATE FOR PALESTINE 1922

The Council of the League of Nations:

Whereas the Principal Allied Powers have agreed, for the purpose of giving effect to the provisions of Article 22 of the Covenant of the League of Nations, to entrust to a Mandatory selected by the said Powers the administration of the territory of Palestine, which formerly belonged to the Turkish Empire, within such boundaries as may be fixed by them; and

Whereas the Principal Allied Powers have also agreed that the Mandatory should be responsible for putting into effect the declaration originally made on November 2nd, 1917, by the Government of His Britannic Majesty, and adopted by the said Powers, in favour of the establishment in Palestine of a national home for the Jewish people, it being clearly understood that nothing should be done which might prejudice the civil and religious rights of existing non-Jewish communities in Palestine, or the rights and political status enjoyed by Jews in any other country; and

Whereas recognition has thereby been given to the historical connexion of the Jewish people with Palestine and to the grounds for reconstituting their national home in that country; and

Whereas the Principal Allied Powers have selected His Britannic Majesty as the Mandatory for Palestine; and

Whereas the mandate in respect of Palestine has been formulated in the following terms and submitted to the Council of the League for approval; and

Whereas His Britannic Majesty has accepted the mandate in respect of Palestine and undertaken to exercise it on behalf of the League of Nations in conformity with the following provisions; and

Whereas by the aforementioned Article 22 (paragraph 8), it is provided that the degree of authority, control or administration to be exercised by the Mandatory, not having been previously agreed upon by the Members of the League, shall be explicitly defined by the Council of the League of Nations;

Confirming the said Mandate, defines its terms as follows:

Article 1.

The Mandatory shall have full powers of legislation and of administration, save as they may be limited by the terms of this mandate.

Article 2.

The Mandatory shall be responsible for placing the country under such political, administrative and economic conditions as will secure the establishment of the Jewish national home, as laid down in the preamble, and the development of self-governing institutions, and also for safeguarding the civil and religious rights of all the inhabitants of Palestine, irrespective of race and religion.

Article 3.

The Mandatory shall, so far as circumstances permit, encourage local autonomy.

Article 4.

An appropriate Jewish agency shall be recognized as a public body for the purpose of advising and cooperating with the Administration of Palestine in such economic, social and other matters as may affect the establishment of the Jewish national home and the interests of the Jewish population in

Palestine, and, subject always to the control of the Administration, to assist and take part in the development of the country.

The Zionist Organization, so long as its organization and constitution are in the opinion of the Mandatory appropriate, shall be recognized as such agency. It shall take steps in consultation with His Britannic Majesty's Government to secure the cooperation of all Jews who are willing to assist in the establishment of the Jewish national home.

Article 5.

The Mandatory shall be responsible for seeing that no Palestine territory shall be ceded or leased to, or in any way placed under the control of, the Government of any foreign Power.

Article 6.

The Administration of Palestine, while ensuring that the rights and position of other sections of the population are not prejudiced, shall facilitate Jewish immigration under suitable conditions and shall encourage, in co-operation with the Jewish agency referred to in Article 4, close settlement by Jews on the land, including State lands and waste lands not required for public purposes.

Article 7.

The Administration of Palestine shall be responsible for enacting a nationality law. There shall be included in this law provisions framed so as to facilitate the acquisition of Palestinian citizenship by Jews who take up their permanent residence in Palestine.

Article 8.

The privileges and immunities of foreigners, including the benefits of consular jurisdiction and protection as formerly enjoyed by Capitulation or usage in the Ottoman Empire, shall not be applicable in Palestine.

Unless the Powers whose nationals enjoyed the aforementioned privileges and immunities on August 1st, 1914, shall have previously renounced the right to their re-establishment, or shall have agreed to their non-application for a specified period, these privileges and immunities shall, at the expiration of the mandate, be immediately re-established in their entirety or with such modifications as may have been agreed upon between the Powers concerned.

Article 9.

The Mandatory shall be responsible for seeing that the judicial system established in Palestine shall assure to foreigners, as well as to natives, a complete guarantee of their rights.

Respect for the personal status of the various peoples and communities and for their religious interests shall be fully guaranteed. In particular, the control and administration of Waqfs shall be exercised in accordance with religious law and the dispositions of the founders . . .

Article 22.

English, Arabic and Hebrew shall be the official languages of Palestine. Any statement or inscription in Arabic on stamps or money in Palestine shall be repeated in Hebrew and any statement or inscription in Hebrew shall be repeated in Arabic.

DONE AT LONDON the twenty-fourth day of July, one thousand nine hundred and twenty-two.

7. From the WHITE PAPER OF 1939
May 17, 1939

In the Statement on Palestine, issued on 9th November, 1938, His Majesty's Government announced their intention to invite representatives of the Arabs of Palestine, of certain neighbouring countries and of the Jewish Agency to confer with them in London regarding future policy. It was their sincere hope that, as a result of full, free and frank discussion, some understanding might be reached. Conferences recently took place with Arab and Jewish delegations, lasting for a period of several weeks, and served the purpose of a complete exchange of views between British Ministers and the Arab and Jewish representatives. In the light of the discussions as well as of the situation in Palestine and of the Reports of the Royal Commission and the Partition Commission, certain proposals were formulated by His Majesty's Government and were laid before the Arab and Jewish delegations as the basis of an agreed settlement. Neither the Arab nor the Jewish delegation felt able to accept these proposals, and the conferences therefore did not result in an agreement. Accordingly His Majesty's Government are free to formulate their own policy, and after careful consideration they have decided to adhere generally to the proposals which were finally submitted to, and discussed with, the Arab and Jewish delegations . . .

2. The Mandate for Palestine, the terms of which were confirmed by the Council of the League of Nations in 1922, has governed the policy of successive British Governments for nearly 20 years. It embodies the Balfour Declaration and imposes on the Mandatory four main obligations. These obligations are set out in Article 2, 6 and 13 of the Mandate. There is no dispute regarding the interpretation of one of these obligations, that touching

the protection of and access to the Holy Places and religious building or sites. The other three main obligations are generally as follows:—

(i) To place the country under such political, administrative and economic conditions as will secure the establishment in Palestine of a national home for the Jewish people, to facilitate Jewish immigration under suitable conditions, and to encourage, in co-operation with the Jewish Agency, close settlement by Jews on the land.

(ii) To safeguard the civil and religious rights of all the inhabitants of Palestine irrespective of race and religion, and, whilst facilitating Jewish immigration and settlement, to ensure that the rights and position of other sections of the population are not prejudiced.

(iii) To place the country under such political, administrative and economic conditions as will secure the development of self-governing institutions.

3. The Royal Commission and previous Commissions of Enquiry have drawn attention to the ambiguity of certain expressions in the Mandate, such as the expression "a national home for the Jewish people," and they have found in this ambiguity and the resulting uncertainty as to the objectives of policy a fundamental cause of unrest and hostility between Arabs and Jews. His Majesty's Government are convinced that in the interests of the peace and well-being of the whole people of Palestine a clear definition of policy and objectives is essential. The proposal of partition recommended by the Royal Commission would have afforded such clarity, but the establishment of self-supporting independent Arab and Jewish States within Palestine has been found to be impracticable. It has therefore been necessary for His Majesty's Government to devise an alternative policy which will, consistently with their obligations to Arabs and Jews, meet the needs of the situation in Palestine. Their views and proposals are set forth below under the three heads, (I) The Constitution, (II) Immigration, and (III) Land.

I.—The Constitution

4. It has been urged that the expression "a national home for the Jewish people" offered a prospect that Palestine might in due course become a Jewish State or Commonwealth. His Majesty's Government do not wish to contest the view, which was expressed by the Royal Commission, that the Zionist leaders at the time of the issue of the Balfour Declaration recognised that an ultimate Jewish State was not precluded by the terms of the Declaration. But, with the Royal Commission, His Majesty's Government believe that the framers of the Mandate in which the Balfour Declaration was embodied could not have intended that Palestine should be converted into a Jewish State against the will of the Arab population of the country. That Palestine was not

to be converted into a Jewish State might be held to be implied in the passage from the Command Paper of 1922 which reads as follows:—

"Unauthorized statements have been made to the effect that the purpose in view is to create a wholly Jewish Palestine. Phrases have been used such as that 'Palestine is to become as Jewish as England is English.' His Majesty's Government regard any such expectation as impracticable and have no such aim in view. Nor have they at any time contemplated . . . the disappearance or the subordination of the Arabic population, language or culture in Palestine. They would draw attention to the fact that the terms of the (Balfour) Declaration referred to do not contemplate that Palestine as a whole should be converted into a Jewish National Home, but that such a Home should be founded *in Palestine.*"

But this statement has not removed doubts, and His Majesty's Government therefore now declare unequivocally that it is not part of their policy that Palestine should become a Jewish State. They would indeed regard it as contrary to their obligations to the Arabs under the Mandate, as well as to the assurances which have been given to the Arab people in the past, that the Arab population of Palestine should be made the subjects of a Jewish State against their will.

5. The nature of the Jewish National Home in Palestine was further described in the Command Paper of 1922 as follows:

"During the last two or three generations the Jews have recreated in Palestine a community, now numbering 80,000, of whom about one-fourth are farmers or workers upon the land. This community has its own political organs; an elected assembly for the direction of its domestic concerns; elected councils in the towns; and an organisation for the control of its schools. It has its elected Chief Rabbinate and Rabbinical Council for the direction of its religious affairs. Its business is conducted in Hebrew as a vernacular language, and a Hebrew press serves its needs. It has its distinctive intellectual life and displays considerable economic activity. This community, then, with its town and country population, its political, religious and social organisations, its own language, its own customs, its own life, has in fact 'national' characteristics. When it is asked what is meant by the development of the Jewish National Home in Palestine, it may be answered that it is not the imposition of a Jewish nationality upon the inhabitants of Palestine as a whole, but the further development of the existing Jewish community, with the assistance of Jews in other parts of the world, in order that it may become a centre in which the Jewish people as a whole may take, on grounds of religion and race, an interest and a pride. But in order that this community should have the best prospect of free development and provide a full opportunity for the Jewish people to display its capacities, it is essential that it should know that it is in Palestine as of right and not on sufference. That is the reason why it is necessary that the existence of a Jewish National Home in Palestine should be internationally guaranteed, and that it should be formally recognised to rest upon ancient historic connection."

6. His Majesty's Government adhere to this interpretation of the Declaration of 1917 and regard it as an authoritative and comprehensive description of the character of the Jewish National Home in Palestine. It envisaged the further development of the existing Jewish community with the assistance of Jews in other parts of the world. Evidence that His Majesty's Government have been carrying out their obligation in this respect is to be found in the facts that, since the statement of 1922 was published, more than 300,000 Jews have immigrated to Palestine, and that the population of the National Home has risen to some 450,000, or approaching a third of the entire population of the country. Nor has the Jewish community failed to take full advantage of the opportunities given to it. The growth of the Jewish National Home and its achievements in many fields are a remarkable constructive effort which must command the admiration of the world and must be, in particular, a source of pride to the Jewish people.

7. In the recent discussions the Arab delegations have repeated the contention that Palestine was included within the area in which Sir Henry McMahon, on behalf of the British Government, in October, 1915, undertook to recognise and support Arab independence. The validity of this claim, based on the terms of the correspondence which passed between Sir Henry McMahon and the Sharif of Mecca, was thoroughly and carefully investigated by British and Arab representatives during the recent conferences in London. Their Report, which has been published, states that both the Arab and the British representatives endeavoured to understand the point of view of the other party but that they were unable to reach agreement upon an interpretation of the correspondence. There is no need to summarize here the arguments presented by each side. His Majesty's Government regret the misunderstandings which have arisen as regards some of the phrases used. For their part they can only adhere, for the reasons given by their representatives in the Report, to the view that the whole of Palestine west of Jordan was excluded from Sir Henry McMahon's pledge, and they therefore cannot agree that the McMahon correspondence forms a just basis for the claim that Palestine should be converted into an Arab State.

8. His Majesty's Government are charged as the Mandatory authority "to secure the development of self-governing institutions" in Palestine. Apart from this specific obligation, they would regard it as contrary to the whole spirit of the Mandate system that the population of Palestine should remain forever under Mandatory tutelage. It is proper that the people of the country should as early as possible enjoy the rights of self-government which are exercised by the people of neighbouring countries. His Majesty's Govern-

ment are unable at present to foresee the exact constitutional forms which government in Palestine will eventually take, but their objective is self-government, and they desire to see established ultimately an independent Palestine State. It should be a State in which the two peoples in Palestine, Arabs and Jews, share authority in government in such a way that the essential interests of each are secured.

9. The establishment of an independent State and the complete relinquishment of Mandatory control in Palestine would require such relations between the Arabs and the Jews as would make good government possible. Moreover, the growth of self-governing institutions in Palestine, as in other countries, must be an evolutionary process. A transitional period will be required before independence is achieved, throughout which ultimate responsibility for the Government of the country will be retained by His Majesty's Government as the Mandatory authority, while the people of the country are taking an increasing share in the Government, and understanding and co-operation amongst them are growing. It will be the constant endeavour of His Majesty's Government to promote good relations between the Arabs and the Jews.

10. In the light of these considerations His Majesty's Government make the following declaration of their intentions regarding the future government of Palestine:—

(1) The objective of His Majesty's Government is the establishment within ten years of an independent Palestine State . . .

(2) The independent State should be one in which Arabs and Jews share in government in such a way as to ensure that the essential interests of each community are safeguarded.

(3) The establishment of the independent State will be preceded by a transitional period . . .

II.—Immigration

12. Under Article 6 of the Mandate, the Administration of Palestine, "while ensuring that the rights and position of other sections of the population are not prejudiced," is required to "facilitate Jewish immigration under suitable conditions." Beyond this, the extent to which Jewish immigration into Palestine is to be permitted is nowhere defined in the Mandate. But in the Command Paper of 1922 it was laid down that for the fulfilment of the policy of establishing a Jewish National Home

"it is necessary that the Jewish community in Palestine should be able to increase its numbers by immigration. This immigration cannot be so great in volume as to exceed whatever may be the economic capacity of the country at the time to absorb new arrivals. It is essential to ensure that the immigrants should not be a burden upon the people of Palestine as a whole, and that they should not deprive any section of the present population of their employment."

In practice, from that date onwards until recent times, the economic absorptive capacity of the country has been treated as the sole limiting factor, and in the letter which Mr. Ramsay MacDonald, as Prime Minister, sent to Dr. Weizmann in February 1931 it was laid down as a matter of policy that economic absorptive capacity was the sole criterion. This interpretation has been supported by resolutions of the Permanent Mandates Commission. But His Majesty's Government do not read either the Statement of Policy of 1922 or the letter of 1931 as implying that the Mandate requires them, for all time and in all circumstances, to facilitate the immigration of Jews into Palestine subject only to consideration of the country's economic absorptive capacity. Nor do they find anything in the Mandate or in subsequent Statements of Policy to support the view that the establishment of a Jewish National Home in Palestine cannot be effected unless immigration is allowed to continue indefinitely. If immigration has an adverse effect on the economic position in the country, it should clearly be restricted; and equally, if it has a seriously damaging effect on the political position in the country, that is a factor that should not be ignored. Although it is not difficult to contend that the large number of Jewish immigrants who have been admitted so far have been absorbed economically, the fear of the Arabs that this influx will continue indefinitely until the Jewish population is in a position to dominate them has produced consequences which are extremely grave for Jews and Arabs alike and for the peace and prosperity of Palestine. The lamentable disturbances of the past three years are only the latest and most sustained manifestation of this intense Arab apprehension. The methods employed by Arab terrorists against fellow-Arabs and Jews alike must receive unqualified condemnation. But it cannot be denied that fear of indefinite Jewish immigration is widespread amongst the Arab population and that this fear has made possible disturbances which have given a serious setback to economic progress, depleted the Palestine exchequer, rendered life and property insecure, and produced a bitterness between the Arab and Jewish populations which is deplorable between citizens of the same country. If in these circumstances immigration is continued up to the economic absorptive capacity of the country, regardless of all other considerations, a fatal enmity between the two peoples will be perpetuated, and the situation in Palestine may become a permanent source of friction amongst all peoples in the Near and Middle East. His Majesty's Government cannot take the view that either their obligations under the Mandate, or considerations of common sense and justice, require that they should ignore these circumstances in framing immigration policy.

13. In the view of the Royal Commission the association of the policy of the Balfour Declaration with the Mandate system implied the belief that Arab hostility to the former would sooner or later be overcome. It has been the hope of British Governments ever since the Balfour Declaration was issued that in time the Arab population, recognizing the advantages to be derived from Jewish settlement and development in Palestine, would become reconciled to the further growth of the Jewish National Home. This hope has not been fulfilled. The alternatives before His Majesty's Government are either (i) to seek to expand the Jewish National Home indefinitely by immigration, against the strongly expressed will of the Arab people of the country; or (ii) to permit further expansion of the Jewish National Home by immigration only if the Arabs are prepared to acquiesce in it. The former policy means rule by force. Apart from other considerations, such a policy seems to His Majesty's Government to be contrary to the whole spirit of Article 22 of the Covenant of the League of Nations, as well as to their specific obligations to the Arabs in the Palestine Mandate. Moreover, the relations between the Arabs and the Jews in Palestine must be based sooner or later on mutual tolerance and goodwill; the peace, security and progress of the Jewish National Home itself require this. Therefore His Majesty's Government, after earnest consideration, and taking into account the extent to which the growth of the Jewish National Home has been facilitated over the last twenty years, have decided that the time has come to adopt in principle the second of the alternatives referred to above.

14. It has been urged that all further Jewish immigration into Palestine should be stopped forthwith. His Majesty's Government cannot accept such a proposal. It would damage the whole of the financial and economic system of Palestine and thus affect adversely the interests of Arabs and Jews alike. Moreover, in the view of His Majesty's Government, abruptly to stop further immigration would be unjust to the Jewish National Home. But, above all, His Majesty's Government are conscious of the present unhappy plight of large numbers of Jews who seek a refuge from certain European countries, and they believe that Palestine can and should make a further contribution to the solution of this pressing world problem. In all these circumstances, they believe that they will be acting consistently with their Mandatory obligations to both Arabs and Jews, and in the manner best calculated to serve the interests of the whole people of Palestine, by adopting the following proposals regarding immigration:—

(1) Jewish immigration during the next five years will be at a rate which, if economic absorptive capacity permits, will bring the Jewish population up to approximately one-third of the total population of the country . . .

(2) The existing machinery for ascertaining economic absorptive capacity will be retained, and the High Commissioner will have the ultimate responsibility for deciding the limits of economic capacity. Before each periodic decision is taken, Jewish and Arab representatives will be consulted.

(3) After the period of five years no further Jewish immigration will be permitted unless the Arabs of Palestine are prepared to acquiesce in it.

(4) His Majesty's Government are determined to check illegal immigration, and further preventive measures are being adopted. The numbers of any Jewish illegal immigrants who, despite these measures, may succeed in coming into the country and cannot be deported will be deducted from the yearly quotas.

15. His Majesty's Government are satisfied that, when the immigration over five years which is now contemplated has taken place, they will not be justified in facilitating, nor will they be under any obligation to facilitate, the further development of the Jewish National Home by immigration regardless of the wishes of the Arab population.

III.—Land

16. The Administration of Palestine is required, under Article 6 of the Mandate, "while ensuring that the rights and position of other sections of the population are not prejudiced," to encourage "close settlement by Jews on the land," and no restriction has been imposed hitherto on the transfer of land from Arabs to Jews. The Reports of several expert Commissions have indicated that, owing to the natural growth of the Arab population and the steady sale in recent years of Arab land to Jews, there is now in certain areas no room for further transfers of Arab land, whilst in some other areas such transfers of land must be restricted if Arab cultivators are to maintain their existing standard of life and a considerable landless Arab population is not soon to be created. In these circumstances, the High Commissioner will be given general powers to prohibit and regulate transfers of land. These powers will date from the publication of this statement of policy and the High Commissioner will retain them throughout the transitional period.

17. The policy of the Government will be directed towards the development of the land and the improvement, where possible, of methods of cultivation. In the light of such development it will be open to the High Commissioner, should he be satisfied that the "rights and position" of the Arab population will be duly preserved, to review and modify any orders passed relating to the prohibition or restriction of the transfer of land.

18. In framing these proposals His Majesty's Government have sincerely endeavoured to act in strict accordance with their obligations under the

Mandate to both the Arabs and the Jews. The vagueness of the phrases employed in some instances to describe these obligations has led to controversy and has made the task of interpretation difficult. His Majesty's Government cannot hope to satisfy the partisans of one party or the other in such controversy as the Mandate has aroused. Their purpose is to be just as between the two peoples in Palestine whose destinies in that country have been affected by the great events of recent years, and who, since they live side by side, must learn to practice mutual tolerance, goodwill and co-operation. In looking to the future, His Majesty's Government are not blind to the fact that some events of the past make the task of creating these relations difficult . . .

8. ZIONIST REACTION TO THE 1939 WHITE PAPER

Statement by the Jewish Agency for Palestine (1939)

1. The new policy for Palestine laid down by the Mandatory in the White Paper now issued denies to the Jewish people the right to rebuild their national home in their ancestral country. It transfers the authority over Palestine to the present Arab majority and puts the Jewish population at the mercy of that majority. It decrees the stoppage of Jewish immigration as soon as the Jews form a third of the total population. It puts up a territorial ghetto for Jews in their own homeland.

2. The Jewish people regard this policy as a breach of faith and a surrender to Arab terrorism. It delivers Britain's friends into the hands of those who are biting her and must lead to a complete breach between Jews and Arabs which will banish every prospect of peace in Palestine. It is a policy in which the Jewish people will not acquiesce. The new regime now announced will be devoid of any moral basis and contrary to international law. Such a regime can only be established and maintained by force.

3. The Royal Commission invoked by the White Paper indicated the perils of such a policy, saying it was convinced that an Arab Government would mean the frustration of all their (Jews') efforts and ideals and would convert the national home into one more cramped and dangerous ghetto. It seems only too probable that the Jews would fight rather than submit to Arab rule. And repressing a Jewish rebellion against British policy would be as unpleasant a task as the repression of the Arab rebellion has been. The Government has disregarded this warning.

4. The Jewish people have no quarrel with the Arab people. Jewish work in Palestine has not had an adverse effect upon the life and progress of the Arab people. The Arabs are not landless or homeless as are the Jews. They are not in need of emigration. Jewish colonization has benefited Palestine and

all its inhabitants. Insofar as the Balfour Declaration contributed to British victory in the Great War, it contributed also, as was pointed out by the Royal Commission, to the liberation of the Arab peoples. The Jewish people has shown its will to peace even during the years of disturbances. It has not given way to temptation and has not retaliated to Arab violence. But neither have the Jews submitted to terror nor will they submit to it even after the Mandatory has decided to reward the terrorist by surrendering the Jewish National Home.

5. It is in the darkest hour of Jewish history that the British Government proposes to deprive the Jews of their last hope and to close the road back to their Homeland. It is a cruel blow, doubly cruel because it comes from the government of a great nation which has extended a helping hand to the Jews, and whose position must rest on foundations of moral authority and international good faith. This blow will not subdue the Jewish people. The historic bond between the people and the land of Israel cannot be broken. The Jews will never accept the closing to them of the gates of Palestine nor let their national home be converted into a ghetto. The Jewish pioneers who, during the past three generations, have shown their strength in the upbuilding of a derelict country, will from now on display the same strength in defending Jewish immigration, the Jewish home and Jewish freedom.

9. THE BILTMORE PROGRAM 1942

Declaration Adopted by the Extraordinary Zionist Conference, Biltmore Hotel, New York City, May 11, 1942

1. American Zionists assembled in this Extraordinary Conference reaffirm their unequivocal devotion to the cause of democratic freedom and international justice to which the people of the United States, allied with the other United Nations, have dedicated themselves, and give expression to their faith in the ultimate victory of humanity and justice over lawlessness and brute force.

2. This Conference offers a message of hope and encouragement to their fellow Jews in the Ghettos and concentration camps of Hitler-dominated Europe and prays that their hour of liberation may not be far distant.

3. The Conference sends its warmest greetings to the Jewish Agency Executive in Jerusalem, to the Va'ad Leumi, and to the whole Yishuv in Palestine, and expresses its profound admiration for their steadfastness and achievements in the face of peril and great difficulties. The Jewish men and women in field and factory, and the thousands of Jewish soldiers of Palestine in the Near East who have acquitted themselves with honor and distinction

in Greece, Ethiopia, Syria, Libya and on other battlefields, have shown themselves worthy of their people and ready to assume the rights and responsibilities of nationhood.

4. In our generation, and in particular in the course of the past twenty years, the Jewish people have awakened and transformed their ancient homeland; from 50,000 at the end of the last war their numbers have increased to more than 500,000. They have made the waste places to bear fruit and the desert to blossom. Their pioneering achievements in agriculture and in industry, embodying new patterns of cooperative endeavor, have written a notable page in the history of colonization.

5. In the new values thus created, their Arab neighbors in Palestine have shared. The Jewish people in its own work of national redemption welcomes the economic, agricultural and national development of the Arab peoples and states. The Conference reaffirms the stand previously adopted at Congresses of the World Zionist Organization, expressing the readiness and the desire of the Jewish people for full cooperation with their Arab neighbors.

6. The Conference calls for the fulfilment of the original purpose of the Balfour Declaration and the Mandate which *"recognizing the historical connection of the Jewish people with Palestine"* was to afford them the opportunity, as stated by President Wilson, to found there a Jewish Commonwealth.

The Conference affirms its unalterable rejection of the White Paper of May 1939 and denies its moral or legal validity. The White Paper seeks to limit, and in fact to nullify Jewish rights to immigration and settlement in Palestine, and, as stated by Mr. Winston Churchill in the House of Commons in May 1939, constitutes "a breach and repudiation of the Balfour Declaration." The policy of the White Paper is cruel and indefensible in its denial of sanctuary to Jews fleeing from Nazi persecution; and at a time when Palestine has become a focal point in the war front of the United Nations, and Palestine Jewry must provide all available manpower for farm and factory and camp, it is in direct conflict with the interests of the allied war effort.

7. In the struggle against the forces of aggression and tyranny, of which Jews were the earliest victims, and which now menace the Jewish National Home, recognition must be given to the right of the Jews of Palestine to play their full part in the war effort and in the defense of their country, through a Jewish military force fighting under its own flag and under the high command of the United Nations.

8. The Conference declares that the new world order that will follow victory cannot be established on foundations of peace, justice and equality, unless the problem of Jewish homelessness is finally solved.

The Conference urges that the gates of Palestine be opened; that the Jewish Agency be vested with control of immigration into Palestine and with the necessary authority for upbuilding the country, including the development of its unoccupied and uncultivated lands; and that Palestine be established as a Jewish Commonwealth integrated in the structure of the new democratic world.

Then and only then will the age-old wrong to the Jewish people be righted.

10. From the U.N. GENERAL ASSEMBLY PALESTINE PARTITION RESOLUTION November 29, 1947

Plan of Partition with Economic Union Part I—Future Constitution and Government of Palestine

A. Termination of Mandate Partition and Independence

1. The Mandate for Palestine shall terminate as soon as possible but in any case not later than 1 August 1948.

2. The armed forces of the mandatory Power shall be progressively withdrawn from Palestine, the withdrawal to be completed as soon as possible but in any case not later than 1 August 1948.

The mandatory Power shall advise the Commission, as far in advance as possible, of its intention to terminate the Mandate and to evacuate each area.

The mandatory Power shall use its best endeavours to ensure that an area situated in the territory of the Jewish State, including a seaport and hinterland adequate to provide facilities for a substantial immigration, shall be evacuated at the earliest possible date and in any event not later than 1 February 1948.

3. Independent Arab and Jewish States and the Special International Regime for the City of Jerusalem, set forth in part III of this plan, shall come into existence in Palestine two months after the evacuation of the armed forces of the mandatory Power has been completed but in any case not later than 1 October 1948. The boundaries of the Arab State, the Jewish State, and the City of Jerusalem shall be described in parts II and III below.

4. The period between the adoption by the General Assembly of its recommendation on the question of Palestine and the establishment of the independence of the Arab and Jewish States shall be a transitional period.

B. Steps Preparatory to Independence

1. A Commission shall be set up consisting of one representative of each of five Member States. The Members represented on the Commission shall be elected by the General Assembly on as broad a basis, geographically and otherwise, as possible.

2. The administration of Palestine shall, as the mandatory Power withdraws its armed forces, be progressively turned over to the Commission, which shall act in conformity with the recommendations of the General Assembly, under the guidance of the Security Council. The mandatory Power shall to the fullest possible extent co-ordinate its plans for withdrawal with the plans of the Commission to take over and administer areas which have been evacuated.

In the discharge of this administrative responsibility the Commission shall have authority to issue necessary regulations and take other measures as required.

The mandatory Power shall not take any action to prevent, obstruct or delay the implementation by the Commission of the measures recommended by the General Assembly.

3. On its arrival in Palestine the Commission shall proceed to carry out measures for the establishment of the frontiers of the Arab and Jewish States and the City of Jerusalem in accordance with the general lines of the recommendations of the General Assembly on the partition of Palestine. Nevertheless, the boundaries as described in part II of this plan are to be modified in such a way that village areas as a rule will not be divided by state boundaries unless pressing reasons make that necessary.

4. The Commission, after consultation with the democratic parties and other public organizations of the Arab and Jewish States, shall select and establish in each State as rapidly as possible a Provisional Council of Government. The activities of both the Arab and Jewish Provisional Councils of Government shall be carried out under the general direction of the Commission.

If by 1 April 1948 a Provisional Council of Government cannot be selected for either of the States, or, if selected, cannot carry out its functions, the Commission shall communicate that fact to the Security Council for such action with respect to that State as the Security Council may deem proper, and to the Secretary-General for communication to the Members of the United Nations.

5. Subject to the provisions of these recommendations, during the transitional period the Provisional Councils of Government, acting under the Commission, shall have full authority in the areas under their control, including authority over matters of immigration and land regulation.

6. The Provisional Council of Government of each State, acting under the Commission, shall progressively receive from the Commission full responsibility for the administration of that State in the period between the termination of the Mandate and the establishment of the State's independence.

7. The Commission shall instruct the Provisional Councils of Government of both the Arab and Jewish States, after their formation, to proceed to the establishment of administrative organs of government, central and local.

8. The Provisional Council of Government of each State shall, within the shortest time possible, recruit an armed militia from the residents of that State, sufficient in number to maintain internal order and to prevent frontier clashes.

This armed militia in each State shall, for operational purposes, be under the command of Jewish or Arab officers resident in that State, but general political and military control, including the choice of the militia's High Command, shall be exercised by the Commission.

9. The Provisional Council of Government of each State shall, not later than two months after the withdrawal of the armed forces of the mandatory Power, hold elections to the Constituent Assembly which shall be conducted on democratic lines.

The election regulations in each State shall be drawn up by the Provisional Council of Government and approved by the Commission.

Qualified voters for each State for this election shall be persons over eighteen years of age who are: (*a*) Palestinian citizens residing in that State and (*b*) Arabs and Jews residing in the State, although not Palestinian citizens, who, before voting, have signed a notice of intention to become citizens of such State.

Arabs and Jews residing in the City of Jerusalem who have signed a notice of intention to become citizens, the Arabs of the Arab State and the Jews of the Jewish State, shall be entitled to vote in the Arab and Jewish States respectively.

Women may vote and be elected to the Constituent Assemblies.

During the transitional period no Jew shall be permitted to establish residence in the area of the proposed Arab State, and no Arab shall be permitted to establish residence in the area of the proposed Jewish State, except by special leave of the Commission.

10. The Constituent Assembly of each State shall draft a democratic constitution for its State and choose a provisional government to succeed the Provisional Council of Government appointed by the Commission. The constitutions of the State shall embody chapters 1 and 2 of the Declaration provided for in section C below and include *inter alia* provisions for:

(*a*) Establishing in each State a legislative body elected by universal suffrage and by secret ballot on the basis of proportional representation, and an executive body responsible to the legislature;

(*b*) Settling all international disputes in which the State may be involved by peaceful means in such a manner that international peace and security, and justice, are not endangered;

(c) Accepting the obligation of the State to refrain in its international relations from the threat or use of force against the territorial integrity or political independence of any State, or in any other manner inconsistent with the purposes of the United Nations;

(d) Guaranteeing to all persons equal and non-discriminatory rights in civil, political, economic and religious matters and the enjoyment of human rights and fundamental freedoms, including freedom of religion, language, speech and publication, education, assembly and association;

(e) Preserving freedom of transit and visit for all residents and citizens of the other State in Palestine and the City of Jerusalem, subject to considerations of national security, provided that each State shall control residence within its borders.

11. The Commission shall appoint a preparatory economic commission of three members to make whatever arrangements are possible for economic co-operation, with a view to establishing, as soon as practicable, the Economic Union and the Joint Economic Board . . .

C. Declaration

A declaration shall be made to the United Nations by the provisional government of each proposed State before independence. It shall contain *inter alia* the following clauses:

General Provision

The stipulations contained in the declaration are recognized as fundamental laws of the State and no law, regulation or official action shall conflict or interfere with these stipulations, nor shall any law, regulation or official action prevail over them.

Chapter 1.—Holy Places, Religious Buildings and Sites

1. Existing rights in respect of Holy Places and religious buildings or sites shall not be denied or impaired.

2. In so far as Holy Places are concerned, the liberty of access, visit and transit shall be guaranteed, in conformity with existing rights, to all residents and citizens of the other State and of the City of Jerusalem, as well as to aliens, without distinction as to nationality, subject to requirements of national security, public order and decorum.

Similarly, freedom of worship shall be guaranteed in conformity with existing rights, subject to the maintenance of public order and decorum.

3. Holy Places and religious buildings or sites shall be preserved . . .

Chapter 2.—Religious and Minority Rights

1. Freedom of conscience and the free exercise of all forms of worship, subject only to the maintenance of public order and morals, shall be ensured to all.

2. No discrimination of any kind shall be made between the inhabitants on the ground of race, religion, language or sex.

3. All persons within the jurisdiction of the State shall be entitled to equal protection of the laws.

4. The family law and personal status of the various minorities and their religious interests, including endowments, shall be respected.

5. Except as may be required for the maintenance of public order and good government, no measure shall be taken to obstruct or interfere with the enterprise of religious or charitable bodies of all faiths or to discriminate against any representative or member of these bodies on the ground of his religion or nationality.

6. The State shall ensure adequate primary and secondary education for the Arab and Jewish minority, respectively, in its own language and its cultural traditions.

The right of each community to maintain its own schools for the education of its own members in its own language, while conforming to such educational requirements of a general nature as the State may impose, shall not be denied or impaired. Foreign educational establishments shall continue their activity on the basis of their existing rights.

7. No restriction shall be imposed on the free use by any citizen of the State of any language in private intercourse, in commerce, in religion, in the Press or in publications of any kind, or at public meetings.[1]

8. No expropriation of land owned by an Arab in the Jewish State (by a Jew in the Arab State)[2] shall be allowed except for public purposes. In all cases of expropriation full compensation as fixed by the Supreme Court shall be paid previous to dispossession.

Chapter 3.—Citizenship, International Conventions and Financial Obligations

1. *Citizenship.* Palestinian citizens residing in Palestine outside the City of Jerusalem, as well as Arabs and Jews who, not holding Palestinian citizenship, reside in Palestine outside the City of Jerusalem shall, upon the recognition of independence, become citizens of the State in which they are resident and enjoy full civil and political rights. Persons over the age of eighteen years may opt, within one year from the date of recognition of independence of the State in which they reside, for citizenship of the other State, providing that no Arab residing in the area of the proposed Arab State shall have the right to opt for

---

[1] The following stipulation shall be added to the declaration concerning the Jewish State: "In the Jewish State adequate facilities shall be given to Arabic-speaking citizens for the use of their language, either orally or in writing, in the legislature, before the Courts and in the administration."

[2] In the declaration concerning the Arab State, the words "by an Arab in the Jewish State" should be replaced by the words "by a Jew in the Arab State."

citizenship in the proposed Jewish State and no Jews residing in the proposed Jewish State shall have the right to opt for citizenship in the proposed Arab State. The exercise of this right of option will be taken to include the wives and children under eighteen years of age of persons so opting.

Arabs residing in the area of the proposed Jewish State and Jews residing in the area of the proposed Arab State who have signed a notice of intention to opt for citizenship of the other State shall be eligible to vote in the elections to the Constituent Assembly of that State, but not in the elections to the Constituent Assembly of the State in which they reside.

2. *International conventions. (a)* The State shall be bound by all the international agreements and conventions, both general and special, to which Palestine has become a party . . .

11. ISRAEL DECLARATION OF INDEPENDENCE May 14, 1948

The Land of Israel was the birthplace of the Jewish people. Here their spiritual, religious and national identity was formed. Here they achieved independence and created a culture of national and universal significance. Here they wrote and gave the Bible to the world.

Exiled from the Land of Israel the Jewish people remained faithful to it in all the countries of their dispersion, never ceasing to pray and hope for their return and the restoration of their national freedom.

Impelled by this historic association, Jews strove throughout the centuries to go back to the land of their fathers and regain their statehood. In recent decades they returned in their masses. They reclaimed the wilderness, revived their language, built cities and villages, and established a vigorous and ever-growing community, with its own economic and cultural life. They sought peace, yet were prepared to defend themselves. They brought the blessings of progress to all inhabitants of the country and looked forward to sovereign independence.

In the year 1897 the First Zionist Congress, inspired by Theodor Herzl's vision of the Jewish State, proclaimed the right of the Jewish people to national revival in their own country.

This right was acknowledged by the Balfour Declaration of November 2, 1917, and re-affirmed by the Mandate of the League of Nations, which gave explicit international recognition to the historic connection of the Jewish people with Palestine and their right to reconstitute their National Home.

The recent holocaust, which engulfed millions of Jews in Europe, proved anew the need to solve the problem of the homelessness and lack of independence of the Jewish people by means of the re-establishment of the Jewish

State, which would open the gates to all Jews and endow the Jewish people with equality of status among the family of nations.

The survivors of the disastrous slaughter in Europe, and also Jews from other lands, have not desisted from their efforts to reach Eretz-Yisrael, in face of difficulties, obstacles and perils; and have not ceased to urge their right to a life of dignity, freedom and honest toil in their ancestral land.

In the second World War the Jewish people in Palestine made their full contribution to the struggle of the freedom-loving nations against the Nazi evil. The sacrifices of their soldiers and their war effort gained them the right to rank with the nations which founded the United Nations.

On November 29, 1947, the General Assembly of the United Nations adopted a Resolution requiring the establishment of a Jewish State in Palestine. The General Assembly called upon the inhabitants of the country to take all the necessary steps on their part to put the plan into effect. This recognition by the United Nations of the right of the Jewish people to establish their independent State is unassailable.

It is the natural right of the Jewish people to lead, as do all other nations, an independent existence in its sovereign State.

ACCORDINGLY WE, the members of the National Council, representing the Jewish people in Palestine and the World Zionist Movement, are met together in solemn assembly today, the day of termination of the British Mandate for Palestine; and by virtue of the natural and historic right of the Jewish people and of the Resolution of the General Assembly of the United Nations.

WE HEREBY PROCLAIM the establishment of the Jewish State in Palestine, to be called Medinath Yisrael (The State of Israel).

WE HEREBY DECLARE that, as from the termination of the Mandate at midnight, the 14th-15th May, 1948, and pending the setting up of the duly elected bodies of the State in accordance with a Constitution, to be drawn up by the Constituent Assembly not later than the 1st October, 1948, the National Council shall act as the Provisional State Council, and that the National Administration shall constitute the Provisional Government of the Jewish State, which shall be known as Israel.

THE STATE OF ISRAEL will be open to the immigration of Jews from all countries of their dispersion; will promote the development of the country for the benefit of all its inhabitants; will be based on the principles of liberty, justice and peace as conceived by the Prophets of Israel; will uphold the full social and political equality of all its citizens, without distinction of religion, race, or sex; will guarantee freedom of religion, conscience, education and culture; will safeguard the Holy Places of all religions; and will loyally uphold the principles of the United Nations Charter.

THE STATE OF ISRAEL will be ready to co-operate with the organs and representatives of the United Nations in the implementation of the Resolution of the Assembly of November 29, 1947, and will take steps to bring about the Economic Union over the whole of Palestine.

We appeal to the United Nations to assist the Jewish people in the building of its State and to admit Israel into the family of nations.

In the midst of wanton aggression, we yet call upon the Arab inhabitants of the State of Israel to preserve the ways of peace and play their part in the development of the State, on the basis of full and equal citizenship and due representation in all its bodies and institutions—provisional and permanent.

We extend our hand in peace and neighbourliness to all the neighbouring states and their peoples, and invite them to co-operate with the independent Jewish nation for the common good of all. The State of Israel is prepared to make its contribution to the progress of the Middle East as a whole.

Our call goes out to the Jewish people all over the world to rally to our side in the task of immigration and development, and to stand by us in the great struggle for the fulfilment of the dream of generations for the redemption of Israel.

With trust in the Rock of Israel, we set our hand to this Declaration, at this Session of the Provisional State Council, on the soil of the Homeland, in the city of Tel-Aviv, on this Sabbath eve, the fifth of Iyar, 5708, the fourteenth of May, 1948.

12. From the LAW OF RETURN 1950

Israel's "Law of Return" was passed unanimously by the Knesset on July 5, 1950.

1. Every Jew has the right to immigrate to the country.
2. *(a)* Immigration shall be on the basis of immigration visas.
   (b) Immigrant visas shall be issued to any Jew expressing a desire to settle in Israel, except if the Minister of Immigration is satisfied that the applicant:
   (i) acts against the Jewish nation; or
   (ii) may threaten the public health or State security.
3. *(a)* A Jew who comes to Israel and after his arrival expresses a desire to settle there may, while in Israel, obtain an immigrant certificate.
   (b) The exceptions listed in Article 2 *(b)* shall apply also with respect to the issue of an immigrant certificate, but a person shall not be regarded as a threat to public health as a result of an illness that he contracts after his arrival in Israel.

4. Every Jew who migrated to the country before this law goes into effect, and every Jew who was born in the country either before or after the law is effective enjoys the same status as any person who migrated on the basis of this law.

5. The Minister of Immigration is delegated to enforce this law and he may enact regulations in connection with its implementation and for the issue of immigrant visas and immigrant certificates.

13. U.N. SECURITY COUNCIL RESOLUTION 242 1967

Text of United Nations Security Council Resolution 242 of November 22, 1967

Adopted unanimously at the 1382nd meeting

The Security Council,

Expressing its continuing concern with the grave situation in the Middle East,

Emphasizing the inadmissibility of the acquisition of territory by war and the need to work for a just and lasting peace in which every State in the area can live in security.

Emphasizing further that all Member States in their acceptance of the Charter of the United Nations have undertaken a commitment to act in accordance with Article 2 of the Charter,

1. *Affirms* that the fulfillment of Charter principles requires the establishment of a just and lasting peace in the Middle East which should include the application of both the following principles:

   (i) Withdrawal of Israeli armed forces from territories occupied in the recent conflict;
   (ii) Termination of all claims or states of belligerency and respect for and acknowledgement of the sovereignty, territorial integrity and political independence of every State in the area and their right to live in peace within secure and recognized boundaries free from threats or acts of force;

2. *Affirms further* the necessity
   (a) For guaranteeing freedom of navigation through international waterways in the area;
   (b) For achieving a just settlement of the refugee problem;

(c) For guaranteeing the territorial inviolability and political independence of every State in the area, through measures including the establishment of demilitarized zones;

3. *Requests* the Secretary-General to designate a Special Representative to proceed to the Middle East to establish and maintain contacts with the States concerned in order to promote agreement and assist efforts to achieve a peaceful and accepted settlement in accordance with the provisions and principles of this resolution.

4. *Requests* the Secretary-General to report to the Security Council on the progress of the efforts of the Special Representative as soon as possible.

14. U.N. SECURITY COUNCIL RESOLUTION 338 1973

Text of United Nations Security Council Resolution 338

Adopted by the Security Council at its 1747th meeting, on 21/22 October 1973
The Security Council

1. *Calls upon* all parties to the present fighting to cease all firing and terminate all military activity immediately, no later than 12 hours after the moment of the adoption of this decision, in the positions they now occupy;
2. *Calls upon* the parties concerned to start immediately after the cease-fire the implementation of Security Council Resolution 242 (1967) in all of its parts;
3. *Decides* that, immediately and concurrently with the cease-fire, negotiations start between the parties concerned under appropriate auspices aimed at establishing a just and durable peace in the Middle East.

15. From the CAMP DAVID ACCORDS 1978

A Framework for Peace in the Middle East Agreed at Camp David

Muhammed Anwar al-Sadat, President of the Arab Republic of Egypt, and Menachem Begin, Prime Minister of Israel, met with Jimmy Carter, President of the United States of America, at Camp David from September 5 to September 17, 1978, and have agreed on the following framework for peace in the Middle East. They invite other parties to the Arab-Israeli conflict to adhere to it.

Preamble

The search for peace in the Middle East must be guided by the following:

—The agreed basis for a peaceful settlement of the conflict between Israel and its neighbors is U.N. Security Council Resolution 242, in all its parts.

—After four wars during thirty years, despite intensive human efforts, the Middle East, which is the cradle of civilization and the birthplace of three great religions, does not yet enjoy the blessings of peace. The people of the Middle East yearn for peace, so that the vast human and natural resources of the region can be turned to pursuits of peace and so that this area can become a model for co-existence and cooperation among nations.

—The historic initiative of President Sadat in visiting Jerusalem and the reception accorded to him by the parliament, government and people of Israel, and the reciprocal visit of Prime Minister Begin to Ismailia, the peace proposals made by both leaders, as well as the warm reception of these missions by the peoples of both countries, have created an unprecedented opportunity for peace which must not be lost if this generation and future generations are to be spared the tragedies of war.

—The provisions of the Charter of the United Nations and the other accepted norms of international law and legitimacy now provide accepted standards for the conduct of relations between all states.

—To achieve a relationship of peace, in the spirit of Article 2 of the United Nations Charter, future negotiations between Israel and any neighbor prepared to negotiate peace and security with it, are necessary for the purpose of carrying out all the provisions and principles of Resolutions 242 and 338.

—Peace requires respect for the sovereignty, territorial integrity and political independence of every state in the area and their right to live in peace within secure and recognized boundaries free from threats or acts of force. Progress toward that goal can accelerate movement toward a new era of reconciliation in the Middle East marked by cooperation in promoting economic development, in maintaining stability, and in assuring security.

—Security is enhanced by a relationship of peace and by cooperation between nations which enjoy normal relations. In addition, under the terms of peace treaties, the parties can, on the basis of reciprocity, agree to special security arrangements such as demilitarized zones, limited armaments areas, early warning stations, the presence of international forces, liaison, agreed measures for monitoring, and other arrangements that they agree are useful.

Framework

Taking these factors into account, the parties are determined to reach a just, comprehensive, and durable settlement of the Middle East conflict through the conclusion of peace treaties based on Security Council Resolution 242 and 338 in all their parts. Their purpose is to achieve peace and good neighborly relations. They recognize that, for peace to endure, it must involve all those who have been most deeply affected by the conflict. They therefore agree that this framework as appropriate is intended by them to constitute a basis for peace not only between Egypt and Israel, but also between Israel and each of its other neighbors which is prepared to negotiate peace with Israel on this basis. With that objective in mind, they have agreed to proceed . . .

16. Palestine National Council Declaration of Independence 1988

In the name of God, the Compassionate, the Merciful.

Palestine, the land of the three monotheistic faiths, is where the Palestinian Arab people was born, on which it grew, developed, and excelled. The Palestinian people was never separated from or diminished in its integral bonds with Palestine. Thus the Palestinian Arab people ensured for itself an everlasting union between itself, its land, and its history.

Resolute throughout that history, the Palestinian Arab people forged its national identity, rising even to unimagined levels in its defense as invasion, the design of others, and the appeal special to Palestine's ancient and luminous place on that eminence where powers and civilizations are joined. . . . All this intervened thereby to deprive the people of its political independence. Yet the undying connection between Palestine and its people secured for the land its character and for the people its national genius.

Nourished by an unfolding series of civilizations and cultures, inspired by a heritage rich in variety and kind, the Palestinian Arab people added to its stature by consolidating a union between itself and its patrimonial land. The call went out from temple, church, and mosque to praise the Creator, to celebrate compassion, and peace was indeed the message of Palestine. And in generation after generation, the Palestinian Arab people gave of itself unsparingly in the valiant battle for liberation and homeland. For what has been the unbroken chain of our people's rebellions but the heroic embodiment of our will for national independence? And so the people were sustained in the struggle to stay and to prevail.

When in the course of modern times a new order of values was declared with norms and values fair for all, it was the Palestinian Arab people that had been excluded from the destiny of all other peoples by a hostile array of local and foreign powers. Yet again had unaided justice been revealed as insufficient to drive the world's history along its preferred course.

And it was the Palestinian people, already wounded in its body, that was submitted to yet another type of occupation over which floated the falsehood that "Palestine was a land without people." This notion was foisted upon some in the world, whereas in Article 22 of the Covenant of the League of Nations (1919) and in the Treaty of Lausanne (1923), the community of nations had recognized that all the Arab territories, including Palestine, of the formerly Ottoman provinces were to have granted to them their freedom as provisionally independent nations.

Despite the historical injustice inflicted on the Palestinian Arab people resulting in their dispersion and depriving them of their right to self-determination, following upon UN General Assembly Resolution 181 (1947), which partitioned Palestine into two states, one Arab, one Jewish, yet it is this resolution that still provides those conditions of international legitimacy that ensure the right of the Palestinian Arab people to sovereignty and national independence.

By stages, the occupation of Palestine and parts of other Arab territories by Israeli forces, the willed dispossession and expulsion from their ancestral homes of the majority of Palestine's civilian inhabitants was achieved by organized terror; those Palestinians who remained, as a vestige subjugated in its homeland, were persecuted and forced to endure the destruction of their national life.

Thus were principles of international legitimacy violated. Thus were the Charter of the United Nations and its resolutions disfigured, for they had recognized the Palestinian Arab people's national rights, including the Right of Return, the Right to Independence, the Right to Sovereignty over territory and homeland.

In Palestine and on its perimeters, in exile distant and near, the Palestinian Arab people never faltered and never abandoned its conviction in its rights of return and independence. Occupation, massacres, and dispersion achieved no gain in the unabated Palestinian consciousness of self and political identity, as Palestinians went forward with their destiny, undeterred and unbowed. And from our of the long years of trial in evermounting struggle, the Palestinian political identity emerged further consolidated and confirmed. And the collective Palestinian national will forged itself in a political embodiment, the Palestine Liberation Organization, its sole, legitimate representative, recognized by the world community as a whole, as well as by related regional and international institutions. Standing on the very rock of conviction in the Palestinian people's inalienable rights, and on the ground of Arab national consensus, and of international legitimacy, the PLO led the campaigns of its great people, molded into unity and powerful resolve, one and indivisible in the triumphs, even as it suffered massacres and confinement within and without its home. And so Palestinian resistance was clarified and raised into the forefront of Arab and world awareness, as the struggle of the Palestinian Arab people achieved unique prominence among the world's liberation movements in the modern era.

The massive national uprising, the *intifadah*, now intensifying in cumulative scope and power on occupied Palestinian territories, as well as the unflinching resistance of the refugee camps outside the homeland, have elevated consciousness of the Palestinian truth and right into still higher realms of comprehension and actuality. Now at last the curtain has been dropped around a whole epoch of prevarication and negation. The Intifadah has set siege to the mind of official Israel, which has for too long relied exclusively upon myth and terror to deny Palestinian existence altogether. Because of the Intifadah and its revolutionary irreversible impulse, the history of Palestine has therefore arrived at a decisive juncture.

Whereas the Palestinian people reaffirms most definitely its inalienable rights in the land of its patrimony:

Now by virtue of natural, historical, and legal rights and the sacrifices of successive generations who gave of themselves in defense of the freedom and independence of their homeland;

In pursuance of resolutions adopted by Arab summit conferences and relying on the authority bestowed by international legitimacy as embodied in the resolutions of the United Nations Organization since 1947;

And in exercise by the Palestinian Arab people of its rights to self-determination, political independence, and sovereignty over its territory;

The Palestine National Council, in the name of God, and in the name of the Palestinian Arab people, hereby proclaims the establishment of the State of Palestine on our Palestinian territory with its capital Jerusalem (Al-Quds Ash-Sharif).

The State of Palestine is the state of Palestinians wherever they may be. The state is for them to enjoy in it their collective national and cultural identity, theirs to pursue in it a complete equality of rights. In it will be safeguarded their political and religious convictions and their human dignity by means of a parliamentary democratic system of governance, itself based on freedom of expression and the freedom to form parties. The rights of minorities will duly be respected by the majority, as minorities must abide by decisions of the majority. Governance will be based on principles of social justice, equality and nondiscrimination in public rights on grounds of race, religion, color, or sex under the aegis of a constitution which ensures the role of law and on independent judiciary. Thus shall these principles allow no departure from Palestine's age-old spiritual and civilizational heritage of tolerance and religious co-existence.

The State of Palestine is an Arab state, an integral and indivisible part of the Arab nation, at one with that nation in heritage and civilization, with it also in its aspiration for liberation, progress, democracy, and unity. The State of Palestine affirms its obligation to abide by the Charter of the League of Arab States, whereby the coordination of the Arab states with each other shall be strengthened. It calls upon Arab compatriots to consolidate and enhance the emergence in reality of our State, to mobilize potential, and to intensify efforts whose goal is to end Israeli occupation.

The State of Palestine proclaims its commitment to the principles and purposes of the United Nations, and to the Universal Declaration of Human Rights. It proclaims its commitment as well to the principles and policies of the Non-Aligned Movement . . .

17. Israel-PLO Declaration of Principles 1993

The Government of the State of Israel and the P.L.O. team (in the Jordanian-Palestinian delegation of the Middle East Peace Conference) (the "Palestinian Delegation"), representing the Palestinian people, agree that it is time to put an end to decades of confrontation and conflict, recognize their mutual legitimate and political rights, and strive to live in peaceful coexistence and mutual dignity and security and achieve a just, lasting and comprehensive peace settlement and historic reconciliation through the agreed political process. Accordingly, the two sides agree to the following principles:

Article I

Aim of the Negotiations

The aim of the Israeli-Palestinian negotiations within the current Middle East peace process is, among other things, to establish a Palestinian Interim Self-Government Authority, the elected Council (the "Council"), for the Palestinian people in the West Bank and the Gaza Strip, for a transitional period not exceeding five years, leading to a permanent settlement based on Security Council Resolutions 242 and 338.

It is understood that the interim arrangements are an integral part of the whole peace process and that the negotiations on the permanent status will lead to the implementation of Security Council Resolutions 242 and 338.

Article II

Framework for the Interim Period

The agreed framework for the interim period is set forth in this Declaration of Principles.

Article III

Elections

1. In order that the Palestinian people in the West Bank and Gaza Strip may govern themselves according to democratic principles, direct, free and general political elections will be held for the Council under agreed supervision and international observation, while the Palestinian police will ensure public order.

2. An agreement will be concluded on the exact mode and conditions of the elections in accordance with the protocol attached as Annex I, with the goal of holding the elections not later than nine months after the entry into force of this Declaration of Principles.

3. These elections will constitute a significant interim preparatory step toward the realization of the legitimate rights of the Palestinian people and their just requirements.

Article IV

Jurisdiction

Jurisdiction of the Council will cover West Bank and Gaza Strip territory, except for issues that will be negotiated in the permanent status negotiations. The two sides view the West Bank and Gaza Strip as a single territorial unit, whose integrity will be preserved during the interim period.

Article V

Transitional Period and Permanent Status Negotiations

1. The five-year transitional period will begin upon the withdrawal from the Gaza Strip and Jericho area.

2. Permanent status negotiations will commence as soon as possible, but not later than the beginning of the third year of the interim period, between the Government of Israel and the Palestinian people representatives.

3. It is understood that these negotiations shall cover remaining issues, including: Jerusalem, refugees, settlements, security arrangements, borders, relations and cooperation with other neighbors, and other issues of common interest.

4. The two parties agree that the outcome of the permanent status negotiations should not be prejudiced or preempted by agreements reached for the interim period.

18. ISRAEL-JORDAN WASHINGTON DECLARATION 1994

A. After generations of hostility, blood and tears and in the wake of years of pain and wars, His Majesty King Hussein and Prime Minister Yitzhak Rabin are determined to bring an end to bloodshed and sorrow. It is in this spirit that His Majesty King Hussein of the Hashemite Kingdom of Jordan and Prime Minister and Minister of Defense, Mr. Yitzhak Rabin of Israel, met in Washington today at the invitation of President William J. Clinton of the United States of America. This initiative of President William J. Clinton constitutes an historic landmark in the United States untiring efforts in promoting peace and stability in the Middle East. The personal involvement of the President has made it possible to realise agreement on the content of this historic declaration. The signing of this declaration bears testimony to the President's vision and devotion to the cause of peace.

B. In their meeting, His Majesty King Hussein and Prime Minister Yitzhak Rabin have jointly reaffirmed the five underlying principles of their understanding on an Agreed Common Agenda designed to reach the goal of a just, lasting and comprehensive peace between the Arab States and the Palestinians, with Israel.

1. Israel and Jordan aim at the achievement of just, lasting and comprehensive peace between Israel and its neighbours and at the conclusion of a Treaty of Peace between both countries.
2. The two countries will vigorously continue their negotiations to arrive at a state of peace, based on Security Council Resolutions 242 and 338 in all their aspects, and founded on freedom, equality and justice.
3. Israel respects the present special role of the Hashemite Kingdom of Jordan in Muslim Holy shrines in Jerusalem. When negotiations on the permanent status will take place, Israel will give high priority to the Jordanian historic role in these shrines. In addition the two sides have agreed to act together to promote interfaith relations among the three monotheistic religions.
4. The two countries recognise their right and obligation to live in peace with each other as well as with all states within secure and recognised boundaries. The two states affirmed their respect for and acknowledgment of the sovereignty, territorial integrity and political independence of every state in the area.
5. The two countries desire to develop good neighbourly relations of co-operation between them to ensure lasting security and to avoid threats and the use of force between them.

C. The long conflict between the two states is now coming to an end. In this spirit the state of belligerency between Israel and Jordan has been terminated. . .

19. From ISRAEL-PLO AGREEMENT ON TRANSFER OF POWER 1994

Preamble

WITHIN the framework of the Middle East peace process initiated at Madrid in October 1991;

REAFFIRMING their determination to live in peaceful coexistence, mutual dignity and security, while recognizing their mutual legitimate and political rights;

REAFFIRMING their desire to achieve a just, lasting and comprehensive peace settlement through the agreed political process;

REAFFIRMING their adherence to the mutual recognition and commitments expressed in the letters dated September 9, 1993, signed by and exchanged between the Prime Minister of Israel and the Chairman of the PLO;

REAFFIRMING their understanding that the interim self-government arrangements, including the preparatory arrangements to apply in the West Bank contained in this Agreement, are an integral part of the whole peace process and that the negotiations on the permanent status will lead to the implementation of Security Council Resolutions 242 and 338;

FOLLOWING the Agreement on the Gaza Strip and the Jericho Area as signed at Cairo on May 4, 1994 (hereinafter "the Gaza-Jericho Agreement");

DESIROUS of putting into effect the Declaration of Principles on Interim Self-Government Arrangements as signed at Washington, D.C. on September 13, 1993 (hereinafter "the Declaration of Principles"), and in particular Article VI regarding preparatory transfer of powers and responsibilities and the Agreed Minutes thereto;

HEREBY AGREE to the following arrangements regarding the preparatory transfer of powers and responsibilities in the West Bank:

[. . .]

Article II

Preparatory Transfer of Powers and Responsibilities

1. Israel shall transfer and the Palestinian Authority shall assume powers and responsibilities from the Israeli military government and its Civil Administration in the West Bank in the following spheres: education and culture, health, social welfare, tourism, direct taxation and Value Added Tax on local

production (hereinafter "VAT"), as specified in this Agreement (hereinafter "the Spheres").

2. For the purposes of this Agreement, the Palestinian Authority shall constitute the authorized Palestinians referred to in Article VI of the Declaration of Principles.

3. The Parties will explore the possible expansion of the transfer of powers and responsibilities to additional spheres.

Article III

Scope of the Transferred Powers and Responsibilities

1. The scope of the powers and responsibilities transferred in each Sphere, as well as specific arrangements regarding the exercise of such powers and responsibilities, are set out in the Protocols attached as Annexes I through VI.

2. In accordance with the Declaration of Principles, the jurisdiction of the Palestinian Authority with regard to the powers and responsibilities transferred by this Agreement will not apply to Jerusalem, settlements, military locations and, unless otherwise provided in this Agreement, Israelis.

3. The transfer of powers and responsibilities under this Agreement does not include powers and responsibilities in the sphere of foreign relations, except as indicated in Article VI(2)(b) of the Gaza-Jericho Agreement.

[. . .]

20. NEGOTIATIONS BETWEEN JORDAN AND ISRAEL

Common Agenda
Washington, D.C. – September 14, 1993

Washington Declaration
Washington D.C. – July 25,1994

Trilateral U.S.-Jordan-Israel
Economic Committee

Established by Pres. Clinton-Crown Price Hassan-FM Peres
Washington, D.C. October 1,1993

TREATY OF PEACE
Arva – October 26, 1994

– Full diplomatic relations.
– Agreed international boundary with minor modifications.
– End to belligerency; cooperation in prevention of terrorism.
– Agreement on allocations of water and the development of new water resources.
– Freedom of access to religious sites; recognition of special role of Hashemite Kingdom over Muslim holy shrines in Jerusalem.
– Freedom of passage by land, sea and air.
– Cooperation in such areas as the economy, transportation, telecommunications, tourism, environment, energy, health, agriculture, war against crime and drugs.
– The problem of refugees and displaced persons will be resolved in agreed-upon negotiating frameworks.

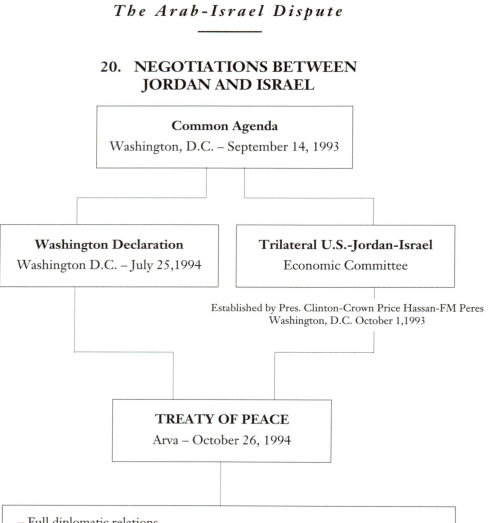

21. NEGOTIATIONS BETWEEN THE PALESTINIANS AND ISRAEL

Declaration of Principles
Washington D.C. – September 13,1993

STAGE I
Interim Self-Government Arrangements

GAZA-JERICHO AGREEMENT
Signed: May 4, 1994

The withdrawal of Israeli administration and forces from Gaza and Jericho, and the transfer of powers and responsibilities to a Palestinian Authority. The Agreement includes:

- Security arrangements
- Transfer of civil affairs
- Legal framework
- Economic framework

TRANSFER OF POWERS
Signed: August 29, 1994

The early transfer of powers and responsibilities in specified spheres, in those parts of the territories not included in the Gaza-Jericho Agreement.
These spheres include:

Education & culture
Health
Social welfare
Direct taxation
Tourism
Other spheres as agreed

INTERIM AGREEMENT & ELECTIONS
Signed: Sept. 28, 1994

A comprehensive agreement on the transfer of powers and responsibilties in the West Bank from Israel to an elected Palestinian Council, according to the following target dates:

- *Dec. 31, 1995:* End of IDF redeployment from populated areas of West Bank
- *Jan. 20, 1996:* Elections to the Palestinian Council
- *March 31, 1996:* IDF redeployment from Hebron
- *June 30 & Dec. 31 1996, June 30, 1997:* Further IDF redeployments in West Bank

STAGE II
Permanent Status

PERMANENT STATUS AGREEMENT

An agreement to determine the nature of the final settlement between Israel and the Palestinians, as follows:

- Talks to begin as soon as possible but not later than 3rd year of interim period (*May 1996*).
- Permanent Status issues to include: Jerusalem, refugees, settlements, security arrangements and borders.
- Permanent Status Arrangement to enter into force after 5th year of self-government (*May 1999*).

INDEX

Index

Index

Index

[redacted]